Poetry in Our Time

Library of Congress Cataloging in Publication Data

Deutsch, Babette, 1895-
    Poetry in our time.

    Reprint of the ed. published by Doubleday, Garden
City, N. Y.
    Includes index.
    1. English poetry--20th century--History and
criticism. 2. American poetry--20th century--His-
tory and criticism. I. Title.
[PR610.D4 1975]   821'.9'109   73-191121
ISBN 0-8371-7309-4

Babette Deutsch, a native of New York, is internationally known as poet and critic. She is the author of ten volumes of poems, of which the most recent is *The Collected Poems of Babette Deutsch* (1969). In addition to critical prose, she has written fiction and juveniles, one of the best-known of the latter being the prize-winning biography, *Walt Whitman, Builder for America*. Her *Poetry Handbook* is now available in a fourth, revised, enlarged edition. Her translations include poems from Rilke's *Book of Hours*, Blok's *The Twelve*, Pushkin's *Eugene Onegin*, the work from the Russian having been done with her husband, Avrahm Yarmolinsky. She served two consecutive three-year terms as Honorary Consultant to The Library of Congress. From 1944 to 1971 she gave a course in twentieth-century poetry at the School of General Studies, Columbia University, from which she holds an honorary Litt. D. Miss Deutsch is a Chancellor of The Academy of American Poets. She is a member of the National Institute of Arts and Letters and of the American Academy of Arts and Letters.

POETRY IN OUR TIME

*A Critical Survey of Poetry
in the English-speaking World
1900 to 1960*

by Babette Deutsch

SECOND EDITION
REVISED AND ENLARGED

GREENWOOD PRESS, PUBLISHERS
WESTPORT, CONNECTICUT

Acknowledgment is made to the following publishers and authors of copyrighted material which appears in this volume:

LÉONIE ADAMS: excerpt from *Those Not Elect* by Léonie Adams.

GEORGE ALLEN & UNWIN: excerpt from "The Embankment" by T. E. Hulme, from *Umbra* by Ezra Pound.

CHATTO & WINDUS LTD.: excerpt from "The Show" by Wilfred Owen, from *The Poems of Wilfred Owen*.

THE DIAL PRESS, INC.: excerpt from "The Death of the Ball Turret Gunner" by Randall Jarrell, published by The Dial Press, Inc.

DOUBLEDAY & COMPANY, INC.: excerpts from "The Years Between" by Rudyard Kipling, copyright 1914, 1919 by Rudyard Kipling and "Many Inventions" by Rudyard Kipling. Reprinted by permission of Mrs. George Bambridge and the publisher; excerpts from *The Lost Son and Other Poems* by Theodore Roethke, copyright 1948 by Theodore Roethke.

E. P. DUTTON & CO., INC.: excerpts from *Five Rivers* by Norman Nicholson, copyright 1945 by E. P. Dutton & Co., Inc.

EYRE & SPOTTISWOODE LTD.: excerpts from "Janet Waking" and "Judith of Bethulia" by John Crowe Ransom; excerpts from "The Subway" and "Seasons of the Soul" by Allen Tate.

FABER & FABER, LTD.: excerpts from *Collected Poems 1909–1935*, *Four Quartets*, and *The Complete Poems and Plays* by T. S. Eliot; excerpts from "My Sad Captains" by Thom

Anchor Books edition: 1963
Copyright © 1963 by Babette Deutsch
*Copyright © 1952, 1956 by Columbia University Press,
New York*

Originally published in 1952 by Henry Holt and Company, Inc., by Columbia University Press in 1956 and 1958, and by Anchor Books in 1963.

This edition is reprinted by arrangement with Babette Deutsch

Reprinted by Greenwood Press, Inc.

First Greenwood reprinting 1975
Second Greenwood reprinting 1977

Library of Congress catalog card number 73-191121
ISBN 0-8371-7309-4

Printed in the United States of America

Gunn; excerpts from *The Cloth of Flesh* by Sean Jennett;
excerpt from "The Anathemata" by David Jones; excerpt from
Springboard and *Poems 1925–1940* by Louis MacNeice; for
"Bowl" and excerpts from *Opus Posthumous* by Wallace
Stevens.

FARRAR, STRAUS & CUDAHY, INC.: excerpts from "Baroque Comment" and "Knowledge" by Louise Bogan from *Collected
Poems 1923–1953* by permission of Noonday Press, Inc., a
subsidiary of Farrar, Straus & Cudahy, Inc.

FUNK & WAGNALLS COMPANY, INC.: excerpts from *High Falcon*
by Léonie Adams.

GROVE PRESS, INC.: excerpt from "The Human Fold" by Edwin
Muir, from *Collected Poems 1921–1951*, copyright © by Edwin
Muir.

HARCOURT, BRACE & WORLD, INC.: experts from "Northern
April" © 1961 by Abbie Huston Evans and "Sunup in March"
© 1953 by Abbie Huston Evans, from *Fact of Crystal*; excerpts
from *Poems 1923–1954* by E. E. Cummings, copyright 1950
by E. E. Cummings; excerpts from *Collected Poems 1909–
1935* by T. S. Eliot, copyright 1936 by Harcourt, Brace &
World, Inc.; excerpts from *Four Quartets* copyright 1943 by
T. S. Eliot; excerpt from "Burnt Norton" from *The Complete
Poems and Plays of T. S. Eliot*; excerpts from *Lord Weary's
Castle*, copyright 1944, 1946 by Robert Lowell; excerpt from
The People, Yes by Carl Sandburg, copyright 1936 by Har-
court, Brace & World, Inc.; excerpt from *Poems and Sonnets*
by Ernest Walsh, copyright 1934 by Harcourt, Brace & World,
Inc.; excerpts from *The Beautiful Changes* by Richard Wilbur.

HOLT, RINEHART & WINSTON, INC.: excerpt from "Acquainted
with the Night" and "Come In" by Robert Frost, from *Complete Poems of Robert Frost*, copyright renewed © 1956 by
Robert Frost; excerpts from "The Olive" and "Is My Team
Ploughing?" from *Complete Poems* by A. E. Housman, copyright © 1959 by Holt, Rinehart & Winston, Inc.; excerpts from
Selected Poems by Mark Van Doren, copyright 1939, 1944,
1948, 1953, 1954 by Mark Van Doren.

HOUGHTON MIFFLIN COMPANY: excerpts from "Invitation to
Miss Marianne Moore" by Elizabeth Bishop, from *North and
South*; excerpts from *Poems, 1924–1933* by Archibald Mac-
Leish.

BRUCE HUMPHRIES, INC.: excerpt from *Rock and Shell* by John
Wheelwright, copyright 1933 by Bruce Humphries, Inc.

Signature of All Things by Kenneth Rexroth; excerpts from *The Selected Writings of Dylan Thomas*, copyright 1939 by New Directions; excerpts from *Later Poems of William Carlos Williams*, copyright 1944, 1948, 1950 by William Carlos Williams; excerpts from *Collected Poems of William Carlos Williams 1906–1938*, copyright 1938 by New Directions; excerpts from *Paterson, Books I–IV* by William Carlos Williams; excerpt from "Orpheus" from *The Collected Poems of Ivor Winters*.

OXFORD UNIVERSITY PRESS: excerpts from *Collected Poems 1930–1960* by Richard Eberhart, copyright © 1960 by Richard Eberhart.

OXFORD UNIVERSITY PRESS, LONDON: excerpts from "The Windhover," "I Wake and Feel," and "The Letters of G. M. Hopkins to Robert Bridges" by Gerard Manley Hopkins.

A. D. PETERS: excerpt from *The Magnetic Mountain* by Cecil Day Lewis.

RANDOM HOUSE: excerpts from *Collected Poems* by W. H. Auden; excerpts from *Collected Poems of Kenneth Fearing*; excerpts from *Selected Poems* and *Solstice and Other Poems* by Robinson Jeffers; excerpts from *Poems 1940–1953* by Karl Shapiro.

CHARLES SCRIBNER'S SONS: excerpt from *Now with His Love* by John Peale Bishop, copyright 1933 Charles Scribner's Sons; renewal copyright © 1961 by Margaret G. H. Bronson; "The Subway," copyright 1937 Charles Scribner's Sons and "Seasons of the Soul" copyright 1945 by Allen Tate, from *Poems 1922–1947* by Allen Tate, copyright 1932, 1948 by Charles Scribner's Sons.

DAME EDITH SITWELL: excerpt from "The Sleeping Beauty" from *Selected Poems* by Edith Sitwell.

THE SOCIETY OF AUTHORS: excerpts from "The Olive" and "Is My Team Ploughing?" by A. E. Housman, by permission of The Society of Authors as the literary representatives of the Estate of the late A. E. Housman, and Messrs. Jonathan Cape, Ltd., publishers of A. E. Housman's *Collected Poems*.

THE VIKING PRESS: excerpts from *Collected Poems* by D. H. Lawrence and *Last Poems* by D. H. Lawrence.

and again
to
Avrahm

Foreword to the Reprint Edition

Were I to update this book, I should take account of the completed work of those poets (too many good ones) no longer in the land of the living, and should change the syntax in writing of them. A look at the later performance of John Hall Wheelock would offer fresh witness to the fact that an aged poet can write with an intensity and a force beyond his earlier powers. Again, the adjective "young" is no longer applicable to some whose further accomplishment asks for comment. I should no longer have reason to call *Chronique* "the most recent" of St. John Perse's poems, or *Thrones* "the most recent addition" to Pound's *Cantos*. It would not now be correct to pair off William Jay Smith and Barbara Howes. The writers of so-called "confessional" poems would require a word. So, too, the rise of the Black poets. This would allow a chance to listen not only to the voices of the descendants of slaves here but also to the voices of those French-speaking Blacks of Africa and Madagascar who so compellingly celebrate *négritude*. Updating is merely tangential to some sins of omission. Prominent among those who would certainly receive attention in a new edition of these pages are such signal makers as John Berryman, Anthony Hecht, and Howard Nemerov.

No changes, whether by way of deletion or addition, would alter the fundamental character of the book. Re-reading it, with a sense of all that has happened, since it was last revised and expanded, to the poetic scene and to human history, I found myself largely in agreement with the self responsible for that work. My wish for it is that the close of the final chapter should have for the reader the validity that it continues to have for the woman who wrote it years ago.

January 9, 1974

Note to the Second Printing

of the Second Edition

In the two years that have elapsed since this edition was published, the poetic scene has suffered a change because of the deaths of four men: Frost, MacNiece, Roethke, and William Carlos Williams. These are recorded, with some other supplementary matter, in the Note to the Index of Poets. It has not been feasible, due to technical considerations, to alter the wording of the text so as to take account of the fact that their work is finished. It has been possible, however, to make a modest number of changes that seemed desirable. Thus, the names of a few poets not mentioned before have been introduced, although, for various reasons, there are notable practitioners who are not discussed. In certain instances there has been some slight amplification, as where later work by established poets has been briefly noticed, or where the fruits of recent scholarship, such as the admirable studies of Yeats and Eliot by Thomas Parkinson and Herbert Howarth respectively, have suggested elaboration.

Babette Deutsch

New York
23 March 1964

Foreword to the Second Edition

When a second printing of this book appeared in 1956, it included a Foreword that was in the nature of a short supplementary chapter to the first edition, issued in 1952. An excerpt from the opening paragraphs seems appropriate here.

"Even in the short time since this volume was first published, the world of poetry has become slightly other than it was. The aged, unaging Walter de la Mare, Wallace Stevens, Dylan Thomas, are dead: their work can now be seen in its entirety. Some established poets have issued their collected works. A few younger or hitherto neglected figures have won recognition from their fellows and from a friendly public. Noting with dry realism 'the trial by market everything must come to', Frost has remarked that a poet's stock rises and drops with the years. As demonstrably Robert Graves asks:

> Could Shakespeare make the less
> Chaucer's goodliness?

and affirms that each poet aims to outdo only his own achievement. A glance at the present scene confirms both observations. . . . Reappraisals continue. Yet it is also clear that the virtuosity of Auden cannot make less Robert Frost's goodliness. It is, of course, impossible to discuss all the ways in which the poets of the English-speaking countries compete with each other and themselves, with their Ancestors, and with their own emerging progeny. Rather than merely catalog their names, I regretfully omitted from the text and from this Foreword many fine makers. In a few instances, at the expense of more admirable work, verse of lesser worth has been considered because it was particularly significant of the period in which it was written."

The Foreword went on to sketch briefly "some aspects of recent poetry, necessarily unrecorded before." The present edition is a revision and an enlargement of the entire volume, including that additional material. Some poets not discussed earlier have found a place here, but far from all who have done fine work receive mention. Where the text has been expanded, it has often been for the sake of a fuller discussion of poets already considered. Thus, the pages originally devoted to Wallace Stevens, whose work came to an end half a dozen years ago, grew into an entire chapter.

The book owes something to private letters from several of the poets included. It owes what value it may have to the conviction that, as Stevens affirmed, "the significance of poetry is second to none." The fullest enjoyment of it, as is the case with the other arts, the sciences, games of skill, comes with the fullest understanding. Most of the time the poet is talking to himself, hoping he will be overheard. But he is talking about matters of endless interest. His subjects are those that Yeats said alone could concern a serious mind: sex and death. He meditates, as Eliot has, on time and eternity, and on the difficulties of communication. Much recent work deals for that reason with the poetic process. Like Robert Penn Warren, the younger poet is occupied with the problem of identity. Like Wallace Stevens, he looks for "a new kind of reality". Though space travelers come to rival frogmen in numbers, though we may learn to jazz the music of the spheres, these subjects are not apt to lose interest for us, as long as we remain human. Nothing can deal with them more meaningfully for the men and women of the twentieth century than the poetry of this century.

Babette Deutsch

New York
17 March 1962

Foreword to the First Edition

This book is about the poetry written during the twentieth century wherever English (or American) is the literary language of the country. Its purpose is to make the poetry more accessible to the intelligent reader. To that end it examines the rise and growth of modern verse. A single volume about the poetry of half a century cannot take all its practitioners into account, but I have tried to deal at length with significant trends and to neglect neither the founders of modern verse, nor fine poets of slight output, nor yet the poets' poets of greater range. Some years ago I wrote a similar book, the first to explore what it called *This Modern Poetry*. The events of the past decade and a half have changed the world and our view of it and have, of course, changed the poetic scene. Some poets, such as Yeats, have completed their life work. Some have shrunk; others, like Wallace Stevens and William Carlos Williams, have gained in stature. New stars, of varying brilliance, have risen on the horizon. The present volume examines the changes that have occurred in the intervening years and registers developments in the author's approach. The form and content of the poems discussed are viewed in relation to the revolutions of the age in which they were composed. The book seeks to show that this poetry has grown, not out of literature, but out of life, and how in turn it nourishes life in these anxiety-ridden times.

Babette Deutsch

New York
March, 1952

A Note

The author wishes to express particular thanks to Mr. Philip Leidy for his generous help in the typing of the original manuscript, and to two poets, one also a distinguished critic: Mr. Kenneth Slade Alling and Mr. Allen Tate, for their sustained and sustaining encouragement in the preparation of the first edition.

B. D.

Contents

Foreword to the Reprint Edition   *xi*

Note to the Second Printing of the Second Edition   *xii*

Foreword to the Second Edition   *xiii*

Foreword to the First Edition   *xv*

A Note   *xvii*

1. *A Look at the Worst*   1
2. *Farewell, Romance*   31
3. *The Glove of a Neighborhood*   59
4. *The Earthly and the Definite*   85
5. *Speech and Song*   129
6. *The Auditory Imagination*   165
7. *Wit as the Wall*   205
8. *The Ghostly Member*   243
9. *The Supreme Fiction*   269
10. *A Vision of Reality*   287
11. *The Forgèd Feature*   321
12. *Alchemists of the Word*   349
13. *Wars and Rumors of Wars*   389
14. *Science and Poetry*   423

Note to Index of Poets   450

Index of Poets   451

Poetry in Our Time

1. A Look at the Worst

The poetry of Thomas Hardy bridges the gulf between the Victorian sensibility and our own. Born early enough to have known survivors of the battle of Waterloo, he lived to witness the aftermath of the first world war and foresee the rise of the second. He studied architecture before he took up the profession of letters, but the most permanent works of man seemed passing things to one who realized that the road he walked had been built by the Roman invaders of Britain and among whose landmarks were the barrows of men of the Bronze Age. His sense of the past was further fed by his being compelled to witness the decay of the agricultural order and its natural pieties, along with the passing of his forebears' faith in an all-wise Providence and that of his close contemporaries in an almost deified Progress. If his gloomy meditations and his conventional technique recall an earlier day, his employment of the homely words of his native Wessex, and, above all, his dramatic irony, ally him with his juniors.

Stephen Spender opens a poem called "Tom's A-Cold" with the picture of a day of rain that "Makes sky and plain one dull pain." The Tom of the title is Thomas Hardy, and the poem avers that: "Such a day was the sum of my life." It goes on, however, to admit that poor Tom's days "Burned with a hidden blaze." Poor Tom was one who, like the Duke's son wearing the mask of a madman in *Lear*, "understood the sick botched lives"; one who hated wars, imperial privilege, dubious creeds. He held that the human need was to know that we know nothing of our

origin or our end, and that we have nothing, unless, in
the poet's curious but pressing phrase, we can "Comfort
that poor condition, man." The monologue says that where
Tom lies, under the rhyming gravestone, his eyes are two
pools climbing

> Through grey reflections to the sky—
> My world asking your world: "Why?"

It was a question that Hardy asked of the universe, and
that was pointed up for him by the events of nearly ninety
years.

In one of his earliest pieces, a sonnet called "Hap",
written at the height of the Darwinian controversy, Hardy
observed that the "purblind Doomsters" might as readily
have strewn blisses about his pilgrimage as pain. Toward
the close of the century he was bitterly acknowledging
himself "one born out of due time", being a man "Who
holds that if way to the Better there be, it exacts a full
look at the Worst." This stubborn refusal to look away
from the facts as they presented themselves to him helped
to differentiate him from the elder Victorians. If he regarded the universe as the creation of a blind Will, without intelligence or pity, he came for a time to put his
hope in what he called "evolutionary meliorism", and to
believe that the Power that had brought the planets and
the pismires into being might yet achieve the awareness
developed by one of the least of its creatures.

He expressed this hope at the close of his most ambitious work, *The Dynasts*. An epic drama of the Napoleonic wars, this unwieldy medley of verse and prose in 19
acts and 130 scenes opens with the query of the Shade of
Earth: "What of the immanent Will and Its designs?" To
which the Spirit of the Years replies: "It works uncon-
sciously as heretofore." As the drama proceeds, the scene
repeatedly assumes the likeness of a vast brain, Space
being conceived as that organ of the Will governing the
universe, and the personages and action of the play as a
portion of its tissues. The finale finds the Spirit of the

Years joining the Spirit of the Pities in a hopeful chorus that has a quaintly Shelleyan ring. But while Hardy can contemplate a future in which the shaping energy of the universe may become aware of the pain suffered by the victims of its blind workings, he is not always certain that It will "fashion all things fair." Past wrongs cannot be righted nor past sufferings canceled, and sometimes the poet wonders what the "Sleep-worker", roused to wakefulness, will do, asking:

> Wilt thou destroy, in one wild shock of shame,
> Thy whole high heaving firmamental frame,
> Or patiently adjust, amend, and heal?

At the close of his life he abandoned belief in the possibility of such amendment.

Examining the body of his work, however, one finds poems that expose the misery of sentient life repeatedly relieved by admission of such refreshments of the spirit as are available. One instance is the lyric in which he speaks of a frail, gaunt, wind-beaten thrush singing "as of joy illimited" in the growing gloom of a winter dusk. As he hears the bird caroling ecstatically in so bleak a scene, he can only think that through his song there trembles a hope of which the listener was unaware. Even though Hardy has no "blessed Hope", he has an eye for the May month flapping "its glad green leaves like wings", for the creatures stirring in the warm mothy darkness of a summer evening, for "the full-starred heavens that winter sees". Torn though he was by his sense of the pain with which all life is fibred, he could yet communicate his sensitive concern for the various aspects of Nature. It is this, above all, that is realized in James Wright's stern, tender lines: "At Thomas Hardy's Birthplace, 1953", which present a telling portrait of the elder poet.

There are moments, rare but no less valid, when Hardy celebrates with gusto the delights of sheer living, as in the song that begins:

> Sweet cyder is a great thing,
> A great thing to me . . .

A more delicate charm attaches to a country song, which, though written in a minor key, opens bravely enough:

> Let me enjoy the earth no less
> Because the all-enacting Might
> That fashioned forth its loveliness
> Had other aims than my delight.

Delight, at all events, is there.

A more frequent mood is that in which the poet declares:

> I never cared for Life: Life cared for me,
> And hence I owe it some fidelity.

Typical is the tune and the tone of one of his last lyrics, written at the age of eighty-six, and entitled, "He Never Expected Much". The sense of a neutral-tinted experience, relying for its color on vicarious drama and accepted with a kind of dreary composure, mars much of Hardy's performance.

It has been contended that passive suffering does not make for poetry, and a large portion of Hardy's work supports this view. Its great fault is a tone of melancholy and negation suggesting a lack of vitality, as distinct from the gentle irony that stiffens his finer lyrics. He allowed himself flat statements in verse that fail to spur the imagination. Or, experimenting with musical effects, he would try a dancing metre inappropriate to his theme, and indulge in such awkward triple rhymes as "listlessness"—"wistlessness". Presenting what he called satires of circumstance, he often stressed the satire so that drama became melodrama, and sentiment, sentimentality. But if he was as uneven as he was prolific, the best of his work shows a grandeur of conception, a rare subtlety of insight.

One of the qualities that endears him to us is his pleasure in paradox. His dramatic lyrics are shot with grim humor. Typical is the piece called "The Curate's Kindness". A broken-down old countryman had looked forward resignedly to the shame of the poorhouse because he would at last be rid of his wife, since he would be assigned to the men's wing and she to the women's. He is ready to drown himself on discovering that the parson has overruled the Board so as not to separate the pair after forty years of wedlock. This "workhouse irony" gains not a little from being presented in the form of a short monologue delivered by the victim in good plain Wessex. From the start the poet used the old regional speech wherever he found no equivalent in received English.

Something of the same acrid savor, as of earth and sweat, is in the dramatic lyrics of D. H. Lawrence. They expose the conflict of feelings in simple human relationships much after Hardy's fashion. Lawrence uses the vocabulary of his native Nottinghamshire, but he prefers freer rhythms. His dialect pieces differ from Hardy's further in respect to tone. The most passionate of them are pitched in the lower key that Hardy reserves for other pieces, and so have a less contrived effect.

An instance is "Whether Or Not", the story of a village triangle. The tale is told in a series of dialogues between the betrayed girl and others: her mother, a neighbor, her betrothed, the widow with whom he lodged and whom he has got with child; these dialogues interspersed with the girl's bitter soliloquies. It opens thus:

> Dunna thee tell me it's his'n, mother,
>   Dunna thee, dunna thee!
> —Oh, ay, he'll come an' tell thee, his-sèn,
>   Wench, wunna he?

The short drumming syllables fairly echo the heart's hard beating. There is no mincing of words as the drama unfolds. The language brutally mirrors the situation. In the end the man rejects both the widow who showed him a kindness his sweetheart refused and the girl whose dream had been "Ter marry wi' cabs an' rice!" He sums it up,

with an honesty the very awkwardness of which makes it
touching:

> I s'll say good-by, Liz, to yer,
>   Yer too much i' th' right for me.
> An' wi' 'er somehow it isn't right.
>   So good-by, an' let's let be!

It is plain enough that, whatever they do, they are not going to be "let be". The piece has an ironic candor that
Hardy could not have bettered.

Not irony so much as a deep sense of the cruelty intrinsic to human relationships, together with a feeling for
the charm of country things, made congenial to Hardy the
work of Charlotte Mew. She wrote several dramatic monologues in the vernacular, of which possibly the best known
is the title poem of her first book, "The Farmer's Bride".
Another touching piece is "The Shepherd's Prayer", spoken
by an old countryman, looking through the farmhouse window from his deathbed. A stanza may show something of
the appeal that her work had for Hardy.

> Turning around like a falled-over sack
> I can see team plowin' in Whithy-bush field and meal
>   carts startin' up road to Church-Town;
> Saturday arternoon then men goin' back
> And the women from market, trapin' home over the down.

The homely simile is one that he may well have envied,
and the rolling cadence has a rightness that his formal
metres did not always achieve. The old shepherd's prayer
to his "Heavenly Master" is that he may "wake in they
same green places" where he "be know'd for breakin' dogs
and follerin' sheep": if he may not walk there and look on
the old faces, he "wud sooner sleep."

Death was a familiar to Hardy, and he dwelt upon the
curious ways in which men greet this inevitable visitant.
There is the farm woman whose first thought, when her
husband is gored by a bull, is for her untidy room, but
who in a fortnight is pining away. There is the lady who

orders her fashionable mourning before her husband breathes his last. A foil to this picture, there is the stricken widower, who is compelled to read a letter on the new Spring modes addressed to a woman who the previous season "was costumed in a shroud." Several Satires of Circumstance deal with the effect of the passing of one member of a triangle on those left behind.

A less astringent irony runs through the ballad of "The Ruined Maid", who is cheerfully contemptuous of the simple friend envying her finery. Similar in tone and diction and lilting rhyme is "The Dark-eyed Gentleman", in which a country woman with a grown son, recalling a complaisant hour of her youth, concludes with an unremorseful glance at her offspring:

> No sorrow brings he,
> And thankful I be,
> That his daddy once tied up my garter for me!

This piece, which recalls a cutpurse song of the sixteenth century, and others even more emphatically are an index to Hardy's delight in balladry. He wrote many songs, not a few of them to those anonymous old tunes that so haunt the heart, at least one to a movement in a Mozart symphony. His posthumous book of lyrics, fittingly called *Winter Words*, includes, along with some of the grimmest poems he ever penned, a thumping if somewhat sardonic "Drinking Song". His feeling for the appropriate cadence was far from impeccable, but his love of melody helped him as well as hindered. As he said of another, one might say of him: "Sing; how a' would sing!"

A poem especially interesting for the management of the rhythm is a late piece called "An Ancient to Ancients". Stanza after stanza nostalgically recalls details of the happy past and the scenes that have forgotten them: "Where once we rowed, where once we sailed," and the damsels who took the tiller were veiled "Against too strong a stare", as in Manet's boating picture.

> The bower we shrined to Tennyson,
>   Gentlemen,
>   Is roof-wrecked,

observes the old man. But he does not forget that others
before him grew old yet remained enterprising fellows,
yea, "Burnt brightlier towards their setting day." His last
word is to youth:

> And ye, red-lipped and smooth-browed; list,
>   Gentlemen;
> Much is there waits you we have missed;
> Much lore we leave you worth the knowing,
> Much, much has lain outside our ken:
> Nay, rush not: time serves: we are going,
>   Gentlemen.

Tremulous though it is with the ghost of the nineteenth
century, once so alive to the speaker, the poem maintains a sturdy awareness of the difference between the
actuality and the spectral memory of it, as well as of the
hungry generation treading on the heels of that now departing. It is doubtful if this piece will have quite the
same value for later comers. Yet the invocation, "Gentlemen", twice punctuating each stanza, making it look,
Janus-faced, at once backward and forward, emphasizes,
by the sharp repetition of that old-fashioned address, the
contrast between what is remembered and what is immediately present to experience. In a somewhat similar
poem, commemorating a native of Wessex who died, an
octogenarian, in the mid-nineteenth century, Hardy evokes
her memories of times more remote, and of how

> With cap-framed face and long gaze into the embers—
>   We seated round her knees—
> She would dwell on such dead themes, not as one who
>   remembers,
>   But rather as one who sees.

The balance here between the long lines and the short
ones helps to contrast the vista enjoyed by the old lady

and the brevity of the moment in which it is glimpsed by those seated round her knees.

Hardy's sense of the pastness of the past was so strong that too often he was able to show a vanished scene or a bygone event only "as one who remembers", but his feeling for history could also serve him well. It did so in a few of the poems that have to do with the Napoleonic wars as recalled by his own elders, and more notably in those dealing with the Boer War and with the first world war, as they impinged on him. As he watched the troops departing from Southampton Docks in 1899, he wondered how long it would be before patriotism would "scorn to stand / Bondslave to realms, but circle earth and seas?" Shortly thereafter he was writing a far less ponderous version of the same theme: "The Man He Killed". Here a simple soldier, who had enlisted in a period of unemployment, offers his stammering reflections on the chances of battle, concluding:

> "Yes; quaint and curious war is!
> You shoot a fellow down
> You'd treat if met where any bar is,
> Or help to half-a-crown."

There is both conscious and unconscious irony in "Channel Firing", resounding lines on gunnery practice that literally wakes the dead. They sit upright, thinking it is Judgment Day. But God rather roughly reassures them and they lie down again, wondering if the world will ever be saner than it was when they were coffined. The skeleton of Parson Thirdly wishes in vain that "Instead of preaching forty year," he had simply "stuck to pipes and beer." This decayed hedonist's regret is silenced by renewed thunders as

> Again the guns disturbed the hour,
> Roaring their readiness to avenge,
> As far inland as Stourton Tower,
> And Camelot, and starlit Stonehenge.

The little leap in "readiness", the heavy spondees in the
final line, as well as the references to the seat of King
Arthur's court, to an old manor associated with violent
men, and to the religious memorials of the early Bronze
Age lit by the same stars that had shone on them thirty-
five centuries since, add to the reverberance. The unconscious irony lies in the date line of the poem: April, 1914.
The penultimate piece in Hardy's last book is a grim comment on the probability of the next conflict, the result,
as he saw it, of the workings among the nations of some
"demonic force" beyond morality as it was beneath consciousness.

His lively sense of evil, nurtured by the public events
of his latter years, makes his work sympathetic to later
poets who have had more intimate experience of the
malign. But his kinship with them is primarily due to the
appreciation of opposite attitudes that makes for irony. It
is peculiarly strong in those poems which imply his feeling
that "delight is a delicate growth, cramped by crookedness,
custom, and fear." Putting aside the weeds, he reveals the
true nature of that delicate growth, for which delight is
one of the happier names: the intimate relation between
man and woman. Some of these lyrics are frankly personal,
among the most touching of them being the reticent, wistful pieces written after the death of his first wife. Elsewhere, with like candor and sensitiveness, he notes the
trivialities that alter for us the color of the weather, the
accidents that change the course of a life, gently exposes
those reasons of the heart that reason does not know.

Hardy's mature lyrics speak to us directly and penetratingly. They reward rereading, even though this uneven
craftsman was capable of confiding the heavy broodings of
his generation to some of the clumsiest verse ever written,
and of sinking into a trough of bathos. Like any poet,
Hardy deserves to be judged by his best work. It shows
an interest in form heightened by his knowledge of music
and of architecture. Further, he had the strength to look
before and after without helpless pining for what is not.

The hunger for myth, like any other, avenges itself when
it is starved, and so some contemporaries flee for suste-
nance to the Church, to an adulterated Buddhism, or to a
secular orthodoxy. But there are others, and Hardy spoke
for them as he looked deeply at "human shows", indulged
in "far phantasies", and acknowledged "moments of Vision". Aware of man's need to order alike his practical and
his imaginative life, and to maintain the precarious balance between them, his own imagination was haunted by
the Sinister Spirit, the Spirit of Irony, and their unsatisfied questioner, the Spirit of Pity.

Hardy wrote several poems in which a naturalistic philosophy is skillfully tallied with elements of the Christian
myth. Among these is "Panthera", a dramatic dialogue the
sources of which the poet traces back to the second century. It concerns a tardy encounter between Jesus and his
presumed earthly father, a Roman officer garrisoned in
Jerusalem thirty years earlier and again at the time of the
crucifixion. Noteworthy also is "The Wood Fire", a blaze
before which sits another Roman who has salvaged the
hacked blood-stained pieces of the cross for his hearth.
Yet this naturalist could offer so deeply felt a tribute to
the power of the Christian legend as that tender lyric,
"The Oxen":

> Christmas Eve, and twelve of the clock.
> "Now they are all on their knees,"
> An elder said as we sat in a flock
> By the embers in hearthside ease.
>
> We pictured the meek mild creatures where
> They dwelt in their strawy pen,
> Nor did it occur to one of us there
> To doubt they were kneeling then.
>
> So fair a fancy few would weave
> In these years! Yet, I feel,
> If someone said on Christmas Eve,
> "Come; see the oxen kneel,

> In the lonely barton by yonder coomb
>> Our childhood used to know,"
> I should go with him in the gloom,
>> Hoping it might be so.

Here the simplicity of the language, even to the use of such old words as "barton" for farmyard and "coomb" for upland valley, the subdued tone, and the quiet verbal music help to create the endearing homeliness and half-shadowy radiance of some medieval Nativity. The purity of feeling is nowise impugned by the half-ironic quality of the last lines, penned in the midst of the first world war, where the word "gloom" carries a double emphasis of figurative meaning not present in his "hoping".

II

Wedded as he was to a dramatic view of things, Hardy was offering high praise when he called a lyric of Housman's the most dramatic short poem in the language. It is a caustic piece of balladry from A *Shropshire Lad*:

> "Is my team ploughing,
>> That I was used to drive
> And hear the harness jingle
>> When I was man alive?"

> Ay, the horses trample,
>> The harness jingles now;
> No change though you lie under
>> The land you used to plough.

> "Is football playing
>> Along the river shore,
> With lads to chase the leather
>> Now I stand up no more?"

> Ay, the ball is flying,
>> The lads play heart and soul;
> The goal stands up, the keeper
>> Stands up to keep the goal.

"Is my girl happy,
    That I thought hard to leave,
And has she tired of weeping
    As she lies down at eve?"

Ay, she lies down lightly,
    She lies not down to weep:
Your girl is well contented.
    Be still, my lad, and sleep.

"Is my friend hearty,
    Now I am thin and pine,
And has he found to sleep in
    A better bed than mine?"

Yes, lad, I lie easy,
    I lie as lads would choose;
I cheer a dead man's sweetheart,
    Never ask me whose.

The chief value of Housman's verse is not its drama,
however, but a kindred quality, a sardonic recognition of
the conflict between the idea and the reality. That conflict is in substance the theme of Matthew Arnold's "Em-
pedocles on Aetna", which Housman in his youth declared
to contain all the law and the prophets. He found the
sum of its wisdom in the affirmation: "Because thou must
not dream, thou need'st not then despair." Although Arnold's poem ends with the philosopher plunging into the
crater, it can scarcely be taken as an invitation to suicide.
It is so, mistakenly, that Housman's lyrics have too often
been read. When, as a boy of thirteen, he was setting
subjects for poems to be written by his brothers and sisters
for their family magazine, the first subject that he chose
was death. He did not participate in the verse-writing on
this occasion, but his sister Clemence produced the following quatrain:

Death is a dreadful thought,
And every person ought
To think of it with reverence
Before they go forever hence.

Housman continued to think of it, if not with reverence, then with respect, and so steadily that his reflections became the object of parody. His lyrics have been condemned not merely for their praise of death but for expressing a habit of mind that dictated the grim admonition: "Let us endure an hour and see injustice done." Yet their tone is often sardonic precisely because they do not ignore the injustice and its stubborn roots. In verse that speaks repeatedly of the soldier's task, the trumpet calls are few and often end on a sour note. The music is apt to be elegiac rather than challenging. But the lyric that bids youth storm the "hell-defended fort", for all its discomfitingly quaint diction and rigid metrics, reminds us of the temper that kept the resistance movements alive, compelling men to continue to assert, in the almost unrelieved darkness of the underground, the values that appeared to be doomed.

His lyrics hold the solace that comes of a candid measuring of man's estate. He is not able to carry the burden of the mystery as far as does Hardy, with all his limitations, or, to name figures nearer the foreground, as far as Yeats, Wallace Stevens, and Hugh MacDiarmid. His picture of the world, like his music, is wanting in depth and complexity.

One finds a similar lack in the work of Edna Millay, a poet of far greater versatility but no larger scope. Like Housman, she won a delighted public by using traditional techniques on familiar themes, while her skillful studding of the lyrical with the daily commonplace gave her verse a freshness that surprised without alarming. She struck a sharper note than Sara Teasdale or that equally delicate and more controlled lyricist, Lizette Woodworth Reese. The girlish ecstasy over the sensuous pleasures of meadow and seaboard, the romantic irony, the light and lovely melodies that enchanted Miss Millay's contemporaries, have exercised a spell over successive generations of girls and boys. She was especially charming when she adopted the rakish air of the Cavalier poets, and absurdly helpless

when she ventured into the forum. The author of a handful of touching songs on the transience of love and the
shortness of life, too often she denounced these griefs with
a petulance from which Housman was free.

For all the slightness of his output, he remains a lyricist
whose mordant phrases have become part of the language
and whose idiom is recalled by poems of a very different
stamp. An example is a lyric more complex than any that
Housman penned, in which Karl Shapiro writes about mail
day in the Pacific theater of war. The fourth stanza is a
reminder, among other things, that

                                            aside from the lads
Who arrive like our letters, still fresh from the kiss
        and the tear,
There are mouths that are dusty and eyes that are
        wider than fear.

It is not the cadence alone that recalls the elder poet's
lyrics on the brevity of a soldier's life. Perhaps it is the
easy use of "lads", a word that keeps recurring in Housman's verse. At all events, the lines suggest the poem in
which he reflects upon those who will die in the glory of
their youth:

The lads in their hundreds to Ludlow come in for the fair,
    There's men from the barn and the forge and the mill
        and the fold,
The lads for the girls and the lads for the liquor are there,
    And there with the rest are the lads that will never
        be old.

The very accent of Housman is sounded by Auden, notably in the song that says: "Time breaks the threaded
dances." And if Auden introduces headaches and worry
and the crack in the teacup into the same lyric, Housman
can talk like any contemporary of frayed collars as well as
of raveled hearts, and conclude a poem about a suicide
with the remark that "dinner will be cold." C. Day Lewis,
in an early essay on the poets of his generation, names as

their literary ancestors Gerard Manley Hopkins, Wilfred
Owen, and T. S. Eliot. Although never ranked with these
as an influence, Housman's name recurs with astonishing
frequency.

Norman Nicholson is a later comer who writes sensitively and sharply of the Cumberland region with the native's delight in its landscape and the contemporary's eye
for the inroads made there by a rapacious industrialism.
Whatever echoes there are in his poems, his voice is his
own. Yet one seems to catch the accents of Housman in
the stanzas entitled "Cleator Moor", which give the un-
lovely history of that mining district, exploited by greedy
owners, fallen into decay during the Depression, but "wick
with men" once more in wartime, "Digging like dogs dig
for a bone," not for life but for death:

> Every waggon of cold coal
> Is fire to drive a turbine wheel;
> Every knuckle of soft ore
> A bullet in a soldier's ear.
>
> The miner at the rockface stands,
> With his segged and bleeding hands
> Heaps on his head the fiery coal,
> And feels the iron in his soul.

Here is the same metrical scheme that Housman used in
the couplets justifying his gloomy verse:

> 'Tis true the stuff I bring for sale
> Is not so brisk a brew as ale;
> Out of a stem that scored the hand
> I wrung it in a weary land.
> But take it: if the smack is sour,
> The better for the embittered hour.

If the use of such homely words as "wick" and "segged" is
closer to Hardy's diction than to Housman's, here is the
sour smack that both commended. One finds it, along with
the latter's stanza form, in the lyrics of some of the

younger poets writing after World War II. Thus, Louis
Simpson, who handles a variety of traditional forms with
grace and vigor, writes about America and the European
scene, about love and war, in poems that sometimes echo
Housman's measures and, in a more sophisticated tone,
his irony.

A great classical scholar, Housman appreciated the spare
directness of Latin verse. His models, however, were neither the Greek and Roman poets nor the admired Matthew Arnold. They were the songs of Shakespeare, the
Scottish border ballads, and the lyrics of Heinrich Heine.
These helped to give his verse its bittersweet savor and
clear melody. Like the old ballad-makers, he knew how to
mingle the fateful and the familiar.

In a period of over forty years he allowed only one
hundred and fifty-three short poems to be published.
Written according to traditional patterns, a sufficient number are saved from dullness by the delicacy of their verbal
texture, by the careful manipulation of rhyme and half
rhyme, as well as by the occasional homely detail and the
ironic touch at the close. Housman knew when and how
to depart from the expected beat, to achieve, in the conventional stanza, effects that delight with their unexpect-
edness. Such are the variations of cadence in an autumnal
poem:

> Tell me not here, it needs not saying,
>   What tune the enchantress plays
> In aftermaths of soft September
>   Or under blanching mays,
> For she and I were long acquainted
>   And I knew all her ways.

The lyric proceeds with a technical skill that makes the
stanzas move as though to the stirring of a changeful September wind. The poem called "Fancy's Knell" has a like
charm, though here it is not the leaves in the wind but
village dancers stepping lightly to the flute that the shifting cadence evokes. In "The Lent Lily" a wealth of exact

rhymes like "array" and "away" is further enriched by
lopped rhymes like "stay" and "playing", half rhymes like
"chilly" and "sally", consonantal rhymes like "hilly" and
"hollow". Like many of Housman's lyrics, this is not wanting in archaisms. That he was capable of plain and passionate speech is instanced by the lines that murmur on
like the millstream under the bridge, heard only by the
man alone with night and hell. He does not know who
made the world but knows that, though his knuckles
bleed, he never soiled his hand with such a deed. They
can rejoice, he says elsewhere, who can be drunk "With
liquor, love, or fights," but those who think must fasten
"Their hands upon their hearts." Some of the bitterest of
his love lyrics have for their theme the fact that the most
faithful of lovers will not be found waiting on Lethe's
wharf. Personal as most of these poems are, they have the
general appeal of their melancholy matter.

Housman died three years and one month, almost to
the day, before the surrender of Madrid blotted out the
hopes of Spanish freedom, and it was early in the century
that his lyric, "The Olive", was first published. Yet it
might well have been called "Elegy for Spain" and have
commemorated the Loyalists and those who died to help
them, betrayed alike by those who would not and by their
false military allies.

> The olive in its orchard,
>   Should now be rooted sure,
> To cast abroad its branches,
>   And flourish and endure.
>
> Aloft amid the trenches
>   Its dressers dug and died;
> The olive in its orchard
>   Should prosper and abide.
>
> Close should the fruit be clustered
>   And light the leaf should wave,
> So deep the root is planted
>   In the corrupting grave.

History has given this lyric an adventitious significance for us: the tree that symbolizes peace is rooted in corruption. Yet, like many of his songs, the poem has a wide validity.

III

Sharing Hardy's view of man's place in the universe, his nerves more keenly attuned than Housman's to the human anguish with which, he reminds us, every inhabited country is clotted, Robinson Jeffers wrote poetry that points up both what is traditional and what is fresh in their work. His own early verse is commonplace in theme and treatment, and it was only with the appearance of the narrative poem, *Tamar*, which catapulted him into fame comparatively late, that he found his style. *Tamar* startled less because of the violence of its theme—the downfall of an incestuous house—than because the drama was set, not in ancient Greece or renaissance Italy, but here and now. The long rolling surflike rhythms, at once more powerful and more controlled than Whitman's, were strange to American poetry. Above all, there was a foreign challenge in Jeffers' doctrine, repeated again and again, most clearly stated in a late lyric:

> Man's world is a tragic music
>   and is not played for man's happiness,
> Its discords are not resolved but by other discords.
>   But for each man
> There is real solution, let him turn from himself and
>   man to love of God. He is out of the trap then.
>   He will remain
> Part of the music, but will hear it as the player hears it.

It is a doctrine against which, as the poet recognizes, men instinctively rebel, yet he insists that they must come to it in the end. Where Hardy's poems present man as part

of the tissues of the vast brain that is mindless Space,
Jeffers has written of him as

> a hardly noticed thought of un-
> happiness passing
> Through a great serene mind.

There are passages in his poems that seem to show a
blind Will at work in the universe, notably in the dramatic poem on the downfall of Christian civilization,
called "At the Birth of an Age". Here a superhumanly tall
figure, abstract and lonely, comes on with a broom, to declare that he is sweeping the Catalaunian Plain for another
battle. Later, after much bloodshed, the Sweeper remarks:

> Some day cabbages and vineyards
> Will spring out of the warriors' inwards.

The final stage direction for this anonymous, almost face-
less figure: "He goes out, absentmindedly sweeping,"
could have been written by Hardy. But Jeffers' poems do
not ask the question that recurs in the work of the Victorian poet: whether the Willer, masked and dumb, can
ever achieve the consciousness with which his cleverest
and cruelest creature is gifted. On the contrary, both the
narratives and the lyrics carry frequent reminders that the
"enormous invulnerable beauty of things / Is the face of
God," and the wise man is he who is able "to live gladly
in its presence, and die without grief or fear knowing it
survives us."

Among Jeffers' recurrent themes are the danger of an
all-too-human love, the self-delusion of man's self-impor-
tance. One narrative after another centers upon incest.
The symbolism that this had for him is apparent in his
treatment of the Orestes story, "The Tower beyond Tragedy". Here Electra, desiring incestuous union, is contrasted with Orestes, who, breaking every human tie, has
climbed the tower beyond tragedy and found release from
the introversion that is the plague of mankind. As in Jef-

fers' other narrative poems, the characters are apt to speak with his voice, use his chosen images, feel with his nerves the torturing persistence of cruelty, respond with his stoic pantheism to the natural scene. His deep-lunged verse, built on a stress prosody, the changing tempo regulated by his feeling for quantity, is peculiarly suited to the prophecies of this Cassandra, the rejections of this Orestes.

As incest, which he equates with man's self-love, is Jeffers' chief theme, so the injured hawk or eagle is one of his major symbols. The rock, that must suffer terrible poundings, shift with the centuries, or crack and wear away, remained for him a tried image of endurance. The wild swan is his image for the beauty of things. But what these poems oftenest depict is the anguish of power blinded or with torn wings. The bird whose blood burns for flight, the wild carnivorous creature, passionate, maimed, and bound, is shown as "the archetype body of life". Jeffers' disgust with humanity was mated to a compassion doubly wounded because it was half scornful of itself. "I like a dowser," he confessed, "go here and there, with skinless pity for the dipping hazel-fork."

His narrative, unlike Hardy's, is always a transparent screen for his own emotion. To appreciate the difference in approach one should contrast the elder poet's dramatic lyrics about the Christian legend with Jeffers' long poem, "Dear Judas", which shows the supposed archtraitor as actually a martyr, who, loving Jesus, sought at any cost to save him from himself. Another instance for comparison is Hardy's elegy on his dog, Wessex, and Jeffers' more discursive poem, "The House-dog's Grave". In both pieces a dead pet addresses the household that mourns him, and neither poem quite escapes the pitfall of sentimentality set by the theme.

A poem that bears more favorable comparison with one of Hardy's takes the form of a dialogue between buried lovers. Here Jeffers adopts a rhymed stanza pattern unusual with him and advantageous to the elegiac tone of the lyric.

"Look up my dear at the dark
Constellations above."
"Dark stars under green sky.
I lie on my back and harken
To the music of the stars,
My dear love."

To the question why he does not lie on her breast as of
old, the answer is that "lonely / Is the word in this country," and the final word he has for her is that the mole is
their moon and worms the stars they observe. Hardy's
poem is a sonnet dated 1867 and entitled "1967". He
foresees that fivescore summers will bring a century which,
"if not sublime", will, at its peak, show "A scope above
this blinkered time." Yet, asks the living lover, what will
that greatness then matter to him:

For I would only ask thereof
That thy worm should be my worm, Love!

If this lyric of Hardy's has a shudder absent from Jeffers' on the same theme, the contemporary's "Christmas
Card" proffers a darker, colder picture than Hardy's parallel poem, "The Oxen". It is not impossible that the difference in tone is due, at least in part, to the fact that while
Hardy was writing about Christmas Eve, 1915, Jeffers was
writing about Christmas Eve, 1940. The giant shadow of
the cross that humanity must bear looms, and looms the
larger for being only vaguely suggested, in this later lyric's
powerful final stanza:

Caesar and Herod shared the world,
Sorrow over Bethlehem lay,
Iron the empire, brutal the time,
Dark was that first Christmas day,
Dark was that day,
Light lay the snow on the mistletoe berries
And the ox lay down at midnight.

The inversions here are meaningful: "sorrow" "iron" "brutal" "dark" "dark"—the words weigh the heavier for their place in the line. The mistletoe is, of course, associated with the Golden Bough that symbolized even, apparently, in druid times, undying life, and the poet says that the snow lay light upon it: the fiery principle was safe. Yet "Caesar and Herod shared the world," and "iron" "brutal" "dark" "dark" are the words that ring in the mind, however softened by the final lines.

Where Hardy was an able dramatist, his junior resembles an actor unable, when giving himself to a part, entirely to divest himself of his own personality. Perhaps for that reason, it is in his lyrics and the more lyrical passages of the narrative poems that his best work is to be found. His plots, mostly woven out of the gossip and old tales of the countryside, enlarged by legendary associations, are overwrought, and have roots in myths so obscure or so literary that they engage the reader only superficially. Moreover, the extravagance of horrors heaped on horror is paralleled by the rhetorical language. If sentimentality is repressed brutality, there are passages in Jeffers' poems which suggest that the converse is also true.

The shorter lyrics, however, gain freshness from being suffused with the influence of a part of America strange to poetry when he began writing. They breathe the air of the seacoast, take in their purview a river valley and the hills beyond it that go down to the sea, the cliffs of the peninsula with their wind-wrenched cypresses, the sweep of the western sky. This landscape, with its haunted habitations, above which broods the inhuman majesty of nature, gave Jeffers something of what the Lake landscape gave a more placid pantheist. His is the poetry of a solitary who sees civilization as "a transient sickness" and is unpleasantly aware of an America "heavily thickening toward empire." But it is poetry strengthened by having its roots in however isolated a part of the American scene. Jeffers celebrated his chosen locality again and again, as where he described Point Joe in his poem of that name:

> Point Joe has teeth and torn ships; it has
>   fierce and solitary beauty;
> Walk there all day and you shall see nothing
>   that will not make part of a poem.

As he watched the shadowlike fishing boats with their
engines throbbing creep out of the fog around the cliff, he
declared that a flight of pelicans is no lovelier, "The flight
of planets nothing nobler." Decades later, the fewest of
those who, aliens as much as Jeffers, wandered across this
region, were able to balance its loveliness and its nobility
against their fear and rage.

He liked to insist that poetry should deal with permanent things and seems to have been pleased by the thought
that "man's needs and nature are no more changed in fact
in 10,000 years than the beaks of the eagles." At the same
time his verse speaks in ordinary language of the incidents
of contemporary life, takes into account the events of the
day. Indeed, *The Double Axe*, composed largely during
the second world war, has much to say about recent history. The poems there set forth his belief that our inter-
vention then and earlier was a terrible mistake, the penalty
for which is still to pay. Savagely he presses upon us the
poisonous fruits of victory, and holds up to the mirror of
human nature its own Medusa-head.

In his effort to retrieve vigor and substance for poetry,
Jeffers sought, as he said, "to attempt the expression of
philosophic and scientific ideas in verse." Unhappily his
work bears witness to the truth of Mallarmé's observation
that poems are made with words, for his tend to be overwhelmed by ideas. These are kindred to the reflections
that shaped Hardy's meditative lyrics, the themes out of
which Housman made his simple songs, the material of
D. H. Lawrence's later verse. For Lawrence the principle
of evil had two centers. One matrix was the soulless machine. The other was self-conscious, egocentric man. Further, he held that God realizes Himself in substance, yet
life has its roots in a profound, mysterious dark, and the

promise of ultimate oblivion is blessed. Jeffers likewise
saw the principle of evil in introverted man and his self-
centered civilization. He saw the universe as the body of
God. He differs from Lawrence in dwelling upon the
cruelty and suffering in the small corner of the universe
that we know. For Jeffers the ultimate values were strength
to endure life with all its ugliness and agony, and the
promise of oblivion as the balance of, the solace for, our
painful consciousness. His ideas are neither unfamiliar nor
unacceptable to the twentieth-century mind. But they are
not always sufficiently wrought into the body of his poetry.
It testifies to the fact that the vitality of a poet does not
depend upon the contemporaneity of his subject matter.
Just as his extravagant imaginings betrayed him into grandiloquence, so his bitter earnestness was apt to make for
flat assertion and iteration. His performance is a warning
against allowing ideas to stalk too pompously on the poetic
stage.

His best work offers a reminder of matters that by
solemn overstatement it tends to obscure. It speaks for a
serenity founded on tragic awareness of the human condition and of the grandeur of the nonhuman universe. One
finds this attitude expressed more often in Chinese poetry than in our own. Possibly this mood was open to Jeffers because the landscape with which he was familiar has
something of the noble austerity that the poet sages of
ancient China sought in their mountain retreats.

Among contemporaries, one finds this temper in certain
poems by Kenneth Rexroth, who is intimate both with the
West Coast ranges and with oriental poetry and philosophy. The opening section of a poem in three parts called
"Lyell's Hypothesis Again" is a case in point.

> The mountain road ends here,
> Broken away in the chasm where
> The bridge washed out years ago.
> The first larkspur glitters
> In the first patch of April

Morning sunlight. The engorged creek
Roars and rustles like a military
Ball. Here by the waterfall,
Insuperable life, flushed
With the equinox, sentient
And sentimental, falls away
To the sea and death. The tissue
Of sympathy and agony
That binds the flesh in its Nessus' shirt;
The clotted cobweb of unself
And self; sheds itself and flecks
The sun's bed with darts of blossom
Like flagellant blood above
The water bursting in the vibrant
Air. This ego, bound by personal
Tragedy and the vast
Impersonal vindictiveness
Of the ruined and ruining world,
Pauses in this immortality,
As passionate, as apathetic,
As the lava flow that burned here once;
And stopped here; and said, 'This far
And no further.' And spoke thereafter
In the simple diction of stone.

There are other lyrics by Rexroth that speak in the same
tone of quiet authority about similar things. He has, however, wandered more widely than Jeffers, both literally
and figuratively, as the scope and variety of his work bear
witness. He is less apt to write in free cadences than in
short unrhymed lines, with attention to the number and
weight of the syllables and to the music of the alphabet.
Although he insists that poetry should do more than communicate, he is rarely didactic. His religious anarchism
finds voice in sardonic bitterness or violent satire. But the
anarchism is less vocal than the unorthodox religiosity of a
man "Lying under the stars, / In the summer night, /
Late, while the autumn / Constellations climb the sky,"

and feeling that the cosmos, present to him in "The faint breeze in the dark pines, / And the invisible grass, / The tipping earth, the swarming stars / Has an eye that sees itself."

It is curious to discover, among poets of a totally different background and approach, brief glimpses of the world as Jeffers views it. Thus, that voluptuary of the imagination, Wallace Stevens, echoes Jeffers almost to a syllable in the line: "It is the human that is the alien," though he goes on in his own fashion: "The human who has no cousin in the moon." The Scottish lyricist, Hugh Mac-Diarmid, who has so much to say about the moon that one almost believes it to be his cousin, ever and again presents that profound sense of the inhuman universe upon which Jeffers harps. MacDiarmid (the pseudonym of C. M. Grieve) writes with a fervent energy, a delicate lyricism, and a glinting humorousness foreign alike to the hermit of Carmel and to later poets of the West Coast. Thus he draws a picture of blue-jowled fishermen hauling on their nets in the wee small hours of a summer morning, shouting to the herring "O come in, and see me," while the herring respond by coming aboard "As if o' their ain accord." There is no anguish here, but a joyful acceptance of the order of things in which destruction is involved with life, as night with day, pain with delight. This, he asserts blithely,

> is the way that God sees life,
> The haill jing-bang o's appearin'
> Up owre frae the edge of naethingness
> —It's *his* happy cries I'm hearin'.

A more somber feeling for the pattern in which man is all but lost broods over other lyrics of his, among them the lines, "Yet Ha'e I Silence Left":

Yet ha'e I silence left, the croon o' a'.

No' her, wha on the hills langsyne I saw
Liftin' a forehead o' perpetual snaw.

No' her, wha in the how-dumb deid o' nicht
Kyths, like Eternity in Time's despite.

No' her, withooten shape, wha's name is Daith,
No' Him, unkennable abies to faith

—God whom, gin e'er He saw a man, 'ud be
E'en mair dumfooner'd at the sicht than he.

—But Him, whom nicht in man or Deity
Or Daith or Dreid or Laneliness can touch
Wha's deed owre often and has seen owre much
O I ha'e Silence left.

Similarly Jeffers fancies

That silence is the thing, this noise a found word for it;
    interjection, a jump of the breath at that silence;
Stars burn, grass grows, men breathe: as a man finding
    treasure says "Ah!" but the treasure's the essence;
Before the man spoke it was there, and after he has
    spoken he gathers it, inexhaustible treasure.

Yet both poets need to find words for it. The Scottish
poet's lyric is part of a long sequence called "A Drunk Man
Looks at the Thistle". This flower is as largely symbolic for
him as the rose was for William Butler Yeats. MacDiarmid's nationalism is more vehement and his intellectual
hunger insatiable. He sometimes finds it possible, however, to twinkle even at these passions. A later version of
the poem cited above ends wryly:

        O I ha'e Silence left,
            —"And weel ye micht,"
        Sae Jean'll say, "efter sic a nicht!"

His concern with it has withstood not merely his wife's
sarcasm but the laughter of time. A late and somewhat discursively learned poem approves Hölderlin because he
sought,

> And often miraculously found,
> The word with which silence speaks
> Its own silence without breaking it.

That word recalls us to a view of the universe at once humbling and exalting. An instance is offered at the close of Jeffers' poem, "Fawn's Foster-Mother". This is a portrait of a withered mountain woman, her face now "furrowed like a bad road" with wagon ruts, who, as a young mother with breasts full of milk, had once nursed an orphaned fawn.

> She is thrown up on the surface of things, a
>   cell of dry skin
> Soon to be shed from the earth's old eyebrows,
> I see that once in her spring she lived in the
>   streaming arteries,
> The stir of the world, the music of the mountain.

This poetry, with all its faults, recalls that music, the discords interrupting it, the silence from which it wonderfully emerges.

2. Farewell, Romance

The poets of the early twentieth century were "full of an unsatisfied hunger for the commonplace." The phrase is Yeats's. It was written not during the severity of his middle period, but in an article that he contributed to a Boston newspaper in 1892. It is further proof, if this were needed, that the poetic renaissance which coincided with World War I, like any other, did not mean a sharp break with the past, but a fresh impulse felt even by those whose work was strongly traditional. The harsh realism of Masefield's early verse narratives startled the public not because it was new but because it had grown unfamiliar. The roots of his poetry went back, as he acknowledged, to the work of Chaucer and, more clearly, to that of Kipling.

The medieval diplomat and the modern storyteller alike respected the vernacular. Both were men of the world, with a lively knowledge of what works beneath its shows. They shared a pleasure in various kinds of craftsmanship. Chaucer's account of the clamor, the color, the bustle of preparation in the yards before a tournament is glorious and down-to-earth, anticipating the sense of realized romance that Kipling found in purring dynamos. Reveling in the right functioning of an engine as he hated its abuse, his verse abounds in tributes to the beauty of steamers and locomotives, to the skill of those Sons of Martha whose care it is "in all the ages to take the buffet and cushion the shock", who see to it "that the gear engages" and who take care that "the switches lock". When Stephen Spender, a quarter of a century later, praises the nobility of pylons and speaks of an airliner with shut-off engines as

More beautiful and soft than any moth
With burring furred antennae feeling its huge path
Through dusk

or of an express train "Steaming through the metal landscape on her lines," rejoicing,

Wrapt in her music no bird song, no, nor bough,
Breaking with honey buds, shall ever equal,

it is from the viewpoint of an observer exalting his aesthetic pleasure in these things. Kipling's verse presents
similar objects with the more intimate delight of a tech-
nician.

In "M'Andrew's Hymn", a long monologue in Scots, he
composed a paean to machinery expressing the religious
veneration of an engineer who finds "Predestination in the
stride o' yon connectin'-rod." A Calvinist, M'Andrew sees
the Hand of God in coupler-flange and spindle-guide. It is
not impossible to interpret Calvinism in secular terms: the
belief in predestination may be a belief in mechanical
cause and effect; the idea of total depravity may be read
as a sense of the stubborn evil in things, the work of what
in contemporary superstition go by the name of "grem-
lins"; and the perseverance of saints may be taken to be
the stubbornly enduring character of engineers that even-
tuates in glory. M'Andrew's engines certainly obeyed the
inalterable, irreversible laws of mechanics. His world was
a divinely ordered machine with a hard core of evil that
only divine Grace could melt.

Spender has said that no poet wrote of the machinery
of a ship with the intelligent sympathy of Kipling until
the advent of Auden. But where the elder singer celebrated the beautiful efficiency of enginery, the poet who
came to the fore in the thirties was compelled to note
"Equipment rusting in unweeded lanes." Of Auden's
group, the one whose early work was distinguished by its
most frequent references to technology was C. Day Lewis.
This is particularly true of his long poem, "The Magnetic

Mountain", where the imagery, in part magical, derives
chiefly from modern technics. Thus he writes:

> Let us be off! Our steam
> Is deafening the dome.
> The needle in the gauge
> Points to a long-banked rage,
> And trembles there to show
> What a pressure's below.
> Valve cannot vent the strain
> Nor iron ribs refrain
> That furnace in the heart.

Here Lewis's metaphors, which Kipling might well have
appreciated, are expressive of a revolutionary dynamism
that the bard of empire would have damned. For Kipling-
esque rhythms one must look to other poets, among them
the American, Karl Shapiro. Though his attitude is more
complex, he writes about "The Gun" in a style the old
jingoist might have inspired. Again, in a piece called
"Buick" Shapiro praises the new motor with Kipling's
loverly delight, comparing it to

> a sloop with a sweep of immaculate wing on her
>   delicate spine
> And a keel as steel as a root that holds in the sea
>   as she leans . . .

He has, too, the elder man's awareness of what went to
the making of this "warm-hearted beauty", now so alien
"from the booming belts" of its birth where it "turned on
the stinging lathes of Detroit and Lansing at night."

In Kipling's verse the machine is viewed as the hand-
some thing it is in the eyes of the technical expert. This
is the attitude that moves him to speak of "our wise Lord
God, master of every trade", address the Deity as "Great
Overseer", and imagine heaven as the region where "the
Master of All Good Workmen shall put us to work anew."

Delight in the work carries over into respect for the worker, whether he is a navvy or a trooper, a pagan water-carrier, a Christian clerk, or even the enemy. It is of the fiber of his verse, showing plainest in the Barrack Room Ballads.

Not only in the jungle but throughout the length and breadth of the earth, these songs repeatedly remind us, "the head and the hoof of the Law and the haunch and the hump is—Obey!" The same moral is implicit in his poem on "The Secret of the Machines", subtitled "Modern Machinery". This is dated by its reference to the S.S. *Mauretania* as "the boat-express". But it remains valid for its injunction, spoken by the machines, to remember the Law by which they live, who "are not built to comprehend a lie":

> We can neither love nor pity nor forgive.
> If you make a slip in handling us you die!

The machine, a physical thing, is itself governed by the laws of nature, which, unlike those made by men, even in the Age of Relativity remain for practical purposes inalterable. The final stanza might have been uttered by the deadliest machine invented. Kipling died nearly a decade before the atom bomb was dropped on Hiroshima. Possibly because he did not witness the progress of World War II, he was the better able to maintain the conviction, expressed in "Recessional" and in his other, less familiar hymns, that the universe, however mysterious, is an ordered mystery, and obedience a primary commandment. His insistence on this is paralleled in recent poetry by his compatriot, Alex Comfort, paralleled because, traveling in the same direction, their views never meet. Comfort reiterates that our world is held together by obedience, but he cannot accept our world, and continues to assert, as in his chilling "Song for Heroes", that "Obedience is death". In lines entitled "Notes for My Son" he points up the need for rebellion with allusions to the martyrdom of Jeanne d'Arc and of Jesus:

> *So that because the woodcutter disobeyed*
> *they will not burn her today or any day*
>
> *So that for lack of a joiner's obedience*
> *the crucifixion will not now take place.*

To Kipling, knowing the terrible mistakes made by even the best of those in authority, it was nevertheless an article of faith that the obedient serve the gods. Nearly half of his "Epitaphs of the War: 1914–1918" are eloquent of that belief. These lapidary epigrams have the firm outline that one associates with some of the antique verse cameos in the *Greek Anthology*, a pathos like theirs, and a wit that they do not often show. Kipling was convinced of the necessity of war, but this bitter patriot's verse was free of blithe romanticizing and sentimental astigmatism. Curiously, one finds its like in the simple quatrain that Roy Fuller wrote during World War II about a native working on an aerodrome and in his dry "Epitaph on a Bombing Victim" which bids the reader not to query his nation that "Was History's confederate."

Because government meant to Kipling the acceptance of an onerous duty, he could be alert to its mistakes and vocal about its ignominy. The lines called "The Settler", with the epigraph: "South Africa War ended, May 1902", carries as much shame as promise in the settler's vow that

> where the senseless bullet fell
> And the barren shrapnel burst,

he will plant a tree and dig a well, and together with his native neighbor atone for "the black waste of it all". If the lines have sardonic overtones sixty years later, there are other pieces that retain their validity. The devotees of the Social Muse, speaking for the forgotten man of the thirties, were little more candid and concrete than Kipling about the ex-serviceman in a postwar world. His Troop-Sergeant-Major turned messenger boy is brother to the apple vendors on the fringes of Hooverville, as is the veteran who thus concludes a detailed account of the treatment accorded him:

> For it's Tommy this, an' Tommy that, an' "Chuck
>   him out, the brute!"
> But it's "Saviour of 'is country" when the guns
>   begin to shoot . . .

He draws more than one picture that in raw truth and gay brutality approximates the Irish ballad of the returned soldier, "Why, Johnny, I Hardly Knew Ye", of which this stanza is typical:

> You haven't an arm and you haven't a leg,
>   Hurroo! Hurroo!
> You haven't an arm and you haven't a leg,
>   Hurroo! Hurroo!
> You're an eyeless, noseless, chickenless egg;
> You'll have to be put in a bowl to beg;
>   Och, Johnny, I hardly knew ye!
> With drums and guns, and guns and drums
>   The enemy nearly slew ye,
>   My darling dear, you look so queer,
> Och, Johnny, I hardly knew ye!

Kipling composed a ballad of Victorian warfare, "The Widow's Party", that follows the same swinging rhythm and is equally frank about the way in which "some was crimped and some was carved, / And some was gutted and some was starved, / When the Widow give the party." The folk song ends with the promise of Johnny's dismayed sweetheart to keep on as her beau this "object of woe". Kipling's ballad concludes with the redeeming assertion that Johnny helped to break a king and build a road:

> A court-house stands where the Reg'ment goed.
> And the river's clean where the raw blood flowed
>   When the Widow give the party.

The stanzas on the improvements in methods of warfare, called "The Benefactors", end on a hopeful note that now has an ironic ring:

> All Power, each Tyrant, every Mob
>   Whose head has grown too large,
> Ends by destroying its own job
> And works its own discharge.

He is steadily concerned with the job well done.

As might be expected, the poet's pleasure in craftsmanship is not least when it comes to his own art. He declares it plainly in one song after another. "The Last Rhyme of True Thomas" relates how Thomas the Rhymer scornfully repudiates the idea that a king can ennoble him, behavior that has proved sympathetic to more than one modern poet of repute. Kipling dreamed of a paradise where each, for the joy of working, "Shall draw the Thing as he sees It, for the God of Things as They are!" He knew that the acorn of actuality may be food for the wild pig, or, imaginatively nourished, grow into a giant oak that will catch the sun and moon in its branches. But lacking that hard, bitter kernel, there will be no tree. With a backward smile at Landor, he asked:

> Ah! what avails the classic bent
>   And what the cultured word,
> Against the undoctored incident
>   That actually occurred?

Perhaps because the undoctored incident was at the heart of his verse, and because that verse gave off the smell of the engine room, the stench of the camp, the garlic and spices of the East, the salt of the open sea, Kipling now and then ventured with impunity into more remote regions and glanced at mysteries, in his punning phrase, "of no earthly importance".

He had no doubt but that "there are nine and sixty ways of constructing tribal lays," and that "every single one

of them is right." His own way was primarily that of the
ballad-maker who is akin to the roving reporter.

> For to admire an' for to see
> For to be'old this world so wide

might have been his slogan. His verse no less than his
prose displays his interest in men and women of different
races, creeds, and colors, in animals, in machinery, and in
verse forms as various as his subject matter. Along with
his curiosity and his great narrative gift went a sense of
rhythm that carries his songs along as on the swing of the
sea, and a feeling for language that can redeem the too
casual or rhetorical diction. The power of his rhythms is
heard diversely in the rolling hexameters of "The Sea and
the Hills", the weighted syllables of "Boots", the familiar
lilt of "The Road to Mandalay", the grave slow movement
of "Gertrude's Prayer". Appropriately couched in quaint
language close to Middle English, this retains all the bitter
force of poetry in modern speech and has a memorable
refrain: "Dayspring mishandled cometh not againe." Prefaced to one of his prose tales is a "Song of the Galley-
Slaves" written in the free cadence that belongs rather to
talk than to song, but held to the pattern of verse by
rhyme and by its desperate burden:

We pulled for you when the wind was against us and
　　　the sails were low.
> *Will you never let us go?*
We ate bread and onions when you took towns, or ran
　　　aboard quickly when you were beaten back by the
　　　foe.
The Captains walked up and down the deck in fair
　　　weather singing songs, but we were below.
We fainted with our chins on the oars and you did not
　　　see that we were idle, for we still swung to and fro.
> *Will you never let us go?*
The salt made the oar-handles like shark-skin; our knees
　　　were cut to the bone with salt-cracks; our hair was

stuck to our foreheads; and our lips were cut to the
gums, and you whipped us because we could not row.
Will you never let us go?
But, in a little time, we shall run out of the port-holes
as the water runs along the oar-blade, and though
you tell the others to row after us you will never
catch us till you catch the oar-thresh and tie up the
winds in the belly of the sail. Aho!
Will you never let us go?

As became a ballad-maker, Kipling used the refrain often
and well. His delight in the lilt of verse, especially that
of the marching song, made him pad his lines to fit the
tune. His weaknesses are plain. So, too, are his gifts. T. S.
Eliot has called attention to the peculiar propriety of the
word "whimper" at the climax of "Danny Deever":

> "What's that that whimpers over'ead?" said
> Files-on-Parade.
> "It's Danny's soul that's passin' now," the
> Colour-Sergeant said.

Eliot uses the word cleverly at the close of "The Hollow
Men", whose world ends "not with a bang but a whimper".
And who are the hollow men, the stuffed men, of Eliot's
poem but sib to Kipling's "Tomlinson".

Later poets writing from the outposts of empire have
not taken the stand of the disciplining adult that inspired
Kipling's imperialism. Their attitude has been rather that
of the rebellious child come of age. This is true of poets
as different from one another as the South African, Roy
Campbell, a Catholic, and John Manifold, an Australian
balladist who puts his faith in revolution. Both have been
able to introduce exotic scenery into their lines as naturally
as did Kipling. Both have written vigorous verse. Neither
measures up to Kipling's originality in working fresh subject matter or his virtuosity in handling traditional patterns.

In the envoy to one of his early books of short stories, he

thanks God for having made him a craftsman and given
him the vision of Eden that allowed him "Godlike to muse
o'er his own Trade", adding in all humility,

> It is enough that through Thy Grace
> I saw naught common on Thy earth.

The lines recall Andrew Marvell's tribute to Charles I
upon the scaffold:

> He nothing common did or mean
> Upon that memorable scene.

One recognizes in Kipling's verse the kingly virtue of re-
viving our sense of uncommon glory. He found it, often,
in the commonplace. Neither the Toryism of which much
of his verse is the vehicle, nor the frequent conventionality
of the pattern, be it that of the popular song or the formal
sestina, impugn the vigor of his best work. Repeatedly
it gives proof that he was a man who believed the wrong
things for the right reasons. It shows, too, that his nerves
were in tune with the times.

His songs never reveal Hardy's desperate sense of the
malign, but one of the last poems he wrote, composed in
1932, and entitled "The Storm Cone", evidences a prescience of the darkness ahead. It describes the signals of
approaching storm in stanzas that throb and shudder, halt
and move on with the laboring, gale-beaten ship. This
seems something larger than the Ship of State, as the
poem concludes sternly that though "She moves, with all
save purpose lost," until she reaches open sea, "Let no
man deem that he is free!" The spirit of this poem is one
to which we must respond, and its traditional form has
again come into favor in some quarters. What chiefly sets
its author among poets of a later day is that the body of
his work reveals a concern with the experiences of the common man in the machine age, a delight in the common
language.

II

John Masefield's early verses tell plain tales of the sea in the jargon of plain sailormen, after Kipling's fashion. Such pieces as "Fever Ship", "Hell's Pavement", the dialogue between a crimp and a drunken sailor called "A Valediction (Liverpool Docks)", are salt-water parallels to the frankest and most tuneful of the Barrack Room Ballads. At least one poem matches in harsh irony Hardy's lines about the dog scratching on its mistress' grave for the bone it had buried there; when the dead sailor has been wrapped up in rotten sailcloth weighted with holystone and dumped into the sea, " 'It's rough about Bill,' the fo'c'sle said, 'we'll have to stand his wheel.' " It was not for nothing that young Masefield had studied Chaucer and delighted in Kipling's verse, nor yet that he had a friend in John Synge. In the preface to his one thin book of lyrics, almost half of which is given over to racy translations, the Irish playwright showed what was wrong with most of the verse in the first decade of the century. He set the poetry of exaltation above any other, but he insisted that poetry needed the strong things of life, to prove that what is noble or tender is not the product of weakness, and he added that "before verse can be human again it must learn to be brutal." These words, written in December, 1908, were largely prophetic. Synge wrote with terrible simplicity of his own broken life. Padraic Colum was sensitively setting down the commonplaces of sufferings endured and small pleasures relished by the Irish peasantry in their smoky cabins and on their boggy roads. Yeats, though scarcely the poet of ordinary things, was soon to turn from the proud, high-flown style of his early lyrics to the proud, severe style of his middle period, and to recall in his own verse the savagery of O'Bruadair and of Swift. These poets, among others, helped to set the tone. It remained for Masefield to produce a narrative poem abounding in brutality and yet emulous of tenderness and exaltation, "The Everlasting Mercy", and its companion piece, "The Widow in the Bye Street".

Both poems deal with the crasser aspects of village life, both are realistic not only in their recital of unpleasant facts but in their freedom from any moral lesson. The everlasting mercy is extended to Saul Kane, drunkard, bruiser, fornicator, through no virtue of his. The widow lives to see her only son hanged for murder—" 'Crime passionel' in Agricultural Districts" the lawyers list it—to have her heart broken, her life wasted, through no fault of hers. Although these poetic narratives are inept and sentimental in their lyrical passages, the dialogue is in the plain language of the prize ring and the public house. The drunken hired man's threat to the farmer in the famous couplet:

> "I'll bloody him a bloody fix,
> I'll bloody burn his bloody ricks"

is a use of common diction in a common situation that would have lifted the hair from Wordsworth's horrified head, but would also have assured him that poets had achieved the courage of his convictions.

A less ambitious but in some ways more satisfactory piece is "Reynard the Fox". This Chaucerian verse narrative has much of the color and excitement of a fox hunt, and gives life to the fox himself. But like the bulk of Masefield's work, the poem suffers from his careless technique. He hoped that his verse would be spoken rather than read, that it would become part of the heritage of the simple folk about whom and for whom it was composed. In the prefatory remarks to his *Collected Poems* he observes somewhat wistfully of himself and his fellows that "Whatever their faults and shortcomings, these poets have been a school of life instead of a school of artifice. However harshly the next school may treat them, that school must be a little livelier for their efforts." The words "lively" and "harsh" recur in the two short pages of this introduction. To look at life closely, as he at first tried to do, was to see it as harsh—for the great majority of mankind squalid in its circumstances, cruel in its processes, meaningless in its conclusion. Within his limitations Masefield sought to make his readers enter more fully into the daily life of the sailor and the farm hand. It meant noting such details as "the stink of bad cigars and heavy drink" in the public house, "the fag-ends, spit and sawdust" on the floor, the "filthy hut . . . without a drain" where mangy chickens with sore necks search the room for crumbs, the gale at sea in which the sails are "whirled like dirty birds". It meant dealing with raw lust, savage stupidity, brutish work, empty deaths.

There is some food for irony in the fact that the man who was to become Laureate of England should have opened his career with a poem consecrating his songs not to the ruler, not to the bemedaled commander, but to "The men with the broken heads and the blood running into their eyes." If he has achieved a place not generally accorded those who choose unsavory subjects, it may be because, for all his knowledge of and sympathy with the deprived, his attitude is not one of rebellion against their evil case, but one of simple tenderness and pity, and his usage is largely conventional. Masefield's narrative poems may be contrasted with the brief piece on "Whitehaven" by Norman Nicholson. He uses the short couplets that Masefield used, and his theme is related to that of "The Everlasting Mercy". Nicholson pictures the seaport mining town and its history in language free of adjectival rot, and rendered livelier by the use of slant rhymes. His is the unorthodox Christianity of the revolutionary, and his clear-eyed, hot-hearted understanding, no less than his virile craftsmanship, is beyond that of Masefield, who has not shown to the same degree what the younger poet calls "the anger of love".

Masefield has been uncritical alike of the Establishment and of familiar verse forms. It remained for poets with keener eyes and ears, wilder blood, quicker minds, to write the short and ugly annals of the poor in a more compelling fashion. He lacks the skill exhibited by his masters. Here is neither Kipling's rich vocabulary nor his incantatory manipulation of the refrain. Instead, Masefield offers a dulling repetition of phrase. For all the rough speech in his early work, he does not have the ear for the vernacular of John Synge, who said he got more aid than any learning could have given him from a chink in the floor of an old Wicklow house that let him hear what the girls in the kitchen were saying. Yet if his verse wants the craftsmanship of his elder compatriot and the earthiness of the Irishman, Masefield's work shows that respect for the school of life with which he was to inspire his own successors.

III

An American poet, contemporary with Masefield, whose work has a certain affinity with his, is that lyrical revivalist, Vachel Lindsay. A native of Springfield, Illinois, Lindsay's feeling for the town, half sentimental, half visionary, is a permanent element in his verse. He saw Lincoln's mournful ghost walking there at midnight in wartime, but this New Jerusalem was to be builded with the help of other venerables as well, Buddha, Confucius, and Swedenborg among them. Lindsay's work is a curious medley of local patriotism and the enthusiasm of a young evangelist, seeking utterance in the mysterious music of which, as he early discovered, Poe was the master. All this indicates no kinship with the British sailor poet, yet Lindsay's verse is suffused with the proselytizing faith of the Quaker lady who rouses the soul of Saul Kane in Masefield's "Everlasting Mercy", and the same poem has passages instinct with the sense of outrage that cries out in Lindsay's lines on the stunted bodies and starved minds of the slum children. The poetry of both men shows a quickness of sympathy half obscured by an oversimplification of social and psychological problems, and of aesthetic problems as well.

Lindsay was apt to identify the evils of our civilization with the brute machine, and to some degree with the Re-

publican party. A few passages in his work, for all their
naïveté, kindle with indignation at the forces that sap the
idealism of youth and the manhood of the poor. "Not that
they starve, but starve so dreamlessly," he says in "The
Leaden-Eyed". His juniors were to say the same things
more penetratingly but with no deeper feeling. There is
an ironical fidelity to fact in his "Factory Window Song"
with its reiterated "Factory windows are always broken."
There is not the sharpness of a later generation of poets
who saw more than factory windows broken.

The rules that Lindsay laid down for himself when he
tramped across the country, trading his rhymes for bread
with small townspeople and farmers, are curiously like the
duties enjoined on the members of a workers' collective
outlined by a much lonelier man who wrote his poetry in
the form of prose parables: Franz Kafka. Lindsay had
something of Kafka's religiosity but not his subtlety. Nor
did Lindsay's conscience extend to his art. His work is
marred by the facile phrase, the stereotyped metaphor, the
tendency to inflation that marks the sentimentalist.

His ethical bias tended to put a curb on his fantasy, but
it was less hampering to his lyrical impulse. His stanzas are
rich in gay sound patterns and have a novel, riotous freedom of rhythm suggestive of the revivalist's shout and the
college yell. He had an ear for the singing game and the
"train-caller in a union depot" as well as for the old hymn
tunes. Thus, "John L. Sullivan, the Strong Boy of Boston"
introduces, along with the mockingbird in the lane, the
shrill voices of the pavements chanting, "East side, west
side, all around the town", "Ring-around-a-rosie", and
"London Bridge is falling down". Lindsay's music ranges
from the rousing drum beat of "Booth led boldly with his
big bass-drum—" and the thousand-throated whisper of
"The Kallyope Yell" to the plangent sweetness of "The
Chinese Nightingale". The skillful use of the pause is especially noticeable in the pieces that he called Negro ser-
mons, such as the half-humorous, half-solemn stanzas on
"How Samson Bore Away the Gates of Gaza". The sim-

plicity of thought and feeling that he shares with Masefield may have helped him to enlarge the audience for his chosen art.

Lindsay, too, wanted a public made up of ordinary people, the people whom he met casually as he tramped from one state to another, preaching his Gospel of Beauty, speaking for a "new localism". He found a slightly more sophisticated audience which enjoyed his showmanship but failed to respond as he had dreamed to the civic ardor that inspired it. Like the man who wrote it, Lindsay's verse was the battleground of a zeal to reform the world and a delight in pure art. The struggle invalidates most of his poems, including the one that brought him recognition: "General William Booth Enters Into Heaven". This moves to the thrumming of banjos, the calling of flutes, the jingling of tambourines, the hard throb of drums. But though Lindsay scored the poem as though thus seeking to enhance the sense of valor or tenderness or exaltation that a given stanza was to convey, he insisted that "poetry is first and last for the inner ear." No such conviction animates the verse written to jazz background music that a later generation was to greet vociferously. The events of the intervening decades transmogrified tenderness and exaltation to satiric rage. As with Jacques Prévert, some of whose work Lawrence Ferlingetti has done into English, hatred of knavery and folly bred an aggressive anarchism.

Lindsay's favorite among his long poems was neither the hymn to General Booth nor the resonant "Congo", absurdly subtitled "A Study of the Negro Race" but rather a study in vowel and consonantal melodies. He may have preferred "The Chinese Nightingale" above his other poems because it satisfied his hunger for tone color and Oriental splendor. As he wrote to Sara Teasdale, the lyricist for whom it was composed, "A ghost-nightingale— thousands of years old—sings in a Chinese laundry for the night-shift—about 4 o'clock in the morning, sings of the most ancient possible days in China." Among the "dragon-mountains" and "rainbow-junks", the laundryman, bowed over his ironing board, hears the clock on his wall, the railroad yard beyond his door, less clearly than the sound of temple gongs and "the howl of the silver seas". The poem has the flaws that Lindsay's work never escapes, but the shadowy visions that float upon the words as upon the smoke of burning joss sticks, the lyrical cadences, have a lasting enchantment.

> "One thing I remember:
> Spring came on forever,
> Spring came on forever,"
> Said the Chinese Nightingale.

An insatiable romanticism of the kind that was to show itself again in the verse of Stephen Benét and Paul Engle, allowed Lindsay to gild the American past with the wonder of legend and to exalt popular heroes, from presidents to prize fighters and movie stars. His starved imagination, attaching itself to the America of the Midwest, led him toward the same jejune fantasy that is shown up in Walt Disney's versions of folk tale. His verse is apt to veil the actualities of American life in an eager optimism. Yet the giants to whom it pays tribute include, along with the orthodox representatives of the native tradition, the forgotten eagle, Governor John P. Altgeld, who had dared to reopen the Haymarket case and pardon the three remaining victims of an affair only less notorious than the judicial murder of Sacco and Vanzetti some forty years later.

In "General William Booth", as elsewhere, Lindsay seems trying to recall, together with the glamour of the bonfires and brasses of the political parades of his boyhood, the image of a renewed democracy which floated like a banner above them for the dreamy eyes of a boy. In his efforts to produce a kind of communal poetry, using words snatched from the street, using chants in which the audience might freely join, he was working to retrieve something of that lost glory.

However naïvely and inadequately, he was seeking to express with the same religious fervor a vision of America kindred to that which trembles and gleams and sings in the ambitious structure of Hart Crane's *The Bridge*. The gulf between the achievement of the two poets is enormous. It may be glimpsed in their treatment of an identical subject, the half-mythical figure of the woman whom Lindsay called "Our Mother Pocahontas" and whom Crane addressed as "Princess". Crane identified her with the American continent. Both poets saw her as a native Corn-Goddess. Lindsay was incapable of Crane's imaginative flights, telescopic imagery, and heavily loaded diction. Yet he remains unique in his generation for having anticipated Crane's dream, and he was among the first American poets to find his materials in the native background, to give currency to popular songs, and to employ, if not without a measure of awkward archaisms, the American language.

IV

Not so much a poet of the Midwest as a poet of America with a strong Midwestern accent, Lindsay has affiliations with such regional verse-makers as Sandburg and Masters, who came to the fore at about the same time. Masters had his roots in the America of Jeffersonian democracy, yet he liked to call himself a Hellenist. His effort in the *Spoon River Anthology* was to combine American provincialism with Greek universality. The germ of the book was the idea of telling the story of an American country town so as to make it the story of the world. He found its prototype in the *Greek Anthology*, that superb collection of poems ranging from Simonides' stern epitaphs on those fallen in the Persian wars to the lyrics of tenth-century Byzantium. Masters' work has greater frankness, if it wants the other virtues of his models.

The town of Spoon River was a microcosm in which he saw the image of the small town of his boyhood, as also of the metropolis he had come to know while practicing criminal law in Chicago. All manner of men and women speak from their graves in this community. Since wanderers from Poland, Germany, and even China, were buried here, various nationalities, too, are represented, and nearly all these people are drawn with something of the savage candor, though never the wit, of Daumier's cartoons.

The book opens with a lyric echoing the cry that haunts the centuries. Masters' prelude lacks the music of more venerable elegies, though his reiterated "All, all, are sleeping on the hill," has a mournful lyricism quite foreign to the prosaic phrases in which he presents the histories of the sleepers. But what sets this poem apart from most of its exemplars is that instead of lamenting great kings and dazzling ladies, or such masters of balladry as Robert Henryson, it recalls Ella, Kate, and Mag, Bert, Tom, and Charley, men who were burned to death in a mine or "killed in a brawl", women who "died in shameful childbirth" or "at the hands of a brute in a brothel". The governing emotion is not pity but bitter pain over the greed, the bigotry, the malice, of men. The memory of the Haymarket riots and their cruel consequences lives on in Spoon River as in Lindsay's poem to Altgeld, but these pages nowhere voice Lindsay's ready optimism. Repeatedly they remind one of Hobbes' description of the life of man in a state of nature: "solitary, poor, brutish, nasty and short". But the people who tell their stories here had lived in no jungle save that of industrial America.

Fairly typical in its grimness is the story of Adam Weirauch, who lost many friends fighting for Altgeld, and lost his slaughterhouse with the rise of the house of Armour. Weirauch entered politics and was elected to the legislature, but he sold his vote on a streetcar franchise and was caught. He ends up by asking whether it was Armour, Altgeld, or himself that ruined him. His unvarnished speech is more usual than the imaginative comment of Mrs. Kessler, who supported her family by taking in washing and learned people's secrets from their curtains, counterpanes, and shirts, felt that "The laundress, Life, knows all about it" and never

Saw a dead face without thinking it looked
Like something washed and ironed.

These epitaphs do not hide any of the stains, the running colors, the rents and patches, in the lives they record. Editor Whedon, a lesser representative of the gentry on whom Ezra Pound pours the vomit of his Fourteenth and Fifteenth Cantos, lies in death

close by the river over the place
Where the sewage flows from the village,
And the empty cans and garbage are dumped,
And abortions are hidden.

Masters makes no attempt to conceal the sewage, the empty cans, the garbage, the abortions. Not the shames of Spoon River alone, but the shames of a nation are exposed. The foul actualities of the Spanish-American War as the soldiers in the swamps knew them are related by a boy who went to uphold "the honor of the flag". Near him rests a veteran of the Revolution, who endured the heartbreaking struggle of the frontier, and whose last word is:

If Harry Wilmans who fought the Filipinos
Is to have a flag on his grave
Take it from mine!

The cruelties of an economic system based on exploitation, the meanness or stupidity of average minds, an inherent weakness of body or spirit, had marred the lives of most of those who came to lie in the Spoon River cemetery. Yet there is Lucinda Matlock, who worked contentedly beside her husband for seventy years, raising twelve children, and who cries out on the "degenerate sons and daughters" of the younger generation:

Life is too strong for you—
It takes life to love life.

There is Fiddler Jones who ended up with forty acres,

> ended up with a broken fiddle—
> And a broken laugh, and a thousand memories,
> And not a single regret.

There is the handful of men and women, among them not
only the astronomy teacher and the students of the Upanishads (one of these "the village atheist"), but the piano
tuner and the gardener, whose minds have learned to soar
and whose feet walk the earth, rejoicing in it.

However they differ in their attitudes and the circumstances of their lives, the characters are seldom identifia-
ble by their speech. The cadences are monotonous and
closer to prose than to song. One exception is the epitaph
of the poet, Thomas Trevelyan. Yet the lyricism of the
lines given to him is defeated by his trite, conspicuously
"poetic" language. Another versemaker here, "Petit the
Poet", remorsefully records his deafness:

> Tick, tick, tick, what little iambics,
> While Homer and Whitman roared in the pines!

Masters himself does not echo their resounding song. More
than the rest of his volumes, this one escapes the weight
of his heavy rhetoric, but there is little relief from its flat
diction. Only after reading the bulk of these stories one
hears the overtone of compassionate objectivity that is the
essence of the book. It is the voice of old Gustav Richter,
who worked all day in his hothouses and in his sleep
seemed to see his flowers transplanted "To a larger garden of freer air." There he heard a Presence, that walked
between the boxes, noting what was needful:

> Dante, too much manure, perhaps.
> Napoleon, leave him awhile yet.
> Shelley, more soil. Shakespeare, needs spraying—

It is the voice of the gardener and the voice of God. It is
the voice of Edgar Lee Masters observing the men and
women of Spoon River. The *Anthology* remains good
realism because, while exhibiting all the ugliness of life

in a small American town of the industrial age, it admits
the beauties that may also flourish there. Unique in the
originality of its conception, it pointed the way for later
poets to execute thumbnail biographies in a stronger or
subtler fashion.

Horace Gregory has written a dozen pieces that hint an
indebtedness to Masters as well as to T. S. Eliot. His
characters are not met with in a small town's cemetery but
on a street corner or in a saloon in a great city. Their language is more metaphorical than that of Masters, their
speech has implications as well as cadences of which he
was incapable, but their cramped ambitions, their crippled histories, their loneliness, their occasional grandeur
are the same. Kenneth Fearing's elegies are simpler and
more savage than Gregory's and generally loud, as his seldom are, with a blatant colloquialism. But he too has
affiliations with Masters. Consider his portrait of the
scrubwoman and the pawnbroker, "Minnie and Mrs.
Hoyne", Minnie who

> doesn't care. Get the money, that's all.
> She could die laughing, some time,
> Alone in the broom closet among the mops and
>   brushes on the forty-third floor.

Witness "Class Reunion" and other elegiac pieces with
more characteristic titles, one of which dates obtrusively:
"Payday in the Morgue", "Love, 20¢ the First Quarter
Mile", "Discussion after the Fifth or Sixth".

The poets were asking, as the Goncourt brothers had
asked themselves half a hundred years earlier, whether
there were people too mean, misfortunes too low, dramas
too foul-mouthed, terrors too ignoble to find a place in
literature. The question became more urgent during the
bleak decades that followed World War I and was angrily
revived after World War II. It was Edgar Lee Masters
who, the year that the first war opened, asked it with peculiar force in *Spoon River Anthology*.

V

The work of Carl Sandburg speaks out of a sympathy
with a more depressed group than that to which most of
the inhabitants of Spoon River belonged. They, with a
few exceptions, were native Americans. It was the Swedes,
the Dagos, the Hunkies, working in the stockyards and the
wheat fields, laying ties on the railroads, whom the author
of *Chicago Poems* put into his verse. He had heard the
voice of the land in its folk ballads and sailor chanties, its
bawdy songs and sentimental ditties. It had spoken to
him in the accents of a fellow coal shoveler in Omaha, a
Mexican Negro in a Texas saloon, a private who fought
beside him in the rain and mud of Puerto Rico, an old
fiddler turned milkman with whom he washed delivery
cans.

Unfortunately the ballad rhythms do not carry over
into his verse. Too often one hears only the speech of the
softhearted police reporter. Nevertheless, Sandburg's performance has much in common with Whitman's. It shows
the same interest and delight in the American scene, as
in all sorts and conditions of men and women. If it does
not celebrate the physical self with the gusto of "Calamus",
it speaks out against a repressive respectability. Its affirmative character shows a tie with the older poet that Allen
Ginsberg, in his "hungry fatigue . . . shopping for images"
in a California supermarket, trying to turn his nightmare
into a vision, cannot as fully claim. Much as Whitman
exalted the divine average, Sandburg tends to deify "the
People". But his verse denounces the betrayers of the people in plainer accents than Whitman's. The famous
phrase about blood, sweat, and tears could be paralleled
in Sandburg's offering of "hunger, danger, and hate" in
the war against the exploitation of man by man. He understood, too, the toll of more orthodox battles, as he brooded
over the victims of the first world war:

Fixed in the drag of the world's heartbreak
Eating and drinking, toiling . . . on a long
job of killing.

Twenty years later he wrote:

The first world war came and its cost was laid
on the people.
The second world war—the third—what will be
the cost?
And will it repay the people for what they pay?

The phrases are those of an editorial rather than of a
poem, but they echo in the memory. So, more painfully
than when it was written, does the early piece in which he
asks what a hangman thinks about when he goes home
from work, and guesses that "Anything is easy for a hangman."

The questions and the answers, the easy colloquialisms,
the harshness and the sudden gusts of sentiment, and of
sentimentality, in Sandburg's first book recur in those that
followed it, including the immense amorphous tribute
called *The People, Yes*. Sandburg could dedicate that
book "to contributors dead and living", most of them
anonymous, because it is largely made up of cant phrases,
slang, stale jokes, tall stories, the jargon of Main Street.
Chicago Poems offers a glimpse of a dead factory girl and
concludes with grim quietness: "It is the hand of God and
the lack of fire escapes." There are just such vignettes of
misery in *The People, Yes*. There the man on the witness
stand, asked if he will swear that what he is about to say
is the truth, the whole truth and nothing but the truth,
gives an answer that fairly covers Sandburg's verse: "No,
I don't. I can tell you what I saw and what I heard and I'll
swear to that by the everliving God but the more I study
about it the more sure I am that nobody but the everliving
God knows the whole truth and if you summoned Christ
as a witness in this case what He would tell you would
burn your insides with the pity and the mystery of it."

For Sandburg the sum of all knowledge is in one word: "Maybe." The sum of human history is in three words: "Born, troubled, died." The sum of awful truth is in five words: "This too shall pass away." He asks, and the answer is implicit in the question: ". . . tell me if the lovers are losers . . . tell me if any get more than the lovers . . . in the dust . . . in the cool tombs." He repeats what the angry young men who succeeded him ignored, that the same emotions are known to the girl who has breakfast in bed and the girl at the sink washing dishes. At the heart of one piece after another is a cry of loneliness, the loneliness of life in a big city or on a farm or in a small town where nothing seems to happen but the shooting by of the express. If there are lines rough with resentment at a society in which millions of people are starving behind a plow or starving behind a counter, there are lines as hauntedly wistful. It is this wistfulness—always on the verge of a mawkishness into which it often falls—that distinguishes Sandburg from his savage juniors, as his sense of the cruelties of the industrial age helps to set him apart from the blithe, barbaric yawper who preceded him.

It is not only Chicago, the "City of the Big Shoulders", to which Sandburg has written a paean. He celebrates, as few have done, the spaciousness of the Midwest, the hospitable soil, "the gold of a ripe oat-straw, gold of a southwest moon", and therewith the outlook of people who live on a land that has been generous to them. They are used to permanencies like earth and stars, things that last longer than skyscrapers and empires.

> The whispering pinks, the buds on the redhaw,
> The blue roofs of the sky . . . stay put.

It is a dimmer way of saying in verse what Yeats said in prose when he declared himself to be Blake's disciple, not Hegel's: "the Spring vegetables may be over but they are never refuted."

Sandburg's sketches of people and places that he wants to remember have a blurred, impressionistic quality. He is

like a man leaning over a bar, who may break into a tune,
a little off-key, but who prefers to talk, a man whose utterance is never as profound as his convictions, because he is
apt to say too much, a man who conveys, almost in spite
of himself, his sense of "the pity and the mystery of it".
What he contributed to American poetry was a renewed
awareness of ordinary life as of ordinary language, including slang as poetic diction of a fresh sort.

However he differed from them in his approach to politics and to poetry, he was the forerunner of the proletarian
poets of a later generation and their successors. There are
pages of Kenneth Fearing's that might almost have come
from Sandburg's pen. His use of Fearing's nervous cinematic technique, even to the use of the counting-out
phrase, is evidenced in a passage from *The People, Yes*:

> One-two-three, five-six-seven every day the police
> seize and the courts order to jail
> this skulker who stole a bottle of milk,
> this shadow who ran off with a loaf of bread,
> this wanderer who purloined a baby sweater in a
> basement salesroom—
> And the case is dismissed of the railroad-yard plain-
> clothes detective who repeatedly called "Stop!"
> to a boy running with a sack of coal and the boy
> not stopping the dick let him have it. "It was
> dark and I couldn't see him clear and I aimed at
> his legs. My intention was to stop him running.
> I didn't mean for the bullet to go as high on
> him as it did."

Again, Langston Hughes was to find words and music,
the music of the "blues", the words of that displaced person, the American Negro, for the brief, often dubious
pleasures, the long griefs of his people, in lines as forthright as Sandburg's. A fairly representative piece is an
early one called "Spitoons". This begins with the admonition: "Clean the spitoons, boy." There is no blinking

the slime in the hotel spitoons, but no refusal of possible
gaiety either.

> Hey, boy!
> A bright bowl of brass is beautiful to the Lord!

Having compared it to the cymbals of King David's dancers, the wine cups of Solomon, the singer shouts:

> Hey, boy!
> A clean spitoon for the altar of the Lord!
> A clean bright spitoon all newly polished,—
> At least I can offer that.
> Com' mere, boy!

This slightly jazzed version of the legend of the juggler of
Notre Dame is frank enough about what the dimes and
nickles of the spitoon-cleaner can buy. Though Sandburg's
influence may have been indirect, it is suggested in other
pieces by Hughes which give the big and little ironies of
life in a Negro version of that versemaker's attitude and
presentation.

Sandburg might have said with Masefield that however
harshly the next school treated him, it was a little livelier
for his efforts. Though he lacks Kipling's craftsmanship,
he shares with that poet, along with such men as Masefield and Lindsay and Masters, a breadth of sympathy, an
indignation born of humanity, that are precious ingredi-
ents of poetry. Their verse revives our sense of the romance of the commonplace, and of the sturdy strength as
well as the bitter lot of the sons—and daughters—of
Martha.

The desire to come to closer grips with actuality, however tawdry or terrible, to express it in words that are as
much of the moment as the feeling that stirs beneath
them, was a quickening element in the work of these poets,
a source of its primary appeal. Of them all, it was Kipling
who best knew how to retain the propriety of his diction
while keeping it plain. To this master, therefore, the debt
of his fellows is greatest. "Time," writes Auden,

that is intolerant
Of the brave and innocent,
And indifferent in a week
To a beautiful physique,

Worships language and forgives
Everyone by whom it lives;

. . . .

Pardoned Kipling and his views . . .

The poet who tries to set down honestly what he sees and feels, and who has command of his craft, earns pardon for the most mistaken opinions. For poetry continues to be written with words, and conscientiously used, they speak truth.

3. The Glove of a Neighborhood

In a caustic sonnet Edwin Arlington Robinson describes New England as the place "where the wind is always north-north-east." It is an ironical picture of the region, not as Robinson himself, but as the outsider sees it. Robert Frost is more direct in expressing his admiration for the countryside that bred both poets. They have more in common with one another than either has with the Midwesterners who shared the glory of the same poetic revival. Both have explored the same distinctive region. Moreover, the work of both exhibits the ethical preoccupation of the New Englander and his habit of wry understatement. The likeness stops there. Frost has lessons for his juniors. Robinson is one of the moderns chronologically, rather than by temperament or performance. He deserves consideration because his best work is finely representative of traditional poetry, because in a few pieces he evoked, as no poet had previously, a landscape with figures familiar to his fellow Americans.

Among his masters were Robert Browning and, if circumstantial evidence means anything, a contemporary of Browning's who wrote neat vers de société, Winthrop Mackworth Praed. If Robinson often wanted the evocative force of the greater poet, he deepened and intensified in similar structures the lesser one's blend of pathos and irony. The American might be humorous about human failings in the fashion of the early Victorian, but he seldom omitted to convey, as a good New Englander, the sense of moral responsibility.

Robinson wrote a number of long narratives in verse, some purporting to deal with his contemporaries, the more famous ones serving up stories from the Arthurian cycle in a less watered fashion than Tennyson's but without the blood and iron of Malory. He had small gift for narrative, and a great temptation to chew a cud of "ifs" and "buts" rolled up into one juiceless ball. Whether his characters move against the drafty, tapestried background of the middle ages or among the furniture of twentieth-century America, they have a habit of talking like their author. Their metaphors, like his, are largely a matter of lights and shadows, of music, discords, and silences. Their diction, like his, is involved and abstract.

The sentence structure that suggests Praed readily falls into hesitancies and restrictive glosses reminiscent of Henry James. The poet had a less sensitive grasp of language than the novelist and a less profound feeling for symbolism, so that his verse narratives are not as poetic as James's greater prose fictions. Nevertheless the two writers exhibit interesting resemblances. Both rely on a gift for creating atmosphere. Both tend to shove the murders and adulteries offstage, and make the action the subject of extended discussion among the characters. Both are preoccupied with the theme, exemplified in the lives of so many New Englanders and at some period in their own, that worldly failure may issue in spiritual triumph, though they recognized how barren even to the victors spiritual victories may sometimes seem.

The Puritan consciousness, the Puritan conscience, are offered repeated, if somewhat obscure, testimonials. Indeed, the pallid gleam of transcendentalism hovers over Robinson's work, from the sonnet called "Credo" that he wrote before the turn of the century to the long narrative in verse that he completed just before his death nearly forty years later. His most involved fictions are a more roundabout way of presenting the unhappy men encountered in his first book, significantly entitled *The Children of the Night*, and of reiterating its melancholy wisdom.

Nor did his philosophy alter from that expressed in his early sonnets to Crabbe, to Zola, to Verlaine, in his flat eight-line "octaves" and in the French forms consecrate to light verse—triolet, villanelle, and ballade—into which he poured the bleak moods and solemn reflections of his youth. It is not alone his concern with the problems that fretted the Victorians that aligns Robinson with the poets of the latter half of the nineteenth century. It is his preference for statement rather than suggestion and his meditative, rationalistic habit of mind. While in one poem after another, though not always explicitly, he pitted Dionysus against Demos, what he appears chiefly to have desired was to retrieve for our bewildered time the New England idealism of a simpler day.

But if he was not a deeply imaginative poet nor a technical innovator, he was an acute explorer of a small corner of his world, concerning himself particularly with those shabby, frustrated, but fascinating inhabitants of it who command our charity and our amusement, our pity and our shamed admiration. One of his familiar character sketches is of "Richard Cory", whose fellow townsfolk "went without the meat, and cursed the bread", to be startled out of their miserable routine when that glittering gentleman "went home and put a bullet through his head." Equally noteworthy is "Miniver Cheevy", a poem that is an ironic variant on Kipling's farewell and hail to romance in "The King" and on Masefield's "Cargoes". Robinson's interest, however, was not so much in the machinery of our civilization as in the man who could not accommodate himself to it.

He produced a number of portraits, some of them done with remarkable sharpness and subtlety. The broken millionaire, "Bewick Finzer", with his cracked voice, his withered neck,

> The cleanliness of indigence,
> The brilliance of despair,

who keeps returning,

> Familiar as an old mistake,
> And futile as regret,

is an unforgettable figure. "The Poor Relation", who might well have been the heroine of one of James's short stories, is a notable picture of reduced gentility. There are some fine strokes here, such as the passing remark,

> She knows as well as anyone
> That Pity, having played, soon tires,

and the almost casual allusion to "The lonely changelessness of dying". In the final stanzas not alone the wheels and the horns, the traffic and the crowds, send up their clamor to shake the poor relation's miserable perch; she hears, and we with her, the noise of time itself.

There are several companion pieces to this in sketches of forgotten gentlemen, like the beggar as memorable for

> His unshaved, educated face,
> His inextinguishable grace
> And his hard smile,

as for the bolus of wisdom that he leaves with his benefactor: that

> all the Peace there is on Earth
> Is faith in what your world is worth,
> And saying, without any lies,
> Your world could not be otherwise.

A more ironic anecdote of Christmas Eve is offered in the sonnet, "Karma", which tells how a financier is recalled by "a slowly freezing Santa Claus" on the street corner to a friend whom in the course of business he had wrecked. Only half sure that he wished his ruined friend back again,

> from the fulness of his heart he fished
> A dime for Jesus who had died for men.

The verb "fished" seems to underscore the contrast between the mean-spirited almsgiver and the Fisher of men. One of the most amiable of Robinson's many derelicts figures in "Mr. Flood's Party". This is a half-humorous, tender picture of a solitary drinker of Tilbury Town, "convivially returning with himself" from his lookout on the hill to his jug, and, when his modest orgy is over, more than ever alone. A refreshing element in the poem is that Eben Flood's few words are uttered in his own huskily quavering voice rather than in that of the poet. Toward the close, as the engaging old toper lifts up his voice and sings,

> Secure, with only two moons listening,
> Until the whole harmonious landscape rang—

the reader shares old Eben's brief hilarity, even while he smiles at it, with possibly, a wry reflection on the man-made satellites that Robinson did not live to see. The saccharin drop in the final lines cannot spoil the poem as a whole, its pathos pointed up by its humor.

Robinson's more ambitious dramatic monologues, such as "Ben Jonson Meets a Man from Stratford" or "Rembrandt to Rembrandt", do not have the authenticity of his New England portraits. At least one of these, "Isaac and Archibald", composed about the turn of the century, anticipated, in its apparent simplicity and its gentle irony, the rural dialogues that Robert Frost was to produce more than a decade later. One is made to see with uncommon clarity two old men, from the viewpoint of a little boy who walked one of them to and from the other's farm, went down cellar with him to fetch cider, sat with the ancient pair in the orchard while they played seven-up and made sly innuendoes on the subject of old age, and listened to each in turn lament, not without pride in his own relative vigor, the senescence of the other. The presentation of the two ancients through the eyes of the boy is an instance of Henry James's indirect method of revealing character, and the piece has many slighter Jamesian touches, such as the phrase about "a small boy's adhesive-

ness / To competent old age," or Isaac's "sweet severity"
that made him "think of peach-skins and goose-flesh".
Yet it remains all recognizably Robinson's own, including
the reference to a transcendental "light behind the stars"
and his characteristic method of seeking to define by nega-
tives and repetitions. The view of Archibald's farm as
seen in the distance among its hackmatacks and apple
trees, with the big barn roof beyond, is almost a description of the poem itself:

> And over the place—trees, houses, fields, and all—
> Hovered an air of still simplicity
> And a fragrance of old summers—the old style
> That lives the while it passes.

Some of Robinson's finest work breathes of this fragrance.
One instance is his sonnet on "The Sheaves", that lay,
golden in the golden weather,

> but not for long to stay—
> As if a thousand girls with golden hair
> Might rise from where they slept and go away.

A mist of nostalgia softens his most brilliant landscapes,
as here, and again in "The Dark Hills", which in six somber, resonant lines evokes a sunset and therewith the sorrow and the wonder that dying splendor can summon.

Robinson was incapable of the savage realism he
praised, though he reiterated the need to look truth in the
face and wrote a few dramatic lyrics, like "The Mill",
stern enough to have been penned by Hardy. The laconic
yet reverberant wording, the domestic scene, followed by
that of the discovered suicide in the barn, strongly rendered with a few strokes, the subdued tone, all contribute
to the darkness of this tragedy in little and enlarge its
significance. Technically, Robinson's work is of interest
insofar as it shows how individual phrasing is an index to
style where a man is using the accepted forms of an older
day. His preference for blank verse and his monotonous
end-stopped lines emphasize the old-fashioned character

of his performance. It is honest, serious work, and represents, in the old phrase, the "application of ideas to life".
Too often the ideas have reference to a world no longer
actual and inadequately realized. Robinson's pedestrian
reasonableness generally prevented him from transmuting
his ideas into the stuff of poetry. Yet his most severe and
delicate sonnets, lyrics, and character studies are memorably wrought "in the old style that lives the while it
passes".

II

The poetry of Robert Frost deals more largely and
more explicitly than does Robinson's with the old rural
New England. But if he finds his material in a pattern of
life that was traditional with his forebears, his poetry is
tougher than Robinson's, partly because it retains a
stronger hold on the immediate facts of experience, and
because its language is not literary.

The people about whom he writes are usually of New
England stock, folk who cultivate their rocky acres with
stubborn courage and bear, until they break, the drudgery
and isolation of their lot. His subjects are the commonplaces of the countryside: apple-picking, hay-making, the
sleep of an old man alone in an old farmhouse, the clean-
ing of the pasture spring. His diction is simple and colloquial. One hears the very intonation of the man who
wonders "if splitting stars / 'Sa thing compared to splitting wood." In the many instances where Frost allows some
rural figure to speak for himself, his lapses into his own
mannerisms are fewer than Robinson's. These dramatic
monologues are spoken by people who might be his kindred or his neighbors. There is verisimilitude in their diction, whether the person speaking is the farmer who sees
no reason for mending the wall between his apple orchard
and his neighbor's pine grove; the farm woman whose mad
uncle was housed in a home-made cage in the attic and
who dimly senses his fate crawling toward her; the man

and wife to whose kitchen the incompetent worn-out hired
hand comes "home" to die; or either one of the middle-
aging pair whose removal from the city to a farm invites
scrutiny of the rewards of more than one way of life and
a glance at the chilling shadows that encroach on each.
Frost has about as much to say of happy wooings and
matings, of friendly encounters and generous neighborli-
ness, as of the bleaker aspects of farm life. This, together
with the fact that his little dramas are enacted amidst the
steady caring for crops and creatures, further distinguishes them from the pomp and circumstance of Robinson's narrative poems, while their humorousness gives
them a salty quality not found in Masefield's tales of the
English countryside.

In one of his earliest poems Frost remarks: "The fact
is the sweetest dream that labor knows." This seems to
echo the thought of another perceptive New England
farmer, who kept one commonplace book for facts and another for poetry, but confessed that he found it difficult to
preserve the vague distinction he had in mind, and concluded: "if my facts were sufficiently vital and significant
—perhaps transmuted more into the substance of the human mind—I should need but one book of poetry to contain them all." Frost's poems repeatedly remind us that
the central fact in nature for himself and his kind is human nature. However interestedly he may observe such
impersonal things as storms and stars, he is apt to relate
his observations to some insight into humanity. Mankind
has consecrated the earth for him, both as a poet and as a
tiller of the soil. "Nothing not built with hands of course
is sacred," he asserts. The hermit of Walden, for all his
aloofness, would have understood what the poet meant.
Certainly Frost's poetry, like Thoreau's prose, reveals not
only an unshakable independence but also an intimate
knowledge of the bases of existence ignored by the city-
dweller and a loverly patience with and delight in the
natural scene.

The grimmer views that this verse presents are relieved

by glimpses of such features of the farmer's day as vivify, if he has the poet's temper, his limited and burdensome routine: the reward of watching the seedling "shouldering its way and shedding the earth crumbs"; the madness of the cow in apple time; the noise of trees; the whirl of snow in which the city withdraws into itself and leaves "at last the country to the country." A distaste for luxury is generally supposed to belong to the New England character, and indeed Frost's poetry has nothing to say of the imagined pleasures of silken Samarkand and cedared Lebanon; yet it celebrates luxuriously the jeweled vision of blueberries in rain-wet leaves, along with such delicious commonplaces of rural experience as the lumps, "like uncut jewels, dull and rough", of scented sprucegum, which

> comes to market golden-brown,
> But turns to pink between the teeth.

All the homely details of barn and farmhouse, orchard, pasture, and wood lot, are illuminated by their particularity. The dry brook

> That shouted in the mist a month ago
> Like ghost of sleigh-bells in a ghost of snow,

though, June being gone,

> Its bed is left a faded paper sheet
> Of dead leaves stuck together by the heat—
> A brook to none but who remember long,

is but one of a score of instances of what the seasons have to give to a man who gratefully accepts the need of being "versed in country things". Not even Burns has written more tenderly of the young life on and about a farm, be it a runaway colt, a young orchard threatened by false spring, a nestful of fledglings exposed by the cultivator, or lads and girls.

Frost's remoteness from things urban, his acceptance of the traditional forms, ally him with the Georgians. Like that British group, he is closer to Wordsworth and

John Clare and to the Dorsetshire poet of rural life,
William Barnes, than to his contemporaries. The term
"Georgian" has come to connote the work of some forty
poets (the academic number seems symbolic), assembled
in successive anthologies, the first of which was published
in 1912. For the most part this verse ignores such features
of our lives as the city and the slum, as it evades our confusions and anxieties. In this respect it differs markedly
from poetry written after World War II by men who are
again willing to employ familiar forms, to speak without
raising their voices, to evoke the homely interior and the
suburban scene. Some of these later poems, not blinking
the bleak detail, breathe the air, chill and foul, of the
times, and present without delusion, as without romantic
extravagance, complexity of feeling. Thus, G. S. Fraser,
with candor and concreteness illumines the private pain
that has become a symptom of the illness of our age. Roy
Fuller, D. S. Savage, Francis Scarfe, are among the contemporary poets who have offered vignettes of ordinary
life as quietly as did the Georgians, but whose lyrics are
crossed, as theirs seldom were, with cruel wit and tragic
ambiguities.

Instead of using what they had learned from their seniors to give form and color to their own experiences, they
took over the very attitudes of an elder generation. There
is testimony to this in Rupert Brooke's extenuation of the
harsh realism in a few of his lyrics: the nausea of the lover
at sea, the hideous close-up of Helen in her old age: "There
are common or sordid things—situation or details—that may
suddenly bring all tragedy, or at least the brutality of actual emotions, to you; I rather grasp relievedly at them,
after I have beaten vain hands in the rosy mists of other
poets' experiences." Like many of his fellows, too often he
beat vain hands in those rosy mists.

Actual, as opposed to literary, emotions broke in brutally upon this nostalgic lyricism when, in 1914, some of
the younger men were caught in the wheels of the war
machine. But aside from those whom the horrors of the

trenches shocked into plain speech, and who must be discussed later, there were several members of the group who stood out from the rest, a few of whom will be considered again in another connection. Chief among these was Walter de la Mare, a poet with an extraordinarily delicate ear and a fine sense of tone color, whose eerie lyrics seem to be haunted by two ghostly presences, Time and the Self. Another was James Stephens, whose verse might have been composed by a leprechaun with a human heart. Yet another was D. H. Lawrence, a poet who was as little of this company as of any other. Lawrence was in passionate revolt against the machine and the mass. He had firsthand knowledge of the ugliness of lower-class life in England, and some of his early poems record it unflinchingly in his native idiom, but, as has been noted, in a fashion closer to Hardy's than to that of such an ethical romanticist as Masefield. His poetry is the work of a man more badgered and more savage than any of the Georgians, including the war poets. Indeed, only insofar as he was in flight, was Lawrence in the same galley.

Robert Frost, on the contrary, though unmistakably an American, is in some respects representative of the group, which numbered several of the friends with whom he spent his journeyman years as a poet. His work takes almost as little account of the industrial revolution and its consequences as does that of his fellows. But it penetrates more deeply than theirs below the surface of rural life. One cannot confuse this twinkling Yankee, who talks of "the trial by market everything must come to", with such poets as Brooke, longing for honey with his tea at Grantchester, or even with Davies, gazing happily at sheep and cows, shadowy pool and sunstruck stone. Frost's view is not that of the congenital vagrant, content with such pleasures as he meets while tramping the roads, any more than it is that of the town-sick romantic, who finds the country as charming as a new mistress. He has for it, rather, the understanding, affectionate, slightly quizzical look that a man gives the wife of his bosom. He continually implies what he says plainly in the description of Hyla Brook: "We love the things we love for what they are."

The world of modern technology is not one with which it is easy to be on the intimate terms that poetry demands. Outcroppings of the old order continue to claim attention, like glacial boulders in acreage staked out for an air field. It is not only for those who work the little farms of his native Italy that Virgil's Georgics are valid after nearly two millennia. Their validity is attested frequently by Frost. Almost equally familiar with the classics and the native scene, in one of his rare poems thick with literary allusions he observes that he thought Lucretius "By Nature meant the Whole Goddam Machinery". In a few other pieces he jocosely introduces a Greek or Latin phrase. He pays obeisance specifically to Virgil in his "political pastoral" entitled "Build Soil", a conversation between two shepherds whom he names after the characters in one of the Latin Eclogues. There is a Virgilian serenity and solidity about much of this contemporary American work, as also a repeated recognition of the tears of things. Where Frost deals with those elements of rural life that have remained unaffected by the rapid technological changes that followed the invention of the steam engine, few poets now writing in English have equaled him, and few of any time and place have surpassed him.

The sense of being at home with nature is paramount in his work. One finds this also in the gentle lyrics of the friend of his youth, Edward Thomas. This victim of the first world war wrote with quiet intimacy about the rural world that he had to leave so early. For him, the men, the beasts, the trees, the implements, that composed his vision of an old grange had immortal things to say. Although he was more subject to melancholy, or perhaps confessed it more readily, there is in some of his poems a sadness that reminds one of Frost in its freedom from self-pity. He communicated his affectionate knowledge of country things and persons in singing lines rich with minute particulars. A like restraint curbing a great intensity marks the few brief poems of Kenneth Slade Alling. He presents "The bookless language / The pageless speech" of an oak in a winter wind as he presents mown hay, seagull, humming-bird, crow, toad, "Locusts, etc.", with a pregnant laco-nism.

A fond familiarity with the land is especially apparent in Mark Van Doren's work. His poems are filled with the appreciation of the minutiae of farm life that is among Frost's contributions to our poetry.

Van Doren, though he has paid the tribute of imitation to more than one of his literary forebears, has put his per-sonal stamp upon some admirable lyrics. A sonnet se-quence celebrating the gradual fruition and relinquishment of late love has passages that lift it out of its conventional groove. He has written several penetrating love lyrics as well as good things in other genres, but some of his best work shows him to be Frost's disciple.

An instance is an early poem called "Big Mare". This gives the odors and essences of meadow and barn as Frost might give them, but shows a deeper tenderness than the elder poet generally admits. Here is the mare in the field at the hour when the old man who used to care for her should be coming. One sees her feeding and, in the cool of the afternoon, starting for the barn, her feet trampling the clover, her breast moving "with superfluous might against the weeds". But there is no familiar shout to summon her,

> No corn upon an aged, trembling hand. . . .
> She hesitates, as if the barn were gone—
> Had never been just here—and gazes long
> At the half-opened door; then stumbles through.

There are nubbins in the box as usual, the salt and the tim-othy. The scene is presented simply; the facts are suffi-cient comment on themselves. But one is made to realize "foolish whispers, not of the hay", "spidery ghosts of fin-gers" caressing her, actual as the feedbox. Only at the close is there a query.

Does a plain mare remember? And how long?
Tomorrow will come a slap and a careless whistle.
Tomorrow will come a boy. Is she to forget?

The piece is the reverse of the poems by Hardy and Jeffers
in which their dogs reflect on life in the houses haunted by
the memory of them. Here is the death of the human as
dimly felt by the animal. There is no taint of sentimentality, but a true inwardness in the clear picture.

The long poem called "A Winter Diary" chronicles a
season in the country with the same affectionate fidelity to
fact. At least one passage combines the homeliness of Frost
with the richness of Keats, who was also remarkable for his
sense of detail. These couplets show the cellar shelves that
had been "layered dust" now "wiped to kitchen neatness"
and holding such clear jellies as

Crab-apple, quince, and hardly-ripened grape,
With jam from every berry, and the shape
Of cherries showing pressed against the jar;
Whole pears; and where the tall half-gallons are,
Tomatoes with their golden seeds, and blunt
Cucumbers that the early ground-worms hunt.
The highest shelf, beneath the spidery floor,
Holds pumpkins in a row, with squash before—
Dark horny Hubbards that will slice in half
And come with pools of butter as we laugh,
Remembering the frost that laid the vines
Like blackened string—September's valentines.

The tally of stored food goes on, naming corn and carrots
and beets, the "seven barrels of apples standing by", and
mention of the woodpile against the wall summons retro-
spectively the scene of autumnal woodchopping. The passage ends with an intimately American picture of the family gathered about the treasures come via the mail order
catalogue. The whole is done with the same humorous
charm, the honesty, the abiding affection, that mark his
shorter poems about country life. Creating atmosphere

with concrete particulars, these couplets have "power against a season's law" and, for more than the poet, keep a certain winter alive. To Mark Van Doren the tasks in field and house are his riches, even to hanging the tools "where they belong", and, symbolically, his description of those chores might be of the tools themselves: "good, clear, shapely, / Solitary things"—to do, and to show his life's companion. One of his happiest poems is ironically called "Country Boredom". He has a good deal to say about trains, too, but it is noteworthy that they are apt to be taking someone home. Particularly memorable are the lyrics that explore, with acuteness and unsentimental delicacy, the relation between members of one household, especially between father and son. Frost, too, has dealt with familiar and familial intercourse, but not with quite the same intimacy. For more recent work of this kind one may turn to such different practitioners as Van Doren's accomplished contemporary, Robert Penn Warren, young W. D. Snodgrass, chronicling candidly a deprived parenthood, George Garrett, recording the pangs that assail even a happy father in the post-war world, and Barbara Howes, whose lyrics could have been written only by a woman. The shadows that hover menacingly over some of her radiant landscapes—only less glamorous than those of her husband, William Jay Smith—help to give depth to the domestic interiors that are painted with uncommon warmth and liveliness.

In Mark Van Doren's verse there is a strain of gentleness that sometimes weakens it, but that may also be the key to his insight into the behavior of men and women, girls and boys. There is no malice in him, and this may help him to accept our unhappy case with Frost's serenity and without his wryness. If Van Doren is more overtly engaged with metaphysics, like the elder poet he keeps returning to the things of earth and the concerns of men here.

As might be expected of verse that dwells upon the

details of the old agricultural order, the attitude expressed
in Frost's pages is a conservative one, in the best as well
as in the less happy sense of the term. His poems assert
the need to conserve, to protect, those values that the
poet has tested and found good.

> New is a word for fools in towns who think
> Style upon style in dress and thought at last
> Must get somewhere,

observes the woman in "The Home-Stretch", speaking, it
would seem, for her delineator. His pieties are those of
one who accepts the routine dictated by nature. He has
not seen fit to alter or to comment on a question that he
put in a poem published some forty years ago:

> How are we to write
> The Russian novel in America
> As long as life goes so unterribly?

A decade later he was reaffirming his conviction of the
necessity for "a one-man revolution"—an increased separa-
tism, a lonely plowing-under of crops and of thoughts. His
admonition to "build soil" ends:

> Don't join too many gangs. Join few if any.
> Join the U.S. and join the family—
> But not much in between, unless a college.

This is dangerously close to the viewpoint of those rugged
individualists who might feel differently if they had to spell
the adjective with an "a". Frost's individualism, however,
is of a sturdier and withal a gentler kind than theirs, as
witness the early lyric called "The Tuft of Flowers". The
poet, going to turn the mown grass to dry, is guided by
hovering wings to a tuft of butterfly weed left by the
mower. The sight makes him reverse the thought of everyone's aloneness with which he had begun his work, and
he concludes:

'Men work together,' I told him from the heart,
'Whether they work together or apart.'

The poem is also a tribute to the virtuous impracticality
that Robinson liked to celebrate. What might almost be
considered a pendant piece, "The Wood-Pile", has to do
with a pile of corded wood left

> far from a useful fireplace
> To warm the frozen swamp as best it could
> With the slow smokeless burning of decay.

The frozen swamp may yield nothing useful from this
heat, the chance passer-by may not profit practically from
his find, yet the lines seem to pose the question as to
whether anything is ever wholly wasted. The very existence
of the poem implies a negative answer. In "West-running
Brook", a homely poetic dialogue that touches on the run-
ning-down of the universe, there is also a reminder of the
resistance to the expense of energy that is so significant a
feature of life's processes. It is only in lines written in old
age that Frost, observing the countless butterflies literally
knocking themselves out over flowering milkweed, remarks
that here "waste was of the essence of the scheme." The
fact, he declares, "must be fairly faced", adding in a footnote that it "shall be in due course." If it were faced
fairly, the reader may reflect, something would be gained,
and the waste thereby diminished. A more familiar
poem tells how, leaving the road at "A scent of ripeness
from over a wall", the poet comes upon an apple tree that
had shed all its fruit, making the ground "one circle of
solid red". He greets the fragrance and the rosiness with
the plea that something may always go unharvested. Here
is not Gerard Manley Hopkins' joyful celebration of the
weeds and the wilderness, but Frost's lyric points the natural ambivalence of this careful husbandman of crops and
words.

He seems to describe his own best verse where he says
of a woodland creature:

> The bird would cease and be as other birds
> But that he knows in singing not to sing,

and again in a poem about a maker of ax helves:

> Baptiste knew how to make a short job long
> For love of it, and yet not waste time either.

In speaking of the people and places that have touched
his imagination, Frost shows the lingering pleasure of Bap-
tiste in his material, yet does not waste words either. He
has the New Englander's reticence, but he has also a less
engaging tendency to play the rustic philosopher. His
aphorisms are often memorable, as when, in that New
England classic, "The Death of the Hired Man", Warren
observes:

> Home is the place where, when you have to go
>   there,
> They have to take you in,

his wife countering by calling it "Something you somehow
haven't to deserve." Thereby the two characters also define themselves, as well as the diverse attitudes, Frost has
said, of opposed political parties and of man and woman.

It is interesting to discover resemblances with the work
of the aged New Englander in that of a young midwest-
erner, James Wright. His poems are straightforward yet
resonant, at once conversational and lyrical. He, too, offers
monologues that turn out to be self-portraits of the speakers, landscapes with figures (sometimes animals) that are
no less lively for their moral import. He is not fearful of
ugly or dreary subject matter, as is evident in the titles
as well as in the body of such poems as "Old Man Drunk",
"In Shame and Humiliation", "At the Executed Murderer's
Grave". James Wright does not blink the more dismal
truths. The first in a sequence of unusual love poems ends
on a statement which has all the stern force of its simplicity: "And things were as they were." It is a paraphrase,
stronger than the original, of the conclusion to one of

Frost's minor dramas: ". . . And they, since they / Were not the one dead, turned to their affairs."

Frost once wrote that meaning is what chiefly matters in a poem. The remark opens the question as to the meaning of "meaning" for him; it would appear to be the prose sense of a conviction arrived at from ripe experience. His weakness is a reluctance to let a poem disclose the conviction without an explicit declaration from the poet. The dry humor that is one of the charms of his verse is most acceptable when it resides in the tone of the poem as a whole, instead of running to inflated whimsy or flat statement. However powerful an element of poetry wit may be, only insofar as it works together with feeling can it achieve its poetic end. Frost knows this as well as anyone, if he does not always abide by it. Like Job in his *Masque of Reason*, he takes the attitude that

> We disparage reason.
> But all the time it's what we're most concerned with.

An obvious instance of his concern with it is the piece called "A Considerable Speck", about what seemed a dust speck but then showed itself to be unmistakably "a living mite" moving across his manuscript. He noticed its suspicion of his pen, and observed how once more it raced toward the wet ink, how it paused, how it crept cunningly on its invisible feet. In the end he let it lie on the sheet until he hoped it slept, a mercy extended less in pity than in recognition that he was dealing with an intelligence:

> I have a mind myself and recognize
> Mind when I meet with it in any guise.
> No one can know how glad I am to find
> On any sheet the least display of mind.

This is worth contrasting with a sonnet by Karl Shapiro on a less happy experience.

> Writing, I crushed an insect with my nail
> And thought nothing at all. A bit of wing
> Caught my eye then, a gossamer so frail

And exquisite, I saw in it a thing
That scorned the grossness of the thing I wrote.
It hung upon my finger like a sting.

He noticed the delicacy of what remained of the mite, a
leg: a "frail eyelash" on which it "climbed and walked
like any mountain-goat." He looked, in vain, for the tiny
head, and his heart cried out in fear at the mystery of
existence, self-love, death:

It was a mite that held itself most dear,
So small I could have drowned it with a tear.

The difference between the two poems is not so much a
matter of form, nor is it in the fact that Shapiro crushed
the insect, while Frost observed his mite and saved it. The
difference lies chiefly in that the elder poet makes the incident an occasion for reflection on intelligence, the
younger, who at first "thought nothing at all", remains
primarily engaged with feeling.

Sometimes Frost's concern with reason tends to invalidate his poetry. Thus, his humorous examination of the
injustice of Job's case, which is, in effect, an examination
of the human condition, errs on the side of too great
reasonableness. It is amusing to conceive of God as having
been provoked into testing the disinterestedness of the
virtuous man because the tempter came to Him and He
was tempted. But Frost's play with the old problem, however entertaining, leaves us with a sense of having been
cheated. And the reason for that, since we are talking of
reason, is that the poem turns so casual a look at what
Yeats called the Vision of Evil. A man may have it and yet
not write great poetry, but the greatest poetry cannot be
written without it. The subsequent *Masque of Mercy*,
which asserts that

the saddest thing in life
Is that the best thing in it should be courage,

concludes with the protagonist's confession that he and Jonah

> both have lacked the courage in the heart
> To overcome the fear within the soul
> And go ahead to any accomplishment.

Frost has gone ahead to considerable accomplishment, the greater because of those poems which confront the anguish of existence and the presence of the malign. This presence is less evident in the grim New England dramas that first established his reputation than in such a late poem as "Design". The first of its ironic contrasts occurs in the opening line: "I found a dimpled spider, fat and white," —where the babyish charm associated with "dimpled", "fat", the radiant innocence symbolized by "white", are alike contradicted by the character of the insect thus described. The contrast is italicized by the fact that the spider is resting on a white heal-all, and holding a moth "Like a white piece of rigid satin cloth—", the deathy "rigid" in juxtaposition to the festive elegance of "satin cloth". The heal-all itself (the very name of the flower is suggestive) is obviously dead, its blue having withered to white. The word "white" occurs five times in this sonnet of more than Petrarchan intricacy, and is further emphasized by being not merely the most prominent rhyme word but also being used twice as an end rhyme. Insistently the poem asks the question explicit in the sestet, whether the happening was due to nothing but "design of darkness to appall?— / If design govern in a thing so small." That darkness should appall by means of whiteness stresses the irony. More often Frost treats the malice of fate with wry humor, as in one of his own favorites: "Provide, Provide".

In a rambling and withal revealing poetic discourse, "New Hampshire", he calls himself "a sensibilitist", one who makes a virtue of his suffering from nearly everything that goes on round him.

> Kit Marlow taught me how to say my prayers:
> 'Why, this is Hell, nor am I out of it.'

There is a renewed, if oblique, recognition of this in the sonnet, written in terza rima, that takes its title from its first and last lines, "Acquainted with the Night":

> I have been one acquainted with the night.
> I have walked out in rain—and back in rain.
> I have outwalked the furthest city light.
>
> I have looked down the saddest city lane.
> I have passed by the watchman on his beat
> And dropped my eyes, unwilling to explain.
>
> I have stood still and stopped the sound of feet
> When far away an interrupted cry
> Came over houses from another street,
>
> But not to call me back or say good-bye;
> And further still at an unearthly height,
> One luminary clock against the sky
>
> Proclaimed the time was neither wrong nor right.
> I have been one acquainted with the night.

The night to which the poet refers here is real enough, but it is also figurative, and the city, which is evidently no metropolis but some New England town, seems to represent some more significant, if less actual, locale. It is like the desert places of which he speaks in another lyric, where he describes a lonely walk in the snow at nightfall, declaring that he can be scared neither by the blank loneliness of the snow-masked fields nor yet by the skies' empty spaces, who has it in him "So much nearer home" to scare himself with his own "desert places". Night and rain recur in Frost's poems with a persistence that sometimes makes it seem as though he had accepted the dark invitation of the woods that had vainly beckoned him and Edward Thomas in youth. Rain, he asserts, in a late lyric, is as strong without as wine within, and "magical as sunlight on the skin", and he proceeds:

> I have been one no dwelling could contain
>   When there was rain;
> But I must forth at dusk, my time of day,
> To see to the unburdening of the skies.
> Rain was the tears adopted by my eyes
>   That have none left to stay.

When these lines were written, dusk had veritably become his time of day. It finds him, as he had promised, only more sure of all he thought was true. He has gone his chosen way, taken the grassy road less traveled by, but the path has not been as zigzag as he would persuade us. In an essay called "The Constant Symbol" he speaks of "a straight crookedness like the walking-stick he cuts for himself in the bushes for an emblem." Who is he? The independent wayfarer, the mind of the poet. Frost's way has been rather a crooked straightness. His poetry has not swerved from its first direction. Abandoning certain archaisms, it has become straightforward, while insofar as it avoids mere prose statement, it has grown richer. Fond as he is of the couplet, perhaps because it so readily lends itself to gnomic utterance, he commands a remarkable variety of forms. He has, too, the master's pleasure in technical skills. Thus, "The Silken Tent" is not only one of his subtlest and most melodious lyrics, it is also a sonnet in one sentence.

That he has come to a fuller recognition of the part symbol plays in poetry is plain not only from his declaration that "poetry is simply made of metaphor," but from the internal evidence afforded by his later work. Not least is it attested by the lyric called "Directive". Here the speaker revisits an abandoned

> house that is no more a house
> Upon a farm that is no more a farm
> And in a town that is no more a town.

The wanderer is content to find himself by losing himself, and ends up drinking the cold brook water out of a broken

cup stolen from the children's playhouse. The waters of
life, the poem appears to say, must be drunk from the cup
of imagination, but lacking the cold actuality, one has
only the broken cup.

Representative of his riper work is the lyric called
"Come In":

> As I came to the edge of the woods,
>   Thrush music—hark!
> Now if it was dusk outside,
>   Inside it was dark.
> Too dark in the woods for a bird
>   By sleight of wing
> To better its perch for the night,
>   Though it still could sing.
> The last of the light of the sun
>   That had died in the west
> Still lived for one song more
>   In a thrush's breast.
> Far in the pillared dark
>   Thrush music went—
> Almost like a call to come in
>   To the dark and lament.
> But no, I was out for stars:
>   I would not come in.
> I meant not even if asked,
>   And I hadn't been.

The poem is written almost entirely in monosyllables, and
with few metaphors: the tricky phrase "sleight of wing",
the reference to "the pillared dark", and the stanza about
the sunset lingeringly reflected in the bird's song, are all.
Accepted for its surface meaning, it has a quiet charm,
but it can also be read figuratively. The light that enlivened other years has faded, and can now be the subject
only of a retrospective lyricism, but the poet refuses to
dwell upon a vanished radiance. He is "out for stars",
which can be seen only in the darkness, he is prepared for
the night, and for the dark finalities that this suggests. The

little twist of the final lines, which shows the speaker aware that his fate is not wholly in his own hands, points up his spiritual independence. What distinguishes this lyric is not alone the simplicity of the diction, the maturity of the attitude, and the reticence with which it is disclosed, but an elusive quality that belongs to all good talk: its tone.

Frost's tone, as here, is not seldom somewhere between the quizzical and the tender. This is also the tone of his "Lesson for Today", offered to young Harvardians in the summer of 1941. The poet, reviewing other dark ages, pauses to glance at and comment on Alcuin's epitaph. The thought that Charlemagne's tutor confided to medieval Latin verse was very like that inscribed on the stones in many an old New England graveyard:

> Pause here a moment, passer-by,
> As you are now, so once was I,
> As I am now, so you will be,
> Prepare to follow death and me.

Alcuin's epitaph differs from this in being more elaborate, more lyrical, and wistfully pious. After some amiable discourse on the subject of dark ages and dark ends, Frost tells the old Yorkshireman's ghost that he too holds the doctrine of "Memento Mori", and were an epitaph to be his story, he'd have a short one ready for his own.

> I would have written of me on my stone:
> I had a lover's quarrel with the world.

As might be expected of a poem entitled a "lesson", it is a shade too hortatory. But it has a quality that is one of the distinguishing features of his work, and that may perhaps be summed up as a somber serenity. This implies not merely an acknowledgment but an acceptance of the incongruities of experience that make for our divided feelings, and gives his poetry a validity its other virtues alone could not command. It may be that Frost came to poetic maturity because he had reached out to the universe not alone, as Yeats had suggested, with the glove of a nation, but often with that of a neighborhood on his hand. His grasp of this special part of the native scene is remarkably different from that of his juniors, among them John Wheelwright and Robert Lowell. These poets regard the familiar genius loci with a more sardonic eye and address it in the compressed allusive language of a later day. They have been haunted, each after his own fashion, as Frost has not, by the ghosts of the Indians massacred, the witches burned, the Quakers tortured, the whalemen drowned, the factory hands maimed, the good shoemaker and the poor fish peddler executed by respectable New Englanders. With a strong religious bias foreign to Frost's almost facetious mysticism, they have been apt to dwell upon the vices that grow thornily in their native region, rather than to note, with him, the cool flowers and tart fruits of its virtues. Nevertheless, Robert Frost, knowing his limited section of New England from its hilltops to the roots of its boulders, came to know what he does of a wider and deeper region.

His love of the earth is matched by his concern with astronomy: he has written more than a score of lyrics that have to do with the heavenly bodies. One of his own favorites among his poems is "Choose Something Like A Star". This is a variant on Matthew Arnold's "Self-Dependence" and its theme is one that William Carlos Williams and Wallace Stevens also found congenial. Frost's treatment of it is straightforward, his speech, notwithstanding a reference to "Keats' Eremite", is colloquial, and his tone characteristically light. The lines mediate happily between the modest planet that we inhabit and the brighter stars. It is memorable, if somewhat too minatory to rank with his finest poems. Some of these fulfill his own formula by beginning in delight and ending in wisdom. There are others that begin in anguish and come, it may be riding on a jest, to the same luminous end.

4. The Earthly and the Definite

"Who recalls the address now of the Imagists?" The question occurs as a rhetorical aside in an apostrophe to the Social Muse, that belated tenth sister, born of the Depression succeeding the first world war. Her story deserves a chapter to itself. So does the school of the lost address. The very poem in which Archibald MacLeish parenthetically dismissed the imagists shows traces of their indelible influence.

The term *"imagisme"*—it was anglicized later on—was coined by Ezra Pound, but the man responsible for much of the theory, as well as for the first specimens of imagist poetry, was T. E. Hulme. Several years before he went to the front, to be killed in 1917, this English thinker was the center of a small group of poets who were feeling their way toward a new method. They were as ready as any realist to take the commonplaces of the young twentieth century for their subject matter, but their primary interest was in what Hulme called "a new technique, a new convention".

The mass of elliptical notes and unfinished essays that he left at his death were edited by Herbert Read and published under the title, "Speculations". In these pages Hulme opposes the new poetry to that of the immediate past by reason of its acknowledgment of human limitations, and by the clarity and precision of its style. He opposes it to the art of the more distant past because it expresses that "change of sensibility" which the machine age had brought about. In a packed original aggressive style Hulme preached the classicism that some of his contemporaries were to practice.

The word has been worn smooth by too much handling, but there is no mistaking what it meant to Hulme and his circle. For them classicism was "verse strictly confined to the earthly and the definite". Yet for all Hulme's emphasis upon the presentation of "small, dry things", for all his insistence that "in the classic it is always the light of ordinary day, never the light that never was on land or sea", he did not forget that emotion is the matrix of poetry. In his discussion of its proper themes he declared that it was useless to work up an emotion about motor cars on the theory that motor cars are beautiful: the emotion must precede the poem. Attacking the matter from the other side, he argued that the work of those versifiers who traffic in the jewels of the past suffers from "a lost poetic content".

Strength of feeling, clear perception of the object, accurate rendering of it, implied for him the accomplished use of imagery. He wanted no decoration, no ornament. If he argued against plain speech, it was because he held that plain speech was inaccurate, that new metaphors, that fancy, make for precision. The five brief pieces which form the complete poetical works of T. E. Hulme illustrate his aesthetic, as witness even so slight a thing as "the fantasia of a fallen gentleman on a cold, bitter night" entitled "The Embankment":

> Once, in finesse of fiddles found I ecstasy,
> In the flash of gold heels on the hard pavement.
> Now see I
> That warmth's the very stuff of poesy.
> O, God, make small
> The old star-eaten blanket of the sky
> That I may fold it round me and in comfort lie.

Looked at closely, these lines might be taken as more than an example of Hulme's theory of poetry, as, indeed, a metaphorical restatement of the changed demands of the art. The imagists would neither go whoring after the frivolous goddesses of the fin-de-siècle poets nor would they celebrate cosmic abstractions. They wanted the warmth of true-tongued feeling; they wanted a sky that had been overextended by "poetic" usage to become once more something they could relate, "star-eaten" and remote though it was, to the shivering human. They wanted words that would give the sting of experience, endured and known. Hence the emphasis on the concrete detail—the object seen, heard, smelled, tasted, and touched, on the metaphor that has the force of a physical sensation. They agreed with Aristotle that for the poet "the greatest thing by far is to have a command of metaphor. This alone cannot be imparted to another; it is the mark of genius, for to make good metaphors implies an eye for resemblances."

The poets whose vehicle is the illuminating image would appear to be at the opposite pole from those who sought, by figures as private as the ritual of an illicit religion, to suggest their responses to the world of "appearances" and the reality that it veiled. Not a Mallarmé, but a Gautier, the man for whom the external world existed, is the imagists' true ancestor. And yet their method may be thought of as a kind of reversed symbolism, bounded in a nutshell and counting itself king of infinite space. The imagist felt that he roused a sufficient sense of wonder by presenting his subject in a single skillfully developed metaphor. Occasionally he abandoned trope altogether, and achieved his effect by the impact of the naked thing-in-itself, not the unknowable ultimate reality, but the essence of the actual.

The nucleus of the imagist group was formed in 1912 by Ezra Pound, H. D. (Hilda Doolittle), and Richard Aldington. Pound stated the principles upon which they were agreed: "1. Direct treatment of the 'thing', whether subjective or objective. 2. To use absolutely no word that does not contribute to the presentation. 3. As regards rhythm: to compose in the sequence of the musical

phrase, not in the sequence of the metronome. 4. To conform to the 'doctrine of the image'." Pound's definition of
an "Image" was "that which presents an intellectual and
emotional complex in an instant of time." Certainly these
poets were concerned with imagery both in the sense of
the ordinary concrete detail and as a means of large evocation.

The first anthology of imagist poetry, which appeared in
1914, bore the title *Des Imagistes*, as though to stress the
contributors' debt to France. The volume included poems
by Pound, H. D., Aldington, Skipwith Cannell, John
Cournos, F. S. Flint, Ford Madox Ford (then Hueffer),
James Joyce, Amy Lowell, Allen Upward, and William
Carlos Williams. The majority of these poets, together
with two later comers, put forth the final, retrospective *Imagist Anthology* issued sixteen years later. Of those
who appeared in both the first and the last assembly,
H. D. and Dr. Williams proved most faithful to the tenets
of the group. Pound re-examined these in his "Few Don'ts
by an Imagiste". His principal articles of dogma were the
stripping away of every superfluous word; the use of concrete detail and abhorrence of abstractions; strict attention
to technique, involving an expert understanding of cadence. The models he suggested were Sappho, Catullus,
Villon, Heine, Gautier, and Chaucer. While Pound, aided
by the discriminating Madox Ford, was the first to rouse
an interest in technical problems, the chief publicist for
imagism was Amy Lowell. She created a number of costume dramas in verse and stimulated experiments in imitation of oriental poetry and in such novel French forms as
polyphonic prose, but she was more important as a propa-
gandist than as a poet. The anthologies that she assembled
were noteworthy for the inclusion of two newcomers: John
Gould Fletcher and D. H. Lawrence. Their work is too
various to fall strictly within the limits of imagism, and
each merits attention as much for his excursions from the
school as for his contributions to it.

Here, indeed, was not a school, in the French sense,

but rather a set of people drawn together by a common dissatisfaction with nineteenth-century poetry and with the realists' answer to its lack, and by a common interest in technical experiment. They were influenced, too, by translations from the poetry of ancient China and Japan, which was now coming to have something of the effect on English verse that oriental brush work and prints had had somewhat earlier on Western painting.

> But since water still flows, though we cut it with our
>   swords,
> And sorrows return, though we drown them with
>   wine,

run two lines in a lyric by Li Po. Another, apparently literal, version has it:

> Drawing sword, cut water, water again flow,
> raise cup, quench sorrow, sorrow again sorry.

If it is impossible to produce an English lyric according to the complex rules governing a Chinese poem, with its strict parallelisms and tone patterns, it is clear that such a poem, even in translation, points the way to significant concision. Most Chinese poems are short, some being in the form of a quatrain which is known as a "stop-short" because the poem stops, but the sense goes on. The Japanese tanka, a five-line lyric of thirty-one syllables, and the briefer haiku, afford further lessons in economy. In lines as spare and telling as those of a Chinese painting on silk or a print by Hokusai, these oriental poems evoke the life of the palace, the serene austerity of a philosopher's mountain retreat, the waste of warfare, the lasting grief, or the moment of delight. More often than not, an apparently simple reference carries a weight of allusion which shows how, out of the image, the symbol may grow.

In the light of later developments, the concentration of imagist poetry seems an easy achievement, while the conflict that raged over free verse fades into the comfortable past. When the struggle was hottest, however, the imagists repeatedly defied their opponents to name the metre in which *Leaves of Grass* was written, or to scan the prophetic books of Blake. They found a modern precedent in the "London Voluntaries" of W. E. Henley, with their musicianly indications of tempo, as they found in his hospital pieces the feeling treatment of anti-poetic subject matter. On the other hand, so fine a prosodist as T. S. Eliot contended that "the ghost of some simple metre should lurk behind the arras in the freest verse, to advance menacingly as we doze and withdraw as we rouse." Other masters of prosody said free verse was indistinguishable from prose. It is, of course, as hard to draw an unyielding line between poetry and prose as between animal and vegetable life. But we can all tell a camel from a camellia, and most people are able to make similar distinctions in the field of letters. A piece of cadenced prose, like Pater's monumental paragraph on the Mona Lisa, may be printed as poetry, but the violence done to the whole is usually recognizable in the fragmentary nature of such a passage. A poem, on the contrary, is complete and self-contained, whether it follow the antique design of a Petrarchan sonnet, the modern elaboration of Auden's "Song for St. Cecilia's Day", or elect the once startling freedoms of a lyric by William Carlos Williams.

In all patterns it is the fulfillment or cheating of expectancy that affords the satisfaction of recognition or the delight of surprise. In metrical verse these pleasures depend on the play between the metre and the superimposed speech rhythm. Free verse depends on the enhancement of the speech rhythm alone. In the hands of the moderately talented, it proved no more remarkable than the run of conventional verse. The masters of vers libre, and their more brilliant satellites, are as readily distinguishable as one speaking voice from another. To some extent this is due to the tone taken and to the choice of subject matter, but it is also due to a difference in phrasing, partly dictated by the poet's individual vocabulary.

The heavily weighted syllables of H. D.'s strophes could never be mistaken for Pound's fluent line, with its preference for the close of a hexameter. Nor could either be confused with the clipped speech rhythms characteristic of Williams.

Not all who called themselves imagists could do so legitimately. Meanwhile, a number of poets of widely different backgrounds, who made no special plea for it, were illustrating the principles of imagism. Among these was Adelaide Crapsey, inventing a form as strict as the haiku: a five-line poem of twenty-two syllables that she called a cinquain, to whose narrow compass she was able to entrust the delicate arbutus or a scene as fit for the heroic dead as the Grand Canyon. There was Lola Ridge, presenting with sympathetic intimacy the green-walled tenements, the flare-lit huddle of traffic, the pressure of stricken, indomitable ghetto life. There was that "hurried man", driven by the hungers of one of life's eagerest stepchildren, Emanuel Carnevali, whose poems mirror with a witty faithfulness the sordid scenes from which he escaped into a hospital and some symptoms of the disease of the times from which he could escape only in death.

There was Thomas McGreevy, creating by indelible particulars scenes that stir the heart. He paid tribute to Li Po, among others, and despite the gulf between the two poets, the dream-haunted Irishman shares with his Chinese confrère a love of landscape, of music and color, as also a wry melancholy, and a gift for conveying the mystery of the actual. Years later the work of McGreevy's younger compatriot, Denis Devlin, was to show an eclecticism fed like his on a knowledge of old Europe, and an appreciation of more than one way of writing verse. Devlin dealt with philosophical and religious themes, but he could also effectively present some small precise scene, be it a boy poised on the edge of a springboard, smashing the silence "in crumbs of glass" as he plunges, a chary government official vis-à-vis a dingy dignified ancient in a low pub on a rainy evening, or a "feast-day of the Republic" at

Annapolis. Though it was not his chief concern, Devlin's work offers fresh reminders of how powerfully the realization of externals, if it is sufficiently intense, contributes to the tone of a poem.

When imagism was still a battle cry, one of its un-avowed adherents was Ernest Walsh, who, like Carnevali and Adelaide Crapsey, died young, with too little work done. His lyrics exploit bodily delight with the frankness of Jean de Meun in the thirteenth century and of such twentieth-century Americans as Williams, Cummings, and Rexroth. In any case, Walsh kept his promise to warn, to urge the living, in words as keen as cognac. And in some poems, like whole fruits in brandy, is preserved the peculiar flavor of those old European towns that are now no more than a memory. Such is his picture of

Mougins

The Post Office was the grandma.
All day in the hot sun its cracked white face
Watched them pass to and from the fountain
        in the square.
The fountain is a friendly saint who heard
        everything
That was said in the square. But the post office
This old woman she knew the secrets they were
        afraid to say
And she kept them. They all passed before
        grandma—
The village dog cleaner gentler and better
        to look at
Than the village children who swarm like
        vermin—old men
With faces that have the dignity of an
        old penny
Women with faces like old sour dishmops
        coming and going
From the public washhouse women like a
        broom worn thin

A broom ready to be thrown away.
Yet somehow the sun passes over this town
Like the hand of an old gentleman over an old
    face that has no worries.

II

The poetry of both Walsh and Carnevali has something
of the vitality, something of the savage exacerbated tenderness, that marks the work of D. H. Lawrence. He attached himself early to the imagists rather because, like
them, he craved immediacy, than because he understood
their principles. He was too subjective to share their interest in technical subtleties, too apt to pour into his poems
the crude emotion of the moment in all its turbidness. Yet
his eye was the alert servant of his feeling, and he had an
ear for personal rhythms. Scattered among his poems are
a few small clear images, like that of the baby asleep after
pain, hanging numb and heavy as "a drenched, drowned
bee", or the slight dawn poem called "Green", which has
the clarity of living green stems through which the sun is
shining. There are pictures alive with color, among others,
the woman bathing in the sunlight by the window, which
glows like a golden Renoir come to life in music, and as
against that, the sullen pigments in which he paints the
Thames embankment at night, where houseless sleepers
lie in huddled disarray, or a somber funeral procession
under the Italian cypresses.

In Lawrence's most powerful work the metaphor takes
on a symbolic value, as in his swan song: "The Ship of
Death". Of the several versions of this poem none is
wholly satisfactory, but all are nobly conceived and deeply
moving. It opens in the conventional metre of blank verse;
as it progresses the rhythm becomes freer, though always
retarded:

Now it is autumn and the falling fruit
and the long journey towards oblivion.

The imagery is appropriately reminiscent of the most ancient hymns we know, those from the Egyptian Book of
the Dead, notably that celebrating the voyage in the Boat
of the Sun. The poem is saved from didacticism and sentimentality by the somber tone, the grave cadences, the
simplicity of the language; and by the adventitious fact
that it was composed by a dying man:

> Oh build your ship of death. Oh build it!
> for you will need it.
> For the voyage of oblivion awaits you.

Lawrence's sense of verbal texture was erratic, at its
strongest in a handful of love lyrics, and in the echoing
rhymes of a few other poems. But he had an instinctive
feeling for cadence, which also showed itself effectively in
his later love poems. His rhythms were not consistently
appropriate and his work suffered from lack of discipline.
Many pages offer mere jottings for the poems that he
never took the trouble to compose. Some of his verse, like
much that was to be spilled out by more helpless in-
valids of a later day, is no more than the groans and
retchings and curses of a sick man, who, however uncertain his diagnosis, knows that he is dragging out his days in
a sick society. Often Lawrence the prophet shouted down
Lawrence the poet. But his attachment to the living world
was too strong to be seriously obscured by his preach-
ments and could be threatened but not destroyed by his
formal ineptitude.

The obverse of the moralist's rage against the arrogant
stupidity of the well-born, the fatuous stupidity of the
rich, the violent stupidity of the mob, was the artist's will
to preserve the integrity of the individual. Bound up with
this was a sensual delight in the earth, in the sun and the
serpent which it brings forth, in the darkness and the miracle of the senses that are alive in the dark. Like Rimbaud, welcoming "every influx of true vigor and tenderness", Lawrence hoped for the restoration of what he
called "the phallic consciousness" in our lives: "the source

of all real beauty, and all real gentleness", and which, he insisted, "is not the cerebral sex-consciousness, but something really deeper, and the root of poetry, lived or sung." This conviction is uttered in "The Wild Common", which opens his *Collected Poems*:

> The quick jets on the gorse-bushes are leaping
> Little jets of sunlight texture imitating flame . . .

"But how splendid it is to be substance, here!" he exclaims, and then: "My shadow is neither here nor there; but I, I am royally here!" The sweeping peewits, the rabbits, the glittering gorse, the water with his shadow, which is more truly the white reflection of his body, quivering upon it, the seven larks singing at once, are all part of his paean. How many of his later poems are iterations of that first statement in "The Wild Common": "all that is God takes substance!" In the same way they continue to assert the lesson of an early piece, a young teacher's word to his pupils, called "Discipline":

> the fight is not for existence, the fight
>   is to burn
> At last into blossom of being, each one his
>   own flower outflung.

Nowhere is this more clearly stated than in one of his last poems, "Flowers and Men", an arraignment of those who kept misunderstanding his demand for the achievement of selfhood. Though marred by its petulant tone, the poem evokes with sparse means the unspoiled life of the flowers he loved. It should be read together with "Bavarian Gentians", wherein he invokes the blue torch of the flower as a symbol of the fructifying dark. His acceptance of death was akin to that which Whitman expressed, and Lawrence used almost the same imagery, with sad serenity taking ship for the longest journey. This, too, meant affirmation. Whatever his irritations with the less amiable forms of life, the only creatures that his heart could not own were the fish, since he ignorantly supposed them incapable of love. But he wrote a delighted poem about dolphins leaping as if around Dionysus' vine-wreathed ship. His celebration of "the bouncing of these small and happy whales" occurs in the midst of his farewells to the world.

For all its flaws, the body of his poetry makes him free of the company of such a great modern as Hardy, such a great forebear as William Blake. He wrote lyrics with the dramatic, forthright, ironical character of comparable poems by the Wessex master. And, after endlessly renewed battles with abstractions, he echoed Blake in declaring the profoundest sensual experience to be the sense of truth and the sense of justice. His final poems are a protest, spoken in defense of true vigor and tenderness, and reminding us of the wise madman who cleansed "the doors of perception" and looked out upon a universe throbbing with energy.

Lawrence's elaborate fantasies about birds, beasts, and flowers offer some of the strongest tokens of his pleasure in the fierce strangeness and variety of the world. Too often, here, as elsewhere, he intrudes himself upon the poem, so that his Tuscan cypresses and grapes, like his ponderous elephants and beak-mouthed tortoises with the Cross upon their shells, are compelled to become an illustration of some aspect of his confused passionate thought. Thus the poem, "Snake", remarkable in certain particulars, hovers between a clean objectivity and a moody subjectivity. Superficially, it is a mere anecdote, beginning simply enough:

> A snake came to my water-trough
> On a hot, hot day, and I in pyjamas for the heat,
> To drink there.

The speaker is annoyed because he must wait with his pitcher. The reader must wait, too, wait patiently and delightedly, to watch the snake drink:

He lifted his head from his drinking, as
        cattle do,
And looked at me vaguely, as drinking
        cattle do,
And flickered his two-forked tongue from
        his lips, and mused a moment,
And stooped and drank a little more,
Being earth-brown, earth-golden from the
        burning bowels of the earth
On the day of Sicilian July, with Etna smoking.

But precisely because the snake is this beautiful gold
color, the watcher hears a voice reminding him that it is
venomous and must be killed. He cannot, however, bring
himself to kill the creature,—is it out of cowardice, per-
versity, humility, or secret gladness that this guest had
come to drink at his water-trough,

    And depart peaceful, pacified, and thankless
    Into the burning bowels of the earth?

Only when the slow, dreamy, godlike thing eases itself
deliberately down into the black hole from which it had
emerged, the watcher, out of an impulse that he but half
comprehends, throws a clumsy log at the water-trough,
and the snake, though perhaps not hit, "Writhed like
lightning, and was gone." Immediately the watcher is over-
come with regret and compares the snake to the albatross,
and wishes him back again, thinking him

    Like a king in exile, uncrowned in the underworld,
    Now due to be crowned again.

The watcher has missed his chance "with one of the lords
of life" and has a pettiness to expiate. The poem is bathed
in an atmosphere of sultry suspense. Words and phrases
are continually repeated, sometimes with slight variations,
like the golden-brown coils of the drinking snake. The
stanza that describes the snake drinking is especially good,
with the contrast between the hissing sibilants and the

"ow" "oo" "o" sounds that have the effect of dark pigments in a painting.

> He reached down from a fissure in the earth-wall
>   in the gloom
> And trailed his yellow-brown slackness soft-bellied
>   down, over the edge of the stone trough
> And rested his throat upon the stone bottom,
> And where the water had dripped from the tap,
>   in a small clearness,
> He sipped with his straight mouth,
> Softly drank through his straight gums, into his
>   slack long body,
> Silently.

Lawrence is too much on the scene in this poem, yet the
uncrowned king of the underworld is paramount, even as
he vanishes. The fact that the snake is a phallic symbol
enlarges the poem's significance, and makes of it almost a
parable.

For an even more powerful presentation of the creature
one must turn to a passage in Robert Penn Warren's dramatic narrative in verse, *Brother to Dragons*. The butchery
of a slave by one of Thomas Jefferson's nephews furnishes
stuff for a story of terror and horror, and for grave elegy,
for tender lyricism as well. Flawed though it is by a tendency to dogmatize and to indulge in inflated writing, this
work nevertheless displays the richness of the poet's resources. His handling of an encounter with a snake is a
minor example of his skill. He shows unforgettably the
"regal insolence and swag" of the black snake rearing out
of the stones, as "with girlish / Fastidiousness the faint
tongue flicked to finick in the sun." A more scrupulous
craftsman than Lawrence, as also a more penetrating
thinker, Warren manages to endow the animal with its
ancient Egyptian and Norse symbolism, while keeping it a
natural inhabitant of the Kentucky mountain where men,
like snakes, are brothers to dragons.

When Lawrence died, William Carlos Williams wrote

an elegy for him that bore witness to their kinship. It is further attested to in poems by Kenneth Rexroth, who has come under the influence of both these elders. For a time he and Williams were associated with the little circle of self-styled objectivists headed by Louis Zukofsky, epigones of the imagists. Rexroth has experimented with various techniques, including that of the "cubist" poetry of Guillaume Apollinaire. Here separate images, separate lines, seemingly unrelated, yet build up to form, for the sympathetic reader, an emotional whole. While not repudiating his early efforts, Rexroth adopts in his mature work a style that answers the imagists' call for palpable definiteness of statement and deep truth of feeling.

Some of his most moving poems are those written in commemoration of his first wife. They are very personal and yet have a wide validity because they deal simply and affectingly with the fact of loss. A sufficiently large part of his poetry meets Ernest Walsh's demand for work "which does not offend or sound false when competing with Death." His verse is more severely disciplined than that of Lawrence, more tenderly nostalgic than that of Williams, and has a larger allusiveness than either found acceptable. It draws upon the subliminal sources that have nourished both.

III

Adam was the first poet, naming the creatures of the Garden. In the region east of Eden the diversities of animal life stir the lurking poet in every man. The shapes and colors of the creatures, their forms of attack and flight, the reminders they offer of the elemental world from which they evolved and of the human consciousness in which they seem strangely to participate, fairly demand metaphor.

Such poetry may not rouse us to the most profound response. Nevertheless, as in Marianne Moore's slender book of which "Nevertheless" is the title poem, life emerges, tough and breathing, out of the calmest perception, if it be sufficiently penetrating. Miss Moore's performance is at the opposite pole from that of Lawrence and she has not even his tangential relation to imagism. Her metric is precise—it has been compared to a minuet—and has elegance, even when her subject matter is an elephant or a steam roller. Her rhymes are part of a design that does not always conform to the meaning of her statements. If her work asks for comment here it is because of those passages recalling Hulme's remark that "The process of invention is that of gradually making solid the castles in the air." Miss Moore does not build ethereal castles, but she observes the inhabitant of a zoological or botanical garden or of a museum case with a particularity that realizes and solidifies the object. She delights in accurate delineation, whether of lizards, buffaloes, or swans. She is especially good at catching creatures in motion: the plumet basilisk: "a nervous naked sword on little feet", the pelican gliding or quivering about: "as charred paper behaves", the motions of the swallowtail: "magnet-nice as it fluttered" through slack airs and fresh, with "strict ears" only for the "piano replies" of the west wind: "Their talk was as strange as my grandmother's muff." This poem about a butterfly and a child, wonderfully free of the mawkishness the subject invites, is a minor triumph of metaphorical precision.

Her observations extend to the ethical realm. Indeed, her reflective preoccupation with it is one of the distinguishing features of her work. As Emily Dickinson is her literary Ancestor, so, clearly, Elizabeth Bishop is one of her descendants. Not for nothing, in her "Invitation to Miss Marianne Moore", does the younger poet try to seduce her friend thus:

> Facts and skyscrapers glint in the
> tide; Manhattan is all awash with
> morals this fine morning,
>   So please come flying.

The poem is not less enchanting because it reads like a witty paraphrase of Pablo Neruda's lament for a dead poet, his former schoolmate, with a like refrain: "vienes volando"—"you come flying." For Miss Bishop, as for Miss Moore, visual acuteness narrows, or perhaps expands, to moral perceptiveness. Thus her lines on "The Imaginary Iceberg" clearly show the berg's dangerous magnificence, its dazzling integrity, so that she can truly say: "Icebergs behoove the soul." The double vision is evident in her longer poem, "The Fish". There is no confusing with another this battered, venerable, and homely catch, his brown skin hanging in strips "like ancient wall-paper" wearing a darker brown pattern of

> shapes like full-blown roses
> stained and lost through age.

Every detail is present. The fisherman, who is the poet, looking at the gills, "fresh and crisp with blood", thinks

> of the coarse white flesh
> packed in like feathers,
> the big bones and the little bones,
> the dramatic reds and blacks
> of his shiny entrails,
> and the pink swim-bladder
> like a big peony.

The poem proceeds, with the same imaginative exactitude of description. And then the observer sees

> that from his lower lip
> —if you could call it a lip—
> grim, wet, and weapon-like,
> hung five old pieces of fish-line,
> or four and a wire leader
> with the swivel still attached,
> with all their five big hooks
> grown firmly in his mouth.
> A green line, frayed at the end

where he broke it, two heavier lines,
and a fine black thread
still crimped from the strain and snap
when it broke and he got away.
Like medals with their ribbons
frayed and wavering,
a five-haired beard of wisdom
trailing from his aching jaw.
I stared and stared
and victory filled up
the little rented boat,
from the pool of bilge
where oil had spread a rainbow
around the rusted engine
to the bailer rusted orange,
the sun-cracked thwarts,
the oarlocks on their strings,
the gunnels—until everything
was rainbow, rainbow, rainbow!
And I let the fish go.

Every detail is right. Every contrast is pointed. The swim-bladder like a big peony: the live organ functioning in the fish's body, is foil for the dead wall-paper flowers of his ancient skin, as the pool of bilge where the oil spreads a rainbow offers two opposed symbols. The rhyme at the end is the trumpet of moral triumph.

Miss Bishop is often the poet of the sea. So, too, is Philip Booth, a young celebrant of the Maine coast and the waters beyond. Sharing some of Miss Bishop's pre-occupations, he has a stronger interest in form and a greater severity. His images are sharp, like things seen in the light of a Maine day, and he has the gift of making physical actualities illuminate his metaphysical voyages. Miss Bishop, a playful poet, alongside the vividly realized details of Floridian flora and fauna, a Paris courtyard in the early morning, a Cuban peasant's shack, offers scenes that her fantasy contrives. These, too, may carry implications far from frivolous, what she sees being, paradoxically, at once "distorted and revealed".

A younger poet, May Swenson, is another woman with an eye for the exact detail that in particularizing a thing carries the mind beyond it. She takes her travels seriously and is less apt than Miss Bishop to show their ironic aspects. If she lacks an equal command of the lyric line, she displays a greater concern for formal experiment. Some of her inventions suggest Apollinaire's *calligrammes*.

The work of Jean Garrigue shows her possessed of a sensibility very different from that of these poets. Intrepid explorer of intensities that she is, she wants their regard for limits, whether of form or feeling. Nevertheless, she too, in poems about the slum, the park, or the forest, unites accuracy of observation with clear moral judgments. There are pictures in her "False Country of the Zoo" that might have been drawn with Marianne Moore's delicate pencil. We move, as from one cage to the next, from one exotic, "outmoded", melancholy creature to another, till, in the final stanza, we come to

The bear, wallowing in his anger,
The humid tiger wading in a pool.
As for those imports
From Java and India,
The pale, virginal peafowl,
The stork, cracking his bill against a wall,
The peacock, plumes up, though he walks as if weighted,
—All that unconscionable tapestry—
Till a wind blows the source of his pride
And it becomes his embarrassment—
The eye, plunged in sensation, closes.
Thought seizes the image. This shrieking
Jungle of spot, stripe, orange,
Blurs. The oil from the deer's eye
That streaks like a tear his cheek
Seems like a tear, is, is,
As our love and our pity are, are.

When she writes, "The eye, plunged in sensation, closes," she might be speaking of the eye in the peacock's tail, ruffled by the wind. But it is rather the eye of the observer, and when that is lidded, "Thought seizes the image." Miss Garrigue finds her subject matter in the give-and-take between the physical presence and the ideas, or more often, the emotions that attach to it. If she wears her feelings upon her sleeve, the embroidery can dazzle. And with what unembarrassed ecstasy she proffers the key to a foreign city or to the gate of a secret garden.

In her early work there are occasional reminders of her pleasure in the devices of Wallace Stevens. He greeted the concrete object as provocation for music and for revery. He would not consider it strictly on its own merits. He must walk round it, lift it up, set it down against a different background, look at it in various mirrors, making resultant magic. When he suggests "Thirteen Ways of Looking at a Blackbird" one is made more conscious of the dozen ways in which the poet cocks his eye than of the blackbird itself. His concern is with ways of looking. The statement recalls the fact that the young British poet, Elizabeth Jennings, calls one collection of her sensitive, candid lyrics A Way of Looking. Stevens' concern is also with the effect of each way upon what is looked at, bird or symbol. A memorable exception is an early piece called

BOWL

For what emperor
Was this bowl of earth designed?
Here are more things
Than on any bowl of the Sungs,
Even the rarest:
Vines that take
The various obscurities of the moon,
Approaching rain,
And leaves that would be loose upon the wind;
Pears on pointed trees,

The dresses of women,
Oxen . . .
I never tire
To think of this.

This is a good example of imagist technique, save for the obtrusion of the poet at the close. Possibly even that reference is unobjectionable, since it wakens the reader to the knowledge that he has his own imperial privileges and may turn the great Bowl round in his own imagination. Indeed, it is not concentration and concreteness, or the exploration of personal rhythms, that was the chief gift of the imagists, so much as a loverly delight in the various aspects of a various world, including the uglier of them.

IV

The fewest self-styled imagists showed consistency in their adoption of the principles of the group. The most faithful have been two Americans who differ in almost every particular: H. D., as Hilda Doolittle preferred to be known, and William Carlos Williams. H. D. did not go in fear of abstractions. Moreover, from the beginning the concern of this expatriate was with a civilization far removed from our own. Looking away from the London streets about her under a befogged sun, she recalled to her generation the sea light of the Greek archipelago. The very exclusiveness with which she dwelt upon an all but forgotten landscape, peopled with figures out of classic story, helped, in more senses than one, to reorient the reader. The flowers that grow sparsely on those rocky headlands, the waves that beat at their base, inviting to dangerous quest, the haunting presences of gods and those too well loved or too well hated of the gods, recur in her pages. Even in her most personal lyrics H. D. paid tribute to those Hellenic originals that fed her poetry.

Nevertheless, her work excludes, along with the material thrown up by contemporary life, some of the major themes of the Greek poets. Until the horrors of the second world war broke in upon her, her subjects were limited to the toll demanded by a rigorous art, the agony of physical passion, a seascape or an orchard as these laid upon the beholder the burden of natural beauty. The narrowness that makes for intensity gives to some of her poems a feverish quality not to be found in the most ardent of Sappho's fragments. UnGreek, too, is her care for the minute detail, the sharpness with which she outlines flower and fruit, the "cyclamen-purple, cyclamen-red" of the last grapes, the crisp line of a shadow at evening, the hot color of a petal, the texture of cliff grass. She did not fully exploit her limited vocabulary and her work displays no glint of ironic wit. But her sensitiveness to tone-color is unquestionable. The poem called "Garden" creates a heavy sense of heat by the labials and dentals in her weighted syllables as well as by the imagery of fruit that cannot drop through the thick air, cannot fall into heat

> that presses up and blunts
> the points of pears
> and rounds the grapes.

Vowels and consonants are employed with delicate suggestiveness in a passage from "Sea Gods" where the speaker promises gifts for their altar, the hyacinth-violet

> sweet, bare, chill to the touch—
> and violets whiter than the in-rush
> of your own white surf.

The vowels in "sweet, bare, chill" vary like the colors of the violets: the repeated "i" in "hyacinth-violet" "violets" "whiter" "white" gives the lightness of these slight flowers; the "in-rush of . . . white surf" carries the sibilance of foamy waters.

H. D.'s rhythms are almost the rhythms of speech, but speech at its most passionate, restrained by the very emotion with which it is charged. She had the classical scholar's sense of quantity. The lines are short, often monosyllabic, yet slowed for emphasis. Rhyme is used sparingly and not always effectively, but only in the longer poems and the verse dramas are the insistent repetitions felt as a flaw. Elsewhere, the frequent spondees, the recurrence of certain phrases, the parallelism of others, produce an effect of symmetry. An instance is the poem entitled "Orion Dead". The lines are spoken by Artemis, savage with grief, not least eloquent at the last:

> I break a staff.
> I break the tough branch.
> I know no light in the woods.
> I have lost pace with the winds.

The poems with which H. D. emerged from a silence of nearly two decades point up her early work alike by their resemblance to and their departures from it. As before, she relied here largely on the short, heavily loaded line, on incantatory phrasing, on pure luminous color. But the old altars were veritably shattered by fire from heaven. The poet left ancient Greece for the rubble-strewn London of the Blitz. The sense of miracle felt by the survivors is symbolized by the flowering of a charred tree in the city. The compelling passages are those which, in a few bare words, present desolation: the sliced wall that reveals poor utensils "like rare objects in a museum", or lines that give the sense of resurrection in the midst of dusty ruin as the survivors cross the charred portico, pass through a doorless frame, like ghosts breathing a heavy air, enter a house through a wall, and see the tree flowering:

> it was an ordinary tree
> in an old garden-square.

The ordinariness is part of the miracle. It does not transpire in the ambitious work of her last years.

V

Unlike H. D., whose concision and concreteness he bet-
ters, William Carlos Williams has remained, both literally
and figuratively, in America. His staccato rhythms are
those of American speech. His material is the American
scene. A handful of early lyrics breathe the brightness and
coolth of the poetic dawn that Pound heralded, and there
are a few other poems in which the imagery, the cadences,
sometimes the foreign subject matter, suggest the old expatriate. But if his work reminds the reader of what
Pound has taught his confrères, Williams repaid his debt
with interest.

The focus of his poetry is the provincial life of the East-
ern seaboard. He is interested in the small towns along
the Passaic, the suburban homes set in their neat grass
plots, the festering, fascinating slums, the roads that carry
a man away from them, the ferry that communicates with
the other shore, the gay, tawdry glitter of the metropolis
beyond, the nearby river, no more and no less challenging
in its loveliness than in its defilement. One feels the understanding objectivity of the physician in his approach
to his subject, whether he presents a modest landscape, an
interior, or a person. What person? Any one of the various
inhabitants of the region: simple housewives, puzzled children, and leading citizens (these the fewest), sick paupers,
crazy whores, and lonely young servant girls,

> colored women
> day workers—
> old and experienced—
> returning home at dusk
> in cast off clothing
> faces like
> old Florentine oak.

More of a realist than Lindsay, more of a craftsman than

Masters and Sandburg, he produces poetry that cuts deeper than theirs. This is largely because Williams believes that the poet's job is to perfect the language so as to make it express his own time, and holds this to be as exacting, as significant, as any task of science.

Beginning with bare notations or pure images, he found his way to a more symbolic style. So naked are some of his poems, however, that an admirer in the opposite camp, Wallace Stevens, called him "a kind of Diogenes of contemporary poetry". One might say that the anti-poetic is the tub in which he took refuge, and that not merely rhyme and metre but sometimes metaphor itself became an imperial interference between him and the sun. Nothing is too slight, nothing too mean, for his attention: the gay pompons on his wife's new pink bedroom slippers, a poor old woman greedily munching plums from a paper bag. His poems have the clarity that one finds in the paintings of his friend, Charles Sheeler, whether Williams writes about water splashing in a clean white sink, and on the grooved drain board "a glass filled with parsley—crisped green" (a poem in which the parsley is wonderfully and vividly contrasted with a memory of girls at the opera), or presents the classic simplicity of a powerhouse above squalid shacks. There is no effort to flatter, to cajole, to enchant the reader. Williams seems to be content with the clear line, the pure color. Or the mangy line, the dirty color, if he is looking at the uglier details of the sick room, or the roads that take him to and from it. Here is the child's innocency of the eye, but qualified by the man's feeling.

Chary though he is of metaphor, Williams does not lack "the greatest thing by far". This is clear in his frequent presentations of the city or of the integrated details of a various experience, as a flower. It is clear in his vision of the sea-elephant as Venus rising from the sea. The lines "To Waken an Old Lady", offer delicate evidence of it:

Old age is
a flight of small
cheeping birds
skimming
bare trees
above a snow glaze.
Gaining and failing
they are buffeted
by a dark wind—
But what?
On harsh weedstalks
the flock has rested,
the snow
is covered with broken
seedhusks
and the wind tempered
by a shrill
piping of plenty.

One can read the dark wind as death, and the broken seed husks as those experiences upon which we feed but that in old age are reduced to the dry husks of memory, or as the meagre but sufficient joys of the last of life. It is not the cold somberness of old age that is emphasized, but its thinness; and the vowel sounds are suggestive of both, an effect to which the rhythm contributes. Half of the poem's charm lies in its tone—the affectionately paternal tone of a middle-aged son to an old mother, tacitly suggestive of the reversals that are brought about by the years. Consider, again, the lines called "The Lonely Street". Here Williams takes a scene as dully commonplace as a suburban street on which girls in early adolescence parade, licking "pink sugar on a stick", and gives it something of the quality of Botticelli's "Primavera". This is partly thanks to the colors: the "light frocks", the white, the yellow, and the repeated pinks. Partly it is because the girls are tall, have a "sidelong, idle look", and seem to float, like the "yellow, floating stuff" one of them wears. Such phrases as "pink

flames in their right hands" and "a carnation each holds
in her hand" contribute to the Botticellian effect. Then,
too, the pattern of vocables is carefully managed, as is the
picture, suggestive both of adolescent silliness and girlish
charm, of foolish pleasures and their grey setting.

Williams prefers simply to present the objects, the
facts, even in his more complex pieces. An example is

THE YACHTS

contend in a sea which the land partly encloses
shielding them from the too heavy blows
of an ungoverned ocean which when it chooses

tortures the biggest hulls, the best man knows
to pit against its beating, and sinks them pitilessly.
Mothlike in mists, scintillant in the minute

brilliance of cloudless days, with broad bellying sails
they glide to the wind tossing green water
from their sharp prows while over them the crew crawls

ant like, solicitously grooming them, releasing,
making fast as they turn, lean far over and having
caught the wind again, side by side, head for the mark.

In a well guarded arena of open water surrounded by
lesser and greater craft which, sycophant, lumbering
and flittering follow them, they appear youthful, rare

as the light of a happy eye, live with the grace
of all that in the mind is feckless, free and
naturally to be desired. Now the sea which holds them

is moody, lapping their glossy sides, as if feeling
for some slightest flaw but fails completely.
Today no race. Then the wind comes again. The yachts

move, jockeying for a start, the signal is set and they
are off. Now the waves strike at them but they are too
well made, they slip through, though they take in canvas.

Arms with hands grasping seek to clutch at the prows.
Bodies thrown recklessly in the way are cut aside.
It is a sea of faces about them in agony, in despair

until the horror of the race dawns staggering the mind,
the whole sea become an entanglement of watery bodies
lost to the world bearing what they cannot hold. Broken,

beaten, desolate, reaching from the dead to be taken up
they cry out, failing, failing! their cries rising
in waves still as the skillful yachts pass over.

Here is a spectacle that cannot be accepted for its surface
values alone, although the seascape first glimpsed is sufficiently brilliant to delight the eye, for all its want of
color. The yachts "contend", but theirs is a conflict as safe
as a tourney and as aristocratic, taking place "in a well
guarded arena", where they are surrounded by sycophant
craft that enhance their own free and fleckless grace. The
crew crawling over them, grooming them, is seen as "ant
like": small, industrious, purposeful, and joyless, in contrast to the graceful futility of the yachts themselves, examples and emblems of conspicuous waste. The race is
not clearly motivated and yet is horribly destructive. The
poem is representative not of contending yachts, however
effectively it exhibits them, but of an inner conflict in the
mind of the poet. He rejoices in the elegance and freedom
symbolized by a yacht race even while he is appalled by
the misery of those who have no share in it, who are, in ·
fact, destroyed by the abuse of the power that makes the
race possible. The poem is not a social allegory, for allegory demands that a definite significance be attached to
the images, as though they were walking sandwich men.
The yachts, the sea, the hands seeking to clutch at the
prows, the broken, beaten bodies, whose failing cries rise
in waves "as the skillful yachts pass over", cannot be thus
plainly placarded. The virtue of the poem is that it leaves
one with a sense of mingled delight and compassion, the

one qualifying the other, the mixed attitude with which
one accepts life itself.

Williams' most ambitious work, the long poem, *Paterson*, is closer to symbolism than anything he has written,
if one excepts the "rococo study" called "The Wanderer"
which takes for its theme the whole duty of the poet. On
the first page of the first section of the first Book of *Paterson* he declares: "—Say it, no ideas but in things—" The
least, the most sordid of them have never lost their fascination for him. Even where they might be expected to ex-
trude like bits of collage, the

```
* * *
* S *
* O *
* D *
* A *
* * *
```

sign in a love lyric, or, in a poem about spring, the "STOP
—GO" signal, the arrow pointing to the "Woman's Ward",
the ice-cream parlor menu, are things that in their bare
particularity enrich the whole.

His fidelity to the thing seen is matched by his ear for
the thing heard. A notation about a cat on a jam closet
uses consonants and rhythm to suggest the deliberate
planting of her tentative paws: the silent footing of the
cat is as plain as the silent music of the bellhop's feet and
the gulls' raucous cry:

> And the way the bell-hop runs downstairs:
>   ta tuck a
>   ta tuck a
>   ta tuck a
>   ta tuck a
>   ta tuck a
> And the gulls in the open window screaming over
>   the slow
> break of the cold waves—

It is all part of the modern symphony that includes the "taraaaaaaa! taraaaaaaa!" of the fishman's bugle, the clank of the freight train and the wind in the sycamore, that tree which is one of the familiar presences in his poetry, as it is on so many American streets. Here is the thing that being thus singled out for appreciation implies the rich pluriverse to which it contributes.

In his prefatory note to *Paterson* the author said that "a man in himself is a city, beginning, seeking, achieving and concluding his life in ways which the various aspects of a city may embody—if imaginatively conceived—any city, all the details of which may be made to voice his most intimate convictions." The subject of this long poem, then, is a town on the Passaic River, and is also Noah Faitoute Paterson, the arkbuilder, the maker, the poet, the person. It shows his development under the tutelage of the city's genius loci as Wordsworth's "Prelude" offers an account of the growth of a poet's mind, however different the presiding local deities and the acknowledgment made them by the minds they helped to shape. It also bears resemblance to the quasi-prose epic in which James Joyce identifies his own native city of Dublin with the mythical tavern keeper whose dreams compose *Finnegans Wake*. Both the sage of Grasmere and the Irish exile wanted to free the language from deadening incrustations. So, too, Dr. Williams, lamenting those who die incommunicado, either because "the knowledgeable idiots" of the universities have reduced language to sapless abstraction, or because common speech has been so debased that the unlearned are inarticulate, cries out: "the language, the language!"

The opening of Book One, "The Delineaments of the Giants", is distinctly reminiscent of Joyce's epic fantasy:

> Paterson lies in the valley under the Passaic Falls
> its spent waters forming the outline of his back. He
> lies on his right side, head near the thunder
> of the waters filling his dreams! Eternally asleep,

his dreams walk about the city where he persists
incognito. Butterflies settle on his stone ear.

From this somewhat conventionally poetic conception the
first part moves rapidly to the curt statement: "—Say it, no
ideas but in things—"

At the start the poet, seeking to achieve, out of particulars, the realization of his inclusive, complex identity,
compares himself, only half ruefully, to a dog,

> Sniffing the trees,
> just another dog
> among a lot of dogs.

The first section of Book Two concludes with the warning,
in plain capitals: "NO DOGS ALLOWED AT LARGE
IN THIS PARK." The following section opens thus:

> Blocked.
> (Make a song out of that: concretely)

This is one of the chief themes of the poem. The metaphors, the analogies, the symbols, are always illuminated
by the concrete instance. Book One begins by defining
"the elemental character of the place" (which is also a
person, the poet), delineating the giant Paterson and the
low mountain stretched womanwise beside him, "The
Park's her head, carved, above the Falls, by the quiet /
river." And it ends with another Joycean reference to the
myth "that holds up the rock" and "holds up the water":

> And standing, shrouded there, in that din,
> Earth, the chatterer, father of all
> speech . . .

But between the first and last passage here are the particulars, some pure lyricism, others in the plainest prose:
newspaper cuttings, scraps of Paterson's history, private letters. And whether the talk is of Mrs. Cumming, the minis-
ter's bride, who fell from the cliff above the Passaic Falls
to her death, or of Sam Patch: "Jersey Lightning", diver

from rocks and bridges, whose body was "found frozen in an ice-cake" in the Genesee River, of the picture of an African chief's nine wives in an old *Geographic,* or of some detail of the familiar suburb, the theme is one: "a search for the redeeming language by which a man's premature death . . . might have been prevented." Counterpointed in Book One are the robin's behest: "Clearly! clearly!" and the poet's harsh: "Divorce!" Book Two, which presents Sunday in the park, "concretely": the poet moving among the park crowd acutely alive to the rich vulgar pathetic reality, Book Two cries: "Marry us! Marry us!" The clarity is in the song and in

> The vague accuracies of events dancing two
> and two with language which they
> forever surpass—

The divorce is between the event and the language that should utter it clearly. The unconsummated marriage is between the eloquence of things and of words, between the pedantic learned and the inarticulate vulgar. Throughout Book Two sounds, now loud, now muted, the voice of the roaring Falls, of the river whose wordless speech the poet would translate into living language, and to which he listens, in vain, shaken with the intensity of his listening. Book Three, "The Library", explores further the theme of the decay of the language. There is too much talk here about the poet's difficulty in handling a worn-out language. Moreover, the prose passages tend to obtrude themselves. Again, one misses the Paterson that made headlines in the labor news. Even though this is William Carlos Williams' city, not the murdered Carlo Tresca's, that aspect of it should have more meaning for a poet with Williams' convictions than is implied in the allusion to "the Paterson strike around the first war". Yet the body of this ambitious poem has the qualities of the work that preceded it. Here, among other virtues, is evidence of an ear for the common tongue: "Come on! Wassa ma'? You got /

broken leg?" cries the old girl dancing in the Sunday park.

"No ideas but in things": and so *Paterson* presents the poet's naked sensibility, which, though it responds to details so as to make them "voice his most intimate convictions", as the author says in his Note to Book One, defies the formulations of the intellect. Obviously Williams is using here the method that Pound employs in his *Cantos*. The poem also resembles the *Cantos* in the way in which it moves between music and plain prose. It is musical not alone in the lyricism of certain passages but in its presentation and recapitulation of themes. Thus the fourth Book, which deals with the "perverse confusions" that come of the failure of language and, less plainly, with the poet as savior, repeats the motifs of the earlier books with the same imagery, even to the African chieftain and his nine wives, and ends with a man by the seashore, walking inland with his dog. Again like the *Cantos*, Williams' poem has been resumed and continued beyond the point at which it was supposed to conclude. Thus seven years (the period seems significant) after the appearance of the Book that was to "complete" *Paterson*, the poet brought out Book Five. Dedicated to the memory of Toulouse-Lautrec, it recalls earlier references to Dürer and Leonardo, among others, gives new prominence to the unicorn tapestries, praises such contemporary painters as Ben Shahn and Jackson Pollock. Scraps of letters from Pound and Allen Ginsberg furnish some of the prose passages. The unrhymed free verse finds a place for a fresh and more formal version of one of Sappho's lyrics. Exalting sexuality, this Book asks: "—the virgin and the whore, which / most endures?" and answers: "the world / of the imagination most endures . . ." For all its awkwardness, *Paterson Five* remains eloquent of Williams' quenchless vitality. His final word here is in praise of "the measured dance", of "Satyrically, the tragic foot".

The tone of the entire poem is only occasionally hortatory, more often conversational, although the large fragments of prose discourse are imperfectly assimilated. If *Paterson* is rarely as good as Pound's major work at its best, it is far more alive than the drearier sections of the *Cantos*. Both poets are concerned with communication, and with the forces obstructing and debasing it. The great difference is that for Williams the time is not antiquity or the renaissance, but now (he sees its old roots); the scene is no foreign country, but is the provincial factory town on the Passaic in all the sordidness of its abused beauty and energy.

Paterson compares favorably with another modern American poem of like scope, *The Bridge*, insofar as it is free of the inflated diction and sentiment that invalidates Hart Crane's work. Partly this is because there is no panting after belief here. On the contrary, the poet insistently repeats, "the sea is not our home"—that Sea of Faith which again beckons the forlorn contemporary. Williams refuses to return, to drown, in what he calls "the blood-dark sea / of praise". The man in overalls with his dog, the worker, the poet, must strike inland. Nevertheless, there is a passage in Book Two that reads like a naturalist's psalm, addressing God in a more honest and intelligible fashion than was possible to Emily Dickinson in her shrewdest pieties. Needless to say, it is a fashion equally foreign to Eliot and to Auden. Here Williams sings unto the Lord a new song in very truth. His is a God who has read *The Golden Bough*, a book that does Him justice, a God who is both the father and "the eternal bride", and in whose composition and decomposition the poet finds his despair.

In such late poems as "The Injury" and "Lear", among others, he salutes the dark that seems so alien to the warmth and color that he has been celebrating wherever found. Witness, too, the poem about "the desolate, dark weeks" when the barrenness of Nature "equals the stupidity of man". Here he asks whether the night into which the heart plunges may not be

> the counterfoil to sweetest
>
> music? The source of poetry that
> seeing the clock stopped, says,
> The clock has stopped
>
> that ticked yesterday so well?
> and hears the sound of lakewater
> splashing—that is now stone.

The observation that the most profound sensual experience is "the sense of truth" seems exemplified in Williams' work as a whole. It is particularly exemplified in this poem, where the truth of darkness and desolation is confronted and bravely acknowledged. The simple imagery, the speech cadences, deepen the significance of the lines.

His work declares the sacredness of the secular. He does not blink the ugly sum of havoc, pain, and loss with which every life is involved, yet, like Yeats, in the midst of tragedy, he can rejoice.

> The descent beckons,
>   as the ascent beckoned.

Thus he opens a poem that faces the deprivations of old age, the cold riddle of death, and that acknowledges the virtue—with all its associations of virility, strength, courage —rising out of despair. In "Journey to Love" he reaffirms his delight in "the gardens of the world", his rage at a dominating waste. He can find in a "tree-friend" the "Counterpart of the void", as René Char says in a poem appropriately translated by Williams. For him facts are flowers "and flowers facts". Here is a man who praises "whatever celebrates the light" as he confronts the darkness.

The poets who regard him as an Ancestor, or perhaps as an admired, bountiful uncle, seldom show a like vigor and immediacy. This may be partly because many of them have violently rejected the world in which the doctor, when not composing poems, was busy delivering babies and healing the sick. Among the exceptions is Denise Levertov. The salt savor that the commonplace holds for this young poet, her response to "the humble rhythms", her natural energy, show her kinship with Williams. Her very effort to escape his influence is a tribute to it.

Williams has found his end in his beginnings. He has devoted himself to the American scene as it met the eye of a doctor practicing in the provinces, viewing not only the Passaic Falls but the citified valley below them, the park and the slums, as the places where, as an old Chinese painter said of landscape, life was perpetually springing. He has kept his ear and his verse alert to the language, in both the literal and the figurative sense of the word. His cadences are his own. He has held to the concision and, above all, to the concreteness of the imagists.

He gives the inner quality of things not by transferring to them his feeling about them, nor by a kind of damp sentiment from which even so inward a poet as Rilke was not wholly free. He gets at the essence, as apprehended not *behind* but actually *by means of* the phenomenon: the reality grasped by devoted concentration on its manifest being. Like St. Augustine, he sees the world arranged by an eloquence, not of words, but of things, many of them ugly. He can therefore accept the turd that the sparrows are sharing and the half-rotten potato on the plate, the garbage scraps left in the sink, along with the sparrows, the smell of cleanliness in a Nantucket bedroom, the "absurd dignity of a locomotive" hauling freight.

There are few contrasts as sharp as that between Eliot's query at the opening of the first of his *Four Quartets:*

> shall we follow
> the deception of the thrush?

and Williams' lines "To A Wood Thrush" that conclude:

> What can I say?
>   Vistas
> of delight waking suddenly
> before a cheated world.

To Eliot, exalting renunciation, in retreat from America
and from the age of which it is expressive, the song of the
thrush here spells deception, even though elsewhere he
may associate it with symbols of fertility. To Williams,
never in retreat, for whom America and the age are part,
if sometimes a tawdry, mean, ugly part, of God's poem,
the song of the thrush spells delight to a world that cheats
itself. With the most unlikely means he continually con-
jures back for us

> Unworldly love
> that has no hope
> > of the world
>
> > and that
> cannot change the world
> to its delight—

VI

When Williams declares: "To me, of course, e. e. cummings means my language," he is not talking of "lower-
case cummings" or of the poet's idiosyncratic way with
grammar, or even of his ear for the vulgar shades of American speech. He is saying that here is a man alive to the
reports of his senses, to the sky above his head, to the earth
beneath his feet: an individual, a person, a lover. He is
praising an alert and sensitive sensuality, a freshness of apprehension demanding a new technique.

Cummings was never associated with the imagists, but
his work exemplifies their principles. The device that particularly links him with those poets who went back to the
Chinese in their search for a style is his combination of a
private punctuation with a unique typography. It makes
some of his poems veritable ideographs. For centuries
writers had tried tricks with typography. A familiar instance is the "tale" of Lewis Carroll's mouse curling down
to a pinpoint on the page. But Cummings was after
sharper and subtler effects. His closest kinship is with

Apollinaire, not the Apollinaire who wrote a lyric about
rain in streaming lines, but the poet who manipulated his
syllables and his very alphabet so as to surprise the observer into instantaneous grasp of an experience. It is an
attempt to do with print what Hopkins tried to do by his
peculiarities of diction, to present the "inscape" of things:
a cat recovering its balance as it falls, a moon emerging
from clouds, a train cutting into a sunset among mountains where a black goat wanders.

Sometimes the arrangement is comparatively simple.
More often his syllables spread out upon the page, with
words like anagrams of themselves to signify a world
slapped with lightning and drowned in the sound of thunder (to translate into dull English), the fierce or delicate
dance of lovers, a grasshopper gathering himself up for a
self-annihilating leap and rearranging himself as a grasshopper, the exalté slobber of a drunk, the glory that clings
to the tinsel on a thrownaway Christmas tree:

                    a thrown a

                    -way It
                    with some-
                    thing sil
                    -very

                    ;bright,&:mys(

                    a thrown a-
                    way
                    X
                    -mas) ter-

                    i

                    -ous wisp A of glo-
                    ry.pr
                    -ettily
                    cl(tr)in(ee)gi-

                    ng

The position of "-very" associates it not only with "silvery" but with "bright" and with part of the mystery of Xmas. The position of "X" helps to suggest the ambiguity of the pretty trash, and the fact that Christmas has made its exit.

Similarly the poem on old Mr. Lyman, ruddy as a sunrise, fresh from a funeral, must be viewed in its entirety. Yet the lines on old Mr. Lyman, once grasped by the eye, can be heard, too, and the rhythm, punctuated by the rhyme, enforces the strength of the portrait. The typography is one of the poet's ways of asserting that things should be regarded as living wholes. Elsewhere the unexpected colons, the parentheses that do not always mean a lunar crescent, the split syllables or the sardonic blanks in certain words, jump at the eye, leaving the ear vacant. Such poems defy reading aloud. But they also demand that the eye take in at a glance what anywhere but on the page would be noticed at a glance.

Some of Cummings' early lyrics have an Elizabethan decorativeness. His later poems make words as abstract as "am" "if" "because" do duty for seemingly more solid nouns. By this process he restores life to dying concepts. "Am" implies being at its most responsive, "if" generally means the creeping timidity that kills responsiveness, and "because" the logic of the categorizing mind that destroys what it dissects. Here is a new vocabulary, a kind of imageless metaphor. It is not a device of which other poets readily avail themselves. Yet in an "Advertisement", satirical in the manner of both Cummings and Fearing, the aloof Laura Riding announces:

> Would now know for private information only.
> Would like now to know who.
> Am who.
> Would like to be informed of others.
> So far each who whom have encountered
> Has been which.

Cummings' practice may suggest that of Gertrude

Stein, but her interest was less in the evocativeness than
in the metaphysics of language. Thus she emphasized
words like "as" "and" "or" to represent abstract relations
and preferred participles for their suggestion of continuity. It is significant that she had so notable an influence
on novelists and almost none upon poets. She was capable
of nice insights, as when she observed: "In the midst of
our happiness we were very pleased," but the proper response to her performance may be found in Scene VIII
from her own mocking and relatively lucid production,
I Like It to Be a Play:

> You were astonished by me.
> All of us complain.
> You were astonished by me.
> Don't you interested trying.
> Don't you interested trying to stammer.
> No indeed I do not.

Only superficially do the astonished stammerings of Miss
Stein resemble the astonishing leaps of Cummings. For
him, apparently mechanical insubstantial words, without
color or weight, suddenly come alive, rise, and shine.

While his rhythms are often traditional, he makes his
own particular music, as in the poem beginning:

> anyone lived in a pretty how town
> (with up so floating many bells down)
> spring summer autumn winter
> he sang his didn't he danced his did.

The alterations of emphasis in this lyric give ordinary
words extraordinary meanings and turn them into a dance
that is also the story of a marriage. An exquisite early
piece, "All in green my love went riding", could well be
sung to some old English air. It has the ballad's tapestry
detail of hounds and stags, of horn and "famished arrow",
together with its parallelisms and repetitions, and the dramatic ending of balladry:

> four lean hounds crouched low and smiling
> my heart fell dead before.

Later love lyrics, composed in metres that can be strictly analyzed, move to the airiest melodies, as that which commences:

> yes is a pleasant country:
> if's wintry
> (my lovely)
> let's open the year

Though it is made up of abstractions: "yes" "if" "both", the poem places them in climates of feeling full of gaiety and tenderness. The half-heard echoes of consonants in "country" and "wintry" in the first stanza, "weather" and "either" in the second, of vowels in "country" and "lovely", "weather" and "treasure", "season" and "sweet one", contribute to the lyricism. Rhythm and signification are of special importance to Cummings, but, among others, his well-known poem about the child's "puddle-wonderful" spring world shows his feeling for the aural values of his vocables, as does the delightful piece on apple stealing which lets us hear as well as see

> the red and the round
> (they're gravensteins) fall
> with a kind of a blind
> big sound on the ground

The accuracy of his imagery becomes more evident when certain of his fantasies are contrasted with similar pieces by other poets.

He has a nose for decay wherever it shows itself. It may be in verse that caters to the stock responses of flyspecked sensibilities. It may be in "the Cambridge ladies who live in furnished souls", those afflicted with the occupational diseases of gentility: blindness and deafness to the natural world. It may be the "notalive undead" who make up "a peopleshaped toomany-ness". He recognizes the fixed grin of death in the insane cheerfulness of the brotherhood of advertisers and high-pressure salesmen. His sales resistance to them is complete, whether their product be red shirts, brown shirts, white shirts with Arrow collars, or shrouds.

He celebrates romantic love with a lack of embarrassment available to few poets in our time, and he has a boy's gusto for the pleasures of the senses and particularly —he was a painter—those of the eye. None of his contemporaries has the same gift for conveying muscular energy. His verse strides, climbs, capers, lurches when it must, recovers itself, shows always the vigor of a lively sexuality.

Cummings shied away from intellection so nervously that he sometimes stumbled. Fearful of any infringement upon a freedom that he equated with his private enthusiasms, he retreated into an isolation from which he hurled witty obscenities at those who seemed to threaten it, making no distinction between real and imaginary enemies. But however big his blind spots, however narrow the compass of his verse, it is a little fountain of delight. His picture of the knife grinder, even to his bell, in one of his several lyrics on that vanishing craftsman, is a self-portrait:

> he sharpens is to am
> he sharpens say to sing
> you'd almost cut your thumb
> so right he sharpens wrong
>
> and when their lives are keen
> he throws the world a kiss
> and slings his wheel upon
> his back and off he goes
>
> but we can hear him still
> if now our sun is gone
> reminding with his bell
> to reappear a moon

Later comers, some of whom, like Cummings, never went to school to Hulme and his circle, also exhibit their principles.

> Quietly let me put aside the imagist's
> Self-satisfaction, the duellist's pride.
> All turns of grace are lost,

says Robert Fitzgerald in the very volume that illustrates their turns of grace and their gift for creating atmosphere out of acutely realized particulars. The work of a few Canadians is equally testamentary, especially that of Patrick Anderson, whether he is writing about a classroom, a bathroom, a skier's mountain, or, in a poem which quenches a thirst other than that it describes, about a

Drinker

Loping and sloped with heat, face thatched and red,
hating his engine boots spraying mechanical pebbles,
he slowly comes through the white blocked light to the
    fountain:
his shirt clinging about him wet and rose
hangs heavily in front with his chest's sour bracket.

He crouches then: he turns with a serious hand
the little wheel: hangs, freckles over the jet
rising in a crush of water towards his burning mouth:
his eyes are wide and grave, his act seems private,
and as his hand spreads on the green stained stone
his massive working throat is a column of pure love.

He tastes with the iron pipe the very roots of water
spreading under the ground, which in multitudinous dirt
and infinite threaded dark are purified—
he draws the long stalk of water up between his lips
and in his sandy mouth there bursts its melting flower.

With beautiful inevitability the poem moves between natural and mechanical images, just as the water, a natural element, mechanically directed, satisfies an animal need, and as the body of the drinker, itself a machine, becomes alive to the joys that crown sensual satisfaction. Anderson's cadences are those of speech, his language is concentrated, the simple experience is apprehended with a fullness that gives it another dimension.

Among those who, whether or not influenced by imagist principles, write poems that exemplify them happily, one should count Gary Snyder. He may be speaking of his work as a forester or as a student of Zen, his scene may be the Sierra Nevadas or Japan; in any event he admonishes himself and us to "Lay down these words / Before your mind like rocks." Like Snyder's poems only insofar as they too are intense candid delineations of things, creatures, persons, places seen and admired, are Tram Combs's simple notations of life in the Virgin Islands. Totally different in substance, yet similar to the tone of these poets in the handling of intimately realized experience, are the quiet lines of Edward Field about such matters as subway graffiti, trees, Mark Twain and Sholem Aleichem.

The finest work of any of these poets betrays no dreaming backward or forward. Like that of Hardy and Frost, it is marked by an acceptance of "the light of ordinary day", but it is apt to be more awake than theirs to the contemporary world. Yet it is not flattened to the picture of that world often presented by less sensitive realists. Its strength comes from an exactness of detail, an illuminating precision of metaphor, a feeling for language, springing from "the root of poetry, lived or sung". Here was neither a style nor a school, but a will to nourish the roots. "Who recalls the address now of the imagists?" Possibly the poets have forgotten it because they no longer need it. They are thoroughly at home there.

5. Speech and Song

"*Und überhaupt stamm ich aus Browning. Pourquoi nier son père?*" (And on the whole I stem from Browning. Why deny one's father?). Thus Ezra Pound in a letter to an inquiring critic. It is significant that, addressing a Frenchman, he should begin with a statement in German. His poems are studded with foreign words and phrases. This is one index to his debt to Browning, who also delighted in languages and literatures other than those that were his birthright. It is because in his search for the appropriate word he chooses that, be it English, French, German, Greek, Italian, or Chinese, which best fits the sense or works as evocative shorthand. His poetry is largely conversational in tone (like so much of Browning's), and, as any cultivated man will do, he uses foreign phrases naturally in the course of conversation. In an early poem called "Mesmerism" he pays laughing tribute to "Old Hippety-Hop o' the accents" as one who had also rejoiced to recover and rework

<blockquote>
pure crude fact
Secreted from man's life when hearts beat hard,
And brains, high-blooded, ticked two centuries since.
</blockquote>

Two centuries and more, for it is as often as not something older than renaissance Italy that rides and sings and climbs fighting through Pound's poetry. He acknowledges his parentage indirectly in his curiosity about men and women whose loves and hates are ancient history, his efforts to resurrect the life that filled the medieval countryside. Indeed, the game of mating, fighting, "barter, lands and houses, Provence knew" crowds his *Cantos* only to a lesser degree than it does such early lyrics as "Provincia Deserta" and the Browningesque piece called "Near Perigord".

Browning is generally considered to have held the serene conviction of his Pippa that all's right with the world, yet his portraits were largely of men and women for whom all was wrong. His novel in verse, *The Ring and the Book*, along with how many of the multifarious characters for whom he found a voice, shows him intimately aware of cruel appetites not to be charmed to sleep by innocent song. The solid detail illuminating the "pure crude fact" was another useful element in the work of this "crafty dissector". Above all, Browning communicated his sense of the drama inherent in the conflict of personalities. His titles alone are eloquent of this: *Dramatic Lyrics, Dramatic Romances, Men and Women, Dramatis Personae, Dramatic Idylls, Parleyings with Certain People of Importance in Their Day*. So might Pound have subtitled his poems and portions of his *Cantos*.

The first of these in the original draft opened thus:

Hang it all, there can be but one "Sordello",
But say I want to, say I take your whole bag of tricks,
Let in your quirks and tweeks, and say the thing's
    an art-form,
Your "Sordello", and that the "modern world"
Needs such a rag-bag to stuff all its thought in . . .

What had Browning said in *Sordello*?

Confess now, poets know the dragnet's trick,
Catching the dead, if fate denies the quick,
And shaming her; . . .

What did Pound say in his original first Canto?

             Ghosts move about me patched with histories.
You had your business: to set out so much thought,
So much emotion, and call the lot "Sordello".

Worth the evasion, the setting figures up
And breathing life upon them.
Has it a place in music?

He goes on talking—is it to Browning or is he talking
aloud to himself?—comparing and contrasting the details.

> And for what it's worth
> I have my background; and you had your background,
> Watched "the soul", Sordello's soul, flare up
> And lap up life, and leap "to th'Empyrean";
> Worked out the form, meditative, semi-dramatic,
> Semi-epic story; and what's left?

The Cantos were to show what was left. The reference to
Sordello was ultimately shifted to the second Canto; much
was cut, altered, rearranged. But Pound had learned from
his master, and bettered by a study of more acerb talents,
the use of a style that permits a man to revivify the experiences that have shaped him. In *The Pisan Cantos*, composed during his incarceration, he could repeat: "Ghosts
move about me" "patched with histories." And he might
have added that he had breathed life upon them. "Has
it a place in music?"

It has become a truism that what Pound taught his
successors was the double awareness of verse as speech
and verse as song. Against the nubbliness of Browningesque diction, the coarse texture of common talk, the
relative harshness of the English tongue, he set what he
had learned of verbal music from having steeped himself
in Provençal lyricism. He is one of the few contemporaries
writing in English whose verse shows what he calls "the-
matic invention". This is, of course, not merely the result
of his close study of the troubadours whose verses were
made to be sung. His inventiveness is helped by the fact
that he has not been bound by the tradition of English
poetry alone. It is largely due to his having an exceptionally fine ear and an instinct of workmanship. There are
Cantos in which he keeps astride two horses at once, one

foot on the back of direct colloquial language, the other
foot planted on the back of the melodic phrase.

The sensitiveness of his feeling for cadence can be as-
sessed only by a careful examination of various poems.
"Night Litany" is a work of incantatory repetitions and
parallelisms, enhanced by measured pauses and the purity
of its verbal music. By these means, and by the subtle in-
direction of its imagery, "the glory" and "the shadow" of
an unearthly beauty is evoked, and one is wholly under
the spell of the starlit city of waters. Waters? As the canals
of Venice to the savage seas that the Vikings battled, are
the grave rhythms of that "Litany" to the vigorously
stressed alliterative lines of his version of "The Seafarer".
This tale of pitiless days and nights follows the tumbling
rhythm of the original Anglo-Saxon, and the rough effect
of the poem is in part produced by the rude alliterative
beat, however much it owes to the subject matter:

> May I for my own self song's truth reckon,
> Journey's jargon, how I in harsh days
> Hardship endured oft.
> Bitter breast-cares have I abided,
> Known on my keel many a care's hold,
> And dire sea-surge, and there I oft spent
> Narrow nightwatch nigh the ship's head
> While she tossed close to cliffs . . .

Set these lines against the delicate, halted iambics in the
"Speech for Psyche", as airily sensuous a love lyric as was
ever breathed, and contrast that in turn with the sharp
brilliance of "The Game of Chess":

> Red knights, brown bishops, bright queens,
> Striking the board, falling in strong "L's" of
>   colour.
> Reaching and striking in angles,
>   holding lines in one colour.

This poem, we are told, is a "Dogmatic Statement Concerning the Game of Chess: Theme for a Series of Pic-

tures", and indeed it summons up for the mind's eye a fine example of cubism. The effect is created as much by the weighted monosyllables and driving dactyls as by sharp verbs and curt adjectives. The participles: "Striking . . . falling . . . Reaching and striking" work to produce an effect of long diagonals. The fact that the rhythm is in every case integral to the context is another index to his mastery of his craft.

Before he achieved his own style, he submitted himself to influences remote alike from Browning and the Provençal troubadours. The most noticeable is that of William Butler Yeats. It is hard to determine how deeply these two poets affected one another. Unlike in background and in outlook, they were kindred in their energy and in their devotion to their art. They shared too, a hatred of mediocrity, which they associated with the vulgar middle-class mind. Pound's contact with Yeats must have fostered his anti-democratic bias. From the beginning of his self-imposed exile to its bleak end, he was more aware of Europe and Asia than of the land he left behind him. He could not but turn gratefully to a poet who opened to him the noble world of Celtic legend, peopled with kings and gods, and who revealed to him

> the subtler music, the clear light
> Where time burns back about th'eternal embers,

and "Nature herself's turned metaphysical." If Yeats, seeking a more athletic style, drew support from Pound's concern with the naked image, it is as obvious that Pound rejoiced in the "strange gain" offered by Yeats's traffic in the mysteries of Celtic story and Hindu philosophy. Both felt strongly the fascination of Japanese ritual drama. There are passages in Pound's early lyrics that might have been written by the Irish poet in the first elaboration of his early style. Such a piece is "The Alchemist", subtitled a "Chant for the Transmutation of Metals" and harking back to the medieval practice of writing alchemical equations with the names of women supposedly endowed with magical powers. Though the names invoked suggest Provence rather than Eire, and though it is not without clear images, it is hooded with the wonder after which Yeats, with his craving for myth and ritual, so eagerly sought.

The widely quoted poem, "The Return", while answering to the imagists' demand for economy and appropriateness of diction, is Yeatsean in its suggestive vagueness. Pound has described this lyric as an "objective reality" having "a complicated significance", leaving the poem open to a variety of interpretations. Yeats imagined that it might signify something like his own philosophy of recurrence. He saw history as a cyclical process, the birth, maturing, and death of one civilization after another, each cycle lasting approximately two thousand years, and each the antithesis of its predecessor: what was fair to the dying civilization being foul to the newborn, the sacred becoming secular, the devilish becoming divine, the changes succeeding one another like the phases of the moon but on the grand scale of the Platonic Year. "You will hate these generalizations, Ezra," Yeats acknowledged in an open letter prefacing his *Vision*, "yet you have written The Return, and though you but announce in it some change of style, perhaps, in book and picture, it gives me better words than my own." He ends by quoting the poem in full:

> See, they return; ah, see the tentative
>
> Movements, and the slow feet,
> The trouble in the pace and the uncertain
> Wavering!
>
> See, they return, one and by one,
> With fear, as half-awakened;
> As if the snow should hesitate
> And murmur in the wind,
>   and half turn back;
> These were the "Wing'd-with-Awe",
>   Inviolable.

> Gods of the wingèd shoe!
> With them the silver hounds,
> > sniffing the trace of air!
> Haie! Haie!
> > These were the swift to harry;
> These the keen-scented;
> These were the souls of blood.
> Slow on the leash,
> > pallid the leash-men!

However ambiguous the prose sense of "The Return", whether it has to do with a fateful reversal, akin to the triumph of Christianity over paganism, or the rise of the machine, or but announces "some change of style . . . in book and picture", its effectiveness is clear. The rhythms are worked out with extreme care to convey the hesitancy of those returning. The very vagueness of "they" in the first stanza contributes to the sense of uncertainty. Are they men or angels, creatures or elementals? The mystery is not lessened as the poem proceeds, "fear" "snow" "wind", cold words all, adding to the chill eeriness, before we learn that "These were" (significantly, they *are* no longer) "the Wing'd-with-Awe". The third stanza sustains the chill grey tone with its colorless "wingèd shoe" and its pale "silver hounds". The ghostliness of the picture seems emphasized by the line: "These were the souls of blood", recalling the strengthless dead come to drink of the bowl of blood offered them in Hades by Odysseus, that he might have speech of them. The final image cancels all thought of power and substance, allows only a troubling glimpse of those dim figures returning, shaken and fearful, from some nameless overwhelming encounter.

No work seems more remote from the technical skill and insinuating delicacy exemplified here than does that of Whitman. The gulf between the two poets is deep enough. Yet one finds Pound paying direct homage to his forerunner in the lines called "A Pact", in which he admits that it was Walt who broke the new wood: "Now is

the time for carving." Pound's first "Salutation", with its
attack on the "generation of the thoroughly smug and the
thoroughly uncomfortable", its conclusion "And the fish
swim in the lake and do not even own clothing." is reminiscent of Whitman's lines written in envy of the clean
shamelessness of the animals. It is not the spirit of the
medieval Courts of Love but of the author of "Calamus"
that speaks in "Commission". To all sufferers from "the
tyranny of the unimaginative", to the young, "smothered
in family", the middle-aged, withering in the deserts of
suburbia, to all victims sacrificed to the idols of the tribe
and the barbarities of middle-class culture, the poet cries
not in Walt's accents but surely with his animus:

> Go like a blight upon the dulness of the world;
> Go with your edge against this,
> Strengthen the subtle cords,
> Bring confidence upon the algae and the tentacles
> of the soul.

The expatriate did not forget his pact: he had commerce
with Whitman to the end. As a wretched old man in the
Pisan prison camp, the author of *The Cantos* harked back
to the pioneering poet more than once.

The difference between Pound and Whitman is not between the democrat who in deep distress could look hope-
fully toward the future and the fascist madly in love with
the past. It is that between the woodsman and the wood-
carver. It is that between the mystic harking back to his
vision and the artist whose first allegiance is to his craft,
and so to the reality it presents.

Distinguishing poetry that addresses itself primarily to
the eye from that which addresses itself to the ear, and
both from the poetry of wit, Pound achieved mastery of
all three. Disgusted with the loose productions of poetas-
ters who had been liberated to no good end, he turned
for relief to the astringency of French verse and the bite
of the classical epigram. It is instructive to contrast the
flat Spoon River epitaphs with Pound's dry comments on

those whom defects of person or of breeding, a dull regard for the conventions, or a cramping family background, reduced to the follies and rascalities with which
Spoon River, too, was familiar. Pound's barb glints in the
sun, the satire, feathered with wit, flies to its mark. Useful
as was Masters' performance, it dates in a way that
Pound's imitations of the ancient satirists do not. The
pleasure to be derived from recognition of his models is
not essential to enjoyment of these sharp characterizations.
Whether he cocks an ear in the direction of Propertius or
of Bertran de Born, glances back at Gautier or at Li Po,
his feeling for words, his unique gift of phrasing, permit
him to turn the matter of these poets to his own use.

One of his early poems, entitled "Portrait d'une
Femme", begins: "Your mind and you are our Sargasso
Sea," and goes on to describe a woman like that seaweed-
threaded tract of water, as ambiguous as she is rich and
strange. With some changes, the piece might almost be
the poet's self-portrait. London and less likely places, both
real and imaginary, gave Pound just such rich oddments
as she owned. He describes her treasures in fond detail,
not without a touch of mockery, ending:

> Idols and ambergris and rare inlays,
> These are your riches, your great store; and yet
> For all this sea-hoard of deciduous things,
> Strange woods half sodden, and new brighter stuff:
> In the slow float of differing light and deep,
> No! there is nothing! In the whole and all,
> Nothing that's quite your own.
> Yet this is you.

The description does not fit precisely. Yet his poetry mingles the lost beauties, the forgotten riches of Provence and
old Cathay, with some of the newest discoveries of the
twentieth century. As for her facts that lead nowhere, her
tales pregnant with what "might prove useful and yet
never proves", these are fairly representative of certain
portions of *The Cantos*, his most ambitious, irritating,

and fascinating performance. It is false to say that nothing "in the whole and all" of his poetry is quite his own, but that which can truly be called his own is not easy to discover and define. Pound is a gifted actor, a man who wears whatever mask he assumes as though it were his own face. He is a superb translator, revivifying whatever he touches. He is an alchemist of words, producing, out of the commonest substances, precious metals and life-giving elixirs. When one peers behind the mask, the actual features seem to have been distorted by it; when the magician disrobes, he looks less like Dr. Faustus than like an unfrocked professor thumbing his nose at the Academy. This does not invalidate the performance of the actor or the power of the magician's enchantments.

One of the happiest instances of these is the group of poems that he calls *Cathay*. There now exists a fairly large body of Chinese poetry in English, done by several careful hands. Pound himself reworked at least one of the Cathay poems, without improving it, in his later collection, *The Confucian Odes*. One returns repeatedly to his early versions. This is not because they are close to the original—only a Chinese poet learned in English verse could vouch for that. His renderings remain fresh because he came to these records of old griefs and rejoicings, love, exile, battle, meetings and partings, with so lively an appreciation of the pictorial character of words, for the physical actuality that is thus communicated. *Cathay* is remarkable because it is at once exotic and immediately real. In these old Chinese lyrics warfare is seen with the eyes of the common soldier rather than with those of the crusading knight or the gay cavalier. This was not as startling as it would have been to an earlier generation, uninstructed by Hardy and Kipling. Moreover, *Cathay* appeared when the young soldier poets were writing out of their own bitter experience of modern warfare. What was unusual was to find poems in which love meant the tender strength of friendship rather than the violence of passion. The background, when Pound presented his translations

to the public, before the century was out of its teens, was
unfamiliar: pine trees, willows, and waterfalls rather than
the scenery of the Lake country or the American prairie;
the mountain temple instead of the country churchyard;
the chattering of monkeys, the music of mouthorgans and
drums replacing the song of lark and thrush, the sound
of viol and flute. But the strangeness was never sufficient
to draw one away from the poem itself.

The secret of Pound's victory over this alien material
is, as always, his technical proficiency. By slowing up a
line with hard consonants for dignity: "Red jade cups,
food well set on a blue jewelled table," or for difficulty:

And what with broken wheels and so on, I won't say
                    it wasn't hard going,
Over roads twisted like sheep's guts . . .

by smoothing a line for gentle gaiety: "With ripples like
dragon-scales, going grass-green on the water," he knows
how to make more meaningful these grim laments and
aching recollections. His favorite cadence, the dying fall
of the end of a hexameter, heightens the music. The conversational tone, the frequency with which a sentence
commences with "And . . .", a trick that his pupils have
learned too well, quickens the intimacy. Cathay, apparently more civilized than Provence, if with its own in-
trigues and brutalities, seems, though more remote, somehow less foreign.

What is the use of talking, and there is no end of talking,
There is no end of things in the heart.
I call in the boy,
Have him sit on his knees here
                    To seal this,
And send it a thousand miles, thinking.

Pound's translations of the Odes—awkward rhymes that
mix his notion of the American vernacular with obtrusive
archaisms—offer nothing that approaches the force of this.

To turn from *Cathay* to the group of poems entitled

"Hugh Selwyn Mauberley" is to turn from the lucid, serious beauty of a Chinese painting to the oblique caustic
line of a sophisticated French drawing. Both exhibit
Pound's concern with technical problems, which set him
to studying not only the descendants of the symbolists
but their predecessors, chiefly the Parnassian who so carefully pared and polished his enamels and cameos. "Hugh
Selwyn Mauberley" is a tribute to Gautier and an attack
on Pound's contemporaries, including those who had sur-
rendered to what, with a flicker of the eyebrow at Miss
Lowell, he called "Amygism". The introductory "Ode for
his Sepulchre" recalls the verse preface wherein Gautier
nodded across the years to Goethe, writing lyrics for a
Persian garden while the cannon shook his windows, and
there are numerous explicit references to the French artist's verse and prose. The whole group of the "Mauberley"
poems is a sardonic commentary on his unfading lines
that sum up the demands of art. Gautier's familiar
strophes are here, but significantly distorted:

> The 'age demanded' chiefly a mould in plaster,
> Made with no loss of time,
> A prose kinema, not assuredly, alabaster
> Or the 'sculpture' of rhyme.

At the same time the ironic accent of Laforgue, the
rougher wit of Corbière, contribute to this attack upon a
machine-made culture, of which Mammon is god and the
publicity agent his prophet.

Two of the strongest poems in the group owe nothing
to the poets of the Second Empire or of the Third Republic: they are Pound's personal utterance as he looks about
him at the results of World War I. Or are these lines about
World War II?

> Died some, pro patria,
>   non 'dulce' non 'et decor' . . .
> walked eye-deep in hell
> believing in old men's lies, then unbelieving

came home, home to a lie,
home to many deceits,
home to old lies and new infamy;
usury age-old and age-thick
and liars in public places.

The poets who came out of the trenches, and some who
were never to come out, spilled over with rage and shame.
Pound packed the story into eight succinct lines. There
they are, the young men who died that "civilization"
might live:

Charm, smiling at the good mouth,
Quick eyes gone under earth's lid.

And here we are, with our civilization, rescued again in
another war. And here is Pound's poem, surviving not
"la cité" but its rubble.

Equally memorable are Pound's versions of such Chinese pieces as the "Song of the Bowmen of Shu" and Li
Po's "Lament of the Frontier Guard":

By the North Gate, the wind blows full of sand,
Lonely from the beginning of time until now!
Trees fall, the grass goes yellow with autumn.
I climb the towers and towers
                    to watch out the barbarous land:
Desolate castle, the sky, the wide desert.
There is no wall left to this village.
Bones white with a thousand frosts,
High heaps, covered with trees and grass;
Who brought this to pass?
Who has brought the flaming imperial anger?
Who has brought the army with drums and with
                    kettle-drums?
Barbarous kings.
A gracious spring, turned to blood-ravenous autumn,
A turmoil of wars-men, spread over the middle kingdom,
Three hundred and sixty thousand,
And sorrow, sorrow like rain.

Sorrow to go, and sorrow, sorrow returning.
Desolate, desolate fields,
And no children of warfare upon them,
           No longer the men for offence and defence.
Ah, how shall you know the dreary sorrow at the
           North gate,
With Rihoku's name forgotten,
And we guardsmen fed to the tigers.

It is centuries since that gracious spring turned to blood-ravenous autumn. The poet's name is still spoken, though not as Pound wrote it, for, working presumably from a Japanese text, he gave Li Po's name as Rihoku. But the guardsmen and even the barbarous kings for and against whom they fought are long forgotten. Their anonymity is a reminder that elsewhere lie bones white with many frosts, "high heaps, covered with trees and grass." And as for the "sorrow, sorrow like rain", the "sorrow to go, and sorrow, sorrow returning", as for the "desolate fields", these are everywhere and always changeless. The mournful cadences, the simplicity of statement, the repetitions, which have the effect of a hopeless litany, work together to make the poem durable.

The very ambiguity of the opening lines is eloquent. "Lonely from the beginning of time until now!" That is how the sandy wind sounds in the ears, tastes in the dry mouths of the frontier guard; but it sounds so, tastes so, because they have been at the North Gate, it seems to them, from the beginning of time, because they, like the wind that speaks for them, have been "Lonely from the beginning of time until now!" The poem opens with a view of the desert. There is a glimpse of a ruined village. It seems to end in the jungle. What it shows from first to last is a wasteland, and history cancels itself in the mouth of the tiger, a man-eating beast, as the man-eating beast that is war devours the meaning of life.

Those of Pound's young confrères who were caught in the wheels of the war machine wrote out of the horror, the disgust, the terrible pity, that filled them, refusing to look away from the human flesh hanging on barbed wire or gone to filth in the bloodied wood. Only in an occasional piece, such as the dreadful compelling lines that Owen called "The Show", were they able to compose the experiences that crowded too close upon them. Pound wrote about the war with the cold anger of one not nearly overwhelmed by it. In his translations from the Chinese he was at a further remove from his subject, and this, paradoxically, appears to have worked to the advantage of the poems. Being a master craftsman, he could more readily make his lines the vehicle of pain and truth. The short pieces that speak directly of World War I are the essence of those sections of *The Cantos* that deal with the same material.

II

This enormous work, still unfinished, has been variously described as a fugue with recurrent themes, as a fresco with two main and several subordinate designs, as a modern Commedia, with the *Paradiso* still to be shown. The analogy with any one of these old art forms could perhaps be worked out, with increasing difficulty as the poem grows in length and opacity. Pound once defined an epic as "a poem including history", adding that only a "saphead" could think he knew any history if he did not understand economics. His own "epic" offers evidence of his concern with these fundamentals. More clearly *The Cantos* are a contemporary development of verse as song and verse as speech, with the accent on speech. For what they come to is the monologue of a cultivated man, acquainted with the culture of more than two or three centuries and one continent, or a dialogue between that man and others whom he summons up out of history, literary and political.

And they want to know what we talked about?
        "de litteris et de armis, praestantibusque ingeniis,"

Both of ancient times and our own; books, arms,
And of men of unusual genius,
Both of ancient times and our own, in short the usual
                         subjects
Of conversation between intelligent men.

The talk, essentially the story of the poet's journey, a
story circling around certain main topics, is largely anec-
dotal. The main topics are related to the scenes in the
giant "fresco", the themes of the "fugue". Although he
was to repudiate it, Pound himself more than once drew
the analogy with the fugal form, saying that the first
"subject" or figure was that of the live man going down
into the world of the dead, the "response" was what he
called "The 'repeat' in history", and the "counter-subject" was "the 'magic moment' or moment of metamorphosis", when the daily breaks through into the divine
world. The first Canto opens with the live man going
down into the world of the dead: Odysseus, escaped from
the wiles of Circe, descending into Hades to have speech
of his comrade Elpenor. The "response" here is apparently
Pound going down to the dead, to have speech of Andreas Divus, whose Latin translation of the Homeric
story he discovered on a Paris bookstall and ultimately
turned into the magnificent English verse of this same
Canto. "Lie quiet, Divus. I mean, that is Andreas Divus,"
he says at the close. Divus, through him, is rescued from
oblivion as Elpenor was rescued by Odysseus. The second
Canto gives the "counter-subject": Dionysus on the ship
that was carrying him off to be sold as a slave, the masts
transformed by his magic to growing vines, his leopards
gliding across the deck, the sailors become dolphins playing about the motionless oars. The story of Dionysus
might be interpreted as a variant on one of Pound's
chief themes: the ugliness of usury, or, as he prefers to
call it, "usura". The sailors who wanted to kidnap the unrecognized god were, if not usurers, men

who set money-lust
Before the pleasures of the senses.

Similarly, the enslavement of Dionysus, god of wine, father of drama, is akin to the prostitution of the arts by
commercialism which makes men candidates for one of
the lower circles of hell.

Repeatedly *The Cantos* might take as an epigraph: the
love of money is the root of all evil.

with usura, sin against nature,
is thy bread ever more of stale rags
is thy bread dry as paper,
with no mountain wheat, no strong flour
with usura the line grows thick
with usura is no clear demarcation
and no man can find site for his dwelling.
Stone cutter is kept from his stone
weaver is kept from his loom
WITH USURA
wool comes not to market
sheep bringeth no gain with usura . . .
Usura rusteth the chisel
It rusteth the craft and the craftsman
It gnaweth the thread in the loom
None learneth to weave gold in her pattern;
Azure hath a canker by usura; cramoisi is unbroidered
Emerald findeth no Memling
Usura slayeth the child in the womb
It stayeth the young man's courting
It hath brought palsey to bed, lyeth
between the young bride and her bridegroom
CONTRA NATURAM
They have brought whores for Eleusis
Corpses are set to banquet
at behest of usura.

Thus a passage from Canto XLV, which Canto LI repeats without the archaisms. The same thing is said in the

sixteenth Canto, pointed up with anecdotes in colloquial language, and in Pound's peculiar version of American, interlarded with scraps of Latin and Greek, the illustrations drawn from history ancient and modern. He continues with the incoherent abruptness of rage, finally presenting the "Eeunited States of America, a.d. 1935" and its millions of unemployed, adult illiterates, vocational misfits, victims of preventable accidents: "Hic Geryon est. Hic hyperusura." The uninstructed scarcely need to be told that Geryon is the monster who guards those evil pockets of Hell where the defrauders lie, and that Dante, on his way thither, encounters the usurers who burn for their violence against nature and against art.

On the heels of this outburst comes an exquisitely lyrical Canto, the subject of which is the vegetation rites connected with the worship of Adonis, reminder of a world unpolluted by a greedy industrialism, yet not without grief, since the weight of a man on the earth is that of a bird's shadow:

Forked shadow falls on the terrace
More black than the floating martin
                              that has no care for your presence,
His wing-print is black on the roof tiles
And the print is gone with his cry.

But if Adonis falls, "fruit cometh after." This myth of resurrection is the countertheme to usury, with which the following Cantos are chiefly occupied.

The talk, however, is not exclusively of this crime against nature; it is also "de litteris et de armis". Homer and Ovid are among the great books, and, as might be expected, the songs and stories of Provence are generously drawn upon, one of the most memorable being that of Cabestan's lady to whom was offered in a dish the heart of her lover. The story is so presented that it evokes the like legend of Ytis, served up to his father Tereus by Philomela, the betrayed wife, and her outraged sister, Procne, who were transformed to birds, one of them a swallow. Other tales of savage passion enter here, gentled by time and art, as that of Acteon, transformed to a stag and slain by Diana for his glimpse of her, naked, by the forest pool; and that of the Provençal poet who ran mad as a wolf for love of the lady called Loba, the she-wolf, and who was hunted and brought to her for healing. These are distant matters, yet they come alive in the verse, kindling a sense of loss in what another poet has called our "middling ways", along with wonder at the "magic moment" of metamorphosis.

As for the wars touched upon in *The Cantos*, they are as often the medieval squabbles of Provence as the American revolution and the first world war. Ranging as he does up and down the centuries, through Europe and the Far East, the poet alludes with equal readiness to conflicts between long-dead Chinese war lords, Italian tyrants, or nineteenth-century American robber barons. Some nine Cantos are concerned with the story of China approximately from 2953 B.C. to 1780 A.D., and they are followed by as many more that deal in the same rambling fashion with the early history of these States.

Prominent among the "men of unusual genius" mentioned in *The Cantos* are Sigismondo Malatesta, Thomas Jefferson, John Adams, Sordello, and the venerable Confucius. There are multiple instances of "the 'repeat' in history", occurring at unexpected intervals. Thus, in Canto V there is reference to the killing of Alessandro de' Medici by his kinsman, Lorenzino, a death that was later bloodily avenged. What interests Pound in this tangled story is not so much the character of the murderer as that of the historian, Benedetto Varchi, "one wanting the facts", trying to puzzle out the truth of the matter. The Canto goes on to describe, vividly, another murder, that of Giovanni Borgia, which was never cleared up, and concludes with Varchi's anxiety as to the motive back of Alessandro's death. Canto XIII seems remote enough from the Borgias and the Medicis, since it has to do with Confucius. A key passage at the close, however, relates

them. It is a rendering in verse of a portion of the Analects that runs: "Even in my early days a historiographer
would leave a blank in his text." The Canto ends on a
paraphrase, rich with references, of other parts of the
Analects, but the parallel between Confucius and Varchi
is clear.

Almost in the same breath with various artists, sages,
and philosopher-kings, sharp allusion is made, as in Villon's *Testament,* to big and little gangsters and ecclesias-
tics, as also to munitions makers, politicians, bankers, and
profiteering publishers, while haunting figures out of legend emerge from the crowded background luminously, to
vanish like ghosts at cock-crow. Odysseus descending into
Hades (as he does more than once in *The Cantos*) is as
close to the poet as his own friends and contemporaries,
Hulme and Gaudier-Bzreska, walking "eye-deep in hell"
in 1914, the shrewdness and power of Kublai Khan, are
no less present to him than the power and shrewdness
that built the house of Morgan.

The reader who wants, if not plot, then something by
way of argument, will find himself at a loss. This in spite
of Pound's claim to have composed an epic that begins
in the dark wood of human error and ends in the light.
The Cantos are the allusive talk, sometimes breaking into
song, sometimes severely didactic, and abounding in free
association, of a poet who moves easily and rapidly from
one country, one culture, one age, one language, to another.

It was all done by conversation,
        possibly because one repeats the point when con-
            versing.

Thus a line in the thirty-eighth Canto, which is prefaced
by a passage from the Paradiso concerning Philip the Fair
and the woe he brought by debasing the coinage, and
which deals with the munitions makers whose wealth
came out of the blood and filth of World War I. "One
repeats the point when conversing": hence the analogy
with the fugal form, where the theme is stated and re-

peated by another voice at appointed intervals, with due counterpoint. There is constant recurrence of the subjects announced at the start: the journey of Odysseus, and especially his encounter with Circe and his descent into Hades to have speech of the dead; the selling of the god Dionysus into slavery. These subjects are open to more than one interpretation, but it seems acceptable to regard the poem as a tale, far less coherent than that of Odysseus, about a journey, the poet's, through ancient times as well as his own.

"Worlds we have, how many worlds we have," the poet sighed in the original draft of Canto I. He would speak with the dead: "ghosts . . . patched with histories". As for the enslavement of the god, that is the work of "the perverters of language" and their employers: the plutocrats against whom he wages tireless war. If this hedonist recurs to Confucius, it is because he saw the link between clear thought, clear speech, good government, and the good life. Moreover, this embattled Kultur-träger, admirer though he has been of individual stirrers-up of strife, has no illusions about war and those who stand to gain by it:

War, one war after another,
Men start 'em who couldn't put up a good hen-roost.

The Cantos are a man talking, sometimes it would appear whispering or humming to himself, about his life. The man is a poet, a maker, and much of his talk is of making. It is no accident that in *The Pisan Cantos* he refers twice to the table that a Negro fellow prisoner built for him, nor that he quotes with gusto the slang phrase of another: "Got it *made*, kid, you got it made." That is what Pound must have told himself when, in his own sharp phrase, the hoar frost gripped his tent.

One great difficulty that *The Cantos* present is that the poet, whether quietly mulling over his memories (Willy Yeats and Bill Williams among them) or speaking aloud of public matters, uses the elliptical speech of a man among his intimates and peers. Further, he has been betrayed by his attachment to certain neglected corners of history, as by his blind rage against those in whom he sees the chief enemies of civilization. He is so outraged by what he sees about him that he has to hark back, only to wash his eyes clean, to the court of Alcinous, or that of Taï Tsong, who reigned benignly in the seventh century, or of the great Lorenzo. The present becomes a blurred palimpsest and the most vivid time in *The Cantos* is the past. There is more proportion in the parts than in the whole. A trivial incident that his special scholarship has made important to him is exalted above matters of larger significance. He pours his blistering wrath equally upon the yellow journalists, the profiteers, the provincial mediocrities, the academic bats, the Jews, and the Fabians. More damaging than the privacy of some passages and the mistaken violence of others is the extreme dullness of the later Cantos. Scraps and orts of the correspondence between Adams and Jefferson, obscure references to minor events in the period of the Han dynasty, pointless stories intended to illustrate the corruption attendant on World War I and the gross vulgarity of those for whom the victory was paid in agony and death, are presented with little apparent design or vital force.

> The highbrows are full of themselves
> learnèd, gay and irrelevant
> on such base nothing stands

run three lines supposedly spoken by a Chinese emperor two thousand years ago. Too often in *The Cantos* Pound is merely learned and irrelevant.

One of his earliest poems acknowledged the existence of

> Some circle of not more than three
> that we prefer to play up to,
> Some few whom we'd rather please
> than hear the whole aegrum vulgus
> Splitting its beery jowl
> a-meaowling our praises.

The thirty-sixth Canto, which begins with a version of
Cavalcanti's learned and lovely canzone, "Donna mi prega",
offers a variant of Pound's youthful confession:

> Go, song, surely thou mayest
> Whither it please thee
> For so thou art ornate that thy reasons
> Shall be praised from thy understanders,
> With others hast thou no will to make company.

But the poet is very much concerned with the need for
understanders. About midway of the great work he prints
two Chinese characters signifying "correct name" and
presumably taken from a passage in Confucius which
reads: "If names be erroneous, things will not be accomplished." Between sneers at the vulgar and indignant out-
bursts at the debasement of culture or opaque references
to dark corners of history, *The Cantos* repeatedly present
pleas for clear and accurate speech in obscure tongues
not always written with scrupulous correctness. "On such
base nothing stands."

At their best, however, they illustrate Pound's supreme
sense of language, his grasp of the exact epithet, the right
cadence, his feeling for the weight and color of words.
Under his handling the stuff of ancient chronicles and
literary legends becomes more alive than the events that
make today's headlines. An instance is the passage where
Acoetes, the unwilling pilot of the ship on which Bacchus
was kidnaped, describes the miracle effected by the god.
It is not the images alone, it is the ghostly sound of the
syllables that help to create the mystery:

> Heavy vine on the oarshafts,
> And, out of nothing, a breathing,
>   hot breath on my ankles,
> Beasts like shadows in glass,
>   a furred tail upon nothingness.

Those lines were written by the same poet who presents a
hell that beats Dante's for blinding hideousness and gag-

ging stench. This is the place reserved by Pound for profiteers, bigots, agents provocateurs, and their kindred. Nearly
three Cantos are devoted to the filth of their Malebolge,
unthinkable, unforgettable:

> Above the hell-rot
> the great arse-hole,
> > broken with piles,
> hanging stalactites,
> > greasy as sky over Westminster,
> the invisible, many English,
> > the place lacking in interest,
> last squalor, utter decrepitude,
>
> > .   .   .   .   .   .
>
> Flies carrying news, harpies dripping sh-t through the
> > air . . .

The horror is the greater by contrast with the cool splendor of the succeeding Canto:

> > In the gloom the gold
> > Gathers the light against it.

It is precisely so that the fine passages glow in the murk.
    Consider, for example, a fragment from the opening of
Canto XLIX. Its lucid beauty, as of an old Chinese
painting, is due alike to the economy of the line, the retarded rhythm, and the liquid consonants:

> Autumn moon; hills rise about lakes
> against sunset
> Evening is like a curtain of cloud,
> a blurr above ripples; and through it
> sharp long spikes of the cinnamon,
> a cold tune amid reeds.
> Behind hill the monk's bell
> borne on the wind.
> Sail passed here in April; may return in October
> Boat fades in silver; slowly;
> Sun blaze alone on the river.

Upon this serenity intrudes the thought of that which is against art and against nature: the abuse of these that Pound, after Dante, sums up in the word USURA. Pound's economic views were formed by a less subtle thinker than Thorstein Veblen. In this Canto, however, he offers an English version of an ancient Chinese lyric finely illustrative of Veblenian irony:

> Sun up; work
> sundown; to rest
> dig well and drink of the water
> dig field; eat of the grain
> Imperial power is? and to us what is it?

The Canto concludes:

> The fourth; the dimension of stillness.
> And the power over wild beasts.

What the first three dimensions are we are not told, nor do we need to know. We are back in the stillness with which the Canto began, back in the stillness of the seventeenth Canto, in the deep sea cave of Nerea, back in the equally haunting forty-seventh Canto, back to the death of Adonis, and to the respite granted by Circe, to the concluding lines, suggestive of more than one legend, yet readily open to interpretation: it would appear to be no goddess, but art itself,

> that hath the gift of healing,
> that hath the power over wild beasts.

More than any poet of his time, Pound illustrates the remark that poetry is made with words. His ideas are extraordinarily muddled. In an effort to rescue and preserve the principles of the Fathers of the Republic, he made propaganda for fascism. In his enthusiasm for social credit, he gave aid and comfort to one of the most antisocial of dictators. Eager to free literature from academic pedantry, he moved toward the future with his eyes turned resolutely backward in the direction of romantic

Europe and the empire of the Mongols. Nevertheless, his insistence on the need for clear speech relegated to the attic where they belonged the superfluities of Victorian verse. His scrupulous craftsmanship, aided by his knowledge of several languages and literatures, has resulted in a fresh realization of the variety that can be obtained in English metrics. In *The Pisan Cantos* he observes: "t o break the pentameter, that was the first heave." His own characteristic cadence is in the line from Canto II: "Ear, ear for the sea-surge, murmur of old men's voices" and the penultimate lines of the last of *The Pisan Cantos*:

> and that Vandenberg has read Stalin, or Stalin,
>   John Adams
> is, at the mildest, unproven.

Even in *The Pisan Cantos*, which look like fragments from a fallen pediment, giving only a partial idea of the structure that it should surmount, there are unforgettable passages. One is Pound's lament for the masterful dead whom he had known and loved, living. Another is the lyric that commences

> The ant's a centaur in his dragon world.
> Pull down thy vanity, it is not man
> Made courage, or made order, or made grace,
>   Pull down thy vanity, I say pull down.
> Learn of the green world what can be thy place
> In scaled invention or true artistry,
> Pull down thy vanity,
>   Paquin pull down!
> The green casque has outdone your elegance.

The force and charm of this lyric lie partly in the echoes of phrases and cadences employed earlier. Sometimes the echoes are the more delightful for being oblique. Thus an allusion to Paquin is a reminder of a phrase in another Canto: "Sunset, grand couturier". There are other backward references in the concluding lines here:

To have, with decency, knocked
That a Blunt should open
        To have gathered from the air a live tradition
or from a fine old eye the unconquered flame
This is not vanity.
    Here error is all in the not done,
all in the diffidence that faltered,

The "fine old eye" burning with "the unconquered flame" was not that of the poet adventurer, Wilfrid Scawen Blunt, but of another keeper of "the live tradition": Henry James. The comma at the close was a printer's error, but inadvertently it accentuates the diffidence, the faltering, the undone. "What's done cannot be undone," says Lady Macbeth. Pound says: The "error is all in the not done." It is hard to tell which thought is the sadder.

Pound came tardily to the knowledge of sorrow, as he reflects in *The Pisan Cantos*:

> *Tard, très tard je t'ai connu, la Tristesse,*
> I have been hard as youth these sixty years.

The line in French is another echo—of St. Augustine's confession: "Too late did I love Thee, O Beauty, so old and so new, too late did I love Thee." The saint is speaking of God, the poet of grief. But he seems to imply that there is something holy about sorrow when it illuminates (which it does not always do), and that it is well not to be "hard as youth", at least when one has come to sixty years. The poet, too, is making a confession: that if he kept the eager mind of a child, he came late to the understanding heart of a man; indeed, it took imprisonment in the neighborhood of the death cells to bring him to it. This understanding deepens the finest passages in *The Pisan Cantos*, where the diction is direct and alive as speech, yet as remote from the careless commonplace, as emotionally affecting, as song.

History is presented by Pound as a struggle between the forces of darkness, represented by the big bad bank-

ers and by the governments in collusion with them, and
the forces of light, represented by the arts and by intelligence in the service of the good society. His prejudices
have remained virulent, his mastery of form is less evident. Originally *The Cantos* were to have numbered one
hundred. The most recent addition to them, *Thrones,*
brings the number up to one hundred and nine: the pro-
posed fresco has been extended so far beyond the original
wall that its coherence is lost, the fugue has become utterly free. *Thrones* was preceded by *Rock Drill,* which
Pound seems to see as swinging open the gates to his
Paradiso. A rock drill is an unlikely instrument for the
purpose. These Cantos hammer on the need for economic
reform as exemplified in the works and days of Senator
Thomas Hart Benton, nicknamed "Old Bullion", who
helped Andrew Jackson in his fight against the Bank of
the United States. Pound's elliptical phrases, in sundry
languages, can teach their lesson only to one who studies
the poet's sources. The Chinese ideographs and Egyptian
hieroglyphs with which *Rock Drill* is handsomely studded
show their functional character only to a learned élite,
notoriously without power. *Thrones* relies similarly on
intimate knowledge of such texts as a work on money and
civilization by another nineteenth-century American:
Alexander Del Mar, and the writings of the Church Fathers as edited, in over three hundred volumes, by Jacques
Paul Migne. Poems to which the reader returns are more
often those that enhance his sense of the world than those
that try to guide him in his dealings with it. Didactic
poetry risks the lapse into doctrinal prose. If the later
Cantos escape that hazard because of Pound's poetic
shorthand, its frequent illegibility cripples communication.

Those who have learned from him include such differ-
ent and seminal poets as Yeats, Eliot, and William Carlos
Williams. Each of these men for his own reasons rejected
Pound's ideas, nor did any of them follow his protean

changes or exert his Pygmalion touch on the cold figures of history and mythology. But they shared his devotion, and their work gives various evidence of the value of his contribution to the craft of poetry.

III

Prominent among Pound's disciples is Archibald Mac-Leish. Lacking the inventiveness and vitality of the poets mentioned above, he went to school to different masters, among them Eliot, St.-John Perse, and, belatedly, the votaries of the Social Muse. From Eliot he took chiefly a tendency to hark back to the vegetation myth that helped to shape *The Waste Land*. From St.-John Perse, evocative pseudonym of Alexis St. Léger Léger, came the exotic detail, the sense of vague immensities and haunting mystery that the French traveler into deserts real and imaginary conveys with an authority denied the American. Though at one time scornfully repudiating the proletarian poets, MacLeish came to accept an equally naïve social optimism, which expressed itself in an oversimplified style. Long before this he echoed faintly the voice of the father of surrealism, Guillaume Apollinaire. One of his early pieces, "Men", is admittedly based "On a phrase of Apollinaire". The phrase, taken from "Cor de Chasse" is simply: "Notre histoire est noble et tragique." MacLeish substitutes: "Our history is grave noble and tragic." The additional adjective, the lengthened line, the softness of the entire poem, are characteristic of the way in which MacLeish tends to dilute the influence of other poets. Were his work as derivative as his critics would have us believe, it could not be so recognizably imitated. Even a parody of it must exhibit its "shimmer", its "musical sound", and its skillful off-rhymes.

MacLeish has made technical experiments that charm the ear with their subtleties. He not only employs consonantal rhyme:

> The northeast wind was the wind off the lake
> Blowing the oak-leaves pale side out like
> Aspen:

he also plays with apocopated rhyme:

> The wind is east but the hot weather continues,
> Blue and no clouds, the sound of the leaves thin,
> Dry like the rustling of paper, scored across
> With the slate-shrill screech of the locusts.
> The tossing of
> Pines is the low sound.

Sometimes he uses rhymes in which there is an elaborate interweaving of consonants and vowels:

> One who has loved the hills and died, a man
> Intimate with them—how their profiles fade
> Large out of evening or through veils of rain
> Vanish and reappear or how the sad
> Long look of moonlight troubles their blind stones—

This is part of the octave of a sonnet in which the rhyme scheme is extremely complicated.

Pound's influence is plain in his early work. There is the attempt to relate the Odyssey, and notably the meeting of Odysseus and Elpenor in Hades, to our own time, laying hold on the physical detail that will put breath into the myth. There is the preoccupation with an America in which he feels himself an exile.

> This, this is our land, this is our people,
> This that is neither a land nor a race,

he writes, in an epistolary poem which speaks more intimately of ancient China and modern France than of home. It is curious to contrast MacLeish's ". . . & Forty-Second Street", a bold sally at giving the character of the liveliest thoroughfare of the largest city in the modern world, with Pound's lyric: "N.Y.". The former poem has a concreteness taught by the elder poet, but it lacks his power of condensation. It suggests his work in its rhythm, in its sharp particulars, in an awareness of antiquity impinging upon the contemporaneous. MacLeish's verse tends to be overly wistful, haunted, as Pound's is not, by a sense of the flowing away of the world. At its best, it shows his lesson learned.

An instance is "Eleven", which presents a theme Pound has never touched, in a reminiscential tone foreign to him, so that it is the more interesting to find here an imagist clarity, a precision of epithet, eloquent of his instruction. In the cool shadow of the tool house the child takes refuge from the adult world among ˙spades and mattocks and sickles, polished helves and glistening tines,

> breathing
> The harsh dry smell of withered bulbs, the faint
> Odor of dung, the silence.

Into this hermitage, at noon, one sees enter the old gardener,

> his knees still earth-stained, smelling
> Of sun, of summer, the old gardener, like
> A priest, like an interpreter, and bend
> Over his baskets.

The reader welcomes the old man with an odd sense of recognition, seeing him through the eyes of the child, who sits there, saying nothing, happy as though he were a nonhuman thing, growing. The comparison of the gardener bending over his baskets to a priest is suggestive of the Eleusinian mysteries, in which baskets figured as symbols of the womb in the mystery of rebirth. But the suggestion is of the vaguest. What is felt is the child's revival as he renews his contact with the dumb secret life of the earth.

The success of MacLeish's ambitious poem, *Conquistador*, is likewise the result of his desire to give the special curve and color of the thing seen, the peculiar tang of the thing on the tongue or in the nostrils. Based on the chronicle of the conquest of Mexico by Bernal Diaz del

Castillo, the most compelling part of this long poem is
the Preface of Bernal Diaz, as he, one of the conquerors,
now poor and blind and old, remembers that conquest.

Old men should die with their time's span:
The sad thing is not death: the sad thing

Is the life's loss out of earth when the living vanish:
All that was good in the throat: the hard going:
The marching singing in sunshine: the showery land:

The quick loves: the sleep: the waking: the blowing of
Winds over us . . .

Remembering equally the hardships, hunger and wounds
and thirst, death agonies witnessed, treachery, abandonment to misery, poverty, and pain.

Technically the poem is of interest as a fine example
of terza rima in English. The skillful use of assonance
and of unexpected feminine endings saves it from monotony. The metre, which is close to elegiac pentameter, is
peculiarly appropriate to the tone of the poem. Further,
just as the inexact rhymes give the terza rima a modern
turn, so the deviations from the classical metre keep the
cadences from seeming antiquated. The poem is wanting
in narrative power and, what would compensate for that
lack, a central theme. MacLeish has suggested that the
experience of the Spanish conquerors has been paralleled
in our own time by "the generation of men who have
moved into and explored and conquered and debauched
the unknown world of modern technics", but the idea of
this parallel does not transpire in the work itself. Its excellence lies in the successful creation of atmosphere and
so in the realization of what the conquest meant physically and emotionally to the men who discovered and
destroyed that alien culture.

Signs of Pound's instruction are to be discovered in the
performance of the most diverse poets. Passages in the
work of Robert Fitzgerald, a man of cultivation as well as
of sensibility, reflect the study of both Pound and Eliot.

The younger man's intimacy with the classics is evident
in his learned allusions, his translations, which include
a new rendering of the *Odyssey*, his ready use of Latin
titles for poems about the contemporary scene. His evocations of the recent past, such as the world of Henry James,
as well as his departures from iambic pentameter, are
among the features of his work that suggest Pound's influence. The lessons that the tireless old pedagogue had to
give are patent, curiously, in a few indigenous pieces, like
the one called "Cobb Would Have Caught It"—a poem
that Pound would never have written. Yet, slight and indelible, it bears the stamp of his teaching in its clear concision, the propriety of the language, the colloquialisms, of
which the expatriate would have been incapable but the
value of which he perfectly understood.

In sunburnt parks where Sundays lie,
Or the wide wastes beyond the cities,
Teams in grey deploy through sunlight.

Talk it up, boys, a little practice.

Coming in stubby and fast, the baseman
Gathers a grounder in fat green grass,
Picks it stinging and clipped as wit
Into the leather: a swinging step
Wings it deadeye down to first.
Smack. Oh, attaboy, attyoldboy.
Catcher reverses his cap, pulls down
Sweaty casque, and squats in the dust:
Pitcher rubs new ball on his pants,
Chewing, puts a jet behind him;
Nods past batter, taking his time.
Batter settles, tugs at his cap:
A spinning ball: step and swing to it,
Caught like a cheek before it ducks
By shivery hickory: socko, baby:
Cleats dig into dust. Outfielder,
On his way, looking over shoulder,
Makes it a triple. A long peg home.

Innings and afternoons. Fly lost in sunset.
Throwing arm gone bad. There's your old ball game.
Cool reek of the field. Reek of companions.

The fewest of those who show a direct filiation from
Pound have attempted to compose a poem of any length.
An exception is Louis Zukofsky, whose work the master included in his *Active Anthology* in the Thirties. Zukofsky's
autobiographical piece, "A", still in progress, sets forth its
themes in discrete images, scraps of remembered talk,
verse, and song. It is curious to find the method employed
in *The Cantos* adapted by a disciple who draws largely on
his experiences as a Jew, and who cites Marx as well as
Spinoza, if he also emphasizes his devotion to the author
of *A Midsummer Night's Dream* and the composer of
St. Matthew's Passion. The anthology mentioned above
features, too, the work of Basil Bunting, whose hard, sad,
candid poems, collected some ten years ago, reinforce the
conviction that they are a notable exemplar of Pound's
teachings, especially the free renderings of Villon and
others. A later comer, Tom Scott, has done seven poems
by Villon into Scots in a fashion that remarkably transmits
the force and much of the music of the originals. A vigorous, tender poet, Tom Scott has had very different teachers, but in his dedication to his language and his art he
follows Pound's precepts. Other men, though as clearly
distinguishable from each other as from their master, are
no less clearly indebted to him for his insistence on certain essentials.

Pound early set down as part of his credo that "bad
technique is 'bearing false witness.'" At the same time,
to the young American "having the instincts and interiors
of a poet", he said: "Put down exactly what you feel and
mean! Say it as briefly as possible and avoid all sham of
ornament. Learn what technical excellence you can from a
direct study of the masters, and pay no attention to the
suggestions of anyone who has not himself produced notable work in poetry. Think occasionally, (as Longinus has
aforetime advised), what such or such a master would

think if he heard your verses." Eliot and Auden obviously obeyed the injunction to "learn what technical excellence you can from a direct study of the masters." So did less prominent but admirable poets. One means of learning has been by way of translation. Witness the patient labors of Hubert Creekmore, and of that intense, sonorous lyricist, Ben Belitt, among many others. Another means has been the putting of old forms to new uses. Thus, the young practitioner, Donald Hall, pays tribute to Pound in a witty "Sestina". It opens with a paraphrase of the first line of the second Canto: "Hang it all, Ezra Pound, there is only one sestina!" A belief, as the poem proceeds to show, of which its author was duly cured.

Partly because Pound drew on such various sources: Browning and Whitman, Homer and the troubadours, Gautier and Li Po, partly because his influence has so diffused itself, one is inclined to recall the lady of the "Portrait" who had no character but that of her rich, strange hoard, and to identify him with this featureless acquisitor. It would be absurd to do so, however apt the title *Personae* that he gave to more than one collection of his poems. A *persona* was the Romans' word for an actor's mask. The poet has worn his mask so that the painted mouth frees a living voice. Nor should it be forgotten that Pound was Eliot's preceptor, called by that poet "il miglior fabbro": the better smith, forger, inventor, and that no little of what later verse-makers have learned from Eliot is due rather to the dishonored expatriate. Whatever his faults, and even if one looks exclusively at the poetry, Pound is far from faultless, he has made a major contribution to English verse. His unduplicable music taught lesser men to find their own. His insistence on the study of the great poetry of various cultures helped to free ours from a dull provincialism. His perceptiveness about the medium in which he works has been a constant reminder that the just epithet, the active verb, if properly presented to eye and ear, to all five senses, can give the quality of a moment or the pressure of an age. He is largely responsible for the charged language that is the feature of poetry in our time.

6. The Auditory Imagination

> And if you will say that this tale teaches . . .
> a lesson, or that the reverend Eliot
> has found a more natural language . . . you
>   who think you will
> get through hell in a hurry . . .

Thus the opening of Pound's mordant forty-sixth Canto, which appeared during the Spanish civil war. Pound does not allow one to get through hell in a hurry. Neither does "the reverend Eliot", who has been steadily occupied with the modern Inferno, and who has been quite as concerned as Pound with the poet's ultimate problem, that of language. Certain verse-men seem to be hunted, if not to hunt, in couples, and so one groups Wyatt and Surrey, Wordsworth and Coleridge, Keats and Shelley, and, in our own time, Pound and Eliot. However different their backgrounds and their development, these two have been united by their passionate devotion to the craft of poetry, and by a disgust for the spiritual pauperization of a society in which love tends to be as thoroughly mechanized as war. Their early association affected the work of both.

Eliot has publicly acknowledged a debt to Pound, especially for his help in giving final shape to *The Waste Land*, and it is interesting to discover how their study of the same models resulted in similar performance. The young Eliot's incisive etchings of "Aunt Helen", "Cousin Nancy", and "Mr. Apollinax" recall Pound's sharp notations on other emblems of a decaying culture. The main part of "Mauberley" has its counterpart in Eliot's repeated

attacks upon the crass vulgarian Sweeney and upon the
nouveau riche who wears so awkwardly the appurtenances
of a tradition to which he was not born, as in "Burbank
with a Baedecker: Bleistein with a Cigar". As late a poem
as "Journey of the Magi", which appeared when the Battle
of Imagism had been reduced to a footnote in literary
history, resembles some of Pound's *Cathay* pieces in its
description of the hardships of the wintry journey:

> And the camels galled, sore-footed, refractory,
> Lying down in the melted snow,

the miserable travelers regretting the terraced summer
palaces and the silken girls carrying sherbet. The poem
begins, typically, with a quotation from a seventeenth-century divine, and ends with appropriate references to the
Epiphany phrased with the ambiguity and the melodious-
ness peculiar to Eliot. In its very cadences, however, as in
its simple sensuous presentation of the details of the pilgrimage, it bears unmistakably the stamp of Pound's influence.

But where Pound lashed out indiscriminately at the finance capitalists, the Babbitts, the professors of literature,
the bought journalists and their buyers, and found salvation in Social Credit and fascism, Eliot has been more
logical in his conservatism. He early declared himself an
Anglo-Catholic in religion, a royalist in politics, and a
classicist in literature. His royalism has not been obvious in his poems. His religious convictions, tinctured
strongly with doubt, have been among his chief themes.
His poetry has centered on the ultimate concerns of the
religious mind, the problem of evil, and the soul of man.
Beginning with "The Love Song of J. Alfred Prufrock",
and continuing on through the *Four Quartets*, Eliot presents as the most appalling aspect of the modern world
the existence of the millions who merely *exist*, not in the
Existentialists' dynamic sense of the verb, but as the inhabitants of the Waste Land: the hollow men, the stuffed

men, for whom the world ends "not with a bang but a whimper."

Eliot is a classicist inasmuch as he has depended rather upon craftsmanship than upon inspiration, and that he was able, at least in the work of his youthful and middle periods, to find what he called "an objective correlative" for his emotion: he neither dumped his feelings into his verse nor expressed them directly. Instead, he found "a set of objects, a situation, a chain of events" representative of his feelings, and set them to his own music. Mean streets and dingy rooms; a middle-aging man, envisaging his head "(grown slightly bald) brought in upon a platter," while the eternal Footman held his coat and snickered, a man whose fearful concern is whether he should part his hair behind, if he dare to eat a peach; the tentative, pitiable and slightly disgusting lady of the "Portrait", who sits serving tea to friends, and notably to a coldhearted, self-possessed young worldling come to say his farewells; the ambiguous but clearly sinister occurrences participated in by the gross Sweeney and his companions; the desiccated old man who is the speaker in "Gerontion", who has been shown to resemble closely old Edward Fitzgerald, translator of the *Rubaiyat*, the work that inspired Eliot's boyhood verse-making—all these are sufficiently remote from the fastidious and cultivated young man who thus objectified his private responses to a sordid and tawdry society. *The Waste Land*, with its shifting vision of those who inhabit a loveless, meaningless world, and, with the exception of the retrospective lyric, "Animula", those poems that immediately succeeded *The Waste Land*, are likewise almost completely depersonalized.

To be objective is to be detached, to be capable of, perhaps impelled to, wit and irony. The romantic cannot allow the intrusion of comedy upon a serious passage, and cries out against the mingling of the noble with the trivial, the elegant with the burlesque. *The Waste Land* abounds in just such contrasts. Following upon the reverberant echo from Shakespeare: "Those are pearls that were his eyes," is the cry of a hysterical woman of fashion, and then:

But
O O O O that Shakespeherian rag—

These juxtapositions are among the features of much of his poetry. Eliot, the critic, is himself responsible for the thesis that the ability to present in a moment, in the twinkling of an eye, contradictory viewpoints, to inquire into his feelings and feel, as it were, with his mind, links the contemporary poet with the English metaphysicals.

The member of this company most acceptable to the moderns is John Donne, whose highly intellectualized poems are complex in their logical structure, startling in their juxtapositions, and no less subtle because they are furnished with homely imagery and tend to a natural, conversational style. His work is supported by different premises, yet it has features congenial to early twentieth-century poets.

Alert intelligences in the seventeenth century confronted a world which, in its disruptions and promises, somewhat resembled our own on the eve of the Age of Anxiety. If the eye, fixed more steadily than before upon the physical universe, saw the possibilities of subduing it, there was also a clearer insight into its intricacies and betrayals. It was not astonishing that the poets should seek to reach truth on her "huge hill, / Cragged, and steep," by going about and about, so that they might, "what the hills suddennes resists, winne so." Nor was it strange that their verse should exclaim or smile sardonically at the difficulties of the climb.

Eliot's close contemporaries and their juniors likewise found it hard to maintain attitudes that had seemed acceptable a short time since. War, in becoming a world industry, involved dislocations and destructions not confined to physical things. The faith in progress was roughly ripped away. And the bitter, skeptical temper that men carried with them from the trenches, along with their lice, their wounds, and their nightmarish memories, was strengthened by new ideas of behavior which taught them to distrust their most familiar responses. The findings of psychiatrists and anthropologists had much the disturbing effect that the teachings of the physicists had had three centuries earlier, or those of the biologists in a previous generation, and the unease of the intellectuals was complicated by the beginnings of the breakdown of the economic order. All this did not happen at once, but it made Eliot's successors hospitable to his own bleak view of a world more troubled than John Donne's and uglier than that which had exacerbated Eliot's French masters.

Much as Eliot has in common with the elder poet, however, he wants Donne's singular force. He offers

> What's not believed in, or, if still believed,
> In memory only, reconsidered passion . . .

more often than the union of powerful feeling and lively imagery with which Donne apostrophizes his mistress going to bed, or his God, as he goes to his own final couch. If Eliot uses the language of ordinary speech, it has not the savage simplicity of "For Godsake hold your tongue, and let me love," but wearily confesses the tedium of the common hours:

> Oh, do not ask, 'What is it?'
> Let us go and make our visit.

It is not only because they obey the strict rules of his chosen form that Donne's Holy Sonnets have a solidity that sets them poles apart from such a piece of penitential music as "Ash Wednesday". Where Donne turned his learning and his sensuality to the resolution in poetry of an emotional conflict, Eliot weaves literary allusions and melodious echoes into his discourse in a fashion that tends to qualify the intensity of the emotion. Unquestionably, however, a large element in his contribution to modern poetry has been the revival of Donne's inquisitorial psychologizing and his conversational lyricism.

It is well known that Eliot praised Donne for "looking into a good deal more than the heart. . . . into the cerebral cortex, the nervous system, and the digestive tracts." So too, looked, if with different results, certain French poets, whose influence upon Eliot is abundantly evident and has, indeed been publicly acknowledged. Prominent among them is Laforgue, who died, acutely conscious of his own physical malady and not unaware of the spiritual malaise of his time, in the crass Paris of the seventies. A line of Laforgue's might serve as an epigraph for the American poet's studies of the barrenness of contemporary life: "Ah! que la Vie est quotidienne . . ." As the young Frenchman ascribed to the moon and the telegraph wires the humiliations lying in wait for the feeble human organism, so Eliot speaks of the evening

> spread out against the sky
> Like a patient etherized upon a table.

Eliot, like Laforgue, mixes the argot of the street with the question phrased to himself by a half-lunatic Hamlet, passes rapidly from the monuments of the past to the tenements of the present, transposes a sentimental velleity into a witty key, and enhances the grand and the tawdry by setting one against the other. Laforgue's response to the lonely tedium of life and the Void that he envisaged after death was a melancholy tinged with irony. This is the tone of the early work of the American poet who was to struggle so hard for faith. Echoing internal rhymes enrich the vers libre of both, a vers libre, which, as Eliot has pointed out, resembles Elizabethan blank verse in its stretching, contrasting, and distorting of a traditional measure. His early poems also pay Laforgue the oblique tribute of paraphrase in several passages. "Rhapsody on a Windy Night" quotes the "Complainte de cette bonne Lune" directly, and the distorted nursery rhyme in "The Hollow Men" may well be an echo of Laforgue's sardonic version of "Sur le pont d'Avignon" in his "Complainte de cette bonne Lune". Several of Laforgue's compatriots were similarly influential. How congenial the images in Corbière's "Paris Nocturne," with its retiring flood, its crabs scraping in the night, its dried-up Styx, must have been to the poet on whom the Missouri and the Mississippi "made a deeper impression than any other part of the world"!

One of the most exquisite lyrics in the *Quartets* opens with the startling and opaque lines:

> Garlic and sapphires in the mud
> Clot the bedded axle-tree.

The first association is with a poem by Mallarmé which contains the line: "Tonnerre et rubis aux moyeaux". But thunder and rubies at the axles, presumably of the sun's chariot, are nevertheless remote from garlic and sapphires in the mud. These appear to derive from another poem by Mallarmé, addressed to the tomb of Baudelaire, and presenting the sepulchral mouth of the Paris sewer "bavant boue et rubis": slobbering mud and rubies. The multiple associations, like a shaken kaleidoscope, assemble the seemingly ill-assorted pieces in a design that recalls the worlds of both of these Parisians. It also hints at the endless struggle of the poet, especially the urban poet, to reconcile ugly particulars and the dazzling wealth of the imagination, fiery as jewels, lamplight, or sunset.

> When 'Omer smote 'is bloomin' lyre,
> He'd 'eard men sing by land and sea;
> And what 'e thought 'e might require,
> 'E went and took—the same as me!

sang the author of the Barrack-Room Ballads. Some centuries earlier Ben Jonson had observed that a poet should "be able to convert the substances, or riches of another poet to his own use." Agreeing with both, Eliot has made his work a storehouse of treasures, chosen fastidiously from the early Elizabethans and the metaphysicals, from various French poets of the nineteenth and twentieth centuries, from Dante and his circle, and less likely sources. Occasionally a knowledge of his originals impairs one's pleasure in his accomplishment. Familiarity with Gautier's poem beginning

> Carmen est maigre,—un trait de bistre
> Cerne son œil de gitana . . .

may distract one from the neatness of

> Grishkin is nice: her Russian eye
> Is underlined for emphasis.

On the other hand, recollection of Gautier's poem about the hippopotamus can only add to one's enjoyment of the satirical paraphrase in which Eliot contrasts that animal, to its advantage, with the True Church. His transmutation of the work of other poets reaches a climax in *The Waste Land*, where the references range from the Buddhist Fire Sermon to the Hebrew scriptures, from musical themes of the Wagnerian music dramas to the wares of the music halls, from Virgil to Verlaine.

This allusiveness is an aspect of the methods and purposes of those symbolists who, by a succession of vague images, transformed as they were perceived like sculptures of cloud, sought to evoke elusive shades of feeling, to suggest a reality beyond the world of sense. For Eliot, his effort directed to similar ends, his mind furnished with the spoils of his reading in several literatures, literary references are inevitable. His poetry sometimes resembles a room lined with mirrors, reflecting not only the glory that was Greece and the grandeur that was Rome, the middle ages and the renaissance, but the gracelessness, the squalor, of modern Paris and London. Moreover, it is a room with windows framing

> such a vision of the street
> As the street hardly understands;

for the poet sees it as part of the long road traveled by Dante in his journey through Hell and Purgatory.

As he walks down the street Eliot may pause for a backward look, turn to stare at a strange face, may even question his destination, but he moves with the assurance of a major poet. His work is remarkable alike for its variety and its coherence. The contrast between his use of cadence and the stanzas that he patterned on Gautier's strict quatrains is no greater than that between the sardonic tone of "Mr. Eliot's Sunday Morning Service" and the humility of "Ash Wednesday". Reversing the usual process, the young poet composed dramatic lyrics that objectified his private feelings, while the mature man writes verse dramas and lyrics presenting without evasion his religious convictions and the doubt that seems to be intrinsic to them, so that between the lines one hears the cry: "Lord, I believe; help Thou mine unbelief." Yet for all the variations in technique and tone, and although a long poem may be the redemption of several fragments, the work as a whole shows a noteworthy integrity. The same images recur with a persistence that gives them a symbolic significance. The poet is perpetually concerned with the themes of sin and redemption. He is almost as steadily occupied with the difference, pointed out in his final Quartet, between "Attachment to self and to things and to persons", detachment, and indifference, which resembles both "as death resembles life". His poetry implies a Heaven if only because it is so intimately involved with Hell, Hell being not a place but a state, the condition of modern man.

II

The Waste Land is a famous picture of Hell, but it is not only as such that it is central to Eliot's performance. Like the lyrics that preceded it, the poem deals with the curse of infertility, and like the poems that were to follow it, adumbrates the peace possible only to those who have resigned themselves to the Will of God. Eliot's feeling for the musical values of poetry is apparent not only, as elsewhere, in the cadences of the poem but in the handling of the main theme. As in a musical composition one may find the contrast between the several parts confided to the orchestration, so here the chief theme is repeated, but always, as it were, by different groups of instruments. The idea, implied rather than stated, that the abuse of love has meant the denial of life, is introduced, complicated, transposed, developed, with an approach to musicianly skill and symphonic effect. Physical barrenness is represented as the counterpart of the spiritual blight that lies upon the Western world. And, like the opposition of the master and servant motifs in classical comedy, where the servant's behavior caricatures the master's, so the inhabitants of the modern Waste Land, the heartless with the toothless, caricature the tragic passions of antiquity. The more closely one examines the poem, the more intricate its design appears, and the more intimately related to the entire body of Eliot's work.

The romantic legend on which the poem is based derives from the fertility myths of Tammuz, Osiris, and Adonis, translated into Christian symbolism. The tale relates how potency is magically restored to the sick Fisher King and fertility restored to a land laid waste by a drought sympathetically connected with his malady. The cure is effected by the Pure Knight, who fares forth to the Chapel Perilous to find the Lance and the Grail, obvious phallic symbols, representing the instruments of life. The legend is shadowed forth in scenes present to the consciousness of Tiresias, the seer who has been both man and woman, who has foreknown and foresuffered all. This Tiresias is aware, moreover, not only of the dooms that Homer sang, but of the history of the ensuing three thousand years, as grasped by a mind that looks at the contemporary world, remembering the work of Freud and Frazer, along with the vision of Dante and the wisdom of the Rig-Veda.

The poem opens with a glimpse of our rootless, dispersed life, and the first characters to be introduced are, appropriately, tourists and exiles. As it continues, it weaves back and forth between the Elizabethan court and London after the first world war, with glimpses of royalty floating on the Thames, slum dwellers in a public house rehearsing the sordid realities of marriage as they know it, the indifferent performance of the sexual act by a typist and a carbuncular clerk, a lady shaking the walls of her richly furnished drawing room with the hysteria of a self-regarding loneliness. Images of Phoenicia and Smyrna, of ancient and modern trade, of Dante's Hell and no-man's land, weird anticipations of the modern Hell of refugees and displaced persons, heighten the contrasts and intensify the atmosphere of futility, waste, and horror. And all these fragmentary scenes, enacted—as the walls of Troy were built and the Long Walls of Athens destroyed—to music, point to the incoherence, the shabbiness, the emptiness, of a mechanized, loveless, barren world. The poem ends with a line from the Buddhist Fire Sermon, the fire being the threefold fever of greed, hate, and infatuation, which must be extinguished before the soul can enter upon its real life.

The allusiveness is not least evident in a famous passage from the Buddha's Fire Sermon. It opens with a reference to Sappho's lyric on evening which brings all things home, bringing the typist home at teatime, to clear away her breakfast, light her stove, lay out the canned food, beside the window where are spread "Her drying combinations touched by the sun's last rays." The allusion underscores the contrast between the dead Greek lyricist's immortalization of love and the contemporary stenographer's facile, futile yielding to the clerk of the one bold stare. The scene is sharply drawn, less than a dozen lines point up the vanity of the clerk, the bored indifference of the typist, the quick termination of the meaningless episode. A phrase of Goldsmith's: "When lovely woman stoops to folly" recalls the disparity between the conventions of the eighteenth century and those of our own, between the sensibilities of a girl who has indulged a rash impulse to surrender and those of one who has tried to alleviate an unappeasable tedium, in vain. The mechanical motions of smoothing her hair "with automatic hand" and putting "a record on the gramophone", as she dismisses an equally mechanical act, are a commentary on our civilization. The passage is followed by a line from *The Tempest*, loaded with reference to the happy love of Ferdinand and Miranda, the final redemption of Alonso, the responsible behavior of Prospero: "This music crept by me upon the waters." The very allusion to waters carries a further hint of the release and fruition that the children of the Waste Land cannot know.

The poem is enriched, too, by those images which are so intrinsic to Eliot's work that they have taken on the character of symbols. In one of his essays he speaks of the mystery that surrounds a poet's imagery, built up as it is out of seemingly trivial irrelevant experiences. "The song of one bird, the leap of one fish, at a particular place and time, the scent of one flower, an old woman on a German mountain-path, six ruffians seen through an open window playing cards at night at a small French railway-junction where there was a water-mill: such memories may have symbolic value," he observes, "but of what we cannot tell, for they come to represent the depths of feeling into which we cannot peer." The six ruffians and the water mill may be found in the "Journey of the Magi". Other images that recur throughout Eliot's poetry are emphatically present in *The Waste Land*. One of the most familiar is that of the drowned Phoenician sailor. The reader meets him quite anonymously in the youthful poem on Mr. Apollinax, as one of the "worried bodies of drowned men". He is first named in the poem "Dans le Restaurant", written in French and translated almost word for word in *The Waste Land*:

> Phlebas the Phoenician, a fortnight dead,
> Forgot the cry of gulls, and the deep sea swell,
> And the profit and loss.

This last phrase takes on another connotation in "Ash

Wednesday", where the tossed soul sees itself "Wavering between the profit and the loss". As for poor Phlebas, he floats up at the beginning of *The Waste Land*, where Madame Sosostris, the "famous clairvoyante" with "the wicked pack of cards" is telling fortunes:

> Here, she said
> Is your card, the drowned Phoenician sailor.

The last words of "Prufrock" are: "we drown". One remembers the Phoenician again as one reads "The Dry Salvages", with its lingering lyrical evocation of the river and the sea, destroyer and preserver. He figures prominently in *The Waste Land* as an avatar of the god whose effigy was annually cast into the sea as a symbol of the failing powers of nature and retrieved as a symbol and insurance of renewed fertility.

Another recurrent figure who appears almost at the beginning of *The Waste Land* is "the hyacinth girl". The phrase is a reminder that this flower is associated with one of the ancient Greek rituals of sacrifice and regeneration. The girl is presented as returning from the hyacinth garden, her arms full, her hair wet, to one incapable of response. There is something familiar about her. She resembles the weeping girl of "La Figlia Che Piange", clasping her flowers to her with a pained surprise, who is to compel the imagination of the poet for many years. One meets her again in "Dans le Restaurant" as the dilapidated waiter's memory of a little girl he had known in childhood: "Elle était toute mouillée, je lui ai donné des primavères." One encounters her, or her double, in the third part of "Ash Wednesday":

> Blown hair is sweet, brown hair over the mouth
> blown,
> Lilac and brown hair.

Exactly what she represents is not clear, but always she evokes the sense of permanent loss involved in a moment

of hesitation, nostalgia for a freshness and spontaneity now
forever uncapturable.

Again, there is the image of the laughing children in
the shrubbery, who appear in one of the minor lyrics, more
shadowily in "Marina", and repeatedly if mysteriously in
the *Quartets*. The first of these, "Burnt Norton", concludes with a passage evoking the same atmosphere, alive
with bird song and sparkling with innocence, that was
created in the lyric "Marina" and in the poem "New
Hampshire":

> Sudden in a shaft of sunlight
> Even while the dust moves
> There rises the hidden laughter
> Of children in the foliage
> Quick now, here, now, always—
> Ridiculous the waste sad time
> Stretching before and after.

The second Quartet, examining the griefs and disappointments of middle age and reaching beyond them to explore
the dark night of the soul, is not without an echo of "The
laughter in the garden". The reference in the third is more
ambiguous, being to

> the unattended
> Moment, the moment in and out of time,
> The distraction fit, lost in a shaft of sunlight,

but it cannot be ignored. And the final Quartet recalls
the voices of the "children in the apple-tree", just before
the concluding lines which identify the rose with the fire
of perfect love that is God.

There is an allusion at the very opening of "Burnt
Norton" to a timeless moment in the rose garden. It is
hinted that the door into the garden was never opened,
and that what is revived is not an actual experience but
one that had been refused, thus suggesting once more the
image of the hyacinth girl. Yet the reality of the moment
of grace is unquestionable, and the poet repeatedly returns

to consider its significance. In looking for the meaning of these references, one must not neglect the first of Eliot's manifestly religious poems, "Ash Wednesday", where he writes:

> The single Rose
> Is now the Garden
> Where all loves end,

a passage associated with the ineffable sweetness, the immeasurable radiance of Paradise as Dante envisioned that "candida rosa". Without allegorizing too precisely, it seems reasonable to see the hyacinth girl as not unrelated (is she their elder cousin?) to the laughing children in the shrubbery, representative of a forfeited fulfillment, a lost innocence, and to regard the rose as like the lotus rising from the surface of the dry pool, "out of the heart of light," in "Burnt Norton": the flower of immortality glimpsed for a moment; for "Then a cloud passed, and the pool was empty." or, as the poet writes in the last Quartet, with what concentration of meaning:

> Ash on an old man's sleeve
> Is all the ash burnt roses leave.

There are other recurrent images and reverberant echoes in Eliot's work, some of which, like the eagles and the trumpets of Coriolanus, the liquid song of the wood thrush, the barnacled crab, and the refuse lying about on vacant lots and deserted beaches, seem part of a recognizable pattern. As all the characters in *The Waste Land* are united in Tiresias, and as the vision of Tiresias is the substance of the poem, so in the epicene blind seer the various dramatis personae of Eliot's poems seem to meet. He is akin to Prufrock, who has "known them all already, known them all": known "the evenings, mornings, afternoons," even if he has not precisely measured out his life with coffee spoons. He is mysteriously related to Gerontion, stiffening in a rented house, "an old man in a dry month, . . . waiting for rain," no less so if Gerontion is envisaged as our benighted civilization. Tiresias is linked even with Apeneck Sweeney, guardian of the horned gate through which true dreams enter; with the Magi not knowing whether they were led all that way for Birth or death; with the ancient Simeon, who had seen salvation, yet was tired with his own life and the lives of those after him; linked, too, with the vague protagonists of the *Quartets*, and more especially with the "familiar compound ghost" encountered as the poet treads the pavement "in a dead patrol": the nameless stranger whose concern, like his own, has been the purifying of "the dialect of the tribe", the urging of "the mind to aftersight and foresight". What else is Tiresias but the embodiment of such prescience and such understanding? The ultimate vision sought by this stranger is that "still point of the turning world" known to the lover, the hero, and the saint, though Eliot would probably grant illumination to the saint alone.

The hint at illumination in the *Quartets* is strikingly close to the experience described as "the anaesthetic revelation". As one reads the comment of a young American philosopher of the eighties on that experience, one seems to be reading a prose version of the first part of "Burnt Norton" and related poems: "The truth is that we travel on a journey that was accomplished before we set out; and the real end of philosophy is accomplished, not when we arrive at, but when we remain in, our destination (being already there)—which may occur vicariously in this life when we cease our intellectual questioning."

In the realm of Eliot's poetry the vision is known only as it recedes, and the actuality then presented to the senses is of back streets inhabited by disreputable creatures who plot happiness and fling empty bottles, straw-brained paralytics going round and round the prickly pear, a world of mechanical motion and bitter drought. Eliot is responsible for what might be called the rat-and-bone school of poetry that was prominent after the first world war. One could multiply instances of it, but the example offered by MacLeish's "The End of the World" should suffice. This

presents a detailed picture of the cockeyed circus that is
our world, when suddenly the top blows off,

And there, there, there overhead, there, there, hung over
Those thousands of white faces, those dazed eyes,
                                        . . . the black pall
Of nothing, nothing, nothing—nothing at all.

The piece is in accord with the conclusion of "The Hollow
Men" and with the passage in *Crime and Punishment*
where Svidrigailov says quietly: "We always imagine eternity as something beyond our conception, something vast,
vast! But why must it be vast? Instead of all that, what if
it's one little room, like a bath house in the country,
black and grimy and spiders in every corner, and that's
all eternity is? I sometimes fancy it like that."

In Eliot's work the rats and bones are emblems not of
the cemetery (the yew tree is often his symbol of death)
but of a civilization in decay. The dust is not that to which
we are consigned by the burial service but that which surrounds the sparrows in the gutters, settles on the furniture
in dingy rooms, is blown about by the draft under the
lodginghouse door, and fills the desert of the spirit. His
interest fastens with peculiar horror on those with a fatal
incapacity for life, those who, like Apeneck Sweeney, are
bored by the relentless cycle of "birth, copulation and
death". The Evangelist saw such as these spewed out of
the mouth of God. Dante declared that Hell would not receive them, for the damned would glory over them, who
were without blame as they were without praise. Eliot regards them with scorn and fear.

An attitude of fear and scorn is evident in the otherwise
far from obvious lines on "Sweeney Among the Nightingales". The images in this early poem, as Eliot has observed, are perfectly distinct, and it achieves the desired
atmosphere of ominous suspense, like that which precedes
a thunderstorm or which hovers over a dinner table during an air raid. Eliot confesses that he doubts if the poem
"means" anything. The reader is free to have his own

doubts in the matter, and, indeed, even a brief examination of the lines reveals more than sordid vignettes and
a sinister atmosphere. Clearly the poem juxtaposes a trivial
intrigue involving Sweeney and his disreputable companions to the central episode in the tragedy of the House of
Atreus. The first quatrain presents Sweeney:

> Apeneck Sweeney spreads his knees
> Letting his arms hang down to laugh,
> The zebra stripes along his jaw
> Swelling to maculate giraffe.

The second stanza sets the tone of menace, especially in
the lines:

> The circles of the stormy moon
> Slide westward toward the River Plate,
> Death and the Raven drift above
> And Sweeney guards the horned gate.

The gate of horn is that through which true dreams come,
as contrasted with the ivory gate through which issue false
dreams. The poet seems to be saying that, in taking account of the ugly objects summoned by the emotion of
horror, he is dreaming true. Characteristically he leaves the
Sweeney story vague, while selecting concrete details that
underscore the atmosphere of sordid stratagem.

> Gloomy Orion and the Dog
> Are veiled; and hushed the shrunken seas;
> The person in the Spanish cape
> Tries to sit on Sweeney's knees

> Slips and pulls the table cloth
> Overturns a coffee-cup,
> Reorganized upon the floor
> She yawns and draws a stocking up;

> The silent man in mocha brown
> Sprawls at the window-sill and gapes;
> The waiter brings in oranges
> Bananas figs and hothouse grapes;

The silent vertebrate in brown
Contracts and concentrates, withdraws;
Rachel *née* Rabinovitch
Tears at the grapes with murderous paws;

She and the lady in the cape
Are suspect, thought to be in league;
Therefore the man with heavy eyes
Declines the gambit, shows fatigue,

Leaves the room and reappears
Outside the window, leaning in,
Branches of wistaria
Circumscribe a golden grin;

The host with someone indistinct
Converses at the door apart,
The nightingales are singing near
The Convent of the Sacred Heart,

And sang within the bloody wood
When Agamemnon cried aloud,
And let their liquid siftings fall
To stain the stiff dishonoured shroud.

The verbal texture of the final quatrain skillfully supports and transcends the prose sense of the passage. The
hollow resonance of "bloody wood" "aloud" and "shroud"
is counterpointed by the sibilants in the final lines, and
by their blunted "i" sounds, while the word "dishonoured" sets the shallow "i" and the full-throated "o's"
in close conjunction. This verbal melody is of course immensely enhanced by the prose sense of the words, while
at the same time contributing to it.

Putting aside its technical excellence, one notes that
here, as in so many other poems, Eliot seems to be exalting the past and sneering at the present scene, harking
back to crime that is dignified by passion and terrible
retribution, and that bears, for the initiate, the symbolic
values of myth. If he is charged with taking an unfair advantage in contrasting classical legend with a dubious and

probably dull anecdote about the unamiable Sweeney, he
might conceivably reply that he could find no living kings
and heroes about whom he cared to write; that the world,
which owned no accredited myth, was governed by
Sweeney and his kind, and that this was the source of the
poet's suffering and the subject of his poem.

It is only in his later work that the tone of shuddering
contempt for the vulgarity and hollowness of his foes and
neighbors gives place to the penitential attitude of a
seeker after God. Now the symbols alter. The Buddhist
Fire Sermon which is intrinsic to *The Waste Land* declares
that the soul must escape from the flames of greed, of
hate, and of infatuation before it can enter upon its peace.
Fire is here the withering element that threatens the spiritual life. In the last of the *Quartets* fire has a double
aspect, that of lust which destroys, that of penitence
which purges. It is noteworthy that Heraclitus, who furnishes the poet with some of his chief themes and many
of his epigraphs, symbolized God as fire. Moreover, Eliot,
who has studied Sanskrit, must be aware of the multiple
meanings associated with the word for fire in that ancient
language. When, in the final lyric of the *Quartets*, he
writes:

> The dove descending breaks the air
> With flame of incandescent terror
> Of which the tongues declare
> The one discharge from sin and error,

one aspect of the dove is that of the bird of annunciation,
and the tongues are at once tongues of flame and those of
prophecy declaring redemption. In Sanskrit "speech" and
"fire" are related words. If the Greek philosopher identified the moving and ordering principle of the universe
with fire, by the same token he identified that element
with the Logos. There is more than one suggestion of
Pentacost here.

The lyric in the last Quartet that symbolizes super-

human Love by flame is followed by a passage that deals
very simply and almost prosily with the right use of words:

> The common word exact without vulgarity,
> The formal word precise but not pedantic,
> The complete consort dancing together . . .

That same passage concludes the poem and indeed, the
entire series of *Quartets*, with the assurance, taken from
the book of a medieval English mystic, that all shall be
well and all manner of thing shall be well,

> When the tongues of flame are in-folded
> Into the crowned knot of fire
> And the fire and the rose are one.

But the fire and the rose are one only "where all loves
end": in the rose of light that is the Paradiso, when the
"Word of no speech" shines and sounds.

Whether he is being lyrically allusive or studding his
symbolical poems with solidly real pictures of "one-night
cheap hotels", whether he makes us hear the pure melody
of "water lapping the bow" or the prosy injunction: "Don't
throw away that sausage," whether he is coldly satirical or
humbly devout, whatever his matter, his form, or his tone,
Eliot has been consistently occupied with a world laid
waste for want of a fructifying faith. The *Quartets*, con-
taining almost all the familiar images, resuming all the
old motifs, express, more simply and directly than any
poem that precedes them, the effort at complete abnega-
tion which seems the ultimate end of the poet's "intolerable wrestle / With words and meanings."

Not the least fascinating element in these poems is the
way in which his effort at religious affirmation seems to be
bound up with his need to find words that will not crack
or break, slip or slide under the burden of what they must
convey. Leaning on the wisdom of the Bhagavad-Gita and
Heraclitus, of Dante and St. John of the Cross, as well as
of the seventeenth-century moralist, Sir Thomas Elyot,
and the fourteenth-century mystic, Dame Julian of Nor-

wich, he looks before and after, apparently seeking to
pour the experience of a lifetime into the mold of his beliefs, realizing that once more he must make "a raid on
the inarticulate", suggesting that the pattern of the poem
adumbrates a larger design. As he strains after the form
that will offer the satisfaction of a resolved chord, tries for
words that will bestow the benediction of stillness, his
understanding approaches that of an Egyptian sage who
flourished ten centuries before our era: "O Amon, thou
sweet well for him that thirsteth in the desert; it is closed
to him that speaketh, but it is open to him who is silent.
When he who is silent cometh, lo he findeth the Well."
The paradox is that Eliot praises the silence in so musical
a fashion. Even those unable to share his faith, who repudiate a God with the features of a sadistically minded
merchant, and who fail to read the sum of human wisdom
in an ascetic renunciation, find themselves yielding to this
incantatory lyricism and receiving solace from its harmonies.

III

When Poe wrote that the music of poetry should be indefinite and suggestive, by its very vagueness producing a
spiritual effect, he was laying the foundation of symbolist
theory. Eliot, going to school to Poe's French admirers,
among others, brought to English verse a fresh appreciation of the aural values of poetry, together with the fascinated horror that Poe felt for the machine and Baudelaire
for Paris and her suburbs. Symbolism took diverse directions in the work of succeeding generations. For Stéphane
Mallarmé, allusions as frail as tulle, sonorities as vague as
the sea wind, under the control of the poet could open the
gates upon a universe lying beyond the bars of appearance. Beyond a suggestive music, another group of symbolists valued telescoped images and witty verbalism. To
them, too, Eliot paid his devoirs. But what is emphatically
clear in his performance is what he has himself called the

"auditory imagination". The importance that this aspect of his art holds for him is indicated in his deferential reference to Milton and Joyce as "the two great blind musicians," and by what he has to say about musical rhythm and structure in discussing Kipling's verse. Nor should one ignore the fact that the poet began by writing "Preludes", however different from those transmitted by "the latest Pole . . . through his hair and finger-tips", and that, on the verge of old age, he produced the *Four Quartets*, which exhibit something approaching musical structure and in other ways recall, though they nowhere equal, the works in which Beethoven seems to say the unsayable.

Eliot defines "auditory imagination" as "the feeling for syllable and rhythm, penetrating far below the conscious levels of thought and feeling, invigorating every word; sinking to the most primitive and forgotten, returning to the origin and bringing something back, seeking the beginning and the end. It works through meanings, certainly, or not without meanings in the ordinary sense, and fuses the old and obliterated and trite, the current and the new and surprising, the most ancient and the most civilized mentality." This "feeling for syllable and rhythm" is not unlike the requirements of the craft set down by one of Eliot's most admired confrères, Paul Valéry. Indeed, he seems to describe the work of the American when he speaks of the poet's task as a consecration to the building of *"a language within the language"*, recognizable by the rhythm and the harmonies sustaining it, and in which "the sound and the sense can no longer be separated, responding to each other indefinitely in the memory."

The definition applies to the great songs of St.-John Perse, whose *Anabase* Eliot rendered into English verse. Perse composes poems which rely almost as much on their sonorous music as on their, literally, farfetched imagery for a bizarre effectiveness. His adopted name is a key to the character of his poetry, carrying as it does associations with the desert, with the hermit's diet or the fragrance of sherbets in a Persian rose garden and the whiff of sweat and leather from a Persian mount after a lion hunt. And, since "la déesse aux yeux perses", the goddess of the blue-green eyes, was Athene, perhaps the name also suggests wisdom. "There is no history but the soul's, no ease but the soul's," he writes, making his song out of ordinary things, frail and empty and useless things, "assembling on the wastes of exile a great poem born of nothing, a great poem made from nothing . . ." Wisdom, these pages remind one, is the merchandise of the soul, that she does not traffic in for nothing, but that may be hers to keep when she has nothing else. There is a largeness of reference about his poems, the titles of which often evoke the forces of Nature. He has described the theme of *Amers* (*Seamarks*) as the evolution of the human fresco around the sea, comparable to the march around an altar. His most recent poem, *Chronique*, centering on the anguish and the hopes of the race, is no ordinary chronicle, but has the strophic and symbolic sweep of its predecessors. St.-John Perse draws upon a background as exotic to his readers as it is natural to him, and abounding in matter unavailable to less traveled poets. Yet such a work as *Anabase*, which proposes strenuous journeys remote from that of Xenophon's narrative, must have had its influence upon the poet who first translated it into English. Not the grave, incantatory cadences, nor the sudden assaults of its metaphors, not its violence and its grace, but the commingling of concrete particulars and mysterious symbols, the references to the meanest animal urgencies and the mind's most exalted aspirations, are of the fabric of the American translator's larger poems.

Eliot's analysis of "auditory imagination", proper to the work of Perse, is, above all, a clue to his personal method. An exquisite instance of a poem in which the meaning triumphs over the ambiguity by virtue of the music is the self-contained short lyric: "Marina". The title, the references to shipwreck and a dramatic recognition, recall the medieval story on which the Elizabethan play of *Pericles* was based. There is at least one allusion to the text of the

play, but it is vague, and the poem is in effect a texture
of sheer melody interwoven with the poet's familiar imagery. Here once again is the "small laughter between
leaves" that rings with a crystal-clear gaiety. Here is the
physical drought that implies the withering of the spirit,
and here the image of the waters that signify the renewal
of life in the fullest sense of the phrase. The reference to
"grace", however slight, assists the implication of a spiritual rebirth, and the wood thrush is the same bird that
figures in *The Waste Land* and elsewhere, the sweetness
and purity of whose "water-dripping song" seem to have
more than a surface significance. Reading these lines, one
remembers too the poet's preoccupation with death-in-
life and recalls Thaissa's question to Pericles: ". . . did
you not name a tempest, / A birth, and death?" as well
as the query of the Magi: ". . . were we led all that way
for / Birth or Death?" These echoes work with and
through the purely aural effects of the lyric to create an
atmosphere of innocence recaptured, of hope revived, that
lends a human warmth to the idea of redemption and
sheds over a natural human experience a miraculous
radiance.

Marina

Quis hic locus, quae regio, quae mundi plaga?

> What seas what shores what grey rocks and what
>   islands
> What water lapping the bow
> And scent of pine and the woodthrush singing
>   through the fog
> What images return
> O my daughter.

> Those who sharpen the tooth of the dog, meaning
> Death
> Those who glitter with the glory of the humming-
>   bird, meaning
> Death

Those who sit in the stye of contentment, meaning
Death
Those who suffer the ecstasy of the animals, mean-
      ing
Death

Are become insubstantial, reduced by a wind,
A breath of pine, and the woodsong fog
By this grace dissolved in place

What is this face, less clear and clearer
The pulse in the arm, less strong and stronger—
Given or lent? more distant than stars and nearer
      than the eye

Whispers and small laughter between leaves and
      hurrying feet
Under sleep, where all the waters meet.

Bowsprit cracked with ice and paint cracked with
      heat.
I made this, I have forgotten
And remember.
The rigging weak and the canvas rotten
Between one June and another September.
Made this unknowing, half conscious, unknown,
      my own.
The garboard strake leaks, the seams need caulking.
This form, this face, this life
Living to live in a world of time beyond me; let me
Resign my life for this life, my speech for that un-
      spoken,
The awakened, lips parted, the hope, the new ships.

What seas what shores what granite islands towards
      my timbers
And woodthrush calling through the fog
My daughter.

One could multiply instances of such allusive music.
The Waste Land is a notable example of "auditory imagi-

nation", with its manifold echoes of poems, prayers, popular songs, the voices of the sages and of the public house, sounding together in a symphony that presents the desiccation and despair of the machine age. So, again, the *Quartets* mingle passages of almost conversational prose with stressed verse and fine old metrical patterns locked with rhyme and substitutions for rhyme, sound and sense playing upon one another to create a moving awareness of a man on the threshold of old age, assembling his memories, reviewing his accomplishment and his failures, seeking to make his soul.

Much as he esteems depersonalized poetry, Eliot has admitted that "what every poet starts from is his own emotions." Indeed, he has acknowledged that intensity is essential to poetry, and has gone so far as to say that right thinking depends upon seeing and feeling truly. In the *Quartets* he comes full circle and speaks quite plainly in his own proper character of his hopes, his disappointments, his resumed efforts. At the same time, so compelling are the purely aural values of these poems that they seem to illustrate a remark made by so different a poet as Wordsworth to the effect that "the matter always comes out of the manner."

Their declarative prose passages notwithstanding, these four poems are as close to music as any poetry Eliot has ever written. They are properly called *Quartets* because they approximate the sonata form, with its statement, development, and recapitulation of themes, and its contrasting movements. The themes are time and eternity, the solitary vision and the difficulty of communication. The movements are naturally not allegro, adagio, scherzo, and fugue, but the structure of each section of one Quartet parallels that of the same section in the others. The poems may also be considered as four voices, each symbolized by one of the four elements, earth, air, fire, water, to which so many meanings attach, and each given added meaning since its name represents a place significant for the poet. Thus "Burnt Norton" is a Gloucestershire manor near which Eliot spent some time. "East Coker" is the Somersetshire village which was the home of his ancestors. "The Dry Salvages" are a group of rocks off the Massachusetts coast that he knew as a boy, and "Little Gidding" was the seat of a religious community, familiar to George Herbert and Crashaw, its chapel now a shrine for devout Anglicans, where the poet went in wartime to pray.

Simply as a technical achievement, the *Quartets* repay scrutiny. The allusions and symbols coming close upon one another's heels and the repeated references in the alternating prosaic and lyrical passages give the effect of counterpoint. The variety of forms employed is only less remarkable than the skill with which they are managed. The lyric which opens the second section of "The Dry Salvages" is but one instance. The symbolic element in this Quartet is water, exemplified in the river—the stream of personal experience, and the ocean—the source of life and the threatening mystery surrounding it, in which the private history is lost. The lyric is a variant of the sestina. The repetitions are less frequent than in the conventional sestina, but the echoes and half echoes are like the murmur of waters, the sound of the sea wind, the voice of the sea, which seems always on the verge of some tremendous "annunciation", the key word in the poem. The lyric is admirable, but not more so than the opening lines of the previous section, with their opposition of the dark pagan mind and the blindness of modern commercialism, their contrast between poetic resonance and prose matter-of-fact:

I do not know much about gods; but I think that the river
Is a strong brown god—sullen, untamed and intractable,
Patient to some degree, at first recognised as a frontier;
Useful, untrustworthy, as a conveyor of commerce;
Then only a problem confronting the builder of bridges.
The problem once solved, the brown god is almost for-
     gotten
By the dwellers in cities—ever, however, implacable,

Keeping his seasons and rages, destroyer, reminder
Of what men choose to forget. Unhonoured, unpropitiated
By worshippers of the machine, but waiting, watching and
    waiting.
His rhythm was present in the nursery bedroom,
In the rank ailanthus of the April dooryard,
In the smell of grapes on the autumn table,
And the evening circle in the winter gaslight.

"Burnt Norton", the first of the *Quartets,* may be read
as a restatement of that passage from St. Augustine's
Confessions which has to do with the mystery of time and
eternity as it presents itself to the thoughtful Christian.
In "The Dry Salvages" the poet returns to the difficulty
inherent in the Christian view.

Men's curiosity searches past and future
And clings to that dimension. But to apprehend
The point of intersection of the timeless
With time, is an occupation for the saint—
No occupation either, but something given
And taken, in a lifetime's death in love,
Ardour and selflessness and self-surrender.
For most of us there is only the unattended
Moment, the moment in and out of time,
The distraction fit, lost in a shaft of sunlight,
The wild thyme unseen, or the winter lightning
Or the waterfall, or music heard so deeply
That it is not heard at all, but you are the music
While the music lasts. These are only hints and guesses,
Hints followed by guesses; and the rest
Is prayer, observance, discipline, thought and action.
The hint half guessed, the gift half understood, is
    Incarnation.

The Incarnation is, of course, the central event for the
Christian. Those who formulated his faith took over from
Judaism the idea of a universe manifesting God's pur-
pose in a dynamic fashion, one divinely ordered event be-

getting another. But if Christianity accepted the Judaic belief in the fundamental significance of history, it took over from other religions the view that men are not actors in a Divine Comedy, with a beginning, a climax, and an end, but that their lives, like the course of the sun and the seasons, are part of a cyclic process, life being renewed by sacrifice, or by a ritual rehearsal of sacrifice. The Birth and the Death that are the subject of the poet's meditations in "The Dry Salvages" and that he touched upon in earlier poems, are not merely commemorated in the Eucharist, but are regarded as an actual re-creation of the past pointing toward the future, so that the past takes on a present reality.

In this belief the poet made his way to the chapel at Little Gidding, in the midst of war, deeply aware of the history of this sad, dedicated place and the history of his troubled times, kneeling, in the wintry dusk, "where prayer has been valid", communing with the dead, for

> what the dead had no speech for, when living,
> They can tell you, being dead: the communication
> Of the dead is tongued with fire beyond the language
>   of the living.
> Here the intersection of the timeless moment
> Is England and nowhere. Never and always.

This final Quartet resumes the motifs and retains the allusions of the others in such a fashion that one is all but overwhelmed by the thickness of reference. As "Burnt Norton" began with the way in which the future is bound up with the past, so "Little Gidding" concludes with the discovery of ends in beginnings, and with a glimpse of the Paradiso that is all but indistinguishable from the laughter-filled garden of happy childhood. For those who cannot share Eliot's pieties, the Quartets, illustrating poetry's double dependence upon speech and song, remain valid for their remarkable employment of "auditory imagination". Nowhere does the poet exhibit it with greater depth and power.

IV

With Pound and Yeats, the most influential poet of his time, Eliot sent younger men on the ways that he had traveled. As he had explored, among others, the divergent roads taken by the symbolists, so, following him, did his contemporaries and his juniors. The fewest showed a like concern with the musical aspect of poetry, and the man most attentive to it was apt to be overwhelmed by it. Conrad Aiken admittedly "learned from Eliot what he had learned from Laforgue", but the pages that show this influence suggest Laforgue's earliest poems, with their solemn dwelling upon death and oblivion, and upon the littleness of man in the cosmic scheme. While more obviously aware of the native scene than his classmate and confrère, Aiken has been concerned above all to make his poetry the vehicle of the more obscure movements of the mind. A recurrent theme with him is the growth of consciousness, helped by the workings of memory, and its final erasure by death. He does not quite achieve the subtler effects of one group of symbolists and rarely exhibits the sharp wit, the bitter veracity of the other. In one of his ambitious long poems he tried to draw an analogy between the organic life of the city and that of the individual, but the pressures of an urban civilization are not felt in his work as intensely as in that of Corbière, of Laforgue, or of the poet who heard "the human engine" wait "Like a taxi throbbing, waiting," and who saw with the inward-looking eyes of the blind.

As Aiken moves up and down strange stairways, and leans, in his pursuit of the psyche, from the windows of haunted rooms, the steps sometimes take him down to the level of melodrama and in an embrasure one may recognize the ghost of the nineties. The long poems, and Aiken has written many, seem longer because of their repetitiousness: the same themes, the same cadences, recur and, in a single passage, the same phrases, the same words.

When he uses iambic pentameter, it wants the variety
that a few contemporaries can give it, and his sonnet se-
quences are equally conventional. Archaic allusions and
devices are apt to weaken the presentation. The smooth-
ness of his verbal texture becomes monotonous; his ob-
session with the word "music" is maddening. Yet the
musical values of his poetry do lay an urgent claim upon
the reader. Aiken can manipulate his vocables so as to
make the morning veritably sing, as in the refrain from
Senlin's song:

> Vine leaves tap my window,
> Dew-drops sing to the garden stones,
> The robin chirps in the elderberry tree
> Repeating three clear tones.

Other long poems of his are likewise interspersed with
lyrics that charm by a graceful simplicity, such as the familiar one that begins: "When trout swim down Great
Ormond Street". These interludes offer relief from the
wordy arabesques of sound in which they are set.

The shorter poems in which he is content to examine a
single phase of a complex relationship, to evoke some one
evasive mood, rather than detail the biography of a mind,
give actuality to the mystery of human intercourse. Certain pieces stand out from the body of his work. George
Meredith and, later, William Ellery Leonard, anticipated
some of his poems concerning crossgrained love and
broken marriage, but Aiken's have a unique powerful severity. His brief dramatic narrative, "The Wedding", makes
venomously short shrift of the history of the protagonists,
evocatively named Tithonus and Arachne. In the lines
called "Goya", which begin matter-of-factly enough: "Goya
drew a pig on a wall.", the poet escapes from the en-
tangling velleities of what he calls "psycho-realism" and
from the meshes of a cloying lyricism into such harsh air
as Goya himself knew. The clipped quatrains, the sharp
stresses, add to the force of the ugly verbs and adjectives.
Here is the painter of the disasters of war. Here is the

hideousness that fed his savage imagination. Seldom, however, does Aiken's performance produce this shudder. It is curious to hear, in the relatively late poem, "The Kid", written in a straightforward idiom around so thoroughly American a figure as William Blackstone (seen as the prototype of Boone and Johnny Appleseed, Thoreau, Melville, and Henry Adams), an echo from the author of "Ash Wednesday": "world whorled in world the whorl of his thought,"—that friend from whom Aiken learned much, but not enough.

The most vigorous and provocative of Eliot's successors have not shown his sensitive auditory imagination. Theodore Roethke's long poems, beginning with "The Lost Son", are among the few works organized on that principle. Roethke's work is his own. His early poems are distinguished not so much by their matter, which is the stuff of boyhood memories and adult disappointments inevitable to a responsive thoughtful man in mid-century America, nor by their form, which is traditional, but by their tone. He manages to escape the pedestrian flatness of some of his fellows and the strained intellectualism of others. He has more to say of the interior landscape than of that without, and writes with particular acuteness of the nameless malaise of the spirit. His work gains from the fact that his childhood was intimately bound up with the life of a Michigan greenhouse, which, physically and otherwise, was to afford the material for some of his best lyrics. Their mere titles: "Root Cellar", "Forcing House", "Moss-Gathering", "Child on Top of a Greenhouse", "Flower-Dump", tell of that relatively unfamiliar world. This furnished the background and the symbols for the long poems that are such notable examples of "the feeling for syllable and rhythm . . . sinking to the most primitive and forgotten, returning to the origin and bringing something back, seeking the beginning and the end."

Shifting cadences and homely images taken from childhood memories of the floriculturalist's world, meanings as evasive as some secretive animal and equally frightening, produce unusual and powerful effects. These poems are an account of the journey through the dark wood— here symbolized by stagnant water, among other forms of death—into the light that clothes the visible in the garments of eternity. The titles of the sections of "The Lost Son", the first of these long poems, are an index to its substance: "The Flight", "The Pit", "The Gibber", "The Return". But only a reading of it, preferably a reading aloud, can give the quality of this reaching into the sub-human depths of the psyche, this literally sensational evoking of the child's pluriverse and the final emergence into light. Here is no Eliotesque vocabulary. The words are simple. Here are no rhythmic echoes, save, where proper, the echo of childish chant and childish speech, as in the eerie stanzas that begin:

> The shape of a rat?
>> It's bigger than that.
>> It's less than a leg
>> And more than a nose,
>> Just under the water
>> It usually goes.

If the poem bears no resemblance to Eliot's work in detail, as a whole it is a remarkable example of his method. This may contribute to the privacy of Roethke's poems. But the dark passages sometimes emerge into clear, touching speech. For a glimpse of what he does in "The Lost Son" one might take the beginning and the end.

> At Woodlawn I heard the dead cry:
> I was lulled by the slamming of iron,
> A slow drip over stones,
> Toads brooding in wells.

Thus the opening lines and this the end:

> It was beginning winter,
> The light moved slowly over the frozen field,
> Over the dry seed-crowns,

The beautiful surviving bones
Swinging in the wind.

Light traveled over the wide field;
Stayed.
The weeds stopped swinging.
The mind moved, not alone,
Through the clear air, in the silence.

> Was it light?
> Was it light within?
> Was it light within light?
> Stillness becoming alive,
> Yet still?

A lively understandable spirit
Once entertained you.
It will come again.
Be still.
Wait.

This section includes a notable presentation of the greenhouse where the roses are still "breathing in the dark" and of the boiler room where other roses, "The big roses, the big bloody clinkers" are pulled out by the fireman. The use of the word "bloody", with its several connotations, including the curse, is significant. Everything here is alive, and it is plain without the poet's word for it that the greenhouse is his symbol "for the whole of life, a womb, a heaven-on-earth". Yet the womb is not "the whole of life", and it is just beyond the greenhouse, in the somewhat dubious light of the open, that experience begins. Roethke has dealt candidly and delicately with its lesser confusions in several early poems, traditional in form though expressive of an awareness peculiar to our own day.

In his later work evidence of a devotion to Yeats is not limited to the pages written in his memory, yet Roethke's individual voice is unmistakable. It sounds in the unillusioned "Elegy for Jane", with its explanatory epigraph:

"My Student, Thrown by a Horse", in his lyrical celebra-
tions of sexuality, in the bleak honesty of detail as in the
luminousness of the sequence called "Meditations of an
Old Woman". Toward the end there is a passage that
might almost be Roethke speaking of himself and his
poems: "A prince of small beginnings, enduring the slow
stretches of change, / Who spoke first in the coarse shorthand of subliminal depths, / Made from his terror and
dismay a grave philosophical language; / A lion of
flame, pressed to the point of love, / Yet moves gently
among the birds." This somewhat baroque imagery is not
typical. However dark his utterance, the language itself is
usually simple. He will use the vocabulary and the cadences of nursery rhyme to carry large meanings. He
makes old truths plain in words of one syllable: "What's
hell but a cold heart?" Not even Eliot has so fully communicated the "terror and dismay" of the dark night of
the soul. Roethke can also suggest the blaze of the mystic's illumination. This does not prevent him from letting
us share his intense awareness of small, quasi-sentient
life, both the lovely and "the ugly of the universe".

What Eliot's feeling for syllable and rhythm brought
back, in its curious workings, was not the apotheosis of
Roethke's later poems. It was chiefly a sense of disorder,
of frustration and waste. This intimate vision of death
is the more horrifying because it is not the physical death
that is part of the natural life cycle, but the death-in-life
of the Waste Land that is our world. Even the *Quartets*,
poems of religious affirmation, are occupied with

> the strained time-ridden faces
> Distracted from distraction by distraction
> Filled with fancies and empty of meaning . . .

The satiric tone in which he first expressed his aversion
from such "tumid apathy" was congenial to the poets writing after World War I. Poetry centering specifically upon
the wars must be considered later. Suffice it to say here
that the spectacle of a no-man's land where the living

floundered among the dead was less appalling to him than the waste where the living dead went through their mechanical motions.

The young men of the thirties, though they found equal cause for disgust, responded to it in a different way. They recognized the chaotic character of a civilization in which the most delicate and complex instruments are made to serve a Stone Age sensibility. The boredom and horror so present to Eliot were present to them, but the glory they envisaged was of another order. Oppressed though they were by the threatening atmosphere of the period between two wars, they were not, like a later postwar generation, "unable to fare forward or retreat". Certainly they did not, or not yet, recede with him into a Church that they saw "blocking the sun". The revolutionary scion of the Boston Brahmins, John Wheelwright, naming Eliot plainly, recalled his famous credo thus:

> Classicist, Royalist, Anglo-Catholic,
> long names for the four-letter word, a snob.

Less gently nurtured poets were less fastidious in their references to him. This was the period when Eliot's feelings and beliefs became almost a stock subject for satire, and his style material for parody, an oblique tribute to the positive character of his style, if not an admission of the need for dealing with those feelings and beliefs. But whatever the younger poets came to reject, their debt to him is evident. It is predominantly to Eliot, together with Pound, that we can trace the lively consciousness of the urban scene, the anti-poetic imagery, the conversational accent, the more fluid rhythms, the cinematic transitions, fade-outs, and close-ups, the irony and complexity, that give a special tone and form to certain contemporary verse.

The revolutionary poets who rejected his view of the necessity for evil in the scheme of things were savagely reminded by the second world war of the permanence and the power of evil. Certainly art that refuses to acknowledge it as intrinsic to the condition of man must fail to satisfy the honest positivist and the thoughtful rebel equally with the believer in the doctrine of Original Sin. A happier age might return to Eliot's poetry to renew the sense of death that gives a balance to life. In death-devoted times there is a salutary stoicism to be won from dwelling upon the fact. Stoicism, however, is not exalted by the theologically minded poet. His attitude, where it is not expressly Christian, is closer to that found in the sacred writings of Buddhism. Irving Babbitt, whom Eliot has repeatedly acknowledged as his teacher, was a great Buddhist scholar. In a commentary appended to his translation of one of the early Buddhist scriptures, Babbitt observed that "a central admonition of Buddha may be summed up in the phrase: Do not raise a thirst!" This comes close to a central admonition of the poet who so consummately described drought. In the lines that Auden addressed to him, on his sixtieth birthday, the younger poet spoke of how, in the midst of outrageous happenings, and, "Blank day after day, the unheard-of-drought," it was he

Who, not speechless with shock but finding the right
Language for thirst and fear, did most to
Prevent a panic.

Possibly. In any case, he did find the right language for aridity. Moreover, these poems, like later work by Eliot that is more emphatically drama than poetry, point to a new regard for his fellows which has relieved a sense of alienation presumably no less painful for its arrogant expression.

As one reads and rereads the *Quartets*, which speak as lyrically as any of his poems and with a so much more human voice, their burden seems not too remote from the cry of the humbled soul in "Ash Wednesday":

Teach us to care and not to care
Teach us to sit still.

The words have a religious connotation here. They might be taken as another way of phrasing Dante's immense line: "*E la sua voluntate e nostra pace*": in His will is our peace. This is the wisdom of the ages that the veriest agnostic can accept, if the Will be taken to be the body of natural law. As for Eliot's words, they could be spoken by any man confronting the dual necessity for action and resignation that is presented to us again and again, on the threshold of maturity, of old age, and of death. This ensures their living quality.

There is no question but that "the reverend Eliot" has found a natural language. If he learned it, in part, from Dryden and from Byron, he has sought—with a very different practitioner and one more compassionate than these models: Hugo von Hofmannsthal—"to introduce profundity into the mundane". Nor is there any poet of his time who composes, when he will, more musically. Life may turn against us, history deceive us, the Christian myth, as other myths have done, may fail us (though to this the poet would not assent). But certain values endure and are never so indubitably stated as by music, an art as solid as architecture and as abstract as mathematics, an art built upon time and yet in essence timeless. The strength of his poetry, especially the *Quartets*, though they also speak a more ordinary language, is that it can remind us of the glories of traditional music and does not ignore the savage noises of a machine civilization to which *musique concrète* is more adequate.

7. Wit as the Wall

The scenery of the Waste Land not unnaturally inspired a desire to escape. But however urgent the need, there were those who knew that, fleeing, they must carry with them the indelible picture of desolation. That knowledge helps to give their work strong overtones of irony. This is one of the distinguishing features in the poetry of the self-styled Fugitives. Confessedly, they "never quite cared to define what they fled from," but they were united in a distaste for "social optimism"—how reasonably, it took a second world war to prove—and in a desire to cultivate their Southern gardens. More than a decade after their association began, in Nashville, Tennessee, and a little less than a decade before the second world war, they attempted to make plain what they fled *to*. In a symposium significantly entitled *I'll Take My Stand* several of the original group, among whom Allen Tate, John Crowe Ransom, and Robert Penn Warren are the most prominent, united with eight other writers, including John Gould Fletcher, to define their position. Appropriately, Fletcher's essay bears an epigraph from Confucius, for what these poets defended was an agrarian economy and the traditional sanctities and amenities of the South before the war, that is, of course, what Southerners call "the war between the States". They agreed in repudiating the materialism of a machine-made culture, and looked back nostalgically to a society in which "the countryman belongs to the land, the landlord to his tenants, the farmer to his laborers, and not the other way about. This is a deliberate reversal of the values in an industrial society." These words are not theirs. They were written by T. S. Eliot, who in the same essay exalted "the insight into a harmony with nature which must be reestablished if the truly Christian imagination is to be recovered by Christians." The Fugitives, who, like other refugees, are now widely dispersed, shared Eliot's dismay at the gulf between economic and moral responsibility, his profound unease at the lack of a unifying myth. They have continued to be painfully conscious of the divorce between man and nature, and of the dominance of an attitude that ignores whatever escapes the scientist's dry categories and sets the practical life of action above that of imaginative understanding, with what results Madrid and Hollywood, Moscow and Hiroshima bear various witness. The break with an established cultural pattern, of which the Civil War and the reconstruction period were the cause or perhaps more truly the symptom, underscored the dilemma for the Southern intellectuals who came to maturity soon after World War I. They were not alone. Young poets elsewhere were struggling with the same dichotomies, even if they came to different conclusions about the best way to deal with them.

Eliot had been one of the first to formulate in English poetry the reaction of a keen sensibility to an age of scientific mastery and moral anarchy. It was natural that his juniors, reacting in a similar way to the same situation, should be haunted by the voice of Eliot and of those who had taught him how to use it. Moreover, they were apt to look at America with the disenchanted eyes of the expatriate. Ransom in his "Amphibious Crocodile" wittily satirized the would-be cosmopolitan provincial, genus Americanus (with a sidewise glance in the mirror at a young Rhodes scholar), in a style deriving from Eliot's "Hippopotamus" and certain of the Sweeney poems. John Peale Bishop's "Aliens" opens like an Eliot "Prelude" and presents people who might be cousins of the Hollow Men:

> They have no silence and they have no love.
> They sit about their nothingness
> As men from habit sit by empty stoves.

Eliotesque rhythms and queries haunt Allen Tate's "Message from Abroad" and indeed are scattered throughout his verse. Such echoes are the result of more than a fond attentiveness to the cadences and tropes characteristic of the Waste Land's geographer. When Tate writes:

> Heredity
> Proposes love, love exacts language, and we lack
> Language. When shall we speak again? When shall
> The sparrow dusting the gutter sing?

the question harks back to the hysterical lady's cry in *The Waste Land*: "Speak to me. Why do you never speak. Speak." as also to Eliot's third "Prelude". This is not because in both instances there is the demand for speech or because both poets refer to gutter sparrows. It is because they are alike obsessed by a physical and cultural dinginess, and know the helplessness of one who would be heard above the empty cacophony. Younger poets used the same imagery to express the same feelings.

Something more difficult than the replacement of rural by urban imagery was involved for these writers. They were confronted by the complexities of a world in which war and revolution competed for attention with the newly discovered spoils of Egyptian tombs, the luxuries of five-and-ten-cent-store princesses, dinosaur's eggs, and the imminence of split atoms, not then seen as a threat, all presented to them by such time-and-space-destroying means as radio and movie. They had to manage this diverse material in the refractory language of a scientific age.

> Christ is dead. And in a grave
> Dark as a sightless skull He lies
> And of His bones are charnels made.

Thus John Peale Bishop. More drily Tate observed:

> Narcissus is vocabulary. Hermes decorates
> A cornice on the Third National Bank. Vocabulary
> Becomes confusion, decoration a blight.

Meaning had gone out of the world, and therewith meaning had gone out of the language. The poet had no adequate symbols for experiences unrelated to any picture of
reality that he held in common with his fellows. He had
to create his own symbols, to find a fresh vocabulary. Hence
the difficulty of much modern work. The problem was not
new. Blake had wrestled with it a hundred years earlier,
and, though injured, his genius had triumphed.

   The dilemma is compellingly presented in the piece
with which John Peale Bishop introduced his selections
from his own work, "Speaking of Poetry":

The ceremony must be found
That will wed Desdemona to the huge Moor.

                    It is not enough—
To win the approval of the Senator
Or to outwit his disapproval; honest Iago
Can manage that: it is not enough. For then,
Though she may pant again in his black arms
(His weight resilient as a Barbary stallion's)
She will be found
When the ambassadors of the Venetian state arrive
Again smothered. These things have not been changed,
Not in three hundred years

                          (Tupping is still tupping
Though that particular word is obsolete.
Naturally, the ritual would not be in Latin.)
For though Othello had his blood from kings
His ancestry was barbarous, his ways African,
His speech uncouth. It must be remembered
That though he valued an embroidery—
Three mulberries proper on a silk like silver—
It was not for the subtlety of the stitches,
But for the magic in it. Whereas, Desdemona
Once contrived to imitate in needlework
Her father's shield, and plucked it out
Three times, to begin again, each time
With diminished colors. This is a small point
But indicative.

> Desdemona was small and fair,
> Delicate as a grasshopper
> At the tag-end of summer: a Venetian
> To her noble finger-tips.
>
> O, it is not enough
> That they should meet, naked, at dead of night
> In a small inn on a dark canal. Procurers
> Less expert than Iago can arrange as much.
>
> The ceremony must be found
>
> Traditional, with all its symbols
> Ancient as the metaphors in dreams;
> Strange, with never before heard music; continuous
> Until the torches deaden at the bedroom door.

The "huge Moor" may be taken as the primitive element in poetry that springs from and is answered by the emotions. Desdemona, delicate and noble, suggests the formal element that gives significance to energy. Othello, barbarous and uncouth, although he "had his blood from kings", valued the embroidery on the famous handkerchief "But for the magic in it": the sensuous, incantatory power of the art is its sufficient reason for the animal nature.

> Whereas, Desdemona
> Once contrived to imitate in needlework
> Her father's shield, and plucked it out
> Three times, to begin again, each time
> With diminished colors.

The mention of the diminished colors is "indicative". The mind requires the subtler pleasures that intellectual assent and technical propriety afford. Unless emotion and intellect, body and spirit, form and substance are joined, the marriage that results in poetry will never take place. It is "indicative", too, that the gentle Venetian merely imitated in needlework her father's shield: the device that had been wrought into the defense of his body had become for his daughter merely the ornament of an accessory. In

various ways the poem reminds us that the great lack of
our time is that we have no commanding myth,

> Traditional, with all its symbols
> Ancient as the metaphors in dreams

to which we can give allegiance. The dispersed character of
Pound's *Cantos*, the religious poems of Eliot, which shore
fragments of Christian and Buddhist ritual against the
ruins of belief, the lyrics that Yeats built upon his own
curious system, the *tour de force* resulting from Hart
Crane's brave effort to mythologize his America, the concern of later poets with Amerindian ritual and belief, are
evidence of this unanswered need.

If Bishop's pages, like those of other cultivated men of
his generation, abound in reminders of modern rootless-
ness, they are free of the aridity that marks much of the
work of his contemporaries. Where these are apt to pursue
the idea at the expense of the poem, John Bishop celebrated physical delight as vividly as spiritual distress. The
green and gold in certain of his early lyrics glow with the
brilliance of the Venetian school, the colors enlivened by
contrast with the shadow of the war that sometimes
reaches across them. One suspects that the frequent references to Venice in these poems are partly for the sake
of the splendor and grace that its remembered greatness
summons up and perhaps also because, as Stevenson long
ago pointed out, the consonant V, along with P and F,
seems to be prominent in those passages in English writing
that delight our ears. These are noticeable in "Speaking of
Poetry", in the lovely lyric called "A Recollection", that
offers a bawdy acrostic, and in "Metamorphoses of M", a
poem as decoratively suggestive as a fifteenth-century
French tapestry:

> I haVe seen your *F*eet gilded by morning
> Naked under your long gown. I haVe seen them
> Kee*P* such state u*P*on the unswe*P*t *F*loor
> I could haVe sworn Venetian artisans

Had all night been awake, Painting in gold,
To set your beauty on aPProPriate heels.

The skillful use of these consonants is to be found in
other poems of his, as in the first and last stanzas from a
symbolical poem on the fall of Rome, in which the sea
appears to represent the uncurbed energy of nature, and
the temples of Neptune the civilized forms that give it
shape and direction:

Night and we heard heaVy cadenced hooFbeats
OF trooPs deParting; the last cohorts leFt
By the North Gate. That night some listened late
Leaning their eyelids toward SePtentrion.

TemPles oF NePtune inVaded by the sea
And dolPHins streaked like streams sPortiVe
As sunlight rode and oVer the rushing Floors
The sea unFurled and what was blue raced silVer.

A handful of translations, from the Greek Anthology,
from Rimbaud, from the Latin of Petronius Arbiter and
the Provençal of Rudel and Bertran de Born, point to the
diversity of Bishop's mentors, and the euphonious quality
of his own verse is an index to what he learned from the
last. Whether he writes of carrots in a still life or of a
sword dance, of an old pink and grey chateau or a primeval
forest in Virginia, the vivacity of his treatment is the same.
There is apt choice of detail even in poems that deal, in
the remote fashion of symbolism, with ideas. There is a
dazzle of golden light, or, in its absence, as in the Connecticut scenes and the poems on the gloomier aspects of
Western history and culture, a vigor not lessened by being
somber. Those of his juniors whose work vouchsafes a like
mixture of sensuous lyricism and intellectualism, a like
awareness of the native scene with reference to the European past, do not write so sparely.

II

An all but overwhelming sense of the past, or of our painful severance from it, is one of the distinguishing features of the poetry of Bishop's Southern friends and contemporaries, first known as the Fugitives, later more commonly as the Nashville group. The feeling for history is clearest in the work of Allen Tate, with its wealth of classical allusion and its emphasis on such themes as the significance of tradition and the disrelation between modern man and the universe. There would seem to be little in common between the Spartans on the sea-wet rock and the champions of the great Southern plantations except an acceptance of the slave system, but it is characteristic that Tate should write a poem in which a Confederate "on the night before the veterans' reunion talks partly to himself, partly to imaginary comrades" and call it: "To the Lacedemonians". Ignoring the abuses entailed by slavery, in an idealizing recollection of Southern chivalry, Tate conceives that what the Confederate soldiers sought to save by their vain deaths was the authority of a noble tradition, so that by analogy they could say:

> Go tell the Spartans, thou that passeth by,
> That here, obedient to their laws we lie.

By the same token, the poet can see himself as Aeneas— not in Italy but at Washington, considering, as he stands in the rain at nightfall by the Potomac, with the great Dome lighting the water, how meaningless, in the face of history, has become the founding of cities:

> Stuck in the wet mire
> Four thousand miles from the ninth buried city
> I thought of Troy, what we had built her for.

Tate's best-known poem, the "Ode to the Confederate Dead", has to do, as he has told us, with "the failure of the human personality to function properly in nature and so-

ciety". It is ironical from first to last, beginning with its
title, for this Ode is presented not as the poet's share in
a public commemoration, but as the reflections of a solitary man at the cemetery gate. Tate's allusions are less
private here than elsewhere, but it is doubtful whether
without the help of his prose explication the reader could
discover what is implied in its crowded symbolism. The
poem was ten years in the writing and, when its final version was completed, failed to satisfy its author. Nor can
it fully content the reader, in spite of the significance of
its theme, its richness of reference, and the technical care
with which the poet manipulates the antiphonal voices of
what Hart Crane called "active faith" and "the fragmentary cosmos of today".

The difficulty with the Ode, as with many of Tate's
thoughtfully wrought poems, is that it carries too heavy a
weight of intellection for the poetry to sustain. What he
has said of R. P. Blackmur might with equal propriety be
said of him, that he is "as a critic . . . a master of ideas;
as a poet he is occasionally mastered by them." Indeed,
Blackmur seems less fearful of emotion and in a few
poems sets forth the plight of the bereaved New Englander
more lyrically and vigorously than Tate does that of the
denuded Southerner. The idea upon which he plays variations in his poems is that the dominant scientific view
has given us an abstract picture of the world which emphasizes man's helpless isolation, while finance capitalism
has degraded or destroyed men's relations with one another, so that we are cut off from the universe and from
our fellows.

In this emphasis, as in other respects, not least the attraction that the Elizabethans have for him, Tate's avowed
debt to Eliot is plain. His scholarship also is great, and
his verse has the crowded intensity, the wry irony that is
associated with some metaphysical poetry. His later work,
not only in its concern with moral values, its exploration
of the contemporary hell, but in its very details, shows
his careful reading of Dante, who seems to mean to many

modern poets something of what Bach has meant to composers.

Although Tate's work gives evidence of his immersion
in that of other poets, it is not wanting in images as original as they are powerful. An instance occurs in the cemetery scene of his "Ode to the Confederate Dead" where
he speaks of "The brute curiosity of an angel's stare" turning the observer likewise to stone. His poems suffer, however, from an extreme privacy of reference. In the preface
to one of his volumes he notes that when he composed the
lines called "Fragment of a Meditation" he saw the Wise
Men who appear at the end "as Herbert Hoover, Miss
Gertrude Stein, and the late Otto H. Kahn", a statement
for which nothing in that ironic piece prepares us, not even
the collocation of the Nativity with the Greek legend of
the birth of the Minotaur. Tate works and reworks his
poems with lapidary care, but his economy is apt to be
expensive, his intellection often excessive, and the lyricism
that might redeem both insufficient. Seldom does one find
such clear melody as in these lines from "Pastoral":

> And there they were by the river
> Where a leaf's light interval
> Ringed the deep hurrying mirror;

more seldom does he achieve the resonant echoes and
arresting off-beat of the too esoteric but admirably wrought
"Seasons of the Soul." A preoccupation with ideas ("poetry
is not made with ideas," said Mallarmé), a cold latinity,
and a weak grasp of the melodic line mark his distance
from Eliot and give his verse a stiffness which though
always dignified is sometimes awkward.

Fairly typical of Tate's heavily loaded diction, as also of
his thinking, is the relatively simple poem called "The
Subway", for which he employs the sonnet form that he
finds so congenial:

> Dark accurate plunger down the successive knell
> Of arch on arch, where ogives burst a red

Reverberance of hail upon the dead
Thunder like an exploding crucible!
Harshly articulate, musical steel shell
Of angry worship, hurled religiously
Upon your business of humility
Into the iron forestries of hell:

Till broken in the shift of quieter
Dense altitudes tangential of your steel,
I am become geometries, and glut
Expansions like a blind astronomer
Dazed, while the worldless heavens bulge and reel
In the cold revery of an idiot.

The poem itself is "harshly articulate" and packed with suggestion. There is the compression of synesthesia in the initial lines, where the "knell / Of arch on arch" implies that the subterranean architecture is the very voice of doom. The phrase "harshly articulate" could refer both to the noise that the cars make as they rush in and out of the station and to the rough fashion in which they are joined.

The conclusion of the octave is heavy with ironic implication. The subway is a major factor in commerce and industry. But this, the religion of the machine age, gives us merely the "shell" of worship, for it has no fruitful connection, as did the old nature myths, with the processes of life. The subway cars move mechanically, "hurled", like the passengers, not of their own will, "Into the iron forestries of hell". Further, the "business of humility" may be read as an ironic commentary on the distance of the subway riders from those who prided themselves on the possession of an irreplaceable soul, yet who went humbly about the business of redeeming it. These ideas are only hinted at; explicitly the octave gives the physical aspect of the subway: its shattering noise and rush. With the sestet we make a transition to the meaning that the subway has in our society. Emerging into the region of skyscrapers that the subway serves, the dazed traveler finds himself in a world of blank abstraction. The sky is hidden from him (as the subway hid the earth that was its sky), and the "worldless heavens" of a blind astronomer are a fit image of the heavenless world of modern man, full of sound and fury.

Although Tate's later poems exhibit richer references, an ampler design, finer craftsmanship, he has enlarged rather than altered his theme. The substance of "Seasons of the Soul", a poem dedicated "To the memory of John Peale Bishop, 1892–1944", is once more, as the poet has attested in a private letter, "a representation of man committing acts of violence against self and nature." The ostensible subject appears to be the difficulty of reconciling oneself to death: the death of the individual, and the moral death that stalks our world. The poem is in four parts: Summer, Autumn, Winter, Spring. Each part is composed of six stanzas of ten lines. Tate had employed the same metric and the same rhyme scheme earlier, but never more effectively. The short line and the recognitions and surprises afforded by the rhymes work for the prevailing mood of painful unrest. Yet the lines that bring the whole to a conclusion are, with their gradually lengthened cadence, indicative of something close to reconciliation. The first section, which might be expected to speak of that fair season when the soul delights in maturity, looks back nostalgically to the timeless summers of childhood, and also makes a bitterly witty allusion to the June solstice when

> Green France was overrun
> With caterpillar feet.

The opening stanza acknowledges the possibility of the mind, "like a hunting king", falling "to the lion's jaws". The word "jaws" is the key word here, repeated at the close of each stanza, and the suggestion it carries is that the fruitful season has become one of ravage. The final stanza, with its image of the astounded centaur from the Inferno, emphasizes the desperate mood: Chiron was astonished to

see a living man in hell. The implication is that that is
where we now live.

The "Autumn" section, although presenting a dream, is
more concrete, more intimate, and more terrifying than
what preceded it. The dream is certainly of Hell: the
Hell of being lost in the past, and not recognized by one's
own progenitors. The entire poem is suffused with the
dark wind of the Inferno. Here it blows from the fifteenth
Canto, where Dante speaks of the dead looking at him
and his companion, knitting their brows, "as an aged tailor
does at the eye of his needle". Tate writes:

> As in a moonlit street
> Men meeting are too shy
> To check their hurried feet
> But raise their eyes and squint
> As through a needle's eye
> Into the faceless gloom,—
> My father in a gray shawl
> Gave me an unseeing glint
> And entered another room!

The reminder of Dante's passage is not due to the simile
alone, but to the fact that in both instances the poet is
being eyed thus puzzlingly by the dead. The repeated
phrase here is "I stood in the empty hall."

In the succeeding section, "Winter", the poet emerges
from the empty hall, where the self meets with no recognition and can go neither forward nor back, to plead with
Venus, "Goddess sea-born and bright", that she come
again to revive those for whom neither Christ nor the
sea gods of the pagan world any longer bear "The living
wound of love". This phrase turns into a grim refrain
about "The livid wound of love", seen now as beastly
sensuality—there is a clear reference to the "Eternal winters" of that circle of Hell reserved by Dante for gluttons
and voluptuaries. The last two stanzas of the section are
also Dantesque in their reference, but have to do with
those who suffer for the crime of self-slaughter. At the

close the poet, drenched with their blood, seems to
identify himself with them,

> Their brother, who like them
> Was maimed and did not bear
> The living wound of love.

In the final section, "Spring", his appeal is not to the
pagan goddess of love but to the "mother of silences". This
mysterious figure has been identified with the mother
whose death was so lamentable a loss to St. Augustine;
but she is more than a human mother, even one who gave
the world two saints: herself and her son. Although she
may also represent the Virgin, and be symbolic of both life
and love, the final stanza seems to emphasize her identifi-
cation with death. As the poem concludes, the maternal
saint fades into a mother whose "kindness" is the final,
the sole refuge for the harried soul, and is shared by all in
the end.

> Then, mother of silences,
>
> Speak, that we may hear;
> Listen, while we confess
> That we conceal our fear;
> Regard us, while the eye
> Discerns by sight or guess
> Whether, as sheep foregather
> Upon their crooked knees,
> We have begun to die;
> Whether your kindness, mother,
> Is mother of silences.

The stanza is beautifully composed, with its recurrent
claim on the attention of this ambiguous "mother". It asks
her first to speak, then to listen, then to look at us, each
demand being followed by a longer, more anguished
phrase indicative of man's plight. The image of the sheep
accentuates the helpless stupidity of the lost. It recalls
that passage in the Purgatorio where Dante describes the

unshepherded souls who had stubbornly resisted the authority of the Church huddling together like timid, silly
sheep; but those were repentant sinners, assured of ultimate redemption. Not so the men in Tate's poem, who
may imitate each other like sheep, but who have no bond,
either among themselves or with the universe in which
they live like displaced persons.

III

The themes that occupy Tate recur, if less obsessively,
in the work of his fellows. Thus not a few poems by Robert Penn Warren revolve about the meaning of experience
for the denuded contemporary. The position is stated in
one of Warren's "Five Studies in Naturalism", which offers the sardonic commentary of a ragged old Mexican on
the grotesque world galloping past him. The tourist, observing both, remarks:

> We could not see his history, we saw
> Him.
> And he saw us, but could not see we stood
> Huddled in our history and stuck out hand for alms.

The contemporary, huddled in his history, sticking out his
hand for alms, is implicit even in a poem that superficially
seems to be no more than a sensational narrative of the old
South, a rough Kaintuck version of the story of Sohrab
and Rustum: "The Ballad of Billie Potts".

Big Billie kept a tavern "In the land between the rivers,"
where travelers were forced to part with their lives if they
would not readily part with their money. Little Billie, his
only child, the darling of the tavern keeper and his wife,
going about his father's business, got into trouble, and was
sent West to save himself and "to try his luck". For ten
years he was not heard from, and then, having struck it
rich, he rode back. As he was nearing home, he met one of
the neighbors and bade him look in on them later: he
wanted to take his time about surprising his Mammy and

Pappy. And indeed they did not recognize Little Billie in
the big red-faced man, "With a big black beard growing
down to his guts / And silver mountings to his pistol-
butts", who came riding up, and who jingled his pockets
so pleasantly. At the suggestion of the old woman, Big
Billie took him down to the spring after supper for a
drink.

> "Just help yoreself," Big Billie said;
> Then set the hatchet in his head.

Later on in the evening the neighbor came by, asking for
Little Billie, who had had no time to reveal himself. Long
after the neighbor had departed and was well out of sight
and hearing, the old couple took the spade to uncover the
hole where they had laid the nameless black-bearded
stranger. The old woman opened his shirt and saw under
the left breast the birthmark that they both knew.

Simple and sensational as the story is in its bare outlines, it is told so as to italicize matters that are not at all
simple. Centering upon the problem of identity, "The
Ballad of Billie Potts" suggests how this is involved with
place and time, history and tradition. It reminds us of
the homelessness of a people pushing westward and de-
spoiling as they went a continent that history had not
marked. It touches, too, upon what Tate calls "the remarkable self-consciousness of our age". The poet does this,
sometimes rather heavy-handedly, by breaking away from
the rude ballad form to insert parenthetical passages similar now to the voice of Eliot in the *Quartets*, discoursing
on ends and beginnings, and again oddly reminiscent of
Kenneth Fearing's sinister repetitive phrasing, his sardonic
colloquialisms. Both point to a rootless man's search for
identity and to blind betrayal.

Some of the poems in which Warren explores our situation are individualized by his gift for the ugly or alarming
detail: the nightmare, with "its great head rattling like a
gourd", occurring in the same piece with grandpa's wen
"Which glinted in the sun like rough garnet or the rich

old brain bulging through." But here is a tendency towards a forbidding privacy, absent from the lyrics that deal with the perennial subject matter of poetry after the fashion of the old metaphysicals. Such are "Monologue At Midnight", "Bearded Oaks" and "Picnic Remembered", scenes in which time and eternity figure more prominently than do the man and the woman who inhabit them, and "The Garden", with its suggestive subtitle: "On prospect of a fine day in early autumn". These poems proffer something of the somber excitement of Marvell's handling of allied themes. The words like the metrics are those long familiar to English poetry, but the propriety of the tone and of the language redeems them from staleness. Here is work that performs the

> sacrament that can translate
> All things that fed luxurious sense
> From appetite to innocence.

What else is art, when it apprehends and enjoys without desire or dread, but such a sacrament.

The work that followed was to be haunted by Warren's concern with the malign. *Brother to Dragons* has been touched upon. Implicit throughout that narrative poem is the confessed yearning "to make communication, / To touch the ironic immensity of the afternoon with meaning." In the book of poems that appeared three years later, the same wish is apparent, together with a bitter awareness of "the malfeasance of Nature" and "the filth of fate". Yet, like Hardy before him, Warren shows himself keenly responsive to the delicacy and grandeur of the natural world, and, in the darkness of the mid-century, he is capable of hope. He uses a looser line here, richer rhymes, the freedoms that a knowledgeable craftsman allows himself.

The tenderness that Warren sometimes shows is of the essence of John Crowe Ransom's work, which is unique in being as gentle as it is perceptive. His poems are distinguished from those of his confrères by their tone, which

has an especial grace and gaiety. His little dramas do not
swell, as Warren's sometimes will, into something close to
melodrama. His lyrics—he has a singularly fine ear—are
not, as Tate's tend to be, angular with hermetic discourse.
Ransom is as sensible as any of his companions of the
plight of man in our world, a plight emphasized for the
Southerner by the relics of a decayed tradition. He does
not hesitate to make this his theme. But his verse has an
energy that quickens his subtlest intellectualizing. His
poems should not be dismembered, it is only the lyric
entire and intact that can convey his meaning. It is his
mixture of wit and feeling that gives so fresh a turn to his
poetry, whether he engage in theological fencing, embroider with extravagant humor on the plain fabric of a
folk tale, or paint a landscape with odd figures who suddenly reach out hands to squeeze the heart. It is not alone
the Jane Sneed and John Black of his "Eclogue" who resemble the lovers of metaphysical poetry in being

> one part love
> And nine parts bitter thought.

Some such duality runs throughout his poems, whether
they have to do with the young or the middle-aged, the tie
that binds those miserably separated or the division between those happily joined.

The same inclusiveness holds for his poems about death,
which are relatively many and various. There is, for example, the death of the little cousin,

> A pig with pasty face, so I had said,
> Squealing for cookies, kinned by poor pretense
> With a noble house. But the little man quite dead,
> I see the forebears' antique lineaments.

The puny ordinariness of the child is not ignored, but the
"deep dynastic wound" felt by the old people whom he
leaves behind is also acknowledged in all its sadness. There
is the death of another child, a small girl, whose mis-
chievousness, once so disturbing, is now felt as a vexing

lack. There is the passing of "Emily Hardcastle, Spinster", her name a pun, for here death wears the mask of "the Grizzled Baron" to whom the stern gentlewoman had been forced to yield, though she had steadily refused the local gentry. It is not impossible to read her story as an allegory of the old South, too fine to yield to mercantilism, too proud to accept a reduced gentility. There is the "lady of beauty and high degree" who, in spite of being

> The delight of her husband, her aunt, an infant
> of three,
> And of medicoes marveling sweetly on her ills,

dies of fever and chills, fortunate, one is assured, no less in the brevity of her illness than in the elegance of her final rites. There is Miriam Tazewell's storm-riven flower garden, and the "Vaunting Oak" whose hollow trunk is darkly emblematical. And there is Janet's hen.

JANET WAKING

Beautifully Janet slept
Till it was deeply morning. She woke then
And thought about her dainty-feathered hen,
To see how it had kept.

One kiss she gave her mother,
Only a small one gave she to her daddy
Who would have kissed each curl of his shining baby;
No kiss at all for her brother.

"Old Chucky, old Chucky!" she cried,
Running across the world upon the grass
To Chucky's house, and listening. But alas,
Her Chucky had died.

It was a transmogrifying bee
Came droning down on Chucky's old bald head
And sat and put the poison. It scarcely bled,
But how exceedingly

And purply did the knot
Swell with the venom and communicate
Its rigor! Now the poor comb stood up straight
But Chucky did not.

So there was Janet
Kneeling on the wet grass, crying her brown hen
(Translated far beyond the daughters of men)
To rise and walk upon it.

And weeping fast as she had breath
Janet implored us, "Wake her from her sleep!"
And would not be instructed in how deep
Was the forgetful kingdom of death.

The disposition of the rhymes, the manipulated uncertainty of the metre, the orotund latinity setting off the curt prose statements—all these are so many devices for bringing out the contrast at the heart of the poem. The tremendous fact of mortality is illustrated by the death from a bee sting of a barnyard pet. The child's reluctance to realize the death of her brown hen anticipates what she will feel as an adult, confronting mature bereavements. At the same time, the mention of death's "forgetful kingdom" is a reminder that Janet will forget, too, although, as the title makes clear, this is her "waking"—she who had slept so "Beautifully . . . / Till it was deeply morning"— to realities undreamed of. The piece is typical of the poet in its quiet juxtaposition of things that seem worlds apart, as also in its unpretentious drama, its gentle wit, and the felicity of its tone.

Among Ransom's gifts is the ability to objectify an idea in the homeliest imagery. The lyric, "Winter Remembered", has a conclusion as unforgettably plain as a line out of Villon:

Dear love, these fingers that had known your touch,
And tied our separate forces first together,
Were ten poor idiot fingers not worth much,
Ten frozen parsnips hanging in the weather.

He does the same thing in the sonnet sequence, "Two Gentlemen in Bonds", the two gentlemen in question representing body and mind, or simply the unfriendly kindred, the brothers Abbott and Paul. There is delightful dramatization of an idea in his portrait of the old man in war paint and feathers dancing with his grandsons "around a backyard fire of boxes". To the chiding of his son, their father, the grandfather responds with a silence that declares: "This life is not good but in danger and in joy.", repents the "middling ways" of his own years of discretion, and promises that he "will be more honorable in these days."

The gentle irony with which the poet treats such material as a familial or connubial difference or a child's tragedy he exercises on the legends of Scripture. Thus in his handling of the story of Judith of Bethulia every element contributes to surprise: the rhythms, which induce a mounting excitement, the distribution of masculine and feminine endings, the interplay of rhyme and off rhyme, the mingling of the fabulous and the commonplace:

Beautiful as the flying legend of some leopard,
She had not yet chosen her great captain or prince
Depositary to her flesh, and our defense;
And a wandering beauty is a blade out of its scabbard.
You know how dangerous, gentlemen of threescore?
May you know it yet ten more.

One becomes, as it were, half habituated to astonishment, and thus prepared for the conclusion, which shows Judith, no less than Holofernes, captive and stricken:

May God send unto the virtuous lady her prince.
It is stated she went reluctant to that orgy,
Yet a madness fevers our young men, and not the clergy
Nor the elders have turned them unto modesty since.
Inflamed by the thought of her naked beauty with desire?
Yes, and chilled with fear and despair.

As one rereads it, the picture reverses itself, and one sees Judith herself, going bravely to an act bred of desperate fear, and returning from it, "inflamed . . . with desire", as she is also "chilled with fear and despair."

Ransom is unmistakably a member of the company that not so long ago was in flight from the confusions of our industrialized society into the comparative peace, the stable simplicities of his native region, but he turns a more quizzical eye upon what he finds there. What other poets strain for, he appears to achieve with felicitous ease. In the "Survey of Literature" which begins

> In all the good Greek of Plato
> I lack my roastbeef and potato,

he cries God's mercy on the writer

> With no belly and no bowels,
> Only consonants and vowels.

A closely knit poem, "Painted Head", asserts that "Beauty is of body." Appreciation of this fortifies his thoughtful poetry, as does his subtle management of consonants and vowels. His remarks on a recently revised poem renew our sense of the vistas in work "about familiar and familial situations; domestic and homely things". Above all, he differs from those with whom he has been associated in qualifying his acerb observation with a discriminating tenderness. He writes about old age: a rheumy old man in an autumnal garden; blue-eyed girls threatened with the fate of a bleareyed "lady with a terrible tongue," once lovelier than them all; the old South, with its eminent mansions fallen into decay; death and the maiden, depicted as "a gentleman in a dust-coat" and "a lady young in beauty". He writes about meetings and partings, loves and quarrels, rough adventures, theological disputes, family intimacies. But whatever his subject, little or large, and with Ransom the little is always enlarged by implication, his tone is right. The glint of irony is there, deepened as well as softened by a sensitiveness without a grain of sentimentality. Only rarely is the poetry faintly obscured by the branching thorns of a wit that more often supports it.

IV

In his diatribe against the metaphysical poets, Dr. Johnson complained that though "their learning instructs, and their subtlety surprises, . . . the reader commonly thinks his improvement dearly bought . . ." Of such intellectual ostentation some twentieth-century admirers of the school may be accused. The reader is to be blamed who would purchase imponderable values cheaply, but the poets are not altogether free of an arid intellectualism, if not a snobbish pedantry. An instance is Laura Riding, an expatriate member of the original Nashville group. Her reasons for writing poetry are what, following Coleridge, she rightly calls "the right reasons": the need to exercise "those faculties which apprehend in terms of entirety, rather than in terms merely of parts." Yet too often she allows her intellect to get in the way of this demanding exercise. That vigorous practitioner, Robert Graves, who long since explored modern poetry with her, is not subject to the same fault. It was Graves who introduced Ransom's early work to the British public, appreciating especially its local flavor. His own verse moves more readily on "Ogrestrand" or in "Pygmy Valley" than in homelier places, and draws with equal ease on the myths of Greece and of Wales. Graves has deprived his public of some jolly Skeltonics and also of a few poems of childhood that are not without a small *frisson*. The sense of the supernatural, whether dragon, demon, ghost, or goddess, haunts his pages. He has professed admiration for "punctilious and intuitive realism". What he often realizes is the eerie and the fantastic. His stout, learned, controversial book about the White Goddess, as he calls the Muse, shows her in her triple aspect of creatrix, preserver, and destroyer. Aphrodite and Artemis, Demeter and Kali are among her names, who is to be served loyally with delight and dread. A scholar, a novelist, a man of letters, Graves protests loudly his devotion to her. As might be expected of her devotee, he writes with powerful directness about sex, with terrifying intimacy about death. He has himself spoken of his poems as having a "hand-made, individual craftsmanship quality", as they do, the result, perhaps, of a certain roughness in the handling of traditional metres, hints of archaism in the blunt diction, and a remoteness from urban life in their background and substance. The fantasy is sometimes gay, the tone not seldom harsh. Years ago Graves wrote a poem about "The Climate of Thought", which he made out to be strangely calm and still, with "The sun, simple, like a country neighbor; / The moon, grand, not fanciful with clouds." This is too wanting in violence and mystery to be the climate of his own poems. Nor does it seem appropriate to the place that his friend Ransom's subtle and finely wrought lyrics inhabit. It is extraordinarily remote from the dry, sad air in which most of Allen Tate's poems have their being.

Despite his inveighing against the abstraction of science, Tate is apt to fit his verse to the Procrustean bed of abstract philosophizing. A recurrent figure in his work is that of Plato's cave, where the prisoners know reality only by the shadow of its shape and the echo of its voice. In the passage from *The Republic* that fascinates the poet it is pointed out that it is the hard duty of those who have escaped into the light of truth to descend again and share the lot of those chained in the cave, though when they try to enlighten these prisoners they will be mocked for their pains. Plato was concerned with government, but the allegory might also have reference to poetry. The poet, like the philosopher, has had a vision of reality that, on returning to the cave, he finds it difficult to convey to those who know only shadows. A scholarly and a scrupulous craftsman, possessed by the sense of loss that haunts the contemporary mind, Tate is as one who goes down to the den with so strong a feeling of estrangement from the pris-

oners there that he can speak to them only obliquely. The
poet need not have a Platonic picture of eternal values to
find communication difficult. He may be a man with a
vision of evil that will not be reduced to the words in
which people transact the ordinary business of the day.
He may be sensible of tensions too complex to be translatable into the language commonly used by men. Often
more learned as well as more perceptive than his fellows,
it is a matter of course for him to load his work with book-
ish references.

Poetry is apt to evaporate in library air, yet the quon-
dam Fugitives and their friends were not alone in writing
verse that smelled, more or less, of the lamp. Appreciating
the obscurity of some of his allusions, the poet may confide in a postscript the basis for the ideas that play through
a poem. Eliot set the precedent in his casual notes to
The Waste Land, in which he stated that the poem owed
much to Miss Weston's work, *From Ritual to Romance,*
and to the Atthis, Adonis, Osiris sections of Frazer's *The
Golden Bough,* and mentioned the various poets and
saints whose words are woven into his text. Pound is less
explicit than Eliot, but it is common knowledge that for a
full understanding of *The Cantos* one should be acquainted with various works, including Andreas Divus'
translation of the *Odyssey,* the correspondence between
Adams and Jefferson, and the details of Lincoln Steffens'
Autobiography. His later sources, such as F. W. Baller's
edition of *The Sacred Edict* of K'ang Hsi and Thomas
Hart Benton's monetary treatises, are more esoteric.

The detached statements that make up so much of
Marianne Moore's verse are the product of her omnivo-
rous reading. Miss Moore possesses a singularly acute eye,
a precise vocabulary, and an intelligence that allows her
to use these tools to advantage. But the mental acquisi-
tiveness that furnishes her verse with some of its most
remarkable details sometimes turns it into a bibliographi-
cal curiosity. Her work is ornamented with quotations
from such sources, among others equally incompatible, as

the defunct *Literary Digest*, the *Decameron*, the diary of
Tolstoi, the rules and regulations of The Department of
the Interior, Pliny, and the advertising section of the New
York *Times*. The gulf between her and Eliot, who is one
of her attested admirers, may be gauged by the way in
which the reading of the one is absorbed into his poetry,
while the reading of the other is so much on the surface
of hers. What she calls her "hybrid method of composition" often results in moral reflections, as in the title
poem of the little book: *What Are Years?* Its subject,
illustrated by the singing of a caged bird, is courage. The
final stanza shows the bird steeling "his form straight up"
and concludes:

>   Though he is captive,
>   his mighty singing
>   says, satisfaction is a lowly
>   thing, how pure a thing is joy.
>   This is mortality,
>   this is eternity.

In a poem about the ostrich she acknowledges that "Her-
oism is exhausting." Elsewhere she exclaims, and everywhere implies with the same exultation: "What is there
like fortitude!" Whether she is looking at steeplejacks or
strawberries, she is concerned with morals.

Admiring propriety, she likens this virtue to the music
of Brahms and Bach: "a tuned reticence with rigour /
From strength at the source." This describes her own work
at its best. Her respect for reticence may help to account
for her syllabic metric, which reveals itself only to the
attentive eye, and her frequent use of light rhymes which
play hide-and-seek. As becomes a woman who exalts humility, her technique is apt to be

>   retiringly formal
>   as if to say: "And there was I
>   like a field-mouse at Versailles."

Perhaps her interest in the ideas informing right conduct

keeps her poems closer to speech than to song. However much she enjoys examining the animal, the vegetable, the mineral, what chiefly attracts her is evidence of mind and spirit. Yet even when she writes on a subject as abstract as the intellect itself, her control of verbal texture is evident. The glitter of a sparkling wit becomes not merely visible but audible in these lines:

> The Mind is an Enchanting Thing
> is an enchanted thing
>   like the glaze on a
> katy-did wing
>   subdivided by sun
>   till the nettings are legion.
> Like Gieseking playing Scarlatti; . . .

Miss Moore is sometimes betrayed by her thirst for knowledge, and sometimes by her ethical bias, into discursiveness or admonition. Her true poems show a fastidious wit in the service of an incisive apprehension.

Like Miss Moore's less traditional exercises, the work of Yvor Winters is fired with moral passion. Not astonishingly, since it is his conviction that a poem, being "a full and definitive account of a human experience", is "an act of moral judgment." The slenderness of his output—songs, sonnets, a small sheaf of longer pieces—testifies to the rigor of his self-criticism. Exhibiting a like austerity of tone, Winters differs from Miss Moore in his willingness to give lyrical expression to an exquisite tenderness. For all his insistence on the rational import of poetry, he has composed images—a few consisting of a single line—that give the quality of a living landscape, of a passing moment, so as to recreate the very motions of Nature, to whom the motions of the mind are irrelevant.

A more passionate but no more earnest moralist, the late John Wheelwright, like Marianne Moore, was at pains to refer readers to the printed sources of his poems. In a single piece he quotes the Hymnal, the Psalter, the Bhagavad-Gita, Oliver Wendell Holmes, Stonewall Jackson, and an anonymous ejaculation made during the Johnstown flood. The "General Argument" appended to his poems is an attempt to clarify the ideas that shape his apostrophes to those of his fellows—Harry Crosby, Hart Crane, for whom the conflicts of modern life proved intolerable; to his martyred heroes: Sacco and Vanzetti; and to his pet hate: the selfish morality of a secularized puritanism.

Again, C. Day Lewis, who also tried to drive metaphysics and revolution tandem, explains that the theme of his "Transitional Poem" is the pursuit of single-mindedness, and notes that certain lines have reference to such sources as the letters of Spinoza, the Old Testament, Dante's Inferno, Wyndham Lewis's essay on *The Art of Being Ruled*, the "Ballad of the Twa Brothers", *The Ambassadors* by Henry James, and the refrain of a music-hall ditty.

I. A. Richards, well known as an exemplar of what he calls "an exploring mind", does not hesitate to furnish glosses and commentaries on his poems. The fact that "the better poems tend to require fewer notes" has, however, been remarked in a note about his own notes on his poems by another Cantabrigian, William Empson. As might be expected, that intensive critic writes poetry demanding a great deal of miscellaneous and sometimes abstruse information, such as the domestic arrangements of ants and beetles, the incidence of chairs in Chinese art, some implications of the theory of relativity. His literary references are as unexpected as they are various. A poem dealing with the absurdities and cruelties at work in a society that calls itself Christian is entitled "Reflection from Anita Loos": to the effect that "A girl can't go on laughing all the time." Naturally, the man who explored *Seven Types of Ambiguity* through their most labyrinthine passages writes what he calls a "clotted kind of poetry", thick with multiple meanings. He has, however, composed a "Poem About a Ball in the Nineteenth Century" that moves as airily and chimes as gaily as the event it describes. Learned, witty, and ironical, Empson is not incapable of directness. A difficult poem on some of the uses of the imagination ends on the memorably plain admonition to "learn a style from a despair." He has employed the light form of the villanelle for a love poem in which the key lines are forcefully simple:

> It is the pain, it is the pain, endures.
> Poise of my hands reminded me of yours.

The echo of Othello's "It is the cause, it is the cause, my soul" does not make them less effective. Another villanelle harps on a theme that could not be more clearly stated to strike home: "The waste remains, the waste remains and kills." The cadence is almost the same, the feeling as strong.

In a sense, some of Empson's younger compatriots may be said to have learned a style from a despair. Without faith, however troubled, without the hope for political regeneration such as inspired much of the poetry of the thirties, they have recorded experiences buttressed by no myth, in language that requires no explication. It is as if the accumulated horrors and incredible inventions of this century compelled concentration on what is near, small, and familiar. The voice of these poets is subdued, as in the waiting-room of a suburban railway station, a hospital, or a prison, rather than on a pier or at an airport. Admiring the restrictions of Empson's forms, notably the villanelle, the quietness of his tone, the lack of extravagance in his diction, they have produced wryly melancholy, witty poems, wanting in the intensity of which this complex poet is capable.

Since the root of poetry is emotional conviction, verse that requires explanatory appendices is apt to be rejected as not poetry at all. In some instances it is not. One can enjoy symbolist poetry without fully understanding it, because the melodic line and the associations stir some manner of response. One cannot relish intellectual verse without understanding it, where it is wanting in tone-color,

offensively angular in rhythm, highly abstract, or deficient
in wit. The simple if engaging verse that deals in ideas is
no preparation for poetry compact of abstruse thought.
The reader who enjoys the sly rhymes of Ogden Nash,
or the tone that Frances Cornford finds for an ironic yet
compassionate detachment, or, again, the pieces by John
Betjeman that he describes as "SLICK BUT NOT STREAM-
LINED" is responding to qualities that appear in good poetry of low tension. But he is not exercising the faculties
that will help him to wrestle with the heirs of Donne.
Here as elsewhere, for the uneasy reader the way to begin
is to begin. Moreover, the difficulty that a poem presents
may be in direct ratio to its significance. Delay of communication is a different thing from failure, and a statement of confusion or dilemma may have the value of
making the confusion meaningful, the dilemma pregnant.
The most comprehensive poetry takes account of the
whole man, and, paradoxically, it can do so only by acknowledging his divided nature. It is the merit of the
moderns who claim kinship with the metaphysicals to have
realized this.

How admirable is their use of irony may be judged by
contrasting the work of the Nashville group with that of a
Southern regionalist who never learned it. Jesse Stuart,
"the man with the bull-tongue plow", has written hundreds of sonnets about himself and his land, his kin, his
neighbors, his loves. Simple in diction as they are in feeling, they show him, as he admits himself to be,

> lowly in a world of living men,
> And ordinary in a world of dead,

especially in a world of dead poets, the more traditional
of whom he often recalls. Stuart has been compared to
Burns, but he lacks just that saltiness which gives Burns'
lyrics their sparkle. The fault lies only partially in his tireless sonneteering, since Dr. Merrill Moore, one of the original Fugitives, composed more than a thousand sonnets, a
remarkable number of which escape triteness.

V

The poets instructed by Eliot were not the first to re-discover the uses of a dry tone, though they have employed it with great effectiveness. It is one of the merits of William Carlos Williams, and of others who learned from the practice of the imagists. As a check upon romantic grandiloquence it is evident in some of the whimsies of Alfred Kreymborg, as in certain more ambitious pieces by "Others": the poets who reminded the public that "the old expressions are with us always, and there are always others."

Aridity is a token of that self-critical intelligence from which the artist has nothing to fear. It is notable in Yeats's later poems, written when he discovered, having swayed his leaves and flowers in the sun, that he might "wither into truth." Pound, for all his savagery, knows that the light barb may be preferable to the shattering spear. Robert Frost gives an astringent slyness to his homely eclogues and in other poems blends wit and somberness in a fresh and intimate fashion.

New England's laureate is one of the admirations of Mark Van Doren, along with the forthright seventeenth-century lyricist, John Dryden, and the acute "sensibili-tist", to use Frost's word, Emily Dickinson. It is not astonishing, then, that he should declare:

> Wit is the only wall
> Between us and the dark.

Van Doren's association with the Nashville group was tardy and tangential. There are several poets who came to the fore even later and who, like the others not of this company already mentioned, produce work that exhibits a similar complex of thought and feeling. Prominent among them is Richard Eberhart. He looks at the world about him and thinks with a kind of baffled intensity about God. No contemporary has written a more memora-

ble poem on death than he in "The Groundhog". He
first sees the dead groundhog lying in the golden fields of
June, and is shaken by the sight. The lines,

> There lowly in the vigorous summer
> His form began its senseless change,

indicate the way in which the poet makes his words work.
The animal corpse undergoes a change that is "senseless"
in that the creature does not feel itself becoming a "seeth-
ing cauldron" of maggots, and that is otherwise "senseless"
to the wayfarer who does not see the meaning of the transformation. "Half with loathing, half with a strange love,"
he pokes the body "with an angry stick" that does "nor
good nor harm", then stands silently watching this object,
trying for control in its presence, and finally kneeling in
prayer "for joy in the sight of decay." He returns in autumn to see "The sap gone out of the groundhog". The
year, we are told, "had lost its meaning", the autumnal
scene is identified in the mind of the poet with the bony
sodden hulk of the creature, and he, in his autumnal wisdom, is deprived of love and loathing. Another summer
takes the fields again, as he phrases it: "Massive and burning, full of life", but when he chances on the spot—significantly, he does not seek it out—there is

> only a little hair left
> And bones bleaching in the sunlight
> Beautiful as architecture.

He watches them "like a geometer" and cuts himself "a
walking stick from a birch." Every line contributes to the
sense of death viewed as part of the pattern, accepted,
and dismissed. The stick is not used to poke the carcass—
there is little to poke—but to make for jauntiness in walking away from it. Three years later he returns.

> There is no sign of the groundhog.
> I stood there in the whirling summer,
> My hand capped a withered heart,

> And thought of China and Greece.
> Of Alexander in his tent;
> Of Montaigne in his tower,
> Of Saint Theresa in her wild lament.

The poem ends not with the groundhog, who is now part of the ground or dispersed in air, but with the saint. The words on which it concludes are "wild lament", but it is not the poet who laments wildly: the pain, like these deaths, is in his thought. Nevertheless, that sounding "lament" contradicts his confession of "a withered heart". It is characteristic of Eberhart that he should be moved by a trivial natural event to think of persons who represent love of power, love of knowledge, love of God. The helplessness of all love seems implicit here, as is the meaning of diverse civilizations and their passing.

Another memorable poem takes its title from the opening line: "If I could only live at the pitch that is near madness". The first stanza makes clear that he seeks the child's world of transcendently intense sensation and expectation, when everything was "Violent, vivid, and of infinite possibility". But there stood mankind in battalions, "stolid, demanding a moral answer." The poem concludes:

> I gave the moral answer and I died
> And into a realm of complexity came
> Where nothing is possible but necessity
> And the truth wailing there like a red babe.

He knows that he cannot return to that high pitch of being, however lively his remembrance of it at moments, but there is a kind of exultation in the acceptance of man's condition which is the essence of maturity. If he lives in the kingdom of necessity, "the truth wailing there like a red babe" is an infant still, and who knows what it will say when it learns to speak?

Although Eberhart uses some received forms and allows himself occasional archaisms, the abrupt elliptical phrase, the frequent absence of rhyme, the rough metrics, give the effect of speech, personal and passionate. To an extraordinary degree he has had his wish: the particulars of the natural world retain for him, late in life, the numinous quality that they have for a child. He concluded a poem called "1934" with the confession: "And ever and still the weight of mystery / Arrows its way between my words and me." He might with equal truth have written that the weight of mystery arrows its way between his world and him. It finds the hearts of those who listen to his words.

A like intensity is articulate in the work of that sophisti- cated craftsman, Stanley Kunitz. He can commence a lyric with a couplet that might have been composed by one of the metaphysicals: "Lovers relentlessly contend to be / Superior in their identity:". Elsewhere he manipulates a parenthesis with the skill of Cummings, introduces the subliminal imagery of Roethke, sets down public ignominy in a witty shorthand similar to Auden's. But his poems would not be mistaken for theirs. In one, written "for money, rage, and love", on the theft of his wallet in a Roman tram, he speaks of wearing his heart "less Roman than baroque", and indeed, he does not shrink from a grand extravagance of language. He is concerned with the perennial themes of sexual love, death, and the self, and he is also alert to the shames of the century in which he explores these themes. There is a wide range in his work. "The Waltzer in the House" is a delicately dancing lyric about a mouse. In savage contrast to this is the poem that speaks of wrath "come down from the hills" to enlist the poet

>   in his brindled generation,
>   The race of the tiger; come down at last
>   Has wrath to build a bonfire of my breast
>   With one wet match and all man's desolation.

More than one page is sweetened by tender references to the poet's father, and more than one is enlarged by al-

lusions to the Platonic Forms. Like other inquisitors of
the soul, Kunitz sometimes deals in obliquities and opac-
ities. They are redeemed by the energy, by the anguished
and pitiless honesty with which he confronts his life and
whatever we share of it.

Another poet whose work asks consideration here for its
wit and its seriousness is Denis Devlin. The title poem to
his book, *Lough Derg*, is more than a bleak evocation of a
shrine, to which come pilgrims for whom "All is simple
and symbol", by a poet for whom much is symbol but little is simple. The poem reviews the decline of faith in
closely packed stanzas that mingle the historical with the
personal, and that, climbing toward Heaven, fall back into
Hell. Devlin defines it thus:

> Hell is to know our natural empire used
> Wrong, by mind's molting, brute divinities.

His thoughts revolved about these ultimates, while his
eyes and ears and nostrils were awake to the gay or filthy
details of the immediate scene. One of his clearest and
saddest poems, which speaks of unhappy love and of children playing "About prophetic dustbins," has the beautifully managed refrain:

> *Breeze blows and the branches sway*
> *Lovers and beloved gently sleep.*

His gift for the sharp image and for the creation of atmosphere has been remarked. He also used provocative ambiguities, sometimes in the form of puns. The difficulty
in severing some phrase or stanza for examination testifies
to the coherence of his poems. In this, as in his more
startling metaphors, and in the complexity of feeling that
his work presents, he shows his kinship with the neometa-
physicals.

More ambitious, learned, and devout than any of the
works considered above is the *Anathemata* of the Welsh
poet, David Jones. It may be roughly described as a revery on the Mass by a Catholic convert. Because Jones

moves freely among diverse cultures and muses reverently
on ancient cults, the poem is one to which even an agnostic can respond. Reflecting on sacred sculptures from
the sixth century B.C. and from the time when Chartres
was built, he writes:

> O yes, technique—but much more:
> the god still is balanced
> > in the man-stones

The lines might serve as an epigraph to his poem, though
the technique is far from as sure as that of the works with
which it bears comparison. Marked by the puns and the
wide allusiveness of *Finnegans Wake*, it shows a firmer
grasp of history than *The Cantos*, a more solidly based
religiosity than the *Quartets*. It calls for notice here because its devout tenor does not preclude the exercise of
wit, and because of the preface and the footnotes, which
show an engaging respect for the reader who has not the
same background as the poet.

The intellectualized poetry of the twentieth century, as
has been noted, did not begin or end with the work of the
Nashville group, but their example and their criticism exercised considerable influence. During the Depression,
which favored the writing of so-called proletarian poetry,
though the sardonic note was not wanting, work of a metaphysical character was in eclipse. But at about that time
the poetry of wit got fresh impetus from a circle that
included W. H. Auden. He has himself described his
formidable talent as that of "a Thinking Type", and in discussing it the poetry of ideas will again require consideration. At this point a word on the subject might well come
from one to whom Tate has more than once paid tribute,
confessedly if somewhat perplexedly

> > proud that an ancestor knew
> The crazy Poe, who was not of our kind—
> Bats in the belfry that round and round flew
> In vapors not quite wholesome for the mind.

"The crazy Poe" gave wholesome advice, however, when he suggested that the poet emulate those old Goths "who used to debate matters of importance to their State twice, once when drunk, and once when sober—sober that they might not be deficient in formality—drunk lest they should be destitute of vigor." At their best, the various poets considered here, appalled at a barbarism more frightful than that of the old Goths, contrive a remarkable balance between vigor and formality.

8. The Ghostly Member

The genius refuses to be classified, the great talents resist classification. Nevertheless, it seems reasonable to group together those who tend to thrust their roots in like soil, to flourish in a like climate, and to produce poems of something the same shape and savor. Those whose work is considered below bear some resemblance to the English metaphysicals or to the French symbolists and differ as widely among themselves as did the members of these two groups. They are united by their concern with the subtler shades of feeling, with the atmosphere not only of a place but of a moment. In trying to seize it they would say with Rilke: "Wie ist das klein womit wir ringern, / Was mit uns ringt, wie ist das gross;": how small is that with which we wrestle, / What with us wrestles, how immense. Sensitive to music, they make much of the aural values of words. Some among them have a piety for splendid monuments and delicate heirlooms, some for the larger vistas of the natural world, all alike repudiating the world of modern technics as a debasement of their heritage. Like other poets, they are intensely aware of time, which they are apt to regard as but the rags of Eternity.

What may first strike the unaccustomed reader in the early work of such a poet as Edith Sitwell is the use of tone-color. The relation of consonants and vowels is studied with a care that is shown for no other element of the poem's texture. The effects to be got out of the manipulation of sound values leads her far from the accepted language of poetry. She will demote the sense of words in the interests of abstract sound. Such verbal play is a slight

thing contrasted with the enormously rich elaborations
that James Joyce achieves in *Finnegans Wake*, where wit
and music serve one another under the surveillance of a
dominating symbolism. It also differs from the word patterns made by Gertrude Stein, a writer whose interest was
largely in the metaphysics of language.

Edith Sitwell has made a moderately successful effort
to elucidate certain passages in Miss Stein's work. Her
own far richer poetry does not show the fear of emotion
that is apparent in her friend's sly portraits and landscapes. Another great admiration of Dame Edith's is Alexander Pope. Her verse resembles his insofar as it is the
product of a cultivated mind accustomed to the amenities
of a less distracted civilization than ours. She exhibits neither the objectivity, the clarity, nor the mechanistic philosophy of the Augustan Age. On the contrary, her poetry, extremely personal, involute, of allusion all compact,
is expressive of a sensibility deeply affronted by our mechanized world. Even in her later, more somber, and exalted
poetry, she works by means of association and suggestion,
though less intensively using what she calls "a new scale
of sense-values". Actually it is as old as the Rig-Veda and
has become as much a poetic commonplace as Baudelaire's
theory of the correspondences between the senses. The
trouble with Dame Edith's perfumes, sounds, and colors
is that their correspondences are sometimes overly private.

One may recognize her imagery when she tries to give
the impression of bunched, rough, furry chestnut leaves
jutting sharply from their branches by writing:

> Hoarse as a dog's bark,
> The heavy leaves are furred.

But can one accept her "Emily-coloured primulas", so-
called because "Emily is a very bucolic name" and primulas remind the poet of "the bright pink cheeks of country
girls"? Whatever associations primulas may have, Emily
does not seem a bucolic name to those who think of it in

connection with the poetry of Emily Dickinson and Emily Brontë.

When Dame Edith's privacies are presented in abstract sound patterns, they are apt to be even less compelling. Many, if not most, readers of English poetry would agree on the associations connected with certain vowels and consonants: the voluptuousness of "l", the thin quality of "i" and "ee", the heaviness of "b" and "d" that affects such words as "mad" and "brood", as well as "mud" and "blood". These associations may not exist for those nurtured in other languages, but they are fairly common with us. Few, however, would be likely to discover without Edith Sitwell's help that in one of her poems "the ethereal quality of the plant-world, the slow growth of the plant, the color and scent of the rose are conveyed by different wave-lengths of the vowels." When she remarks on "the fat sloth of 'musty Justice'" or "the round body and concentration of 'pomp'" or "the softness and shapelessness of 'loll'", it is apparent that associations quite divorced from the sound of the words are playing an unrecognized part. In relying on her personal responses to given assonances and dissonances, she has often warped the imagery of a poem and destroyed the melodic line.

An instance is the long poem, "Gold Coast Customs", a baroque study of a society that the poet can compare only invidiously with those dedicated to primitive cannibalism. It expresses her horror at a world in which "man is part ravenous beast of prey, part worm, part ape, or is but the worm turned vertebrate." The piece writhes with disgust for the greed of the nouveaux riches, anguish at the debasement of the poor. But the ghastly imagery of brutishness, plague, and decay loses its vividness in the building of abstract sound patterns, and the awkward rhythms fail to suggest, as they are meant to do, the grotesque character of the modern metropolis. The poetry here is not equal to the emotion of one who suffers with what Edith Sitwell calls "the wounded and suffering soul" of the contemporary world. She cannot properly express her painful consciousness of the boorish countries surrounding the parks and gardens that shine and blow in her lyrics of nostalgia or affirmation.

It is not strange that this descendant of the Conquerors should repeatedly have sought the key to a fabulous past. With her fingers upon it, she can work enchantments recalling those of the poet who knew how to build palaces to music. This is especially true of a long poem dedicated to one of her brothers and revivifying the lost world of their childhood. It is called "The Sleeping Beauty". The old fairy story is said to symbolize the awakening of the earth from its winter sleep at the kiss of the princely sun. For Edith Sitwell the legend seems to signify that winter of the spirit which has fallen upon a beauty injured not by the point of a spindle but by the invention of the spinning jenny and all the uglier consequences of the industrial revolution. Mysterious, delicate, not without humor, the poem takes on the coloring of a fairy tale told before a drawing-room fire in the dusk. The magic of one passage lies partly in its lyricism and largely in imagery that suggests at once the elaborate yet delicate decoration of Chinese porcelain, the quaint charm of a tapestry portraying a medieval French fable, and the sunny simplicity of Greek mythology, as seen by a child. Curiously, none of the diverse images seems to quarrel with another, but all together take one into enchanted country.

> Where reynard-haired Malinn
> Walks by rock and cave,
> The Sun, a Chinese mandarin,
> Came dripping from the wave.
>
> "Your hair seems like the sunrise
> O'er Persia and Cathay—
> A rose-red music strange and dim
> As th'embalmèd smile of seraphim,"

He said to her by the white wave
In the water-pallid day
(A forest of white coral boughs
Seemed the delicate sea-spray).

"In envy of your brighter hair—
Since, Madam, we must quarrel—
I've changed the cold flower-lovely spray
To branches of white coral;

And when, white muslin madam, you
Coquette with the bright wind,
I shall be but thin rose-dust;
He will be cold, unkind."

The flowers that bud like rain and dream
On thin boughs water-clear,
Fade away like a lovely music
Nobody will hear,

And Aeolus and Boreas
Brood among those boughs,
Like hermits haunting the dark caves
None but the wise man knows.

But Malinn's reynard-colored hair,
Amid the world grown sere,
Still seemed the Javanese sunrise
Whose wandering music will surprise
Into cold bird-chattering cries
The Emperor of China
Lying on his bier.

Fully to enjoy this poetry, one must yield to the spell of
skillfully managed vocables and fluid images rich with reference. Submission means the freedom of a region as fair
as it is fantastic and one to which the poetry of Edith
Sitwell's brothers, Osbert and Sacheverell, also but less
persuasively invites us. Her own early work offers these
pleasures when she is not helplessly attacking the crude
materialism of the tycoon and the profiteer but re-creat-

ing some part of the past, and when, foregoing extreme privacy of association, she puts her technical skill at the service of a robust, exhilarating humor or a subtle and instructed sensuousness.

There are times when her poetry knocks at the gates of that universe to which Traherne and Blake bore radiant witness, the miraculous region that Dylan Thomas said, ". . . all my five and country senses see." The great gates swing on their hinges for Edith Sitwell in the poems written among the thunders and fires of World War II. It is as though these broke in upon the artificial eighteenth-century world for which she felt the attraction and repulsion of kinship, and led her back to celebrate the innocent animalism, the shining insights of childhood with the religiosity of middle age.

Some of the familiar imagery recurs, but with enlarged significance. We walk in country places, where we meet Venus shrunken to a crone, or among fair grounds, where we come upon the bleeding, baited bear; we are overtaken by a terrible darkness; we live with the Spider and the Ape, which assume the heightened stature of evil gods, or we lie down in filthy rags with the Bone, emblem of death, for sole companion. This is the Inferno where flesh and spirit alike are starved, though it seems more like Rimbaud's Hell than like that we have more recently explored, and it recedes before the light of a new sun. The song of the gardener in "The Sleeping Beauty" grows to a hymn which reconciles the older nature myths with that of Christianity. The poet remembers herself as "a golden woman like those who walk / In the dark heavens"—but "now grown old", she sits by the fire and sees the fire turn cold, yet watches "the dark fields for a rebirth of faith and wonder." Towards the close, with reborn wonder and faith she exclaims:

> O wheat-ear shining like a fire and the bright
>   gold,
> O water brought from far to the dying gardens!

Not all the chilling songs "for those who die of the cold
. . . within the heart of Man" can obliterate the radiance
of that "first lover of the world", the Wanderer for whom
the old earth joyfully waits. Again and again the poet
exalts the life-giving planet, and recalls the myth of
Demeter in a fashion that suggests her self-identification
with the corn goddess, seen as another old woman who
lives in the light of the sun, or perhaps she is the sleeper
at last fully awakened to the world of spiritual beauty.

Citing various religious thinkers, the philosopher who
preferred the world as Idea to the world as Will claimed
that the surrender of the will, the mortification of personal desires, and the acknowledgment of the identity of
the self with the kernel of the universe were attitudes in-
evitably linked together. There are passages in Edith Sitwell's later poems which, tinged with quietism, though
not with asceticism, point to a sense of such mystic union.
This, in spite of the Yeatsean poem, one of the most moving she has written: "The Poet Laments the Coming of
Old Age", wherein she cries out that she has lost the "gold
seed of folly" that would have taught her how to bear the
terrible reversals of old age; lamenting

> That the gold-sinewed body that had the blood
>   of all the earth in its veins,
> Has changed to an old rag of the outworn world
> And the great heart that the first Morning made
> Should wear all Time's destruction for a dress.

Her final word is one of affirmation: "great is the earth's
story," she asserts, and continues serenely:

> The world's huge fevers burn and shine, turn cold,
> Yet the heavenly bodies and young lovers burn
>   and shine,
> The golden lovers walk in the holy fields,
> Where the Abraham-bearded sun, the father of all things,
> Is shouting of ripeness . . .

Elsewhere she asks—a rhetorical question—if God can con-
tract Himself to

                        the scope of a small flower
Whose root is clasped in darkness . . . God in the span
Of the root and light-seeking corolla . . . with the voice
    of Fire I cry—
Will He disdain that flower of the world, the heart of
    Man?

These later poems find an echo in the work of the members of the Apocalypse group, who formulated their religious and humanist credo on the eve of the second world
war.

Not the least notable fact about Edith Sitwell's later
work is the abandonment of purely abstract sound, with a
correspondingly greater control of cadence. The poet con-
fides her hope, her belief, to a simpler and more ample
line. There are instances of exquisite lyricism, especially
in certain Songs, and the recurrent image of the summer
rose evokes some of its richest associations. To many, the
dark lyrics called forth by the second world war will speak
with an intimacy that the mystical poems cannot have,
yet even the agnostic must surrender to the spell that she
knows how to weave out of consonants and vowels as out
of shapes and colors and bright old threads of legend. She
sings a "Green Song", and in the midst of death hers is
the poetry of the living: the light of the sun, the sap in
the leaf, the warm fluid in the vein, which this poet, like
the physician who discovered the circulation of the blood,
conceives as the seat and instrument of the soul.

She does not favor austerity and this makes for discursiveness. It also makes for an extravagance of imagery that
sometimes almost overwhelms the poem. Not only have
the syncopated rhythms and delicate vocables of her
youthful verse given place to a long sonorous line; even
those poems that dwell on spiritual themes abound in
sensuous figures. She is one who would say with Traherne
that "by the very right of your senses you enjoy the world

. . . It is of the nobility of man's soul that he is insatiable." Yet Edith Sitwell indulges in capitalized abstractions as discarnate as Platonic Ideas, and in a few passages permits an equally fleshless scientific vocabulary to obtrude itself awkwardly. Conventional Christian references lessen the power of some poems otherwise luminous with a serene pantheism.

Nevertheless, it is easy to appreciate what Yeats meant when, trying to choose a group of her poems for an anthology that he was making, he complained that one was so dependent on another that selection was "like cutting a piece out of a tapestry." The comparison is apt. Edith Sitwell's poetry has at once the sumptuousness and the naïve simplicity, the splendor of color, the abstract flowers, and the symbolic beasts, even the humorous detail, belonging to that historied art. Indeed, her habit of introducing old images in new settings, repeating old themes with fresh emphasis, makes her work appear like a series of tapestries, some of them patched with fragments from an older fabric. And, like the medieval hangings that kept the cold away from secular kings and princes of the Church, the finest of her poems have a luxurious beauty that serves to grace the bareness, to diminish the chill of a bare, cold age.

II

The preciousness that one finds in certain of her poems may be charged against the work of others considered here, and is not least evident in the lyrics of one who saw it as a threat.

> Go study to disdain
> The frail, the overfine,

commanded Elinor Wylie in "Minotaur", a poem praising animal innocence and recognizing its brute matrix. Yet, like Edith Sitwell, this poet combined a sympathy for

Blake's profound simplicity with a delight in the décor of a period hostile to Blake's premises.

Working closely within the tradition, Mrs. Wylie had the craftsman's concern for phrasing, and for the sensuous qualities of words. Her poem, "Bronze Trumpets and Sea Water—On Turning Latin into English", is eloquent of this. She cherished her nouns and adjectives as she did such ornaments of life as rich stuffs, fine china, tooled volumes, gardens, jewels. Her avowed devotion to Shelley never fooled her into believing that he was her proper model. By the same token, though as homesick as Dame Edith for the dignities and beauties of an irrecoverable age, she rejected that poet's means of recapturing them.

One may gauge the distance between these two by examining such a piece as "Miranda's Supper", the account of a Virginian lady's recovery of the treasures she had buried at the coming of the Northern invader, and contrasting it with Miss Sitwell's treatment of similar themes. Mrs. Wylie's couplets have the sparkle of the silver, the delicate colors of the porcelain, of the heirlooms they describe. Miss Sitwell's lyrics hover elegiacally about "a land, austere and elegant" and with a longer, nobler history than Miranda's. She introduces us to its gardens and its castle, which "seemed an arabesque in music", and achieves effects more magical than Mrs. Wylie's smooth numbers produce; but abruptly she breaks the spell. The rhythms become jerky because in working out her abstract designs she ignores the larger pattern of the melodic line, or she presents superimposed images like the lines of a blurred palimpsest. Sometimes she obtrudes a flat statement such as "When we were young, how beautiful life seemed!"—a gaucheness from which Mrs. Wylie was saved by her habit of ironic self-contemplation, though it also prevented her from plunging as deep or soaring as far as this like-minded poet.

One of Mrs. Wylie's early lyrics sang of Love the lamb-like and the leonine in the pure tones of the *Songs of Innocence*, and with inklings of the *Songs of Experienee*.

But here was clearly no masculine voice. It was as feminine as that of a previous traveler who went companioned by the single hound of her own identity. These alliances are natural. Inasmuch as Blake was in rebellion against his century, he was in sympathy with those earlier poets who had lived not in time but in Eternity. Emily Dickinson, almost as much a heretic in her generation as Blake in his, was their true descendant. Her poetry exhibits a nice mixture of wit and intensity. Elinor Wylie shared her belief that

> The Myrrhs and Mochas of the mind
> Are its Iniquity,

and that

> Much madness is divinest sense
> To a discerning eye,

as she shared the conviction that every human soul is its own "indestructible estate". Both women, like Blake before them, were at home in the company of the physician who had once felt through all his fleshly dress "Bright shootes of everlastingnesse", and the shoemaker's son for whom "something infinite behind everything appeared: which talked with [his] expectation and moved [his] desire."

Elinor Wylie used familiar forms, the carefully wrought lyric, the ballad, the ode, producing, among other things, a sonnet sequence that memorably celebrates a tragic passion. Characteristically, while the tone of the sequence is gravely romantic, the introductory sonnet is threaded with a sad irony. Having played variations on the theme of loyalty and betrayal in love, it concludes:

> These words are true, although at intervals
> The unfaithful clay contrive to make them false.

This ironic note, like her lament for a frivolity that prevented her from sharing "with Donne a metaphysical frolic", as well as the many poems pointed with self-

mockery, amplify the evidence of her tutelage by that inquisitorial lover and passionate penitent.

That she was a metaphysical poet in the wider sense of
the term is shown by such a lyric as "O Virtuous Light",
desperately acknowledging the mystic's danger, the austere
"Birthday Sonnet", fittingly composed the day before her
death, and the poem entitled "This Corruptible". Here
the Mind, the Heart, and the Soul discourse with deceiv-
ing urbanity upon the dissolution of the body. The Mind
is scornful of the Body's claims to anything more than
food and rest. The Heart, weary of this "fustian cloak",
would gladly put it off for "embroidered archangelic plumage". But the Spirit, wiser than both, addresses the Body
with a half-wry tenderness:

> O lodging for the night!
> O house of my delight!

and pleads with it to endure yet another day. It is the
Body, the unlucky slave, unkindly used by these whom
it serves, that will in the end escape

> In some enchanting shape
> Or be dissolved to elemental nothing.

Those others, Mind and Heart and Spirit, are forever captive to themselves, whereas the Body is bound to be released, its substance transformed, its shape quite altered.
The poem concludes, compassionately and chillingly:

> " 'Tis you who are the ghost,
> Disintegrated, lost;
> The burden shed; the dead who need not bear it;
> O grain of God in power,
> Endure another hour!
> It is but for an hour," said the Spirit.

The poets grouped together here have been able to
write of spirit without embarrassment. The suspicion that
attaches to the word is felt least by those who can answer
the altering seasons, whether of nature or of the personal

life, with something of the religious exaltation communicated by the devotional poets of the seventeenth century, an emotion tempered, for some, with critical audacity and psychological penetration. Whatever their period, however individual their voices, such writers fasten their attention upon the mystery of being, and especially upon that which chiefly bears witness to it, the imaginative faculty. They are the victims and the devotees of an awareness which, as in the poem just cited, recognizes its own limitations. And they are sufficiently appreciative of the miracles open to "the chief inlets of soul in this age", as Blake called the five senses, to keep from being trapped by a mysticism that denies the flesh, along with the world and the devil. The harmony that they feel, however darkly, to be governing the universe allows them to believe with him that "Eternity is in love with the productions of time."

The lyrics of Walter de la Mare are largely illustrative of this. He was early associated with the Georgians, and the landscape of his poetry is often theirs: the rural solitude at which W. H. Davies delighted to stand and stare, a significantly far Arabia, as romanticized as James Elroy Flecker's "Gates of Damascus", W. J. Turner's Ecuadorian mountains, or, more simply, "the quiet steeps of dreamland", but whether domestic or remote, affording respite from immediate pressures. Like the Georgians, de la Mare made accepted forms the vehicle of familiar feelings. There is something closer to Victorian pathos than to the panic of the Age of Anxiety in his insistence upon loss: the grief of aging, the stab of personal extinction, the sacrifice that fancy lays upon the altar of knowledge. These regrets speak the language and move in the measures of an elder day. "The flames Hell has kindled for unassoiled sin" could singe only those who walk in the limbo of the nineties. One accepts his archaisms and inversions for the sake of the quaint melody of which they are often a part. His lines on "The Titmouse" seem almost the embodiment of that small shy bird, jangling "a glass-clear wildering stave". This is de la Mare's own crystalline music. Like any sweet thing, it tends to cloy. Yet he stands apart from his fellow traditionalists, superior to them alike in sensibilities and in technique. He has the skill of an Ariel in evoking an air that is no sooner gone than it begins again. This is partly due to his tone-color, partly the effect of the irregularities that he introduces into his metres with a grace that recalls the Elizabethan lutanists.

The theme upon which he plays the most delicate variations is that of personal identity in an impersonal universe. He harps upon the miracle of selfhood, memory, imagination, the riddle of oblivion.

> Each instant is my universe;
> Which at a nod may fade again.

> At the last slumber's nod, what then?

he asks, in a lyric called "Evening". Yeats puts the same query in "What Then?", an autobiography crammed into four short stanzas. There the ironic refrain: " 'What then?' sang Plato's ghost. 'What then?' " takes on dimension from the prose simplicity of the rest of the poem. The salty power of the Irish poet's verse is not to be found in de la Mare's pages.

Those pieces in which he sought to confront the sordid ugliness of modern life are failures, though he could be sardonically sharp about situations occurring in a timeless rural setting. Rarely does he achieve the Hardyesque quality of the little lyric called "Crops", about the farmers who cut their rye, their wheat, their barley, respectively,

> And where day breaks, rousing not,
> Father Weary's cut his throat.

His irony is apt to be obvious, as in the poem about the child who shudders away from the blood-blubbered hare on the kitchen table, only to stare delightedly as a team of artillery thuds gaily by, "And then—the wonder and tumult gone—" to dream a moment, and run back to her mother with the request: "Please, may I go and see it skinned?" The realism that is gilded o'er in his more dramatic verse did, strangely enough, guide his excursions into metaphysics. His concern for truth here is recognized by his most distant juniors. Thus, the Australian balladist, John Manifold, in the same poem in which he sings the praises of the Soviet laureate, Vladimir Mayakovsky, writes admiringly of "That tough old pixy Walter de la Mare."

There is a gentle but genuine authority in the lyrics that lament the closing of the shades of the prison house upon the child's world of fantasy, the blunting of the child's senses. The poems that do not pose the riddle of the universe are likely to celebrate its various if familiar beauties: star and flowering weed, bird song and music box. The monitory note in the final stanza of the poem called "Fare Well" is hidden punningly in its title too:

> Look thy last on all things lovely,
> Every hour. Let no night
> Seal thy sense in deathly slumber
>   Till to delight
> Thou have paid thy utmost blessing . . .

Who does this will fare well, the poet appears to say. His eerie music is the less compelling only because he has not looked with equal intentness upon all things ugly.

Herein the lyrics of the "tough old pixy" differ from those of a man whose earthy whimsicality earned him the title of the pixy's Irish cousin: the leprechaun. James Stephens often wrote in a metaphysical strain about "the living ever-waking Will", and about the miracle of creation, be it that of the Demiurge or of the poverty-stricken poet. He could sing as airily as any bird of what transpires "In the bud of the morning, O!" What makes his poetry unique is the sympathy it shows for creatures less than human. Sometimes his lines leap with the gaiety of a weanling kid. But they can hunch and shiver, too, with all the

Little things that run and quail
And die in silence and despair;

Little things that fight and fail
And fall on earth and sea and air;

All trapped and frightened little things . . .

The wretchedness that pursues not only the mouse, the
linnet, and the hare, but the starved cart horse and his
loose-lipped, sly-eyed driver, was harshly present to the
poet. He knew, too, those waste places where the soul
moves like a naked man in the lion-haunted night. This
compassion for the terrified, the bruised and bereft, gov-
erns the phrasing of his stanzas, with repetitions that are
like the steady throb of a hurt, the recurrent stab of a fear.
It gives a rank strength to his versions of eighteenth-
century Irish poems. If it does not make his pantheism
plausible, it clears Stephens of the charge of a self-delud-
ing seclusiveness.

Edwin Muir was as intimately acquainted as James
Stephens with the grimness of rural, the squalor of urban,
poverty. But comparatively little of this enters into the
Scotsman's poems, many of which, like the Irishman's,
dwell upon the wonder of creation. One would expect
Muir, as Kafka's translator, to acknowledge the obduracy
of the enigma dealt with by that poet in prose, and to be
haunted by the dread that it inspires. Yet Muir's lyrics,
composed for the most part in traditional forms or in
Yeatsian trimeters and tetrameters, recurring to familiar
legendry, and frequently burdened with archaisms, affirm
a renewed exaltation. It is quieter than that of a like-
minded American, John Hall Wheelock, who asserts: "Age
is the hour for praise." Perhaps the difference is in small
part due to Wheelock's happier fortunes and also to his
having been bred and tutored by the sea, while the Scotsman's work is set in a country landscape, more placid in
spite of the mythic presences that frequent it for him.
There is an undercurrent of sadness in Muir's poems, as

he meditates on the brevity of each man's journey through time (the road is one of his recurrent symbols) and on the innumerable generations and their passing. But despite the burden of the mystery, there is staunch acceptance. One of his last lyrics, praising man's capacity for hope and charity, declares: "Strange blessings never in Paradise / Fall from these beclouded skies." Elsewhere he admits that

> public trouble and private care
> Faith and hope and love can sever
> And strip the bed and the altar bare.

Yet the same poem carries a refrain that might be the epigraph to his work:

> "I lean my cheek from eternity
> For time to slap, for time to slap.
> I gather my bones from the bottomless clay
> And lay my head in the light's lap."

Muir has been praised by Kathleen Raine for "the quality of his poetic thought" in an appreciation upholding Coleridge's view of poetry "as a mode of thought rather than a mode of expression". Her own work is the vehicle of thoughts about what Muir called "the order of the spiritual universe" and expresses a sensibility akin to his. She differs from him in important respects. She often employs a rhymed free verse that is foreign to him, and she is less ready than he to summon up figures hallowed for some, hollow for others, by reason of their ancient Greek or Scriptural associations. Her poems are wanting in the tenderness of Muir's more intimate lyrics, in his compassion for those abused and deprived. Identifying as she does with the creatures and with the forces of nature, Kathleen Raine is a woman whose pity tends to lapse into self-pity. But she holds with Muir that "the ever-recurring forms of nature mirror an eternal reality." Central to the poetry of both is a sense of that "eternal reality" as the goal of the human pilgrimage and the source of pure joy.

Kathleen Raine's poems gain in depth and subtlety because they keep returning to the actualities that embody
the mystery of the physical universe and of conscious selfhood. Not alone the stars, the mountain pool, the rock,
the fish, the bird, but the chromosome and the nucleus of
the atom are integral to her vision of the world, which she
regards as the Word màde flesh. Close as she seems to
Blake, she appears to have escaped his confusions, and she
is not at all eager to dethrone Nobodaddy. She is separated from the old visionary by a feeling of the gulf between the self and the Other. And yet she seeks to embrace it, though she is forced to ask how a house so small
can contain a company so great. There are darker poems
here than Muir's tributes to melancholy. Miss Raine acknowledges the death and dismemberment that is intrinsic to our experience, the moments when she finds "ambiguous nothingness" seemingly everywhere and everywhen.
Yet her supreme certainty is that, though the bird, like
all flesh, is dust, "the deathless winged delight" survives.

Something of the same conviction is implicit in the
poems of the octogenarian American, Abbie Huston Evans.
She shares Kathleen Raine's interest in the natural world,
its myriad-faceted immensity, its unfathomable processes.
But she is religious in her sense of the bond linking her
with nature, rather than in Miss Raine's fashion, which
mingles a mystical transcendence with orthodox Christianity. There is, too, the difference of the respective backgrounds of the two poets. Not surprisingly, Miss Evans'
imagery is occasionally reminiscent of Emily Dickinson's,
as when, for her, gentians "put blue in italics" or "long-
legged winds like boys / Race down pastures to the sea".
Unlike her New England forerunner, however, Miss Evans
tends to prose statement. Her work remains poetry because of its scope, and because of her gift for word-music
and for the evocative image, as when she hears "the birds
make whittlings of sound" at a March sunrise, which she
first sees as a "blazing bale in the thicket" and then "as
it were the great bird of day" that "nests for a moment of

time on the floor of the swamp." Like all the marvels, little and large, of sky, earth, and sea that Miss Evans beholds, this makes her meditate on vaster marvels. She is one who would "Deliver the thing itself, its sting or nothing." And to a large degree she does, partly because, contemplating with relish or joyful awe that part of the world it was granted her to know, she never claims to realize more of the universe than one can of an iceberg, which shows only a poor fraction of itself to the dazzled beholder. The title poem of her latest book is "Fact of Crystal" and several of the inclusions might own to the same name. Her wisdom seems to have grown in the dark, till it took on a crystalline quality. It helps to give her poems their hard luminosity.

III

An eye that peers below, within, and above, seeking by that inclusive look to comprehend the unseen, seldom dwells discriminatingly upon particulars. Kathleen Raine names the various natural forms and the aspects of nature so as to assign them places in a larger design, but not in a way that presents the special quality of a certain scene, a certain creature, a certain unrepeatable hour. One of the gifts of Léonie Adams, who is likewise occupied with ultimate themes, is the ability, which Miss Evans also manifests, if less clearly, to extract the essence of the temporal and show it involved with what is beyond time. No contemporary has recorded more subtly than Léonie Adams the movement of the hours as sky and earth body them forth. She is as no other the poet of light, whether it be that of the day that "comes wildly up the East," or of the moon: "The harrier of clouds, a flame half-seen," or of the "Evening Sky":

How now are we tossed about by a windy heaven,
The eye that scans it madded to discern
In a single quarter all the wild ravage of light,

Amazing light to quiver and suddenly turn
Before the stormy demon fall of night;
And yet west spaces saved celestial
With silver sprinklings of the anointed sun.
The eye goes up for certitude,
Driven hither and thither on that shifty scene
To the dome closing like impenetrable hoar,
And down from the cold zenith drops abashed;
O desolation rent by intolerable blue
Of the living heaven's core,
Nor death itself at last the heavenly whim.
For how can an eye sustain
To watch heaven slain and quickening, or do
To stretch in its little orbit and contain
Sky balancing chaos in an inconstant rim?

Just as the eye's little orbit contains "sky balancing chaos",
so within the bounds of a short lyric Léonie Adams holds
"heaven slain and quickening". More than the miracle of
physical vision is suggested here. The wild beauty and
mystery of the evening sky confronting the small, intensely
conscious spectator are so presented as to make us realize
that as the eye apprehends what is beyond the grasp of
every other sense, so the mind has the power to imagine
what the eye has never seen. Her "venerable silver-throated
horn", her legendary boat drifting up the river like a swan,
her hares and falcons, have wandered out of Yeats's country, but she writes by the light that illumined the world
of earlier, more confident religious poets.

Different as is her approach to the heavenly spectacle
from that expressed in their devotional works, she frequently recalls the tone as well as the imagery of the
author of *Centuries of Meditations* and of the poet who
could say, as simply as if he were speaking of the aurora
borealis,

I saw Eternity the other night
Like a great Ring of pure and endless light,
All calm, as it was bright . . .

Tuned to the finest vibrations of the play that goes on in the supernal theater, Miss Adams pays due tribute to the dramatist—time.

Poems having to do with the conjugal quarrel between body and soul, even more than those describing sunset and moonrise, may be expected to have an ethereal quality. The same airy atmosphere bathes those lyrics in which Miss Adams deals with one of the great commonplaces of verse, love between man and woman. Her concern is with the more subtle states of communion or division between lovers. The scene is furnished by unearthly elements, the pang quickened or assuaged because it is endured in sight of "The sky, that's heaven's seat".

Miss Adams' debt to the metaphysicals does not include the conversational idiom and the ironic wit that makes the chief of them congenial to many of her fellow-poets. Nor does she extend her purview to take in such grosser and uglier aspects of even the most private world as are present to W. B. Yeats, or to her junior, Elder Olson, much of whose work is singularly close to hers in structure and texture. But if Miss Adams does not range widely, she cuts deep, as witness a poem which anticipated Elinor Wylie's "This Corruptible", treating the same theme from a different vantage point.

BIRD AND BOSOM—APOCALYPTIC

Turning within the body, the ghostly part
Said, *When at last dissembling flesh is riven,*
A little instant when the flesh is cast,
Then thou most poor, steadfast, defeated heart,
Thou wilt stay dissolution, thou thus shriven,
And we be known at last.

This holy vision there shall be:
The desolate breast, the pinioned bird that sings;
The breast-bones' whited ivory,
The bird more fair than phoenix-wings.
And hurt, more politic to shun,

It gentles only by its sighs,
And most on the forbidden one
Drop pity and love from the bird's eyes;
And what lips profit not to speak,
Is silver chords on the bird's beak.

Alas!

At the dream's end the ghostly member said,
Before these walls are rotted, which enmesh
That bird round, is the sweet bird dead.
The swan, they say,
An earthly bird,
Dies all upon a golden breath,
But here is heard
Only the body's rattle against death.
And cried, *No way, no way!*
And beat this way and that upon the flesh.

In this lyric, Mind and Heart have nothing to say, and it
may be assumed that "the ghostly member" represents
thought and feeling, together with all the other faculties
that distinguish each soul from every other. The poem,
composed by a finer craftsman than Mrs. Wylie, is pitched
in a higher key than "This Corruptible" because of the
stress upon the moment of death. The pang of separation
is sharpened by the knowledge that the spirit fails even
before the body dies. The legendary swan song ("Some
moralist or mythological poet," wrote Yeats, "compares the
solitary soul to a swan") is choked by the death rattle.
Here is a bitter note not sounded by those older poets who
taught Léonie Adams her subtle and compelling music.

Her later poems are prefaced by a couplet of Blake's:
"The child's toys and the old man's reasons / Are the fruit
of the two seasons." Léonie Adams is exquisitely aware of
the seasons and their changes. Her titles alone are evocative: "Words for a Raker of Leaves", "Grapes Making",
"Recollection of the Wood", "Light at Equinox", "The
Summer Image", "The Font in the Forest". As she offers

the atmospheres, the hues, the brightness and shadows of each stage in the natural cycle, she intimates the meaning it can have in the life cycle of the man or woman attuned to it, and so in the building of the soul. There are deep resonances here. In certain poems there is something hermetic, too; the involutions of her thought, her increasingly compact syntax, demand the closest attention. It is rewarded by the richness and the sensitivity of her response to love and loss, to the playful child and the thoughtful old man, to snowy field and budding bough, sunlight, moonlight, and the two twilights.

Her feeling for tone color is superior to that of most of the poets considered here, as is her careful phrasing. She handles the conventional stanza with originality and delicacy, varying the length of a line or the position and character of a rhyme, often creating emphasis by unobtrusive repetition. So scrupulous is her sense of the proper placing of vowels and consonants that it seems as though, reft of every connotation, a poem of hers would remain melodious. If her performance is close to that of poets of the seventeenth century, by the same token hers are some of the finest lyrics composed in the twentieth. Two qualities align it with contemporary work. Her crammed syntax, sometimes reminiscent of Gerard Manley Hopkins, charges her words in a fashion peculiar to our time. Similarly, she resembles certain contemporaries in her pitiless, probing self-awareness. Only one of her poems, "Radio and Katydid", acknowledges the machine age. What is notable is that here, as elsewhere, searching insights into the quality of an ostensibly trivial experience illuminate it in a profoundly suggestive way.

Her work is allied to that of Louise Bogan, another lyricist whose output, though slender, is sufficient to declare the distinction of her verse and point to the tradition from which it stems. Miss Bogan's themes are the reasons of the heart that reason does not know, the eternal strangeness of time in its periods and its passage, the curious power of art. Her mood is oftenest a somber one, relieved not by gaiety but by a sardonic wit. She is primarily a lyricist. Not for nothing does the word "song" recur repeatedly in her titles, as, among others, "Juan's Song", "Chanson Un Peu Naïve", "Song for a Slight Voice", "Song for a Lyre", "Spirit's Song". It is the spirit's song that Louise Bogan sings, even when her subject is the body. The texture of her verse is strong and fine, her images, though few, are fit, her cadences well managed. Her lyrics display her gifts more happily than do her excursions into free verse, yet even an imperfect example of this shows of what durable stuff her poetry is made.

Written in unrhymed cadence, without so much as a verb to support its structure, "Baroque Comment" simply and memorably presents the conflict at the heart of things. To that which is recognizably evil: "loud sound and still chance, . . . the empty desert, the tearing beasts, . . . the lie, anger, lust, oppression and death in many forms", it opposes those things which are good: "Ornamental structures, continents apart, separated by seas", the works of art and of nature at its happiest, consecrated deeds and objects,

> Speech proud in sound; death considered
>   sacrifice;
> Mask, weapon, urn; the ordered strings;
> Fountains; foreheads under weather-bleached hair;
> The wreath, the oar, the tool,
> The prow;
> The turned eyes and the opened mouth of love.

Implicit in her work is the opposition between a savage chaos and the world that the ordering imagination, whether directed by the intellect or the heart, controls.

These poems point, more clearly than do the fastidious lyrics of Léonie Adams, to the dark gulfs, the sheer cliffs about which the mind hovers in vain. Often and gracefully as Miss Bogan bids passion farewell, it returns, as inexorable as a shadow, or as the sea's ponderous pulse, till death seems a lighter thing. Yet few poets have spoken

of death with so sure a touch. An instance is the early
lyric called "Knowledge". The speaker, tutored in the little warmth of passion and the brittleness of treasure, concludes:

> I'll lie here and learn
> How, over their ground,
> Trees make a long shadow
> And a light sound.

The lines describe Miss Bogan's poetry, which, for all its
light sound, casts a long shadow.

An almost palpable darkness hovers over many of the
lyrics of Marya Zaturenska, which move from the innocent
fairyland of a romanticized child's world toward a place
peopled by haunted men and women, and their fearful, august companions, demons, angels, sibyls, gods. Her lyricism
lacks the austere quality of Louise Bogan's. That she has
read the metaphysicals with a fond attentiveness, the epigraphs and the names of her poems bear witness, as does
the tone of those religious lyrics which have the quality of
pastels. But her dream-charged imagery, twined with roses
and with serpents, belongs to another country of the mind.
She may briefly recall to us the forgotten beauties in the
old book of nature, bid us "Remember Paradise and its
perfect climate," more often she will suggest "the Gothic
terror". Her poetry has an old-fangled quality, even as she
acknowledges the risk we run when we listen to the voice
of the past, or glances at the fact that "disaster lies in
wait / For the heart and for the state."

Even so aloof a lyricist as Elinor Wylie was aware of impending disaster. Mrs. Wylie died the year before the Depression of 1929. She was spared the implicit threats and
actual horrors of the Russian purges, the Spanish Revolution, the preludes to the second world war, and the ruin
that followed. Nevertheless, one feels that her poem
"Doomsday" was no mere literary exercise. "The end of everything approaches," she announced, and though its first
sound, to her pretty ears, was like nothing more terrible

than "the wheels of painted coaches" drumming on a turn-
pike, it soon became a "creeping thunder", loud as tumbling glaciers or the first murder. No such dread annunciation is heard in the lyrics of the rest of this little company,
with the possible exception of Miss Zaturenska, who, like
Edith Sitwell, even in the midst of World War II was able
to point to the mystic's refuge.

That refuge is not completely open to the poet, as has
been ruefully pointed out by a practitioner of the art who
belongs to a monastic order. For the mystic, the world and
the flesh are walls that separate him from God. For the
poet, they are the substance or the lenses of his vision.
Moreover, the aesthetic experience can include, and for
the greatest artists, does include, a consciousness of evil
that, unlike the religious, he cannot gloss over or extenu-
ate. The poets grouped together here are united by the
fact that their rarefied intense perception verges on the
illumination of the mystic. The keenness and subtlety of
their apprehension leads them to marvel at the motions
of the mind, and the lyrics to which they confide that
feeling remain a source of delighted wonder.

9. The Supreme Fiction

The poetry of Wallace Stevens, concerned though it is with ultimates, is distinguished by a secularism that is never solemn. His feeling for the elegant, the exotic, the barbaric, his verbal play, may occasionally invite comparison with the work of Edith Sitwell, but his distance from her is plain. Never thinking of himself as a visionary, he could brighten his most abstruse passages with a glancing wit. Stevens was not the mystic, but the metaphysician in love with this world. If he emphasizes the way in which poetry presents particulars so as to build what he calls "a transcendent analogue", it is because the poet's ordering of experience seemed to him potentially more significant than the philosopher's.

He differs from Eliot, that "upright ascetic" in Stevens' phrase, not only in this belief, nor in his delighted apprehension of being, but in the nature of his poetic capital. Reading Eliot, one is increasingly conscious of the number and variety of other writers whose work he has cleverly looted. Reading Stevens, one admires his use of an independent fortune. His learning is so unobtrusive as to be all but irrelevant. Thus, his note on the circumstances under which rationalists in square hats might take to sombreros entertains readers ignorant of Pascal's remark about "les docteurs" with their "bonnets carrés."

Like that of several other Americans, his work owes a debt to the French. Among those with whom he shows an affinity is the short-lived adventurer, Guillaume Apollinaire. Stevens was not guided by the father of surrealism into the caverns of the subconscious, nor did he hail the

phonograph and the radio for the impetus that they might
give to poetry. Yet his meditations on his art occasionally
read like a postscript to the essay on *"L'Esprit nouveau
et les poètes"* that Apollinaire published in 1918. One
might fancy Stevens having a hand in some of the Parisian's more fanciful lyrics, such as "Bestiary". A link between the two may be found in a festive epithalamium that
Apollinaire composed for his friend, André Salmon, where
he wrote that "fondés en poésies nous avons des droits sur
les paroles qui forment et défont l'Univers." Stevens happily exercised his rights in words that make and unmake
the universe. He demanded that the diction of poetry be
big and gay. His poems have the verve of one for whom the
window opens like an orange: "Le beau fruit de la
lumière."

Their luminosity is heightened by a concern with physical light which resembles that of a painter. Even when he
is not poking fun at dullards, he likes a radiant palette.
Some of his more somber themes occur in poems as alive
with color as a canvas by Matisse or Tamayo. He concludes an abstruse meditation with the simile: "Like rubies
reddened by rubies reddening". He begins another: "It was
something to see that their white was different, / Sharp
as white paint in the January sun." In the dismal thirties
he confessed that Marx had "ruined Nature for the
moment." But before that encroaching misery he was able
to picture "Nature as Pinakothek", a picture gallery furnished with motifs for incessant thought. It was natural for
him to write of "A sunny day's complete Poussiniana",
of "weather by Franz Hals", to say that an intellectual satisfaction is "as pleasant as the brush-strokes of a bough, /
An upper, particular bough, in, say, Marchand." The colors, of course, are only part of the glamor; he responds to
the special quality of a scene as the sensibility of the artist
recreates it. Among his titles that suggest paintings are
"Study of Two Pears", "Woman Looking at a Vase of Flowers", "Angel Surrounded by Paysans"—the angel being a
Venetian glass bowl and the peasants the commoner ob-

jects in a still life that Stevens admired for its assertion of
the painter's virility. Nor can one overlook "The Man with
the Blue Guitar", in which the guitar was borrowed from
one of Picasso's canvases. Blue predominates in the scenery
of Stevens' poems, associated, as here, with the adventures
of the mind.

A like painterly concern with the world, physical and
metaphysical, is found in the poems of Charles Tomlinson, a British admirer, though too individual to be an
emulator, of Stevens. "The hardness of crystals, the facets
of cut glass; but also the shifting of light, the energizing
weather which is a result of the combination of sun and
frost—these," he has said, "are the images for a certain
mental climate, components for the moral landscape of my
poetry in general." He too has paid his respects to the
French: Laforgue and Mallarmé, but his declared homage
is equally a "valediction". It is not the street, it is the
mountain (his "Cézanne at Aix" is as economical as Cézanne's watercolors, monumental and changeful like their
subject) that imposes itself on this poet, whose horizon is
nevertheless not bound by it. He asserts that "The imagination cannot lie. It bites brick;"—even beside the Med-
iterranean. Similarly, appreciating "Civilities of Lamplight", he salutes the untamed from which, through its
ordering, it is a haven: "the darkness held / But not dismissed." That phrase characterizes his poems. His description of their moral landscape implies color, and it is perhaps not surprising that this is often a hot southern or a
cool northern blue. Pleased and teased by many of the
same things, Tomlinson in his treatment of them is less
discursive than the master of the blue guitar, and his tone
is more often austere, though, naturally, the younger poet's
achievement is comparatively slight.

The songs that Stevens played on his astonishing instrument might take their key from the tropical and sub-
tropical landscapes that he liked to use as backdrops for his
reflections. His titles set the scene: "Fabliau of Florida",
"Hibiscus on the Sleeping Shores", "Some Friends from

Pascagoula", "Academic Discourse at Havana". How variously he celebrates what he calls the venereal South: "The
young emerald, evening star" above Biscayne Bay, "The
big-finned palm / And green vine angering for life", the
brilliant motions of a morning off Tehuantepec! The rosy
chocolate and gilt umbrellas in "Sea Surface Full of
Clouds" are no childhood confection but a present bright
particularity. It is characteristic that the slopping sea, the
morning gaily hueing the deck, the shifting shapes and
colors, the magical repetitions, like the changes in imagery
and in aural values, are all employed to produce an effect
of sovereign conjuration and show, at the close, "fresh
transfigurings of freshest blue." His later observations are
of things as near home as "Dutch Graves in Bucks County",
the resting-place, though the poem does not tell us so, of
his own forebears. But even when revery gaily illuminated
by metaphor gave place to overly abstract revery about the
meaning of metaphor, he could still take for his *point
d'appui* an orange-seller snoring beside his basket in the
Havana moonlight.

Stevens found in the Floridian landscape or some simpler and more remote locale a refuge from the tawdriness
of "the typical industrial suburb" that he evocatively
named Oxidia. The sound of it secretes meanings, suggesting rust, barren ugliness, and, as well, accidie, the
medieval word for the hopeless sloth that is, in more senses
than one, the deadliest of sins. But whatever any foreign
scene might offer, he had a strong attachment to his own
roots, which thrust down into eighteenth-century Pennsyl-
vania as well as into twentieth-century Connecticut. He
took pains to explain to his Italian translator, Renato Pog-
gioli, that his "ai-yi-yi" was no more Spanish than Pennsyl-
vania Dutch, as were "this-a-way" and "that-a-way", which
he related to "dieser Weg". Pleased with inventing the
"thin men of Haddam", he commented with satisfaction
on the "completely Yankee sound" of the town's name,
which is actual. Certainly no regionalist, and even more a
mental than a physical traveler, Stevens, recommending

that the poet look hard at particulars, could not ignore the indigenous and the local. Taking for his theme the heightening of "the vulgate of experience", he called an early poem "Tea at the Palaz of Hoon" and a late one "An Ordinary Evening in New Haven". As he revolved in his mind the actual and the imaginary, the visible disorder and the desirable design, the lunar melancholy and the sun's largesse, so he considered the interdependence of *beauté* and bareness in matters of language. His concern was the compounding of the literary language with the vernacular, and of the imagination with the world as given. He wanted an ivory tower with "an exceptional view of the public dump and the advertising signs".

In his most successful poems the auditory and the visual imagination play together with contagious *élan*. There was humorous self-deprecation in his calling his first book *Harmonium* and in giving the name of a humbler instrument to the title-poem of another. The music that he makes sometimes recalls that achieved on John Cage's prepared piano. It can also shake with "thunder's rattapallax", utter bird cries, produce the autumnal sound of rhododendrons rattling their gold. One could compile a poetic handbook of his aural inventions, including the names of the characters in his discourses on Dichtung und Wahrheit. The tone color of certain titles, amplifying or transforming their prose sense, further indicates his feeling for abstract sound. "Hymn from a Watermelon Pavilion" is like the hummed refrain of a spiritual. "Peter Quince at the Clavier" chimes as delicately as a harpsichord. Stevens' pleasure in sound effects is still more evident where no reference to music is intended. Such lines as

> Soon, with a noise like tambourines,
> Came her attendant Byzantines

show less virtuosity than those in which he seems to be playing a tiny clavilux, as in the opening of "Bantams in Pine-Woods":

> Chieftain Iffucan of Azcan in caftan
> Of tan with henna hackles, halt!

His playful handling of vocables is more prominent in
his early work. Yet one of his last poems, "St. Armorer's
Church from the Outside", speaks in a characteristic
phrase of "this *vif*, this dizzle-dazzle of being new". He
had a Joycean twinkle for such matters:

> We enjoy the ithy oonts and long-haired
> Plomets, as the Herr Gott
> Enjoys his comets.

The reference to the Herr Gott is typical. Stevens did not
embellish his verse with foreign literary tags after the fashion of Pound and Eliot. Simply, as they did also, like any
cultivated cosmopolite, he used whatever tongue seemed
appropriate, called the moon "the bijou of Atlas", talked of
birds singing and pecking "from sheer Gemütlichkeit", demanded "a beau language". This is not a habit that his
juniors have found acceptable, although Jean Garrigue
does speak in one of her lyrics of a design "irregular and
clair", "douce ropes", "a belle cool din", quite in Stevens'
fashion.

With the first world war the view became a grimmer
one. Stevens rejected some of the few poems that it oc-
casioned, speaking more readily of the dark days between
the wars. The pensive guitarist confronted an earth that
was no longer a mother to men, but

> An oppressor that grudges them their death,
> As it grudges the living that they live.

He was forced to consider what it meant

> To live in war, to live at war,
> To chop the sullen psaltery.

Yet in the midst of the general misery of World War II
he was able to greet the evening star and show it flashing

with a transcendent immediacy that was a renewal of life. The poem that so vividly presents it, "Martial Cadenza", does not blink what was happening in the stricken countries, but it mentions them only to ask what this star had to do "with the world it lit, / With the blank skies over England, over France / And above the German camps?" Elsewhere he inquired: "Of what value is anything to the solitary and those that live in poverty and terror, except the imagination?"

Stevens shared with a poet of more frugal means the realization that to maintain "festival . . . In an unfurnished circumstance" is to possess "an Estate perpetual / Or a reduceless Mine". He painted, as barely as would William Carlos Williams, the Northern winter:

> It is deep January. The sky is hard.
> The stalks are firmly rooted in ice.

These lines are as hard and dry as what they describe. The title of the poem suggests famine in the rural South: "No Possum, No Sop, No Taters". The poem gives that sunlessness, that destitution, hints at a larger famine, and, at the same time, summons its opposite. "Snow sparkles like eyesight fallen to earth," and the image recalls the famous line: "Brightnesse falls from the ayre," from the poem written "In Time of Pestilence". The brightness falls, but it is there. As Stevens' poem proceeds, it shows how the imaginative re-creation of reality, even at its harshest and most poverty-stricken, enriches life and makes it sparkle.

For all his elegance and opulence, he craved the antipoetic, as animals crave salt.

> The hair of my blond
> Is dazzling,
> As the spittle of cows
> Threading the wind.

The lines are from "Depression Before Spring". The subject of "The Man on the Dump" is the materia poetica, the need to throw out trashy conceits that clutter the mind

and smother the senses, and Stevens illustrates his theme
by giving the crude particulars of the dump, where the
poet sits "among mattresses of the dead, / Bottles, pots,
shoes and grass . . .", revolving his thoughts and making
unique music of them. "Bare earth is best. Bare, bare," he
insists in "Evening without Angels". His own poems seldom answer to that description. He is too much engaged
with the textures and tonalities of skyscapes, seascapes,
landscapes, as the seasons or the hours alter them, and
with his thoughts about the nuances of an intent responsiveness. Nakedness could never mean destitution to him.
Witness that remarkable early poem, "The Snow Man",
perhaps the coldest ever written, which compels the reader
to identify himself with "the listener, who listens in the
snow, / And, nothing himself, beholds / Nothing that
is not there and the nothing that is." In a later poem he
asks if there is

>   an imagination that sits enthroned
> As grim as it is benevolent, the just
> And the unjust, which in the midst of summer stops
>
> To imagine winter?

Summer is the season that he celebrates with the greatest gusto. Then, "Without evasion by a single metaphor",
he can fix the sun "in an eternal foliage / And fill the
foliage with arrested peace." Its fulness is eloquent for
him of something richer than its honeyed warmth, large
beyond its towering splendors. An instance is the lyric,
"The Woman in Sunshine":

> It is only that this warmth and movement are like
> The warmth and movement of a woman.
>
> It is not that there is any image in the air,
> Nor the beginning nor end of a form:
>
> It is empty. But a woman in threadless gold
> Burns us with brushings of her dress

And a dissociated abundance of being,
More definite for what she is—

Because she is disembodied,
Bearing the odors of the summer fields,

Confessing the taciturn and yet indifferent,
Invisibly clear, the only love.

For the most part the language is simple here, the phrasing conversational, the tone light; yet the very appearance of the formal couplets on the page helps lift the statement out of the ordinary. Only a careful look at the lines reveals their felicities. Though they evade representation of the woman, the title gives her the peculiar vividness with which a painter sometimes invests a figure in a landscape. The poem itself has warmth and movement. It offers the radiance of a summer day and the motion that paradox invites: the mind turns and turns, looking at the contraries that compose a truth. Then, too, by remarking that certain things are not present, Stevens reminds himself and us of the absent actuality. The effect of the verses about the unfortunate who, going up the stair, met a little man who wasn't there Stevens gets more happily. To say, "It is not that there is any image in the air" is to summon possible images. To speak of "a woman in threadless gold" is to make the texture of that mysterious weave almost palpable. So the larger negations as well are transformed into something realized. Most significant is the final couplet, another way of stating Stevens' conviction that poetry is "the supreme fiction" because it enhances reality. He speaks, in "Credences of Summer", of its personae playing "the characters of an inhuman author". He has less to say, however, of the author than of the play, and in such a fashion that the poet appears as a collaborator.

The epigraph from Mario Rossi that he placed before "Evening Without Angels" might almost be engraved over the portal to his own work: "The great interests of man: air and light, the joy of having a body, the voluptuousness of looking." Almost, for the voluptuary is a speculative one, given to considering the distinctions between the Order of Ideas and the Order of Nature, dancing on his knees and interrogating like a ventriloquist the famous twins: reality and appearance, the objective and the subjective. There is an echo of Rossi's remark in the twentieth section of "The Blue Guitar", in which, as the poet explained in a letter, he apostrophized the air and called it his only friend. He needed "a true belief, a true brother, friendlier than the air. The imagination (poor pale guitar) is not that. But the air, the mere *joie de vivre* may be."

He kept returning to the sufficiency of a world that was stripped of falsifying myths. Implicit in his work is the conviction stated forthrightly in "Esthétique du Mal":

> The greatest poverty is not to live
> In a physical world, . . .

The metrical stress italicizes the idea that not to live in a physical world is not to live. He is more emphatic about the destitution of those who live nowhere else. He insists that the tune to be played upon the blue guitar must be "Of things exactly as they are." This is another way of declaring what Kipling said aforetime, that Heaven is where each "Shall draw the Thing as he sees It for the God of Things as They are!" It is also a way of demanding "imaginary gardens with real toads in them". The requirement has repeatedly been attributed to Yeats by Marianne Moore, who is now widely credited with it. Stevens relished her acute particularity, but his luxurious exploring is as remote from her moralizings in verse as his secularism is from Yeats's devotion to esoteric magic. Where the Irish poet saw the world as a conflict of opposites, the American often found a necessary harmony between them. He continually reminds us of this. Further, for Stevens the most intimate, the most significant relation is that between the gift of the senses and the mind that embraces it, in any shape, with love. Repeatedly he invokes "The liaison, the blissful liaison / Between himself and his environment /

Which was, and is, chief motive, first delight" for himself. He exalts imagination, but we are not allowed to forget that the imagined depends on the real "as a man depends / On a woman, day on night. . . ." The poet is literally and figuratively nowhere without the reality that Stevens voluptuously apostrophizes: "Fat girl, terrestrial, my summer, my night," and that only the irrational distortions of feeling allow him to name, "my green, my fluent mundo."

And so he praises the personal response to the sounds of an autumn evening, the colors of a summer afternoon, the cry of a bird at dawn, the movements of wave or wind, praises the feeling which so vivifies each item of experience that it becomes an essential part of a greater whole. Stevens held that because the poet enriches the sensibility of others by his own, he makes "the paradise of meaning" what it is. To be deprived of such seeing, such hearing, is to be left with "the sky divested of its fountains." Hence poetry is the supreme fiction, without which the world would be an empty place. Like his Professor Eucalyptus, he knew that "The search / For reality is as momentous as / The search for god." Making it his intense, enduring, happy concern, he found poetry the closest approach to religion, not a melancholy substitute. Rather, it is a means of "Contriving balance to contrive a whole." The balance is between the abstracting mind and "The flesh, the bone, the dirt, the stone", between "The wind of Iceland and / The wind of Ceylon", between the fact and the poet's enlivening fictions. "We say God and the imagination are one . . . / How high that highest candle lights the dark.", he exclaimed, as he stood on the brink of Stygia, the darkest river.

He was too steadily occupied with the gross actuality of being and, more often, with its transformation, to dwell on the thought of death, though it figures in his last poems. Among the early pieces there is, of course, the salutation to "The Emperor of Ice-Cream", which he himself liked for its gaudiness. The brilliance, the musical

hullaballoo in *Harmonium* are apt to outshine and out-
sing the tone of those other poems in which he sets forth
the "Domination of Black", composes an elegiac "Sonatina
for Hans Christian", walks, not discomfited, the paths of
the cemetery. He treats the theme more resonantly years
later, considering "Two forms that move among the dead,
high sleep" and "high peace":

> Two brothers. And a third form, she that says
> Good-by in the darkness, speaking quietly there,
> To those that cannot say good-by themselves.

Even toward the close of his life the fact that he was
about to be banished from the world's table was of less
moment to him than the joy of his continued soliloquy
with "the interior paramour" in a darkness lighted by a
sense of the imagination's power. Only in "Madame la
Fleurie" does he speak of a man weighted down "with the
great weightings of the end." Black is dominant here in a
way that it could not be in the poem that speaks of the
hemlocks and the harshly crying peacocks. And earth is
"a bearded queen", is the mother, waiting to devour him
and what he saw. This dread confrontation is singular in
the corpus of Stevens' work.

It contrasts remarkably with his most widely antholo-
gized poem, "Sunday Morning", which sets forth a philosophic humanism. Death is not clothed in horror here,
but, on the contrary, is acknowledged to be "the mother
of beauty". The poem begins serenely:

> Complacencies of the peignoir, and late
> Coffee and oranges in the sunny chair,
> And the green freedom of a cockatoo
> Upon a rug mingle to dissipate
> The holy hush of ancient sacrifice.

Across a day that "is like wide water, without sound" float
the pungent odors and gay colors, like "things in some
procession of the dead,"—only to rouse the lady watching
them to ask whether she shall not find in them, and in

their like, bright or somber, "Things to be cherished like the thought of heaven?" The original version of the poem closed on a picture of men hymning the sun, "Not as a god, but as a god might be," and praising life the more boisterously for knowing the finality of death. Later, Stevens added two stanzas, and rearranged the others. Here the final image is not of men who rejoice in the sun and salute the brief dews of morning and of evening, but shows "casual flocks of pigeons" making

> Ambiguous undulations as they sink
> Downward to darkness, on extended wings.

The implication is that the poet accepts, as before, the humanist's view, exercising what has been called "the courage of the intelligence", though possibly finding it more saddening to maintain. The conclusion, and especially the last line: "Downward to darkness, on extended wings." seems symbolic of Stevens' attitude.

Like the men in this poem whose secular piety issues in praise of the light of the summer morning, the poet rejoices in the sun, making it glitter so festively and fully that sometimes it seems a surrogate for the world and its poetry. Sunlight is blessed because it makes the sea sparkle, the river flash, with miraculous liveliness, and because it covers the rock with bloom. The rock is a recurrent symbol in his pages. In "Credences of Summer" he asserts: "The rock cannot be broken. It is the truth." And he goes on to equate that truth with summer and its sustaining verities. In "The Rock", the piece that gives its title to the last section of his *Collected Poems*, it takes on a more various and a larger meaning, and is finally shown as that reality which it was his labor, as it was his joy, to discover and enhance. The rock occurs again in a late piece, the title of which describes his own loftiest work: "The Poem that Took the Place of a Mountain".

He did not aim to utter "somewhat above a mortal mouth". On the contrary, he declared:

>To say more than human things with human voice,
>That cannot be; to say human things with more
>Than human voice, that, also, cannot be;
>To speak humanly from the height or from the depth
>Of human things, that is acutest speech.

He preferred to speak from the height. To a degree this
lessens the inclusiveness of his work. The exigencies of
ordinary living play a minimal part in it. His window
might offer a clear view of the dump, but he did not
visualize it as often and as variously as he did the sea beyond it and the sky above. His melancholy is a matter of
the weather. He considers loss, pain, and grief, notably in
"Esthétique du Mal", and it is there that he offers a sovereign remedy:

>Natives of poverty, children of malheur,
>The gaiety of language is our seigneur.

In his effort to arrive at an understanding of the poetic
process and to celebrate its bestowals, he was apt to forget
the demands he had made on modern poetry: that it
"learn the speech of the place", face the men and meet
the women of the time, "think about war". His final demand was that it should "find what will suffice." Stevens'
ideal was the supreme poet described by Santayana: "He
should live in the continual presence of all experience, and
respect it; he should at the same time understand nature,
the ground of that experience; and he should also have a
delicate sense for the ideal echoes of his own passions, and
for all the colours of his possible happiness."

Stevens never ceased to speak of these matters, sometimes rather discursively. It is neither in the rich elaborations of "The Comedian as the Letter C" nor, for all its
incomparable passages, in his "Notes Toward a Supreme
Fiction" that he maintains himself at the peak of his performance. He finds what will suffice in those shorter
poems, and in parts of the long ones, where he stops talking about the nature and the possibilities of poetry, to

record, with inwardness and felicity, his liaison with his environment, whether physical or metaphysical.

The "Notes" commence with the statement that the supreme fiction must be abstract, go on to say that it must change, and conclude by remarking that it must give pleasure. Stevens' requirements are close to the old doctrine that poetry should move us, teach us, and delight us. His first injunction is not, as might be supposed, an attack upon concrete particulars. On the contrary, it is a demand for the poetry of things abstracted from our preconceptions and our myths, for the sun without the incredible trappings of Phoebus. His own poems, until he stood on the threshold of old age, are less apt to move us deeply than to instruct and, above all, to give pleasure.

Partly this is a matter of his technical skill. He could, when he chose, write a poem about dawn that is as simple and stirring as an Amerindian chant. "The Brave Man" (who is the sun) is presented with the incantatory repetitions and parallelisms, the natural wisdom, of primitive poetry. Sometimes Stevens made a notation in free verse. More often he played variations on a theme or composed long poems in formal structures, such as the "Notes". This is in three parts, each of ten sections, made up in turn of seven three-line stanzas, and has both prologue and epilogue. He preferred traditional metrics, but escaped monotony by his individual phrasing, the arrangement of his vocables, a generous vocabulary further enriched by witty neologisms. He delights us equally with the eccentric propriety of his actual flora and fauna and that of his tropes, with the originality of his aural patterns and the scope of his phantasy.

In the end, it is for this that we return to a poet who sometimes dismays by withdrawing into a private revery, sings a small song that we cannot readily follow, or lets a problem in aesthetics usurp the poem. Part of the appeal of his work is that it was composed by a man who was no less a sensualist because he was a voluptuary of the mind. That is what makes it inimitable. Others may use his cosmopolitan lingo, or show, like that enthusiastic experimenter, José Garcia Villa, a like pleasure in luxurious metaphors. A few of his juniors may even look at the world with something of his imaginative freedom, as does the eminent craftsman, Richard Wilbur, asserting:

> My eye will never know the dry disease
> Of thinking things no more than what he sees.

Wilbur's verse, like that of Stevens, is charged with responsiveness to the lustres and tones of a physical world most happily furnished, and shows him alert to less perceptible matters. His scenes are alive with light, be it the light coined by "the minting shade of the trees" that shines on clinking glasses and laughing eyes, or one of a wintrier brightness. He manipulates his stanzas with musicianly effects. His poetry engages the eye, the ear, the mind. More often and more intimately than that of Stevens, it speaks of human things. Wilbur's poems are not similarly weakened by abstract meditations, yet for all their wit and their athleticism, they lack the infectious hilarity, as also the grandeur, of Stevens' major structures. The same must be said of other contemporaries, who may remind us of Stevens insofar as their décor is often elegant and their technical skill delightfully apparent. A younger practitioner, W. S. Merwin, is distinguished for a virtuosity which shows him to have learned the lessons of diverse masters but hints at no specific indebtedness. It invites mention here because of an early piece "On the Subject of Poetry". The speaker, confessing that he does not understand the world, describes a man slouched by the millpond at the end of the garden, listening to the revolutions of a wheel that is not there. The unrhymed cadences of the poem, as well as its implications, lead one into Stevens' country. So, too, does the image of the man by the millpond, perfectly motionless, "For fear he should disturb the sound he hears / Like a pain without a cry, where he listens."

None of Stevens' juniors has celebrated being with a

like sensual precision, sparkle, and energy. None has made as much of the situation of the imaginative man in a world that excites and defies the imagination. Wallace Stevens' poetry is crippled neither by a blind faith nor a hunched atheism. In "The Idea of Order at Key West", a poem that should be compared and contrasted with Wordsworth's "Solitary Reaper", Stevens exclaims: "Oh! Blessed rage for order, . . ." It is this rage, its frustrations as well as its partial satisfactions, that is sensed in so much of his work. The stanza that precedes the exclamation bears quoting in full:

> Ramon Fernandez, tell me, if you know,
> Why, when the singing ended and we turned
> Toward the town, tell why the glassy lights,
> The lights in the fishing boats at anchor there,
> As the night descended, tilting in the air,
> Mastered the night and portioned out the sea,
> Fixing emblazoned zones and fiery poles,
> Arranging, deepening, enchanting night.

Though the poet chose the name of his companion arbitrarily, for those who have an association with it, the lines gain in depth. Ramon Fernandez, an avowed humanist, did not hesitate to italicize his *"scorn for all religion"*. At the same time he declared that "the courage of the intelligence does not constitute a refusal of the tragic, but, quite the contrary, *represents a utilization of the tragic* . . . It is the others who are the wastrels, the hedonists of anguish, the deserters of the infinite." Stevens was no deserter of the infinite. His rage for order impelled him to write poems that were big and gay, small and frivolous, as well as some that were melancholy or grave. His most powerful work suggests that the truly sufficing poem, uttered from the height or from the depth of human speech, would be to the region we inhabit what the universe might be to God.

10. A Vision of Reality

Like Blake, whose disciple he claimed to be, William Butler Yeats was a religious man who lived in an age of reason like a wealthy exile. Outraged by the principles of scientific determinism, yet unable to accept the creed of any church, he early made up a religion of his own out of the tradition that poets and painters and more systematic myth-makers had handed down from one generation to another. If, as he said in a lyric composed before the nineteenth century had entered on its last decade: "Words alone are certain good.", it was because they could summon up the superb personages of legend and folklore created out of men's longing for a superhuman nobility. The same thought dictated the admonition in a poem written a few months before his death:

> Irish poets, learn your trade,
> Sing whatever is well made . . .

His earliest lyrics, however, embroider pre-Raphaelite flowers on the hem of Irish legendry in the palest colors. They give no hint that the young poet carried a copy of Whitman in his pocket. Was this dreamer the boy who had planned to describe in his first book, like another Thoreau, the changes undergone in the course of a year by the creatures of some hole in a rock? In middle age Yeats was to elaborate a belief in the conflict at the heart of the universe, a struggle of opposites mirrored in the heart of man. Perhaps this belief had its origin in his understanding of the contraries of his own nature, the hunger for a myth that would satisfy his idealizing imagination, the hunger for the concrete that would feed his sense of actuality.

Rereading those dim old lyrics about the Rose of the World, the Rose of Peace, the Rose of Battle, written in a style learned from Pater, one recalls another of Yeats's masters, the French poet for whom, when he said "a flower", there magically arose the flower that is absent from all bouquets. For Yeats this vague Platonic pattern was perhaps more real than the flower that throughout the centuries had been associated with youth and first love and that the Christian Church took from Aphrodite to give to the Virgin. He identified the Rose of his poems of the nineties with the Intellectual Beauty celebrated by Spenser and Shelley, and yet he could not imagine it removed from human sufferings. Even as he called upon the Rose to "come near, come near, come near—", he broke off, crying that the rose-breath leave him a little space unfilled, lest he have no ear for common things.

Nearly thirty years later his father, to whose exaltation of personality above character his own work owed incalculably much, was to tell him that his poetry was at its best when the wild spirit of his imagination was wedded to concrete fact. It was "poetry in the closest and most intimate union with the positive realities and complexities of life," the old painter affirmed, that the world was waiting for. And he went on to say that while his son's comments on life showed him wonderfully alert to concrete fact, when he wrote verse he, as it were, put on his dress coat and was willing to "forget what is vulgar to a man in a dress-coat." This recalls the lyric in which Yeats consigned his coat embroidered with old mythologies to the fools who had snatched that resplendent garment, declaring that there was more enterprise in walking naked. In one of the more naked later lyrics he confessed that when he was young he

> had not given a penny for a song
> Did not the poet sing it with such airs
> That one believed he had a sword upstairs.

The time came when he had a veritable sword upstairs, the five-hundred-year-old blade wrought by a Japanese craftsman and encased in flowered silk from a lady's court dress. The sword was one of the chief ornaments of his tower room and had its proud place in his verse. But though his references to it are rich in symbolism, the tightened rhythm, the solid detail, the straightforward speech in which his allusions are couched, show that he came to acknowledge in all their ugly ambience "the positive realities and complexities of life."

When he became involved, however indirectly, in Ireland's political struggle, he adopted a looser, unrhetorical cadence and a plainer phraseology. He continued to find the source of his art in the dream of an Ireland united culturally as well as economically, and in the native scene, as also in the visions that came to him sleeping and waking. Thus he yoked together two parts of a personality which almost seem two selves: the mystical and the practical, the attentive Platonist and the active patriot, though where his predecessors had put their verse in the service of their country, Yeats's nationalism served his art. He may have sought escape into fairyland, into a medieval credulity, on the peaks of legend-haunted mountains, but his forced absorption in Irish actualities, bewildering as these often were, kept him from losing his hold on the present world. It was his final boast that all that was said or sung by himself and his two fellow artists, John Synge and Augusta Gregory, had come from contact with the soil, and that they three

> alone in modern times had brought
> Everything down to that sole test again,
> Dream of the noble and the beggar-man.

The half-crazed beggars who fill certain of his ballads with their quarreling, snoring, and singing stir the imagination as do their opposites.

Only extraordinary power could keep intact a personality that had to reconcile recluse and man of action, symbolist and realist. As one turns to the work of his maturity and his old age, one sees Yeats reversing the usual process, to draw upon springs of energy that his youth did not find. There is symbolism here too, not always easy to read. But there is a saving concreteness, a response to sensual experience, that flushes his abstractions with life. His last songs were rooted no less in lust and rage than in a passionate dedication to the things of the spirit. The amazing vigor of his mature work is a kind of fighting strength. It offers fresh proof of his conviction that the most nearly perfect poem, like the most nearly perfect life, results from the conflict of opposites.

Louis MacNeice, like other critics, finds the poet seeking his "Mask", but smiles watching him try it on. MacNeice declares most good poetry to result from "an unconscious collaboration between Jekyll and Hyde", Jekyll being the poet as he would like to be, and Hyde the self that he wishes to suppress. He observes that "in T. S. Eliot Hyde is the yogi-man, but in Yeats Hyde is Common Sense." Certainly there was an intermittent battle between the yogi-man and common sense as Yeats systematized his beliefs, and sometimes the yogi-man triumphed. Yet however absurd the details and some of the principles of his private cosmology, he exemplified his understanding of the artist's search for his opposite. Keats, he reminds us, though deprived of all the luxury of the world, "the coarse-bred son of a livery-stable keeper—" made "luxuriant song". And a greater than Keats, who had the advantage of possessing a myth that he and his fellow men could alike accept, was at odds not only with his fellow citizens and his intimates but with himself. Yeats tells the story with his new-won concreteness and all his old exultation in nobility:

> Being mocked by Guido for his lecherous life,
> Derided and deriding, driven out
> To climb that stair and eat that bitter bread,
> He found the unpersuadable justice, he found
> The most exalted lady loved by man.

Yeats delighted in his work because Dante "as poet saw all things set in order", because his intellect served his most exalted object of desire, "compelled even those things that opposed it to serve, and was content to see both good and evil."

The controlled duality, the capacity to look unflinchingly at both good and evil, that Yeats himself achieved is patent in the work of his maturity, and can be glimpsed even in so early and relatively slight a piece as the lyric called "September, 1913" with its refrain:

> Romantic Ireland's dead and gone,
> It's with O'Leary in the grave.

The poem, though less harsh and less stirring than the lyrics that grew out of the Easter rising, the civil war, and the grim years that followed, is direct enough, and nevertheless seems a denial of the very death it laments. Yeats was now aiming at a "style like speech, as simple as the simplest prose, like a cry of the heart." But that cry in all its clarity was for the revival of romantic Ireland, and for whatever can enrich men's lives by ennobling their imagination.

Yeats was unique in his generation in deliberately rejecting the scientific approach and the stoical skepticism that the age fostered. He confessed that he did not always understand the phantasies that form so large a part of his poetry, nor always interpret them the same way. If the poet is puzzled about the meaning of his poem, it is not astonishing that the reader should be at a loss. When the poet also traffics in cabalistic magic and oriental mysteries, the modern mind is bewildered and repelled. Yet the body of Yeats's verse gains almost as much as it suffers from his wayward medievalism. The mixture of Celtic legend, Hindu philosophy, and sheer superstition that makes up the religion he created for himself served him better in the end than their more honest way of thinking served other poets. The reason for this lies not in the details of his system of beliefs, to which he gave only emotional credence, his intellect, like the wicked King John of the nursery rhyme, living its life aloof. His poetry triumphs because, to employ a distinction as valuable as it is venerable, it is the product not of Fancy but of Imagination. Hardy, Robinson, Jeffers, are also imaginative rather than fanciful poets, but in Yeats the modifying, unifying energy is greater, ranges more easily between the ideal and the physical world.

One finds this powerful faculty at work in the lyrics written in the first decade of the century, when the poet turns from the cloud-pale eyelids and dream-dimmed eyes of legend to look his beloved in the face. One finds it in such a poem as "The Fisherman", in which the meaning seems to be something for a man as simple as the Connemara peasant to take in his net. In the plainest words the poet states the disappointment of his ambition to write for his own race and his desire to write instead for an ideal audience, represented by the figure of the freckled man in rough grey clothes going up to a grey hilltop "at dawn to cast his flies". One recalls Po Chü-i, who is said to have recited his verses to an old peasant woman and changed any word that she failed to understand. But if Yeats's lyric is plain, it is also dense with meaning. The vulgar crowd in the street is far from the sun-freckled man in homespun on his solitary height and from the dawn that is at once part of his experience and symbol of an inhuman power. The poet's hope and the ugly reality he found take on clearer contours side by side; the self-seeking mob and the self-sufficient fisherman are likewise defined by juxtaposition; yet, toward the close, the real and the ideal qualify one another, since the fisherman, though we can see him plain, is

> A man who does not exist,
> A man who is but a dream.

It is for this imaginary audience that the poet would write one

> Poem maybe as cold
> And passionate as the dawn.

This *is* the poem it describes. Yeats has so manipulated rhyme and cadence, so interwoven imagery and symbolism that, just as the cold mountain stream takes coloring from the warmth of the sky, and the figure of the fisherman puts on greatness against the wonder of the natural scene, the ideal is humanized and the real transfigured. The poetry of Yeats's middle period and his old age is equally "cold and passionate", a conjunction of attributes that seems incredible until one examines the work in which they exist together.

He had the capacity with which he credited Donne for being as metaphysical as he pleased, without seeming, like Shelley, unhuman and hysterical, because he could be as physical as he pleased. No poet of our time has such sensual vigor, a vigor that brought both pathos and a certain healthy coarseness into the work of his old age. This physical exuberance ("Exuberance is Beauty," said Blake) irradiates and redeems from unreality even his more abstract poems. The greater part of his work consists of lyrics on personal themes or poems in which the importance of his "system" is an obscuring if not an obscurantist element. Yet he remains a major poet. This is not only because one finds traces of his influence in the performance of juniors as diverse as Ezra Pound, Allen Tate, and W. H. Auden, nor is it because his work is an indestructible whole and deserves to be read as such. Nor is it because his imaginative power was so great. It is also because the body of his writing springs from "the root of poetry, lived or sung." His scorn of those who peep and botanize upon the flowers growing from that root is well illustrated in his lyric on "The Scholars".

Not alone in his love lyrics, indeed, less there than elsewhere, does one find the frank celebration of sex as a thing of beauty and joy. Always that acknowledgment is suggestive of something more significant than the satisfaction of personal desire. Thus in "Leda and the Swan" he imagined "the annunciation that founded Greece as made to Leda, remembering that they showed in a Spartan temple, strung up to the roof as a holy relic, an unhatched egg of hers; and that from one of her eggs came Love and from the other War." The poem presents with superb inwardness and energy the girl in the sexual embrace of the divine bird. Also, and most powerfully, it evokes the story that followed from that union, the beauty of Helen, daughter of the swan, which wrought a ten years' war, and after nearly three thousand years can still quicken the imagination, the tragedy of the house of Agamemnon, which has become a theme for those physicians and philosophers most curious about the workings of man's mind.

LEDA AND THE SWAN

A sudden blow: the great wings beating still
Above the staggering girl, her thighs caressed
By the dark webs, her nape caught in his bill,
He holds her helpless breast upon his breast.
How can those terrified vague fingers push
The feathered glory from her loosening thighs?
And how can body, laid in that white rush,
But feel the strange heart beating where it lies?

A shudder in the loins engenders there
The broken wall, the burning roof and tower
And Agamemnon dead.
                                    Being so caught up,
So mastered by the brute blood of the air,
Did she put on his knowledge with his power
Before the indifferent beak could let her drop?

The sonnet, technically impeccable, renews its power with every reading. Its economy is remarkable: one and a half curt lines,

The broken wall, the burning roof and tower
And Agamemnon dead

suffice to recall the *Iliad* and the *Oresteia*, while the line that speaks of Leda "mastered by the brute blood of the air" unites every aspect of the act of love with the sense of the supernatural that is intrinsic to the poem and that realized love summons up. Nor should it be forgotten that the poem is built upon Yeats's belief that love is in very truth controlled by "the prophetic soul / of the wide world dreaming on things to come."

II

From his youth on, Yeats was fascinated by magic and mystery. He was therefore delighted to discover, when, a few days after his marriage, his wife attempted automatic writing, that she seemed to be in the hands of what he called "unknown communicators". He came to believe that they might be "the personalities of a dream" shared by his wife, himself, "occasionally by others". The chief themes in those writings are not new. Yeats had set them forth in various poems and plays, in an essay on "Magic" written at the turn of the century, and again in two essays completed in 1916, a year prior to the event. There he had classified men as belonging either to the type that achieves perfection from conflict with self or the type that achieves it from conflict with circumstance. He had also given an account of what he believed concerning the state of the soul before birth and after death, convictions largely colored by Hindu philosophy. His two types of men are, of course, those distinguished by psychologists as introvert and extravert, and much that he had to say about memory and dream, when trying to formulate what his wife had written down together with what he believed about the universe and the psyche, could be substantiated in the findings of the psychopathologists. Thus, Freud observed the help furnished by many myths and fairy tales for the understanding of certain typical dreams, and Jung postulated a Collective Unconscious as the source of legend and private dream life. Yeats finally systematized the automatic writings in the light of his wide reading and his acute knowledge of men, a light unhappily clouded by benighted theories. In his introduction to A *Vision*, the

involved and abstract book in which he set these matters
forth, he acknowledged that his arbitrary symbolism might
repel the readers he most valued, but concluded on a note
of diffident stubbornness such as might have been used by
the proponent of a new scientific hypothesis.

The systematization seems to have been unsought by
the mysterious "communicators". When Yeats offered to
spend the rest of his life interpreting what they bade his
wife write, the answer was "No; we have come to give you
metaphors for poetry." This they did, whether one conceive
of them as disembodied spirits or the poet's preconscious
thoughts. Some of these metaphors had long been a familiar element in his poetry. They now became a dominant
feature of it, and indeed, the very substance of certain
poems. Three figures, in addition to the fictive Robartes
and Aherne, recur in his work: hunchback, fool, and saint.
These represent respectively the intellectual, "jealous of
those who can still feel"; the thoughtless, aimless, natural
man, jealous of those who can act with intelligent effectiveness; and he who, unconcerned with thought or deed, rejoices to submit himself to "the total life of humanity".
His saint resembles the poet.

For a fuller understanding of these poems, it should be
recalled that Yeats saw history as the birth, maturing and
death of one civilization after another, symbolized by the
phases of the moon, each cycle of two thousand years reversing its predecessor. This cycle, sometimes called the
Great Wheel, was part of the astrologers' Magnus Annus
or Platonic Year, the 26,000-year period that it takes for
the planets to resume their positions. The Great Wheel
has twenty-eight spokes for the moon's phases, representing the phases of history. The peaks of the Christian era
Yeats placed in sixth-century Byzantium and the time of
the Italian renaissance. He used the same celestial symbol
for psychological types, the moon governing the life of the
inward-looking artist, the sun, which does not figure in his
diagrams, that of the man of action. Whether or not the
soul would become the world's servant, it chose whatever
task was most difficult.

Byzantium represented to Yeats the supreme example of the Unity of Being which the subjective man might achieve. Hence he could write of Justinian's city, before the Emperor opened St. Sophia and closed Plato's Academy, as a place where "maybe never before or since in recorded history, religious, aesthetic and practical life were one." The poem "Sailing to Byzantium" recalls this thought and is thick with allusions to his "system", such as the perne, or spool, and the gyre, emblems of his belief that "Each age unwinds the thread another age had wound." Fire seems to have symbolized Anima Mundi, the source of men's dreams and desires. Contrasting natural delight with the ecstasy known only to the mind, the poem evokes the marvels of his sacred city. There the world as Will can be at rest, lost in the music of the world as Idea.

SAILING TO BYZANTIUM

I

That is no country for old men. The young
In one another's arms, birds in the trees
—Those dying generations—at their song,
The salmon-falls, the mackerel-crowded seas,
Fish, flesh, or fowl, commend all summer long
Whatever is begotten, born, and dies.
Caught in that sensual music all neglect
Monuments of unageing intellect.

II

An aged man is but a paltry thing,
A tattered coat upon a stick, unless
Soul clap its hands and sing, and louder sing
For every tatter in its mortal dress,
Nor is there singing school but studying
Monuments of its own magnificence;
And therefore I have sailed the seas and come
To the holy city of Byzantium.

III

O sages standing in God's holy fire
As in the gold mosaic of a wall,
Come from the holy fire, perne in a gyre,
And be the singing-masters of my soul.
Consume my heart away; sick with desire
And fastened to a dying animal
It knows not what it is; and gather me
Into the artifice of eternity.

IV

Once out of nature I shall never take
My bodily form from any natural thing,
But such a form as Grecian goldsmiths make
Of hammered gold and gold enamelling
To keep a drowsy Emperor awake;
Or set upon a golden bough to sing
To lords and ladies of Byzantium
Of what is past, or passing, or to come.

This lyric is simpler but less resonant than the later
poem called "Byzantium", which magnificently concentrates the images that are the vehicle of Yeats's metaphysics, and half fulfills his hope of some day waking those
"dry astrological bones into breathing life". The more
accessible poem originally appeared in the volume entitled
The Tower, itself a symbol of the meditative life that
Yeats, the gregarious man pursuing his opposite, so often
celebrated. The title poem in that book is frankly autobiographical, concrete, harsh, and witty. Although it concludes with the poet's quiet decision to make his soul, it
begins with a bitter comment on old age, which he compares to the torment inflicted on a dog, "A sort of battered
kettle at the heel." In the very midst of the poem he cries
out:

O may the moon and sunlight seem
One inextricable beam,

a cry that can only mean the desire not to divorce intellectual from physical delight. Insist as he might upon the indestructible beauty of Byzantium, the city of heavenly contemplation, he kept returning to the question asked in one of his verse plays:

> Why must these holy, haughty feet descend
> From emblematic niches?

and to the answer: "For desecration and the lover's night." In one of his last poems, recalling the superb images that haunt the poems of his youth, he acknowledged that he must now abandon them, to

> lie down where all the ladders start
> In the foul rag-and-bone shop of the heart.

One may perhaps define the poet's undertaking as the conduct of a traffic between the two worlds that Santayana calls the realm of matter and the realm of essence. The vast claims made for poetry by the romantics of the nineteenth century and later by certain critics and practitioners of our own day, alike imply some such conception. I. A. Richards, declaring that it "is a perfectly possible means of overcoming chaos," and John Crowe Ransom affirming that it "intends to recover the denser and more refractory original world which we know loosely through our perceptions and memories," recall us to the relation that obtains between the two realms. For, as even the romantics sometimes appear to have understood, and as the materialists never forget, it is through the existence of the physical self, the locus of our sensations and emotions and thoughts, and the substantial inhabitant of the realm of matter, that the mind creates and recognizes a disembodied value. And it is not seldom the sensual world that startles and kindles the imagination. The poet, sensitive to the values in the ideal universe and to the solicitations of the physical world, speaks of both. Since he deals with words, which are things in themselves, to be seen on the page and sounded with the voice, and also signs of absent things, he is the more aware of his dual allegiance. Yeats achieved a fusion of energy and vision and technical competence that allowed him to ply unhampered between the planes. His poems suggest the proposal to straddle two universes.

Newton once compared himself to "a boy playing on the seashore", diverting himself by finding "a prettier shell than ordinary, whilst the great ocean of truth lay all undiscovered" before him. Yeats hated everything that Newton represented to him, and took pleasure in repudiating the man of science even when admitting a similar interest in the factual world. In a late lyric entitled "At Algeciras—A Meditation upon Death", having spoken of the "heron-billed white cattle-birds" that crossed the Straits to rest "in the rich midnight" of the trees, he recalls the evenings of his boyhood, when he would carry back from another tide line, not those of Newton's metaphor, but actual shells from the shore at Rosses. The final stanza of this short poem, with its very real boy, nevertheless implies Newton's metaphor, and the great undiscovered ocean of truth that vainly summons a man about to die.

> Greater glory in the sun,
> An evening chill upon the air,
> Bid imagination run
> Much on the Great Questioner;
> What He can question, what if questioned I
> Can with a fitting confidence reply.

The opening lines here carry more than their surface meaning, since the sun is Yeats's image for the active life, while the "evening chill" suggests the coming of a larger night than is about to descend upon the Algeciras sands. The poem implies that age and the approaching shades had revived Yeats's boyish interest in the natural world. This is emphasized by the tone of the first stanza, which, while creating the atmosphere of grave beauty that bathes the scene, does not shrink from a naturalistic view of the herons feeding on the parasites that feed upon the Moroccan flocks and herds.

Such an attitude is in keeping with the evocative "Dialogue Between Self and Soul", which again sets forth the antinomy between involvement in the active life of the world and withdrawal into the tower of the mind. The Self has the final word. Yeats says as plainly as possible that he would be "content to live it all again": to endure once more not only the miseries of growing up but the struggles and ultimate disappointments of manhood, the assaults of enemies both within and without. It is in this poem that he first makes reference to the crime of birth, claiming,

> as by a soldier's right
> A charter to commit the crime once more.

One wonders whether he had found Schopenhauer quoting Calderon to the effect that man's greatest crime is to have been born. The allusion recurs in the cycle of lyrics called "A Woman Young and Old", the woman asserting that

> where the crime's committed
> The crime can be forgot.

Repeatedly in the later poems Yeats affirms the fundamental character of the natural order. His tower, "powerful emblem" of the contemplative mind and its objects, the imagination and its creatures, was, he admits, built by a bloody arrogance. Earlier in his sad reflections upon the decay of ancestral houses, he had written:

> Some violent bitter man, some powerful man,
> Called architect and artist in, that they,
> Bitter and violent men, might rear in stone
> The sweetness that all longed for night and day,
> The gentleness none there had ever known . . .

He goes on to ask whether the gardens where the peacock sets delicate feet upon old terraces, whether the lawns and graveled paths where the slippered philosopher may be at ease and children find "a delight for every sense", in subduing violence, take away greatness too.

The central idea in this poem is intrinsic to his poetry and finds expression in another dialogue entitled "Ego Dominus Tuus". Here he repeats some of the things that his father was saying to him in letters from America, as where the old man observed of another Irish writer: "If he cannot do his best without having some one to assail or cajole or persuade then he is of the prose writers—and only incidentally a poet. The true poet is all the time a visionary and whether with friends or not, as much alone as a man on his death bed." Yeats paraphrased his father's observation thus:

> The rhetorician would deceive his neighbors,
> The sentimentalist himself; while art
> Is but a vision of reality.

Yet his mythology, as he once said, was rooted in the earth. What else is the meaning of the justly famous poem, "Among School Children", which presents labor as blossoming or dancing where the body is not bruised to pleasure the soul, and concludes on the question:

> O chestnut tree, great-rooted blossomer,
> Are you the leaf, the blossom, or the bole?
> O body swayed to music, O brightening glance,
> How can we know the dancer from the dance?

His realism and the continuity of his thought are nowhere more strongly evidenced than in this poem. Witness the stanza recalling Plato and the solider Aristotle (who, as the poet says, was privileged to play the whip on the bottom of the great Alexander), and "world-famous, golden-thighed Pythagoras", fingering

> upon a fiddle-stick or strings
> What a star sang or careless Muses heard:
> Old clothes upon old sticks to scare a bird.

The juxtaposition of the fiddle-stick and the frame of the old scarecrow is a further hint at the interdependence of body and spirit that is the theme of the poem. The lines anticipate those in "Sailing to Byzantium" about the aged man who is but "A tattered coat upon a stick". They also suggest the opening of that poem with its live birds in live trees, and the final stanza, with its repudiation of this "sensual music" for a golden bird upon a golden bough. Surely this is the "bird born out of the fire" which inhabits the eternal city of the imagination.

These poems bear comparison with an early lyric, called "The Three Hermits", composed when Yeats was reforming his style. The first old hermit laments that he keeps falling asleep when he should be praying. The second, while rummaging for a flea in the most naturalistic fashion, argues that after death souls are given what they have earned, and those who have loved God once "are not changed to anything" except maybe

> "To a poet or a King
> Or a witty lovely lady."
> While he rummaged rags and hair,
> Caught and cracked his fleᵃ, the third
> Sang unnoticed like a bird.

The third old hermit, "Giddy with his hundredth year," is nearest to the only holiness that the poet himself recognized, that of the myth-making mind. But this sacred abstraction is free of the deforming character of Christian asceticism. If soul must clap its hands and sing the louder "For every tatter in its mortal dress", of what should it sing but of human history and the unchristened heart? That the scarecrow of old age can scare away the golden bird, or deprive it of its proper theme, is suggested in more than one poem, notably in the refrain to one of his last lyrics. This affirms the deepening joy, the full heart, of an old man, but concludes by declaring

> he has need of all that strength
> Because of the increasing Night
> That opens her mystery and fright.
> Fifteen apparitions have I seen;
> *The worst a coat upon a coat-hanger.*

Is the skeleton a fitter emblem of mortality?

Those last lyrics testify to Yeats's sustained vitality. Some are full of violence, a few recall the lyrics of his youth but show greater delicacy as well as greater power. Among their beauties is the use of the refrain, which is one of his most paraded bequests to his juniors. It gives many of these poems something of the incantatory quality of the litany or the pathos and force of old balladry. Occasionally he went directly to that source, as in the lyric built upon what may be the earliest English dance song in existence: "Ichaun of Irelaunde". The original manuscript is a fragment that probably came from the notebook of a strolling minstrel. Sometimes Yeats found his refrain closer at hand. Those to the "Three Marching Songs" are more effective in the original version. Yeats wrote them for the Blueshirts, under the mistaken impression that this fascistic group might have an aim such as his own: to unite the members of a cultivated aristocracy, who are above fear, the poor who are beneath it, and the artists, whom, as he wrote, God has made reckless. Discovering that the Blueshirts were far from sharing his lofty dream of nationhood, he rewrote the songs so that no party might sing them.

His sympathies with the fascists were fed by his fear of democratic rule. In spite of his devotion to the memory of the Socialist poet, William Morris, he held that reform could not affect the cyclical process of history, and hated reformers, hated the

> levelling, rancorous, rational sort of mind
> That never looked out of the eye of a saint
> Or out of **drunkard's eye.**

He had nothing but contempt for the vulgar optimism that is "the opium of the suburbs" and he saw democracy as the triumph of mediocrity, of the prudent and the small-minded, who could not share his joy in all that is extravagant, reckless, and noble. His political views were influenced by his conviction that conflict is the source of all that is creative. He had, too, the timid man's admiration of violence. Yet what he sought was "Traditional sanctity and loveliness".

It was in a strain of nostalgia for a noble tradition that he was writing almost a decade after the March on Rome and two years before Hitler took power. This was the dream that had inspired his prayer for his daughter, when he asked that she be allowed to rejoice in the fruits of custom and ceremony. Looking at the portraits of his friends in the Municipal Gallery in his old age, he cried out

> in despair that time may bring
> Approved patterns of women or of men
> But not that selfsame excellence again.

More bitterly he reflected on the theme in another late lyric:

I came on a great house in the middle of the night,
Its open lighted doorway and its windows all alight,
And all my friends were there and made me welcome too;
But I woke in an old ruin that the winds howled
      through;
And when I pay attention I must out and walk
Among the dogs and horses that understand my talk.
O what of that, O what of that,
What is there left to say?

No poet has made more than he of that bereaved question. Nor has any so wonderfully mingled the sweet and the harsh. Chemists analyzing an artificial rose scent found it to be made up, in a 1–8 range, as follows: fragrance 6, acidity 5, burnt smell 2, caprylic (resembling that of a goat or a wet dog) 3, a complexity the peculiarity of which seems illustrated in those last lyrics. If they do not exhibit the superb control of Yeats's greatest work, there is no feebleness, and they fully sustain the tenor of his poetry.

III

Led astray though he sometimes was by wishful dreaming, he was also, happily or unhappily, capable of dreaming true. Philosophers, from the authors of the early Vedas to Vico and Spengler, watching the revolutions of history, have thought of civilizations as flowering and withering like a plant or a planet. Many of Yeats's finest lyrics are founded on an analogous belief. One of the most notable, "The Second Coming", is dominated by the idea, elaborated in A *Vision*, that we are nearing the end of an era. In that curious prose amalgam of astrology and metaphysics, history and psychology, he described the representative man of the period as a person of great strength and initiative, whose object was "to so arrange prohibitions and habits that men may be naturally good, as they are naturally black, white or yellow." The period closing our era he envisaged as one of "a subconscious exhaustion of the moral life, whether in belief or in conduct . . ." He foresaw the supremacy of mechanical force, the artificial unity of Europe: "only dry or drying sticks can be tied into a bundle," and a conflict between secular and religious thought, which would usher in an age the antithesis of our own. However confused his prophecies and however dubious their sources, much that he said by the way is obviously applicable to events that Yeats, dying before the fall of Barcelona, did not live to witness, and to figures that had not achieved their full historical importance when he was writing.

"The Second Coming" is more remarkable than A *Vision*, not simply because it has the depth, coherence, and intensity of poetry, but because it is strikingly prophetic.

It was written in 1921 or a little earlier, when the foulness
and energy of fascism were only beginning to be apparent, years before the emergence of Stalinism and before it
seemed credible that Nagasaki and Hiroshima would present an adequate picture of hell, or the heirs of Bach and
Schiller exhibit in all its horror the exhaustion of the moral
life. Indeed, it is only post facto that the poem can be
read as prophetic, and the prophecy that we read into it
is more precise than what Yeats intended. Yet he himself,
writing to a friend in 1936 of his sense of reality deepening with age and his increasing "horror at the cruelty of
governments", spoke of "The Second Coming" as having
"foretold what is happening."

The opening lines suggest at once the spinning of our
era to its close and the dominance of the falcon, that
"gloomy bird of prey" which images the narrow logic of the
intellect, and which the spirit can no longer master. The
second stanza is more obscure, loaded as it is with the
poet's private symbols. Spiritus Mundi is the Great Mind
and the Great Memory that Yeats saw as the source of the
instinctive life of all creatures, and of man's imaginings as
well. He identified Nature with the Sphinx, whose riddle
was solved by the Greeks and from whom the process of
Western civilization was an escape. His vision of the new
dispensation that is to follow the impending breakdown
is of a monster like a huge sphinx at Gizeh, with the body
of a lion and the head of a man, its "gaze blank and pitiless as the sun," whose light symbolized unimaginative
activity.

The Second Coming

Turning and turning in the widening gyre
The falcon cannot hear the falconer;
Things fall apart; the centre cannot hold;
Mere anarchy is loosed upon the world,
The blood-dimmed tide is loosed, and everywhere

The ceremony of innocence is drowned;
The best lack all conviction, while the worst
Are full of passionate intensity.

Surely some revelation is at hand;
Surely the Second Coming is at hand.
The Second Coming! Hardly are those words out
When a vast image out of *Spiritus Mundi*
Troubles my sight: somewhere in sands of the desert
A shape with lion body and the head of a man,
A gaze blank and pitiless as the sun,
Is moving its slow thighs, while all about it
Reel shadows of the indignant desert birds.
The darkness drops again; but now I know
That twenty centuries of stony sleep
Were vexed to nightmare by a rocking cradle,
And what rough beast, its hour come round at last,
Slouches towards Bethlehem to be born?

This poem is perhaps more terrifying than when it was first
written, later events having given it a clarity and emphasis
that originally it could not have.

Yeats's mind appears to have been as hospitable to visions as that of less imaginative men to dreams of the
night. He was, however, no mystic. If he lacked Kierkegaard's suspicion of mystical ecstasy (the Danish theolo-
gian wondered why one who had no respect for reality in
general should not be equally distrustful of that particular
moment when he was affected by the higher experience),
Yeats was not guilty of self-deceit. He knew that he was
himself, as he said of Blake, "a man crying out for a mythology and trying to make one because he could not find
one to his hand." He had, however, a clearer insight into
his own part in the fabrication. Inclined though he was to
erect his "system" into an unimpugnable philosophy, he
was also able to regard it with something of the candid
humility with which the scientists whom he so little understood regard their abstract structures. And though his
"system" has the absurdities of a home-made myth, it has

also the validity of myth. It is an imaginative ordering of experience that makes it possible "to hold in a single thought reality and justice." Yeats indicated much the same objective in a letter written six months before he died: "To me the supreme aim is an act of faith and reason to make one rejoice in the midst of tragedy." He added, with his usual corrective realism: "An impossible aim . . ."

The tragedy he envisaged was not a personal one, though every victory must seem vain to a man on his death bed. Lamenting the meanness that he saw crawling over all that he held precious, he was yet eager to go on living, eager to get at the truth regarding ideas that continued to vex him, feeling that he was just beginning to understand how to write. His attitude toward the Great Questioner was far from submission. Though his epitaph carries an injunction to

> Cast a cold eye
> On life, on death,

Yeats wrote no quietist verse. A man to whom consciousness is so precious, and for whom the creative imagination is a constant theme, must look upon death as an enemy, though not, like old age, a horror. The fact that Yeats could speak of the psyche as betrayed into life did not alter the reluctance to depart that inspired some of his finest poems. In 1926 he was asking:

> What shall I do with this absurdity—
> O heart, O troubled heart—this caricature,
> Decrepit age that has been tied to me
> As to a dog's tail?

A year later he was crying out:

> Consume my heart away; sick with desire
> And fastened to a dying animal
> It knows not what it is; and gather me
> Into the artifice of eternity.

He was to follow this poem with the "Dialogue Between
Self and Soul", in which he reviewed the distresses of the
better part of a lifetime, only to declare that he cast out
remorse, nay, was shaken from head to foot by the sweetness that flowed into his breast. In one of his last lyrics
he prayed to seem "a foolish, passionate man". His passion
was for a discipline which, in the phrase he took from
Hugo, would transform the mob into a people, and his
folly was to credit a vision that allowed him to unite in-
compatibles. It was a folly not very different from the
shrewdness of the scientist who employs contradictory theories to explain different aspects of one phenomenon.

As a young man he had thought that if he could be sin-
cere and keep his language natural, he would, should good
luck or bad luck make his life interesting, be a great poet.
Every requirement was fulfilled. Though he dramatized
himself continually, as his theory of the Mask implies, he
kept his integrity. His poetic idiom was increasingly natural. He liked to repeat a phrase he attributed to Aristotle: "to think like a wise man but to express oneself
like the common people." As for luck, though later he
would have given it another name, his life was made interesting by both the good and the bad. He knew private
griefs and public disasters. Yet he also knew intimacy with
some of the finest minds of three generations, friendships
unparalleled, the praise of his peers as well as the highest
public honors for his work, joy in a son and a daughter and
in powerful poems of his own making at an age when many
fail. Sincerity, plain speech, and an interesting life combined to make him a poet, but it was a further element
that lifted him head and shoulders above his fellows.
Throbbing with physical energy, his poems open the gates
to the heavenly city of the imagination; pervaded by the
fact of death, they affirm life at its peak of excellence.
Though he worked hard at his verse, there is no sense of
strain in his lyrics—instead, an apparent ease that allows
humor as well as the sharp play of wit. He was able to sustain the tension between contradictory forms of experi-

ence. Further, he maintained his intensity while keeping
his language natural. That is how he was able to achieve
within the limits of his work the supreme aim that he
called impossible: here is poetry to make one rejoice in
the midst of tragedy.

IV

As a young patriot, Yeats dreamed of a Castle of Heroes
that was to be built on an island in the middle of a lake to
which Irishmen worn with labors for their country might
go for refreshment of body and spirit. The Castle was never
more than a dream that he shared with Maud Gonne. Nor
did he fulfill his hope of giving long life to the figures of
native legendry. They moved out of his own poems, to be
replaced by the splendid but quite human figures of his
friends, and seem not to have found refuge elsewhere. His
effect on Irish culture was powerful, but not at all what he
had imagined it would be. He was the moving spirit of the
Irish literary revival. To that revival, with its glorification
of heroic virtue, have been attributed the revolutionary
events of Easter Week, 1916. Whatever his share of responsibility for the course of Irish history, his responsibility
for the break with Ireland's literary past is clear. His influence seems least obvious in the work of his own countrymen, though it is apparent here and there in the turn
of a phrase, the gleam of an image, and chiefly in the removal of rhetoric and other impurities.

Outside of Ireland, modern poetry is a hall of mirrors
for Yeatsian images, a cave of echoes for Yeatsian cadences.
His two great bequests, according to Auden, were the release of regular stanzaic verse from iambic monotony and
the transformation of the type of poem composed for a
special occasion into a serious piece of both personal and
public interest. Auden has himself used these legacies well.
He might have noted a third, that of the refrain, which
Yeats took over from the pre-Raphaelites and handled
with a fresh effectiveness that is the envy and despair of

his juniors. Practitioners of the art of verse who differ in
more particulars than the degree of their craftsmanship
have tried this incantatory device with widely varying success. What all of them conjured up was the ghost of Yeats
that strode off, laughing.

The only Irish writer of Yeats's stature was likewise
deeply concerned with words and music, with myth, and
with what it meant to be an Irishman, yet he did not mini-
mize the extent of the gulf between himself and his older
confrère.

> But I must not accounted be
> One of that mumming company—
> With him who hies him to appease
> His giddy dames' frivolities
> While they console him when he whinges
> With gold-embroidered Celtic fringes . . .

sang James Joyce, in his sly parody on Yeats's "Address to
Ireland in the Coming Times". Here with humorous contempt and invincible pride Joyce reasserted his dissociation
from his dreamy compatriots. But the young Dubliner was
one of them insofar as he exiled himself "to forge in the
smithy of his soul", as the famous phrase goes, "the un-
created conscience of his race", devoting his own dreams
and those of his heroes to the land he left.

Joyce composed a handful of lyrics as slight and plangent as the poems of Verlaine, lyrics in which one seems to
catch the accompaniment of struck or plucked strings, the
low voice of the clarinet. The rest of his poetry, aside from
a couple of satires, takes the ostensible form of prose.
Ulysses, though it might be considered a modern epic, is
too remote from verse to be treated here. *Finnegans
Wake* is too close to poetry to be omitted from consideration. Yet since its scope approximates that of such poems
as *The Aeneid, The Divine Comedy,* and *Faust,* in a general survey such as this it can receive only an appreciative
glance.

Finnegans Wake might be described as the self-portrait

of a mind during a single night, when the unconscious
plays with history in the form of dreams. But it is no ordinary night; indeed, it is more like a night of Brahma in
Hindu mythology, lasting for thousands of years. And the
mind is no ordinary mind. The dreamer, H. C. Earwicker,
may be identified with Howth Castle and environs, but
more than the historic memories associated with Dublin
are in that giant's head. His nocturnal phantasy is furnished with the myths of the race of man. Ostensibly a
plain Dublin tavern keeper, dreaming of the hod carrier
Finnegan's fall from his ladder and the corpse's revival by
spilled whisky, he goes through countless metamorphoses,
as does Finnegan, who comes again as Finn Mac Cool, the
heroic warrior of ancient Ireland, among other avatars.
Earwicker's wife, Anna Livia Plurabelle, is likewise a protean creature. She is the female principle, and she is also
the river Liffey (Amnis Livia is its Latin name), the
beauty made of many beauties as the river is formed by
the confluence of many streams. She may also represent the
flow of history, the river of Time itself. As the two washerwomen—themselves semi-mythological figures—recount her
story to the paddling of dirty clothes on the stones, they
bring the names of a hundred rivers into their talk. One of
them cannot hear well, for the cotton in her ears: "It's that
irrawaddyng I've stoke in my aars. It all but husheth the
lethest zswound," she says. This is not a mere rendering
into lisping brogue of the words: "It's this here wadding
I've stuck in my ears. It all but hushes the least sound."
It is the evocation of Lethe, the stream of forgetfulness,
in a sentence that recalls the Aar River in Switzerland, the
Stoke in England, the Irrawaddy in Indo-China, the Zuyder
Zee, and possibly the strait between Zealand and Sweden
called The Sound, as well as the "Z" shape of winding rivers everywhere.

The book is thick with the ambiguity of dream. The
reader has no chance to orient himself before he is
snatched from the scene, since time, too, is telescoped: the
past impinges on the present, and the sense of dream life

is enhanced by the way in which the objects presented merge into one another and emerge from one another with the illogical rapidity of associated images. These objects have the immaterial quality of things in dreams. But —and in this respect they take on the character of conscious thought—one hears them more readily than one sees them.

Joyce's ear was keener than his eye. His short poems are snatches of pure if archaic lyricism, as even the opening lines prove:

> Rain on Rahoon falls softly, softly falling,

> Bid adieu, adieu, adieu,
> Bid adieu to girlish days,

> Wind whines, and whines the shingle,
> The crazy pierstakes groan;
> A senile sea numbers each single
> Slimesilvered stone.

The music of *Finnegans Wake* is more suggestive, as in the famous passage at the close of the chapter on Anna Livia, where the gossip of the washerwomen in the falling dusk (are they two Dublin chars or are they Life and Death?) eventually flows into the voice of the river muttering to itself over the stones under the elm tree:

> Can't hear the waters of. The chittering waters of. Flittering bats, fieldmice bawk talk. Ho! Are you not going ahome? What Thom Malone? Can't hear with bawk of bats, all thim liffeying waters of. Ho, talk save us! My foos won't moos. I feel as old as yonder elm. A tale told of Shaun or Shem? All Livia's daughtersons. Dark hawks hear us. Night! Night! My ho head halls. I feel as heavy as yonder stone. Tell me of John or Shaun? Who were Shem and Shaun the living sons or daughters of? Night now! Tell me, tell me, tell me, elm! Telmetale of stem or stone.

> Beside the rivering waters of, hitherandthither-
> ing waters of. Night!

"Telmetale of stem or stone"—the tale is not only of the
elm that may be identified with the Tree of Life and the
stone that symbolizes death, but of change and permanence in their several aspects, of time (represented by
Shem and "the Gracehoper") and space (represented by
Shaun and the Ondt: the ontal world that is the ant in
the fable); as it is also the tale of Mercy and Justice.

Every word is packed with meanings that are illuminated by the work as a whole. It is most eloquent where it
is most lyrical. Curiously, the few pages of the *Wake* that
have been rendered into basic English retain something of
the fine rhythms of the original. Here truly are "Melodiosi-
ties in pure-fusion by the score". But the author does not
always obey the injunction of Shem the Penman, that
son of Anna Livia who strangely resembles James Joyce:
"Here keen again and begin again to make soundsense
and sensesound kin again." Since the book is written in an
English which is full of Irishisms and which draws wittily
upon half a dozen other languages to build its telescoped
meanings, the results are often baffling.

Among the paraphrases of nursery rhymes in which it
abounds is one that suggests a metaphorical description of
Joyce's method: "Hadn't he seven dames to wive him?
And every dame had her seven crutches. And every crutch
had its seven hues. And every hue had a differing cry."
One may think of the soul as a lame beggar—Yeats represents it thus in a play—and conceive of it as companioned
by the body, which goes on crutches, too, but those
crutches: sensations, perceptions, emotions, stump along
in Joyce's dream in multiple colors and with multiple
cries. As always, a larger interpretation is possible. Here,
as later in the *Wake*, the reference may be to that ancient
cosmology which compared the world we know to the
colors into which sunlight is fractured. Alone for the seer
is everything radiant with the unbroken light of reality.

The ordinary man submits, with Faust: "Am farbigen Abglanz haben wir das Leben": it is only in colored reflections that he knows life. Joyce expresses a like thought in a more naturalistic if more obscure fashion.

The book is not less cryptic because, behind the proliferating puns and under the wavering appearances of a dream, the *Wake* hides an elaborate intellectual structure, of which the architects seem to have been Vico, Carl Jung, and Einstein. It is the story of a fall and a resurrection, beginning with a thunderclap, its opening paragraph the conclusion of its unfinished final sentence. Thus it recalls the Italian philosopher's theory of the cyclical nature of history, and on every page gives emphasis to his view of the significance of language as an instrument of power, verging upon magic. Moreover, the *Wake* is a tissue of myths and legends, recurrently taking us back to the childhood of the race when, as Vico and later thinkers would have it, man had not yet lost the mythopoetic faculty. In theme and substance the book is largely illustrative of what Jung calls the Collective Unconscious, source of primitive myth, childish fantasy, and adult dream life. It is not alone in the "Fable of the Gracehoper and the Ondt" that Joycean hieroglyph combines with riotously resonant language to juggle the concepts of time and space with a bow and a wink in the direction of Einstein. In fact, the *Wake* is the nearest literary approach to a fourth-dimensional picture of the world that we have.

It opens with a view: "riverrun past Eve and Adam's, from swerve of shore to bend of bay, brings us by a commodius vicus of recirculation back to Howth Castle and Environs." But it is less pictorial than musical. One might conceive it as a huge chorale, that begins with a multilingual word for thunder, and closes, inconclusively (the end of the final sentence on page 628 must be looked for on page 1), with the murmur of Anna Livia as the failing stream of her life and her memories flow into the cold mad salt all-fathering Ocean.

The whole monstrous piece of Rabelaisian Jabberwocky,

with its sonorities and lilting rhythms, occasionally punctuated by rhyme or moving in metre, its polylingual puns and its intricate symbolism, reaches down to memories and anticipations astir like subsea life in the waters of sleep. Like *Ulysses*, it may be read as a commentary on the workings of the average sensual mind as perceived by a man of genius. It is a heroic attempt, and, in view of the demands it puts upon even the patient and the learned reader, possibly a vain one, to master material that has never been handled so intimately in literature. By the very multitude of its meanings, the book tends to make meaning meaningless, and to discourage all but the most passionate pilgrims through its "meandertale". Yet this medley of languages, songs, jokes, fables, and myths, with all its obscurities, offers sights not to be otherwise obtained of the fall and the rise of more than physical systems.

However one looks at it, the *Wake* bulks enormous. There is something Homeric about its size and scope. But unlike any of the works with which it is roughly comparable, that of Rabelais excepted, it is hugely entertaining. The chorus of the song from which it takes its name is its proper epigraph:

> Whack. Huroo. Take your partners.
> On the floor your ankles shake.
> Isn't it the truth I've told you,
> Lots of fun at Finnegan's wake?

Difficult though it is to decipher, irritating as are its sometimes adolescent excursions, much of it may be aptly described in one of Joyce's neologisms as a "grand funferall". Its aggressively lively humor ranges from the witty transpositions of familiar quotations to a wealth of gay bawdry. Not alone its Dublin locale and the nationality of the dreamer and the Finnegan of his dream, but a ribald heartiness unquenched by its mournful understanding, gives the work its peculiarly Irish quality.

The poetry of perhaps no other people is as rich in wit and humor. One finds this strain in the savage songs of the seventeenth-century poet, David O'Bruadair, who was as apt at cursing a stingy barmaid as Antoine Raftery was at praising his bright-haired love. The "unending, rebellious bawl" that O'Bruadair lets out, his translator avers, "would be the most desolating utterance ever made by man if it was not also the most gleeful." The poet who turned that bawl from Irish into English verse was James Stephens. The sparkling vein that runs through Irish poetry crops out in the strict lyrics of Jonathan Swift, who also turned his hand to rendering poems from the Gaelic. More than two centuries later it brightens the firm stanzas of Oliver St. John Gogarty (the disgruntled Buck Mulligan of *Ulysses*), manfully praising women, wine, and song. W. R. Rodgers has written verse that fairly throbs with the "bells and hullabaloos" of joy that ring in the tingling flesh of spring, the sluice of autumn winds. Where there is not blitheness, there is often a wry wit, as in the lyrics of Thomas McGreevy, the mystery-burdened poems of Denis Devlin, or the work of Louis MacNeice, which is more eloquent of his own time than of his native place.

Gaiety, blithe or bitter, is a sign of vigor, and for all the keening in Irish poetry, a saving energy is a permanent element in it, from what we know of its brave pagan beginnings, through the anonymous balladry of the Shan Van Vogh ("the old woman" who is Ireland), down to the verse of her youngest sons and daughters. John Synge's sense of drama invigorated the least of his few lyrics. Joseph Campbell and F. R. Higgins are among those who have shown strength and tenderness in reporting the homely details of Irish life in town and countryside, and more especially that of the plowers and tinkers who are also met with in Padraic Colum's early verse. Like many of their fellows, including such a comparative newcomer as Patrick Kavanagh, these are they whose hearts make free

> To praise the very men
> To whom a rhyme
> That took a morning's work
> Were waste of time.

There is nothing labored, however, in the body of Irish verse, which, down to the lyrics of so recent a poet as Valentin Iremonger, is unashamedly tuneful.

At its best, the poetry of Yeats's younger compatriots is both inward and racy in its realism. Nor should it be forgotten that it was he who, in spite of all his hungry mysticism, brought back a sense of the actual to Irish verse. The "main symbols" that he confided to an intimate: "Sun and Moon (in all phases), Tower, Mask, Tree (Tree with Mask hanging on the trunk). Well," He handled freely. However formidable the Tree of Knowledge of Good and Evil, what blazed largest for him was the Tree of Life. One fancies him gleefully quoting Mephistopheles' remark that all theory is grey, "Und grün des Lebens goldner Baum." If his thinking was sometimes abstruse, he detested the abstract intellect, preferring to keep in his definition of water "a little duckweed and a few fish," having "never met that poor naked creature H_2O." He strengthened his juniors everywhere by acknowledging the Vision of Evil, by his unique union of exaltation and candor, by the sustained energy and intensity of his utterance. Yeats shared von Hofmannsthal's appreciation of the discipline of ceremony. The Irish master might also sometimes have been moved to echo the Austrian when he asked how poetry could bring from the abyss "anything more than human feelings, when poetry itself is nothing more than the language of men!" The more one reads the work of these poets and their kin, men and women alike, the more readily one responds to that wild voice crying down the centuries:

> I am of Ireland
> And the holy land
> Of Ireland:

Good sir, Pray I thee
Of sainted charity,
Come and dance with me
    In Ireland.

11. The Forgèd Feature

A man's **Ancestors** are thrust upon him, but he chooses his ancestors. They belong to the past that is acknowledged, with which there is felt to be a living connection. Thus, young men who came of age as poets in the thirties claimed kinship with Gerard Manley Hopkins. They recognized in this Jesuit priest of the age of Victoria an earnestness and an energy like their own, and an attractive independence. Indeed, it was only in 1918, when the poetic revival promised a hospitable attitude toward Hopkins' experiments, that his friend Robert Bridges first brought out a volume of his poems, drawing them forth from the obscurity that had shrouded them during the lifetime of the poet and for three decades after his early death. Since then the greater part of his writings, in both prose and verse, has been published; his work has been the object of scholarly scrutiny; and W. H. Auden, though declaring him to be a minor poet, unable to influence later men in any fruitful way, has produced a long poem written in the tumbling rhythm to which Hopkins had recalled attention.

Certainly, if indirectly, Hopkins' exploration of the neglected vein of Anglo-Saxon verse has affected contemporary work. He was himself incited to it by an extraordinary sensitiveness to sound, which led him to write with less care for the eye than for the ear. Ironically enough, though he worked in almost complete isolation, becoming, and that posthumously, a poet's poet, all the while he was trying to bring poetry out of the closet, away from the printed page, to where it would rejoice the listener like the sea and the skylark that one of his lyrics praises. As he told the future laureate, he wrote to be heard, and he assured this doubting Thomas that if one took breath and read his verse as he wished to be read, with the ears, it became all right. His experiments with prosody illustrate that delight in individuality which is so strong an element in his work. This governed, too, his disgust with archaisms and poetic diction, his interest in dialects and in the wording as well as the rhythms of common speech, his pleasure in puns and slang. Here, as elsewhere, he singled out for attention whatever was "counter, original, spare, strange;". It was his intense appreciation of selfhood that made him recognize in the "great scoundrel", Walt Whitman, a mind nearer his own than that of any living man. His passion for individuality was at the root of his admiration for Duns Scotus, the medieval schoolman who saw in the "thisness" of each thing the principle of its being, and whose theory of knowledge, with its emphasis on the individual, the concrete, the substantial, was basic to the empirical foundations of secular science.

Hopkins' performance was nothing if not singular—like his corn shooks at harvest "barbarous in beauty". But by a not uncommon paradox, the difficulties that he made for his readers were largely the result of a desire for full communication. It was to this end that he exploited the less usual resources of language and of rhythmic pattern.

For centuries the charm of English verse has been the contrast between an exact metrical scheme and natural speech rhythms. Differences in the individual poets' vocabularies are to be reckoned with, and rhythm will alter according to whether a poem demands homely Anglo-Saxon words or an abstract latinity. But with all its freedoms, a traditional feature of English verse is the number of syllables in a line. The fundamental principle of Hopkins' prosody is reliance on the number of stresses in a line. This was no new departure. It looked back to Anglo-Saxon usage, with its two stresses to each half line, emphasized by alliteration, as in *Piers Plowman*:

In a sómer séson   Whan sóft was the sónne

It was the foundation of nursery rhymes and old anonymous balladry:

> For Wetharryngton my hearte was wo,
>   That ever he slayne shulde be;
> For when both his leggis wear hewyne in to,
>   Yet he knyled and fought on hys kne.

Skelton, the tutor of the prince who became Henry VIII,
had used this rhythm merrily; Milton had employed it to
some extent for the grave choruses of *Samson Agonistes*;
Jonathan Swift had played with it. It was revived by a
master of verse in "Christabel". Hopkins adduced Milton's
example in trying to make his method clear, and though
he discussed it learnedly in detail, summed it up simply
enough by stating that it consisted "in scanning by accents
or stresses alone, without any account of the number of
syllables . . . one stress makes one foot." As in music you
may have one whole note to a measure, followed by a flock
of sixteenths, so here you may have a foot of from one to
five syllables, any seeming inequality being compensated
for by the timing and the employment of rests. The stanza
is scanned as a whole. One is reminded of Lawrence's
comparison of metre to "a bird with broad wings flying
and lapsing through the air." He confessed that he could
not tell what pattern he saw in any poetry "save one complete thing", yet that he seemed to find the same number of long lingering notes in each line. Hopkins' emotion
often dictated rapid, hurdling, soaring, suddenly dropping
measures, and it was perhaps this rush of feeling that
made him so frequently choose the image of a bird "flying
and lapsing through the air".

He called this prosody "sprung rhythm" because it has
an abruptness not common in verse in which the speech
cadence is counterpointed against the underlying metre.
In writing to Coventry Patmore about that poet's essay on
metrical law, Hopkins showed inadvertently that his culti-

vation of sprung rhythm was bound up as much with his feeling for individuality as with his musicianship. Stress was, he remarked, so elementary an idea that it scarcely allowed of definition; "still this may be said of it, that it is the making a thing more, or making it more markedly, what it already is; it is the bringing out its nature." If his poetry was written to be heard, it was because the sound pattern seemed to him its essential, individualizing element. In some notes on rhetoric he defined poetry as "speech framed to be heard for its own sake and interest even over and above its interest of meaning." The phrase "for its own sake" may have been an unintended pun, since the word "sake" held special significance for him. He once explained it as "the being a thing has outside of itself, as a voice by its echo, a face by its reflection, a body by its shadow, a man by his name, fame, memory, *and also* that in the thing by virtue of which especially it has this being abroad, and that is something distinctive, marked, specifically or individually speaking, as for a voice and echo clearness; for a reflected image light, brightness; for a shadow-casting body bulk; for a man genius, great achievements, amiability, and so on." If he cared for the particular element that distinguished a thing to the ear of the listener or the eye of the beholder, he cared even more for the inner nature that so revealed itself. Thus he dwelt upon what he called the "inscape" of speech. This word of his own coining was never precisely defined, though he compared it to the principle of melody in music, of design in painting. He seems to have meant by it the intrinsic quality of an object, a scene, a personality, which set it apart from all others and by which its selfhood was most clearly manifested.

How deeply his idea of verse as "inscape of spoken sound" influenced his handling of it is self-evident in his work. There is also the testimony of his letters and papers. He kept repeating that poetry, as a living art, was made to be performed, by which he meant to be recited, though not in a rhetorical fashion. His sonnet, "Spelt from Sybil's

Leaves", was intended to be almost sung, and he spoke of it as "most carefully timed in *tempo rubato*." Now tempo rubato, literally "stolen time", is irregular: for the sake of greater expressiveness one note is retarded and another quickened without altering the time of each measure as a whole. The sonnet in question is probably the longest, as to lines, ever written.

> Earnest, earthless, equal, attuneable, ′ vaulty,
> voluminous, . . stupendous
>
> Evening strains to be time's vast, ′ womb-of-all,
> home-of-all, hearse-of-all night.

Thus it opens, impressively, in spite of a plethora of adjectives. Carefully marked throughout, it can yet be read otherwise than according to the author's indications, as a piece of music to be interpreted variously by different performers. The significant fact is that Hopkins regarded the sonnet as something in the nature of a musical composition. It is noteworthy that whereas the writing of a poem was a slow process for him, he could make tunes under almost any circumstances.

When he turned Jesuit he burned everything he had written, resolved to make verses again only at the instance of his superiors. This incentive came when the steamer *Deutschland* was wrecked, carrying down with her five nuns who had been exiled from Germany in its *Kulturkampf* against the Church. Hopkins broke a ten years' silence with that remarkable piece of devotional rhetoric, "The Wreck of *The Deutschland*". Unquestionably the subject moved him deeply, but there is evidence that, had a different theme offered itself, he would have welcomed the opportunity afforded him to experiment with a new rhythm that had long been haunting his ear. His innovations were too startling to be acceptable and the poem was not published in his lifetime. There were disturbing elements in it other than the use of stress prosody, if indirectly related to it. Since the stanza was regarded as an

individual entity, it allowed for linked rhymes, such as
are common enough in humorous verse but unlooked-for
in religious poetry. An instance is the chiming of "leeward"
with

> drew her
> Dead.

Then, too, the sound pattern of his poem, with its emphatic alliteration, echoes, and parallelisms, encouraged
his unorthodox handling of syntax. Sometimes there is a
natural deviation from usage, as in the abruptness of

> They fought with God's cold—
> And they could not and fell to the deck
> (Crushed them) or water (and drowned them) or rolled
> With the sea-romp over the wreck.

More often the musical effects as well as the desire for
immediacy and precision compel the language into altogether unfamiliar ways, as where the empurpled skies become the "dappled-with-damson west", or a word is
wrenched apart: "Brim, in a flash, full!" or an article is
dislodged by the force of the rhythm or the meaning or
both and floats free, almost symbolically, as in the description of the sailor pitched to his death:

> They could tell him for hours, dandled the to and
> fro
> Through the cobbled foam-fleece, what could he
> do
> With the burl of the fountains of air, buck and the
> flood of the wave?

Hopkins had made some study of "cynghanedd", the elaborate consonantal and vowel harmonies of the Welsh
bards, which he imitated in such a phrase as "Warm-laid
grave in a womb-life grey". The Welsh also gave him authority for the dropping of articles and pronouns and the
use of compound words. Theirs was a poetry composed to
be chanted. It was natural that it should influence a man

who wrote to be heard. It was natural, too, that the difficulties that this poem presented to those accustomed to reading verse with the eye balked even so conscious a craftsman as Bridges.

Yet with all its apparent roughnesses, "The Wreck of *The Deutschland*" was, as its author declared, "very highly wrought". It was in its considered elaboration that Hopkins' prosody differed from those rugged and prosaic rhythms of Whitman's that seemed to him so like his own. The American, standing above the Platte Canyon in Colorado, had hailed the genius loci of that wild "inscape" of nature as his familiar:

I know thee, savage spirit—we have communed together,
Mine too such wild arrays, for reasons of their own;
Was't charged against my chants they had forgotten
      art? . . .

But thou that revelest here—spirit that form'd this scene,
They have remembered thee.

Hopkins, for all his professed love of the wilderness, was not happy with a savage art. He weighed and timed his stanzas with the attention of a musician. He planned a scholarly work on Greek metre that would take him into a more general study of metrics, and was to be based on such exact sciences as physics and mathematics. He spoke of this projected book as "full of new words, without which there can be no new science".

What he said of scientific discovery he might with greater validity have said of poetry, that it cannot be new without new words. His own abounds in them. Even so simple a lyric as that on the Inversnaid waterfall gives us the roaring foaming torrent in more than its rollicking rhythm and its bouncing echoes. He is not content to remind us of the Hebrides by the introduction of Scottish words. He must invent his own language. Thus he speaks of the small stream's "rollrock highroad", of a "windpuff-bonnet of fawn-froth", of "the beadbonny ash that sits

over the burn", which suggests at once the tree comely
with red berries and the bubble-beaded stream beneath.
He relished racy folk speech, insisted that a poet's style
should be of his age. Poetry, he knew, should not be an
obsolete tongue but, as he put it, "the current language
heightened".

He did not always succeed in avoiding the poetical, in
the derogatory sense of the term. The lushness or prissi-
ness of some of his lyrics are a reminder of the less congenial aspects of the Victorian sensibility. Nevertheless,
his work compares favorably with the performance of his
friend, Bridges, who appears to have learned more from
Hopkins than he could teach.

Bridges' major work, *The Testament of Beauty*, is a po-
eticized version of the ideas set forth with greater propriety and persuasiveness in Santayana's essay on "Ultimate Religion". The vague title of the poem is a clue to
one of its weaknesses. In his praise of the laureate, Robert
Hillyer hints inadvertently at the lack in his poetry:

> Take Robert Bridges, laureate forever,
> Calm as the sea and flowing as a river,
> Who knew his source and end, but also knew
> The homely country he meandered through.

Hopkins was not one to "meander". He worked for intensive compression. His indirections always aimed at being functional. He was of his own age, and an acute critic
of his contemporaries. His best work shows that none of
them delved deeper than he for the richest possible vein of
English speech. The strangeness of his vocabulary is in
part the result of his plumbing for those effective folk
words that have been lost to the literary language. In the
sonnet that he wrote on Purcell's music, a subtle comparison with the motion and markings of a sea bird's plumage
calls out the North-country word "wuthering" with its double suggestion of the sound and the rush of wind. Sometimes he prefers the dialect word to its literary equivalent,
as where he speaks of a "tucked" rather than a "plucked"

string, a "ruck" rather than a "rut". In the Inversnaid lyric the "windpuff-bonnet of fawn-froth" is said to turn and twindle over the black pool. The verb "twindle" means "to twin" and is happily expressive of the way the bubbles of yellowish foam are paired as they race. Perhaps Hopkins chose it partly for its aural associations with "twinkle" and "dwindle". His words are apt to be packed with an almost Joycean richness of reference and call up ideas only tangential to the expressed sense.

There is such ambiguity in the lyric, "Spring and Fall". Spring is represented by the young child, Margaret, grieving over the falling leaves. The sense of the poem is that when she is old enough to accept autumn as part of the natural scheme of things, she will realize the true springs of grief, those intimate changes and losses involving very selfhood that the passage of time means. The idea of the Fall, in the religious sense of the word: "the blight man was born for" is also implicit here.

> It is the blight man was born for,
> It is Margaret you mourn for.

The tone is one of a sad and tender wisdom, that without sharpening to the ironical manages to avoid the pitfall of the sentimental. Familiarity with the poem deepens appreciation of it, and offers the covert reminder that the basic meaning of the word "leaf" is to strip, break, or injure, so that the foliage becomes an emblem of loss. To ask the child:

> Leaves, like the things of man, you
> With your fresh thoughts care for, can you?

is to ask whether, young as she is and inexperienced in such sad matters, she can glimpse the significance of leave-taking.

II

One is inclined to read multiple meanings into Hopkins' phrases, knowing from his own exposition of his poems how much he could make of a word. In "Spring and Fall" the language is unusually simple, except for the line, "Though worlds of wanwood leafmeal lie;" and even there the neologisms need no glossing. Where the poet does make difficulties for the reader with words of his own coinage it is in the effort to render fully and immediately the "thisness" of a thing. For Hopkins it was at once a duty and a delight to praise the Creator in praising His creation. To do so was to point to the inscapes of flowers, skies, birds, faces, to those individualizing traits which were so hard to define, partly because of their uniqueness, partly because he saw them as intrinsic to the inexpressible pattern in the mind of God. Like his unknown contemporary, Emily Dickinson, with whom he had so much in common, he wrenched the language to convey a unique insight. Undeceived as to the obscurities that he found it impossible to avoid, he held that poems dark at first reading should explode. His own lyrics are seldom to be understood as rapidly as they are read, and though they may explode, are apt to yield more light the more carefully they are scrutinized. One of his own favorites among his lyrics is a case in point.

"The Windhover" is a poem to be read with the ears, surely, but there are far deeper implications than this windy music reveals at first hearing. The bird, kin to the American sparrow-hawk, is the falcon or kestrel. While in the title Hopkins chose to give it the local name descriptive of its hovering flight, in the body of the poem he refers to it as a "Falcon", capitalizing the word to emphasize the symbolism, and he makes the most of the courtly associations of falconry. Dedicated "To Christ our Lord", the sonnet expresses the poet's central convictions.

The Windhover

I caught this morning morning's minion, king-
   dom of daylight's dauphin, dapple-dawn-drawn Fal-
   con, in his riding
   Of the rolling level underneath him steady air, and
   striding
High there, how he rung upon the rein of a wimpling wing
In his ecstasy! then off, off forth on swing,
   As a skate's heel sweeps smooth on a bow-bend: the
   hurl and gliding
   Rebuffed the big wind. My heart in hiding
Stirred for a bird,—the achieve of, the mastery of the
   thing!

Brute beauty and valour and act, oh, air, pride, plume, here
   Buckle! AND the fire that breaks from thee then, a billion
   billion
Times told lovelier, more dangerous, O my chevalier!

   No wonder of it: shéer plód makes plough down
   sillion
Shine, and blue-bleak embers, ah my dear,
   Fall, gall themselves, and gash gold-vermilion.

The octave presents the bird poised in mid-air, balancing, as it were, on the wind. The opening lines seem to
say of the falcon what Hopkins wrote in his journal of the
waters at Holywell, a place of pilgrimage on the Welsh
coast: the bird, like the wellspring, is "the sensible thing
so naturally and gracefully uttering the spiritual reason
of its being." The falcon does this too insofar as, in functioning thus perfectly, it exhibits its selfhood and reflects
the Creator. At the same time the bird, as a "sensible
thing", flying and rejoicing in its flight, the natural and
graceful creature seen and rejoiced in, is placed in opposition to all that is above and beyond brute nature. Do not
air and wind, breath and spirit, go back to the same root
meanings? In a later lyric Hopkins compares the Blessed

Virgin to the air we breathe, a comparison that one recalls
in reading the lines of "The Windhover" where the
"world-mothering" element seems something finer than
the atmosphere of earth.

The words "valour" and "pride", though not opposed,
are distinguishable. "Valour" suggests physical prowess;
"pride" carries connotations of majesty and moral propriety. The noble purport of "air, pride, plume" is enhanced
by the exclamation "O my chevalier!" The word "chevalier" held special significance for a poet who thought of
himself as a soldier of Christ.

Brute beauty and valour and act, oh, air, pride, plume, here
    Buckle!

This literally clinches the image. If the obvious meaning
of "buckle" is to fasten on armor, the word has other
meanings: to crumple or bend to the breaking point, and
also to grapple or engage, as, in Scottish or North of England dialect, it means "to marry". The falcon in its glorious motion is an instance of "brute beauty" everywhere,
and here an image of spiritual beauty. In the person of
Christ the two "buckle", being one. But since the world
reflects God imperfectly, the falcon as a type of physical
excellence is no match for the type of moral grandeur, and
so in the contrary sense, the two, contending, "buckle".
"AND" it is precisely when the image of "brute beauty"
suggested by the bird weds, surrenders, "buckles", to the
image of divine grace, that a fire breaks from him, far
more resplendent than the gleam of his wings in the morning light. An infinitely "more dangerous" fire, too, the
perils of the spiritual life being greater than those that a
soldier of fortune has to face.

The language is so highly charged that it asks for analysis, though the poem is so closely integrated that to dis-
member it is almost to destroy it. The octave of this sonnet cannot be appreciated without understanding of the
sestet, although it is wholly different in tone and seem-

ingly different in intention. The vision of the bird re-
buffing the big wind in its mastery of the elements all
but contradicts what the sestet says about the way in
which the self, serving, *is* served by submission, obedience,
sacrifice. Yet there are oblique hints of the conclusion at
the start.

> how he rung upon the rein of a wimpling wing
> In his ecstasy!

The "wimpling wing" may suggest a nun's wimple. The
word "rung" is more allusive. It recalls the term in falconry
for the bird's upward spiraling, but the word used by
Hopkins means rather to linger in the ear or the memory,
or to sound, like a bell, perhaps rung in triumph, perhaps
a summons to prayer; "rung" is also used in speaking of a
coin thrown on a counter to test it, and so suggests the
testing of a man's soul, an idea borne out by the sestet.

The windhover is called "morning's minion": the favorite child, the servant of the morning, as Christ is the son
and servant of God. He is "daylight's dauphin" as Christ
is, accepting the sun as the image of the Trinity, its substance representing God: the power that begets life,
its light, Christ: the intelligence that sustains life, its
warmth, the Holy Ghost: the love that beautifies and vivifies creation. However one interprets it, more can be read
into the poem than its surface meaning.

> My heart in hiding
> Stirred for a bird, . . .

What stirs the heart is not only "the achieve of, the mastery of the thing!": it is dread of the powers against which
the bird contends. The watcher knows the brevity of any
physical triumph. But one may also read into the lines a
sense of this brutish world's threat to the understanding,
and the thought that spiritual triumph may come of pain
and loss.

A passage in a sermon by Hopkins the priest illumines
more fully the work of Hopkins the poet. Speaking of

Christ, he said: "Poor was his station, laborious his life, bitter his ending: through poverty, through labour, through crucifixion his majesty of nature more shines." This might be taken as the text of "The Windhover", or as a prose gloss upon it. Elsewhere, commenting on the *Spiritual Exercises* of Ignatius Loyola, he declared that "a man with a dungfork in his hand, a woman with a slop-pail" gives God glory, if the worker means to do so. The plow pushed steadily against the dark resistance of the soil it furrows, the crumbling ember among the ashes in consenting to extinction, just as the coarse work dutifully done, like the majesty of Christ's nature in the dark circumstances of his life and death, "more shines". The image of the sacrificed God seems implied in the last line of the poem, where the falling embers are said to "gall themselves, and gash gold-vermilion". Although "gall" is used as a verb and not as a noun, it carries shadowy suggestions of the bitter cup accepted in the Garden of Gethsemane, the cup of wine mixed with vinegar offered to the man on Golgotha. It is typical of Hopkins that he should turn a transitive verb into an intransitive one to suit his purposes. This use of "gash" underscores the passive nature of Christ's victimage. Not the least remarkable thing about the poem is the way in which it powerfully presents the bird exulting in sheer physical delight and makes that sensuous body function as an argument for the imitation of Christ, whose greatest degradation, the cross, was also, for the devout believer, his highest flight. Further, if one accepts the medieval symbolism of the Trinity, is it not true that the understanding is crucified anew in every age? Socrates, drinking the hemlock, Boethius, dying in prison, Huss, burning at the stake, Lauro de Bosis dropping from his lone plane, the numberless anonymous members of the Resistance, they too are exalted by their crucifixions. The savior returns, the race of man is redeemed, the sacrifice is renewed.

To examine separately either the substance or the pattern of this poem is of course to do it violence. Yet tech-

nically alone it repays study. Like so many of Hopkins'
pieces, it takes extraordinary liberties with the form of
which it remains a striking example. Here is that strict
thing, a sonnet, written in sprung rhythm, with many "out-
riders" or extra, slack syllables not noted in scanning. The
first line ends on a hyphen, so that perforce the reader
rushes on without even so much of a pause as the line
arrangement of poetry seems to require. Moreover, the
predominant foot, rare in any English poem, is a stressed
syllable followed by three unstressed ones, as in the compound word: "dapple-dawn-drawn". The rhyme scheme
too is unusual. It is apparently Petrarchan, with the conventional abbaabba octave and the sestet also on two
rhymes: cdcdcd. But the octave is so arranged that the
"b" rhyme is a weak version of the "a" rhyme: "king"
chimes with "riding". The whole sonnet is a rich tissue
of elaborate harmonies. This is evident even in the first
two lines, broken off from the exuberant sentence that
they introduce:

I caught this morning morning's minion, king-
    dom of daylight's dauphin, dapple-dawn-drawn Fal-
    con, in his riding . . .

The alliterative consonants are obvious enough, but the
ear catches before the mind recognizes the vowel echoes
in "caught" "dawn" "drawn", as well as in the initial syllables of "dauphin" and "falcon", latent in the first syllable of the repeated "morning". There are blunted echoes
of the four "ings", and the short "i" of "minion" "dauphin"
"in" recurs, ending with the same consonant, once voice-
less, once voiced, in "this" and "his". So much, and it is
only a fraction of what might be said, for the aural pattern
of the poem.

    The form demands notice not merely because of its in-
trinsic interest but also because it illustrates the give-and-
take between freedom and discipline that is part of what
this sonnet, in the common phrase, is "about". Of the less
than eighty complete poems that compose Hopkins' lit-

erary legacy, thirty are sonnets, but it is characteristic of
his dual allegiance that of these thirty, more than half
were written with the large liberties that he took with
"The Windhover". The first lines of a few should suffice to
show this: "Look at the stars! look, look up at the skies!"
or "Summer ends now; now, barbarous in beauty, the
stooks arise" or "Yes. Why do we all, seeing of a soldier,
bless him? bless", or again, the longest sonnet ever made:
"Spelt From Sibyl's Leaves".

"The Windhover" is also worthy of notice because, like
the greater part of his work, it exemplifies the practice of
the seventeenth-century men whose imagery implied their
belief in an ordered universe with a recognized hierarchy
of values, and who saw in the simplest and coarsest things
instances of general truths. So Hopkins can compare the
flaming out of God's grandeur to the "shining from shook
foil", its gathering greatness to the ooze of oil, and therewith compose a sonnet that paraphrases one of his comments on the *Spiritual Exercises*. His "curtal" sonnet, the
simplest he wrote, "Pied Beauty", is a variation on this
theme.

A writer of metaphysical poetry, in every sense of the
term, Hopkins seems nevertheless not to have been influenced by the members of that company. He was
strongly attracted by the work of George Herbert, but his
admirations sent him scurrying in the opposite direction
from their object. His verse is closer to that of Thomas
Traherne, who held that God may be known only through
His creation; that the creation becomes most significant
when perceived by the mind of man; that man's duty is
continually to re-create the world in his mind and so give
it back to the Creator. To love the world He made as He
loves it is to arrive here and now "to the estate of immortality". Traherne's poetry is less remarkable than his
prose writings, which, with the radiant delight of a child
and the power of the Psalmist, declare the glory of God.
Those glowing metaphors express the same sense of "the
world's splendour and wonder" that one finds repeatedly

in the poetry of Hopkins. Indeed, such was the poet-priest's relish of what appealed to ear and eye, nostril, palate, and sensitive fingertips, that even a lyric on the beauty of poverty and the excellence of renunciation has a Keatsian tinge. Sensuousness crops up in the most unexpected places, as in the unlikely image spilled out in the midst of "The Wreck of *The Deutschland*":

> How a lush-kept plush-capped sloe
> Will, mouthed to flesh-burst,
Gush!—flush the man, the being, with it, sour or sweet,
Brim, in a flash, full!

Undeniably, however delicately, sensual delight suffuses the lyric comparing the Virgin to the air, and all naturally crowds the poems in praise of spring bloom and harvest weather, lark song and rushing stream, aspen or ash boughs taboring the skies. Yet with the fewest exceptions these poems illustrate the idea that mortal beauty serves to point to "God's better beauty, grace". Bridges deprecated the fact that Hopkins' poems displayed "the naked encounter between sensualism and asceticism". The encounter is rather between the sensuous pantheist and the athlete of God, and it is as naked as the meeting of wrestlers or lovers.

This conflict may have impelled those "terrible" sonnets that have the force of a cry torn out of the dark night of the soul. They were composed when Hopkins had become to himself, in St. Augustine's words, "a land of hardness and much sweat". The nature of his despair was such as only a religious can know, yet, like so much religious poetry, declares the most human of passions. "Wert thou my enemy, O thou my friend," he asks,

> How wouldst thou worse, I wonder, than thou dost
> Defeat, thwart me?

One of the most striking of these sonnets begins: "Not, I'll not, carrion comfort, Despair, not feast on thee;". It con-

cludes on a note of appalled recognition of what he had
won from the struggle during

> That night, that year
> Of now done darkness I wretch lay wrestling with
> (my God!) my God.

But the poem speaks with equal intensity of the anguish
of that year-long night when death, envisaged as final,
seemed the only good. Powerful as is the imagery in this
sonnet, with its presentation of the poet's lion-limbed Ad-
versary, the metaphor in another is more telling because
less exotic:

> O the mind, mind has mountains; cliffs of fall
> Frightful, sheer, no-man-fathomed. Hold them cheap
> May who ne'er hung there.

Like most of these poems, this offers no gleam of consola-
tion. "No worst, there is none." Here only carrion comfort
avails: the thought that death ends all life "and each day
dies with sleep." The homeliest images occur in one of
the last of these confessions of misery.

> I wake and feel the fell of dark, not day.
> What hours, O what black hoürs we have spent
> This night! what sights you, heart, saw; ways you went!
> And more must, in yet longer light's delay.
>   With witness I speak this. But where I say
> Hours I mean years, mean life. And my lament
> Is cries countless, cries like dead letters sent
> To dearest him that lives alas! away.
>   I am gall, I am heartburn. God's most deep decree
> Bitter would have me taste: my taste was me;
> Bones built in me, flesh filled, blood brimmed the curse.
>   Selfyeast of spirit a dull dough sours. I see
> The lost are like this, and their scourge to be
> As I am mine, their sweating selves; but worse.

This recalls one of Donne's Holy Sonnets. In both poems
the hard throb of the alliterative phrasing is the same.

God's most deep decree
Bitter would have me taste . . .
Bones built in me, flesh filled, blood brimmed the curse.

These lines are paralleled by:

Batter my heart, three person'd God; for you
As yet but knocke, breathe, shine, and seeke to mende:
That I may rise, and stand, o'erthrow mee'and bend
Your force, to breake, blowe, burn and make me new.

Here is the same religious despair, the same energy of
feeling forcing the rhythm out of its natural course.

III

The first poets to heed Hopkins' lessons were those
whose chief theme was not the spiritual drought of the
solitary, but the shame of a social class that had refused
or abused the responsibilities of power. There are traces of
his influence throughout Auden's early verse, and the same
poet has sounded clearer echoes than Hopkins of the
rhythm of *Piers Plowman*, a poem that he had cited as
warrant for his own practice. Appreciation of Hopkins'
technique is attested by Louis MacNeice's more turbulent
rhythms and more conspicuous sound patterns, especially
in his onomatopoetic pieces on air bombardment, as also
in a *tour de force* of music in the service of wit and pathos, commemorating the death of his cat. C. Day Lewis's
youthful work draws obviously upon Hopkins, whom he declares to be one of the ancestors that his generation honored by imitating. The fourth section of his early poem,
"The Magic Mountain", which is built on the conceit that
the lodestone, Marxian theory, is drawing us toward a re-
generated society, is prefaced with a quotation from the
Jesuit poet's sonnet, "Peace": "He comes with work to
do, he does not come to cool", a gentler version of Christ's
announcement that He came not to bring peace, but a

sword. The Messianic motif is further suggested because Lewis employs the image of the windhover at the opening of the poem and again in the third part, where the falcon symbolizes both the joy of a new era and the airman who flies in the van of it, who fights for its coming. Rarely does Lewis's language have the muscular quality present in the Jesuit's most spiritual lyrics. Indeed, one of the major differences between Hopkins and his late-come pupils is that their work lacks the testimonies to physical energy, physical responsiveness in which the priest's poems abound.

Coming to maturity, as these Britishers did, in the decade after World War I, their early poetry was revolutionary in more ways than one. Everywhere about them they saw signs of the decay of the established order. Confidently they anticipated its fall. They expected that after necessary conflict and its attendant miseries, a rehabilitated society would rise upon the rubble of the old. They had not yet been discouraged by evidence of the leukemia that was eating away the life of the communist hope. Another decade was to make corruption plain. But history had not then uncovered it, and to these young men "communism" suggested the glow of dawn. The ignominy that now beclouds the word shows how the debasement of morals is involved with the debasement of language. "If names be not correct, language is not in accordance with the truth of things. If language be not in accordance with the truth of things, affairs cannot be carried on to success . . . proprieties and music will not flourish . . . punishments will not be properly awarded." When this happens, "the people do not know how to move hand or foot," Confucius observed twenty-four centuries ago. Pound's *Cantos* play variations on this theme. Certainly to be a communist in the thirties did not imply adherence to the devious line of the small self-aggrandizing group who, after Lenin's death, made the policy of the Soviet Union. It meant simply the belief that the common ownership of the instruments of production was a prerequisite to an equitable distribution of goods and to establishment of a humane social order.

Possibly one reason for the attraction Hopkins exercised over these young poets was that, however indignant he might be with "fools of Radical Levellers", he held the curse of his times to be the existence of the many who had no place in the commonwealth, sharing "care with the high and obscurity with the low, but wealth and comfort with neither", as he lamented in explaining his gnarled sonnet upon the unemployed. In a letter to Bridges written shortly after the suppression of the Paris Commune he confessed: "Horrible to say, in a manner I am a Communist. Their ideal bating some things is nobler than that professed by any secular statesman I know of (I must own I live in bat-light and shoot at a venture). Besides it is just.— . . . The more I look the more black and deservedly black the future looks, so I will write no more." Bridges failed to answer and when, after a lapse of three years, Hopkins wrote again, he expressed the fear that his friend had been disgusted with his "*red* opinions". He had, himself, "little reason to be red: it was the red Commune," he said, "that murdered five of our Fathers lately—whether before or after I wrote I do not remember." Nevertheless he concluded bravely: "So far as I know I said nothing that might not fairly be said." This conviction is only implicit in his poems. The letter in which he stated it at length was not published until 1935. Yet its mere existence makes intelligible the bond between twentieth-century poets whose theme was the union of mankind in a new economic setup, iconoclastic in its assumptions and scientific in its bias, and the Victorian Tory, living in the closed circle of the Catholic tradition, who celebrated the single, unique individual.

Hopkins' prose writings bear out the testimony of his poetry to the strength of his feeling for selfhood. In the notes that he took on the *Spiritual Exercises* he dwelt on the irreducible, peculiar nature of consciousness, speaking of "that taste of myself, of *I* and *me* in all things, which is more distinctive than the taste of ale or alum, more distinctive than the smell of walnutleaf or camphor, and is incommunicable by any means to another man (as when I was a child I used to ask myself: what must it be to be someone else?) . . ." Nothing explained or resembled this, and the fact that other men felt likewise merely multiplied the wonder. For himself, no resemblance existed: "Searching nature I taste *self* but at one tankard, that of my own being." The word "self" is stamped on page after page of his poems like his personal seal. Thus, writing of Purcell's music, he exclaimed:

It is the forgèd feature finds me; it is the rehearsal
Of own, of abrupt self there so thrusts on, so throngs the
    ear.

Even when he considers the human will submitting itself to the command of conscience, he refers to that voluntary sacrifice in these terms:

The selfless self of self, most strange, most still,
Fast furled and all foredrawn to No or Yes.

His poem on the resurrection speaks of man as Nature's "clearest-selvèd spark".

A like insistence on and delight in individuality is expressed by Hugh MacDiarmid, who can find nothing harsher to say of his fellows than that they are wanting in selfhood. His hymn to energy and intelligence written in synthetic Scots presents anti-Christ as the man in the street, who is like everybody else. MacDiarmid is as much at home with the plain man as with his intellectual peers. It is the conforming dullard with whom he refuses commerce:

O the Devil is naething strange.
His face is the crood's or oor ain
When we cease to be oorsel's
And become 'like abody' again . . .

One suspects that Hopkins, with what dismay, would have found in this turbulent lyricist a mind as sympathetic

to his own as Whitman's, and a power kindred to his own
in the Scotsman's handling of language. MacDiarmid, for
all his concern with Mind, knows well enough that "It's
soon, no'sense, that faddoms the herts o' men." He makes
the most of the sounds, as well as the sense, that Scottish
can give him. Thus for the gentle quarreling noises of
brook water he uses onomatopes like "Cougher, blocher,
boich, and croichle,". He rejoices in the economy of Scottish, which can pack a season into three syllables, as in
the word "yow-trummle", literally "ewe-tremble": the cold
spell that comes at the end of July after sheep shearing.
Among other words that do duty for a whole English
phrase are "blawp": a dull yawning look, "dabberlack": a
leek-like piece of seaweed, "peerie-weerie": diminished to
a thread of sound. It is not only MacDiarmid's happy use
of his native tongue and his folk song rhythms that suggest Hopkins. There is his overt expression of the "red
opinions" that the Jesuit confided to a private letter. Thus,
the Scotsman writes a lyric to "The Dead Liebknecht",
the Spartacist victimized by the Germans, and celebrates
the idol of the Russian communists in more than one
hymn to Lenin. There is also MacDiarmid's evident delight in nature's wilder inscapes—trees and waters, earth
and sky, the uncertain or headlong movement of a mountain stream, the moon like a weird pale crow above the
spinning earth, the tough willows that never come down
from their stormy moods; there is his hurrahing in the
Hebridean harvest as he watches the herring fishers, when
the catch swims in as if of its own accord. And there is the
counterpart of Hopkins' darker humours, when sand
churns in his ears, the grave of all mankind opens before
him, and he groans that no man can know his own heart
until life's tide uncovers it,

> And horror-struck he sees a pit
> Returnin' life can never fill.

The horror is the greater since MacDiarmid cannot retreat, like Hopkins, into the shelter of a creed, much less

of an established church. The Scotsman speaks of God sometimes with a wit like Emily Dickinson's, more often in the spirit of the Upanishads. But there is no quietism in his religion. He once affirmed in a like image the splendor of what Jeffers called "this wild swan of a world". He is as ready to see "The Octopus Creation . . . wallopin' / In countless faddoms o' a nameless sea." His insatiable curiosity and immense learning have fed metaphysical speculations not possible to the Jesuit poet. MacDiarmid sees himself and his beloved Scotland spun round on the Great Wheel, along with "The helpless forms o' God and Deil". For him the Tree of Life is a more valid symbol than the Cross can ever be.

Imbrued as the poetry of Hopkins is with the idea of sacrifice, there is another element of his religious thinking that has affected the poets of a secular age. The opening sentence in the *Spiritual Exercises* of Loyola runs: "Man was created to praise, reverence, and serve God our Lord, and by this means to save his soul; and the other things on the face of the earth were created for man's sake, and in order to aid him in the prosecution of the end for which he was created." Whether or not one believes in such a self-regarding Deity, there come to almost every man hours when the wonder of the world so seizes him that he can echo Hopkins, declaring that all things "are charged with love, are charged with God and if we know how to touch them give off sparks and take fire, yield drops and flow, ring and tell of him." This is the theme of his sonnet, "God's Grandeur", and is implicit in how many other of his poems. Some like impulse of affirmation is clear in those modern pieces that most nearly suggest filiations from his work.

There are the scenes that W. R. Rodgers draws with audacious fidelity and alliterative force, although he is said to have composed these poems without knowledge of Hopkins' work. His "Autumn" poem is especially remarkable for its gusto, its rushing rhythms that lift and pause, its rich rhymes and assonances, its plain imagery. He de-

scribes landscape and skyscape in the hurl of autumn with
an answering hurl of feeling:

> Going out, those bold days,
> O what a gallery-roar of trees and gale-wash
> Of leaves abashed me, what a shudder and shore
> Of bladdery shadows dashed on windows ablaze,
> What a hedge-shingle seething, what vast lime-splashes
> Of light clouting the land.

He speaks of his heart fitting and following the changes in
trees, grasses, and clouds with the shifts of the wind and
compares its motions to that of the bird above him in a
fashion recalling "The Windhover". Nor is he less close to
the manner of Hopkins when he descends from the heights
in more senses than one and describes himself as

> dryly shuffling through the scurf of leaves
> Fleeing like scuffled toast . . .

One of Rodgers' best-known poems, "Awake", is a summons to the wind "That with hag hands hugs the hooked
hawk down" to fall,

> all welded and one, clap
> Wieldy water, scap, and valley gap
> Together, and detach man from his map;

—a challenge that combines Hopkins' feeling for the wild
with his sense of the iniquity of the social order. But
where the Victorian, the more he looked, saw the future
look "more black and deservedly black", the poet writing
in the midst of World War II boldly commanded his fellows to

> clear the careless ground before us
> Of all the dry and tindery increment
> Of privilege,

bidding them "Awake! before it is too late."
Denis Devlin's world was wider and worldier than the

Jesuit's, and his faith spoke with less assurance, yet his
poems have touches that are pure Hopkins. Another Irish
poet, Leslie Daiken, rejoicing in spring on St. Stephen's
Green, uses just such compound words as Hopkins invented, and delights in the ducks quite as the older poet
did in his iridescent-throated pigeons. A stanza should
prove how close in apprehension the two are.

> Headbobbling drakesheen
> from greenshot velveteen
> and a wineplush breastlapping
> and prestdown ducktapping
> from flat bills nippling.

Again, Richard Eberhart describes the landscape about
"Summery Windermere, sweet lake!" with a feeling for its
look and air and an eager abruptness of speech such as one
finds in Hopkins' lyrics on the fells and falls he loved. One
cannot read Elder Olson's "Essay on Deity" without being
reminded of the Jesuit poet's elaborate poem on the Virgin. The more exuberant, overly hortatory work of the
Canadian, Ralph Gustafson, carries reminders of the
world as the priest saw it, "charged with the grandeur of
God." One hears, however diminished in intensity, echoes
of Hopkins in such a poem as "A Canticle to the Waterbirds, Written for the Feast of St. Francis of Assisi, 1950"
by Brother Antoninus, the California poet, William Ever-
son, a lay brother in the Dominican Order. The poem
employs the looser line of Whitman rather than sprung
rhythm, but is not therefore too remote from Hopkins'
practice. It follows him in the coinage of new words:
"Open your waterdartling beaks, / And make a praise unto
the Lord." For the lay brother, as they might have for
the Jesuit priest, the waterbirds' "imponderable grace"
was Godgiven "to *be* His verification", that these lesser
ones "in the rich hegemony of Being, / May serve as testament to what creation is, / And what creation owes."

Whether or not directly influenced by Hopkins' experiments, those moderns who have what Joyce called "an ear-

sighted view" of things sound out "The roll, the rise, the carol, the creation" with which the elder poet longed to fill his "lagging lines". No epigraph from Hopkins' *Notebooks* is needed to show how sympathetically Richard Wilbur has read him. One fancies that the Jesuit would have welcomed Wilbur's lyric on "Grace", physical as well as theological: the grace of tossing lambs, of Nijinsky pausing in mid-air, and

> the dining-car waiter's absurd
> Acrobacy—tip-fingered tray like a wind-besting bird
> Plumblines his swinging shoes, the sole things sure
> In the shaken train . . .

It is not the "wind-besting bird" that points up the kinship here, but rather the skillfully managed rhythm, the pun, the humorous sensitive delight in motion that, being functional, is graceful in both senses of the word. Wilbur's later work, like his earliest, is rich in such verbal play as delighted Hopkins. He enlivens his words with multiple meanings, his metaphors with kinetic imagery. And, as Hopkins wished to be read with the ears, so too, Richard Wilbur composes in a fashion that demands aural sensitivity if the poem is to be fully comprehended. His braiding of rhyme, cross-rhyme, assonance, and alliteration is one of the fine features—when too rich, one of the defects —of his melodious verse. He is not fearful of introducing angels (for Hopkins "the very cheapest thing in literature") into his poems, but he can do so because he recognizes, with one of the Church Fathers who provided him with the title, that "Love Calls Us to the Things of This World". The title poem of his first volume, *The Beautiful Changes*, is a fresh asseveration of the way that the elder poet saw the beautiful,

> Wishing ever to sunder
> Things and things' selves for a second finding, to lose
> For a moment all it touches back to wonder.

He mentions a forest changed "By a chameleon's tuning his skin to it;" and a mantis, on a green leaf, making "the leaf leafier," thus stressing the "instress" of the thing seen. In the final lines Wilbur has described what is essentially the poet's gift: that of offering things for a second finding, and changing all it touches back to wonder. His responsiveness—not qualified but quickened by his sense of history—to present beauties is finely expressed in the poem, "For the New Railway Station in Rome". This contrasts notably with the Roman sonnet by Hardy, subtitled "Building a New Street in an Ancient Quarter". The elder poet fastens upon the nobility of the ruins that declare: "Dunces, Learn here to spell Humanity!" Wilbur, admiring the functional excellence of the new edifice, asks: "What does it say over the door of Heaven / But *homo fecit?*"

The mingling of delight with awe is not often felt in our wintry age. We are apt to respond more readily to Hopkins' "terrible" sonnets than to his hosannas. Yet the very ambivalence of his moods helps to make his work sympathetic, since it bears witness to tensions that are increasingly real to us. Those poets pay him the finest tribute who are most unlike him, being unequivocally themselves. Thus Ted Hughes, speaking almost as though through clenched teeth of the more brutal aspects of rural life, has an earnestness that, however remote from Hopkins in the savagery of its candor, bespeaks his temper. Earnestness—which must not be confused with solemnity—was the quality that he prized above all others. Perhaps he valued it the more because he was dimly conscious of betraying it when his verse fell into the sweet melt of Victorianism. Certainly being in earnest with one's work must have seemed to him the strongest assertion of identity. Such poetry, though it may sometimes be faulty, cannot be false.

12. Alchemists of the Word

The religious poet who must live in the climate of an irreligious age is a kind of spiritual Crusoe. He has to forage for himself to get the materials that such men as Dante and Milton took as a matter of course. Yeats solved the problem after a fashion, sheltering in a cosmology of his own making, but he built his system with a fine disregard for science and the machine. Eliot, on more familiar terms with these fundamentals of our civilization, but unable to accommodate himself to them, has moved about them uneasily, and, not willing to resign his knowledge for Yeats's own-wayish dream, took refuge in the established Church. Neither solution was possible for the young poet who believed that poetry must build upon the contemporary mind and include "all readjustments incident to science and other shifting factors related to that [contemporary] consciousness." The essay by Hart Crane in which this assertion is made is little more than a restatement, in twentieth-century terms, of Wordsworth's remarks on the subject matter of poetry. Crane understood the problem more clearly than did Yeats, and dealt with it more overtly than did Eliot. He was greatly gifted, but being neither as well equipped nor as mature as either, his solution was not satisfactory.

When Crane was commencing work on his major poem, *The Bridge,* he was vehemently repudiating what he called Eliot's "stern conviction of death" as expressed in "The Hollow Men". He differed from Eliot not merely in being a poet of affirmation and wanting to include the machine in his full assent to the spirit of his times, but also in finding the sources of his inspiration in such indigenous writers as Whitman, Melville, and Emily Dickinson. He paid the last-named oblique tribute by mentioning her in *The Bridge*, remarkably enough, in the same breath with the dancer, Isadora Duncan. But however strong the attraction that her poetry held for him, he could not answer the twinkle in her irreverent eye. Wanting her sense of irony, he maintained a distance from her greater than from the other Americans to whose poetry his own was linked.

What Crane shared with Whitman was, among other things, a pleasure in the native scene. He thought in terms of the American continent, its rich variety, its huge expanse. Whitman, too, had felt the impact of mechanical invention and had responded to it with a hearty "Hurrah for positive science!" He had said, in other words, what Crane wrote in his essay about the necessity for making machinery a natural and accepted part of modern poetry. The stimulus that the author of "Calamus" found in his intimate relations with streetcar conductors and ferry pilots, Crane got from the taxi drivers and sailors who figure in his poetry as in his life. The religiosity of the two men seems to have had like roots and to have expressed itself similarly. Whitman's prose as well as his poetry declares his sense of a strong bond with the universe. There are passages in Hart Crane's work that also bear testimony to a blissful self-identification with all that is. In one of his letters he gives an account of an instant of mystic transport that made him exclaim "I have known moments in eternity."

The cry followed his description of the experience known as "the anesthetic revelation". To the uninitiate it is almost as remote as the rapture of the Buddha under the bo tree, the trance of the saint. Crane arrived at it by the purely physical means of sitting in the dentist's chair under the influence of ether. An analogous reaction is recorded in James' *Varieties of Religious Experience*. Describing her anguished vision during an operation under insufficient anesthesia, a woman wrote that she "seemed to be directly under the foot of God", who thought no more of making her suffer "than a man thinks of hurting a cork when he is opening wine, or hurting a cartridge when he is firing." God, she thought, "was grinding his own life out of my pain." The purgatorial section of *The Bridge* has lines that seem to point to a similar illumination that accompanied Crane's suffering in his ether dream. "Kiss of our agony Thou gatherest," he cries, not once, but twice. Where Whitman, full of gusto and serenity, sauntered into "cosmic consciousness", Crane appears to have climbed, perilously, on the wings of wine and music, to tumble like a repetitious Icarus from his uncertain regions of cloud. The more extravagant pages in *The Bridge* read as if he were straining to feel the emotions of the good grey poet with the exacerbated sensibility of Edgar Allan Poe.

He had much in common with this ancestor of the symbolists. He shared with him and his successors an urgent concern with technique. If Crane's exploration of Elizabethan blank verse did not carry him as far as it did Eliot, it definitely affected his performance. He compressed his metaphors accordion fashion like the most elliptical of French lyricists. He incorporated into later poems precious fragments of discarded pieces, turned the discoveries of others to his own uses, and was constantly reworking his material. Then too, as had the symbolists, he tried to capture the aura of a mood, the atmosphere of a psychological situation. Witness "Wine Menagerie", or the more fantastic "Paraphrase", which was composed on waking out of a drunken sleep to a dazzling morning in the belief that he was dead.

He would have agreed with the author of *The Poetic Principle* that the music of poetry should be indefinite and suggestive and should produce a spiritual effect. He would not have agreed that it is impossible to produce a long poem, although perhaps there was such an admission in his final desperate act. His major work, *The Bridge*, runs to more than one thousand lines. Poe had declared: "that degree of excitement which would entitle a poem to be so called at all, cannot be sustained throughout a composition of any great length. After the lapse of half an hour, at the very utmost, it flags—fails—a revulsion ensues—and then the poem is, in effect, no longer such." The excitement demanded here is that which, in Poe's phrase, elevates the soul. Granted his premise, it is easy to see why *The Bridge*, with all its grandeur of intention and its passages of splendor, was a failure. Crane could not maintain either in himself or in his poem the requisite level of exaltation. In forcing himself to achieve it he exhausted his energies and invalidated his work.

One of the fundamental differences between Whitman and Poe was in the response that each made to science. Crane appeared to swing from one attitude to the other, but in reality he was as impatient of the scientific approach as he was ignorant of its findings. Whitman welcomed scientific developments as a means of coming closer to the secret of the universe, a secret that he was assured was a beautiful one. Poe, though he was attracted by astronomy and was so enamoured of the deductive method that he became the father of the Whodunit, recognized the threat of scientific seclusiveness. He saw it as the enemy of poetry. Before the machine he felt the same fascinated terror that invades certain parts of the very poem in which Crane celebrates the triumph of the engineering mind.

The Bridge is on the whole affirmative in tenor, and so accepts machinery, notably the airplane, as an instrument of progress, a means to subtler and nobler communication. But the poem also takes account of the ugly aspects of our mechanized existence. There are passages that present the machine moving upon humanity with senseless relentlessness as in Poe's stories about mechanical horrors. Science and technology are plainly to be feared when they are not imaginatively controlled. But Crane did not realize this. He seems to have been the victim of an unreasoning terror of forces that he scarcely tried to understand. The contemporary, of course, cannot have—as Dante did—an inti-

mate knowledge of the processes that circumscribe and determine his daily routine. Moreover, if there is any
material unfit for poetry, it is the abstractions on which
that knowledge is founded. Nevertheless, the poem to
which Crane devoted his best energies could not be shaped
by a man with such a loose hold on the facts governing the
mechanized world whose furthest limits he was exploring.
The Bridge sometimes reads as though the poet were trying to compensate for lack of factual detail and for the
ignoring of natural laws by obtruding the vocabulary of the
powerhouse and using the inflated language of the deliberate visionary.

The belief that the poet must be a visionary, must make
himself a visionary, Crane took from another precocious
provincial, Arthur Rimbaud, himself the heir of Baudelaire and therefore of Poe. In the nearly ninety years since
he stopped writing, the fierce vision of the boy who cried
that the poet is "truly Thief of Fire" has illuminated the
work of realist and surrealist alike. The doctrine that Rimbaud set forth in his youthful letters and in the vehement
prose that he repudiated with equal poetic vehemence has
become a commonplace of the schools. The poet is an explorer of unknown realms of consciousness. He is a seer,
a maker, an inventor, an "alchemist of the word". Rimbaud was no thin-blooded dreamer. He expected a ma-
terialistic future. In his middle years, when he had rejected poetry permanently, he was to long for a son who
would grow into a famous engineer, made rich and powerful by science. But above all, he was what psychologists
call an eidetic, one with unusually vivid mental images.
His were extraordinary not only because they were vivid
but because they were exquisite or horrible, or a grotesque
mélange of the two. And if the visions did not come to
him, he went out of his way to capture them by means of
potent drugs, as less gifted versemakers were to do later.
Sensations and ideas swarmed to him like so many genie
that he had cunningly enchanted. His poetry anticipated
the kaleidoscopic shifts and dislocations of the movie, the

crosscurrents of the radio, but with an extravagance possible only to the willfully deranged mind. Crane's poetry,
in its charged hyperbole, its half-colloquial, elliptical notation of the actual and the imagined scene as they crowd
upon a shelterless sensibility, in its straining to reveal
transcendent truth, while intent on being "absolutely modern", is a belated, slightly hollow echo of Rimbaud's.

It has, however, an indigenous quality that separates it
from work centered, as much contemporary poetry has
been, upon purely literary experiences. The native element in it is not confined to the poem that he regarded as
an American *Aeneid*. It is present in his lyrics, one of
which is addressed to Melville, another to Emily Dickinson, in his casual references to New York streets and to
the Connecticut countryside, in the baseball scores, the
roof garden, and the "religious gunman" of his poem on
imagination entitled "For the Marriage of Faustus and
Helen".

This was preceded by a more accessible if far less ambitious poem about poetry, called "Chaplinesque". These
lines center upon Chaplin's old movie, "The Kid". They
take their start from the close of Eliot's fourth "Prelude",
which, presenting several images of a sordid city street,
speaks of the fancies that curl around them, and particularly

> The notion of some infinitely gentle
> Infinitely suffering thing.

Crane takes as this infinitely gentle, infinitely suffering
thing the stray kitten that Chaplin picks up from the door-
step, to shelter in "warm torn elbow coverts". As Crane
recognized, the pathos of this piece verges on bathos. But
it does nevertheless evoke Chaplin's touchingly hopeful,
helpless pantomime. For Crane the tramp's "meek ad-
justments", his side-stepping and smirking, the "pirou-
ettes" of his "pliant cane", represented, as he wrote in
1921, "the futile gesture of the poet in the USA today."
The kitten crying in the alley and rescued by a ragged out-

cast symbolizes poetry. Superficially, this is the old-fashioned romantic view of the poet as the lost vagabond.
Actually, the lyric is realistic enough. It was written when
the reaction against the first world war and its aftermath
was finding vent in Parisian Dada, and filling the intellectuals everywhere with the conviction that nothing made
sense—especially the idea of becoming a poet in a money-
mad world. The weakness of "Chaplinesque" lies not in its
assumptions but in the weakness of the kitten as symbol:
the sensibility of a poet, however starved and abused, is
analogous to something more alert, mature, and human.
But the closing lines are significant. "The game enforces
smirks," but Chaplin's audience has seen

> The moon in lonely alleys make
> A grail of laughter of an empty ash can, . . .

What, one might ask, is the Grail doing in this alley? The
reference is more meaningful than it seems. Crane shows
the moonlight hallowing an empty ash can so that this
takes on the aspect of a sacred symbol. Further, the nick-
name of Parsifal, who figures in a modern version of the
Grail legend, was "the guileless fool". There are moments
when Chaplin is both the guileless fool and the gentle
knight. And the Grail was, of course, a symbol of longevity
and fertility. Chaplin, clowning it in lonely alleys among
the empty ash cans of a cold starving world, is akin to the
poet who restores life to the dead world of money and
machines.

Hoping everything from poetry, like the young Rimbaud before him, Crane felt a sense of alienation, amount-
ing almost to nausea, from the commercialized environment in which he was forced to make a living. Hungry
for a philosophy that would support his poetic credo, he
snatched at whatever offered. He believed that he had discovered a solid metaphysical structure when he came upon
the turgid transcendentalism of Ouspensky. The rapture
with which Rimbaud filled him was due as much to the

intoxication of the young Frenchman's dream as to the
technical innovations in his poems. The more so since
Crane was not on intimate terms with these in the original. Naturally, Crane responded with eagerness to the
work of those poets who had been in his own plight.

By the same token, he recognized a kindred spirit in
Samuel Greenberg, a half-literate boy who died in a charity
hospital at the age of twenty-three without ever having
had a line published. A poem of his called "The Tempest", written in his unidiomatic yet surely poetic style,
has lines eloquent of Crane's feeling:

> I live in an age where the age lives alone,
> And lonesome doth it rage
> Where the bard dare not come.

Not alone Greenberg's isolation and his devotion to
poetry drew Crane to his work. Greenberg, whose mother
tongue was Yiddish, got drunk on the dictionary. Words
had the same effect on Crane. He studied Greenberg's
manuscripts eagerly and incorporated passages from them
into his own poems. In the process they underwent a curious transmutation. Thus Greenberg wrote: "Silhouette set
the scepters roving." In the second of the six lyrics that
Crane called "Voyages" he gave the line this turn:

> Take this sea then, enlisted by what sceptres
> Roving wide from isle to isle have churned—

In the final version of the poem he apostrophizes the sea
as one

> The sceptred terror of whose sessions rends
> As her demeanors motion well or ill,
> All but the pieties of lovers' hands.

The only detail he kept of the original was the word
"sceptres" and he even changed that to an adjective, but
he retained the feeling of Greenberg's line. The sea is
not only royal and majestic. It is in continual movement,

and is the cause as well as the means of "roving". The "sceptred terror" of the sea's sessions carries the sense of fateful gestures in the original line. Crane's phrase enhances the terror associated with this symbol of the powerful Unknown.

The second "Voyage" is one of the most admirable instances of his poetic shorthand. It opens with a metaphor which evokes the sea as "this great wink of eternity". The sea may be conceived as a vast eye, looking at the universe and able to reflect what is beyond the compass of the human eye, or perhaps winking at the dazzle that confronts it. The phrase may imply that the sea, a thing "Of rimless floods, unfettered leewardings", allows as large a glimpse of eternity as is allowed in the wink of an eye. Crane explained the lovely phrase, "Adagios of islands", as conveying the image and rhythm of a boat coasting slowly in an archipelago, adding that it also ushers in a world of music.

Voyages II

And yet this great wink of eternity,
Of rimless floods, unfettered leewardings,
Samite sheeted and processioned where
Her undinal vast belly moonward bends,
Laughing the wrapt inflections of our love;

Take this Sea, whose diapason knells
On scrolls of silver snowy sentences,
The sceptred terror of whose sessions rends
As her demeanors motion well or ill,
All but the pieties of lovers' hands.

And onward, as bells off San Salvador
Salute the crocus lustres of the stars,
In these poinsettia meadows of her tides,—
Adagios of islands, O my Prodigal,
Complete the dark confessions her veins spell.

Mark how her turning shoulders wind the hours,
And hasten while her penniless rich palms
Pass superscription of bent foam and wave,—
Hasten, while they are true,—sleep, death, desire,
Close round one instant in one floating flower.

Bind us in time, O Seasons clear, and awe.
O minstrel galleons of Carib fire,
Bequeath us to no earthly shore until
Is answered in the vortex of our grave
The seal's wide spindrift gaze toward paradise.

Music plays through the lines of this poem partly by
reason of the sensitive handling of vocables and of exact
and inexact rhymes, partly because of the reference to the
bells off San Salvador, the lines about the sea "whose
diapason knells / On scrolls of silver snowy sentences,"
and the phrase presenting the southern stars as "minstrel
galleons of Carib fire". Crane often used the double stimulus of alcohol and music to compel his daemon. His interest in the whole range of music, from the classics, both
old and new, to jazz, is apparent throughout his work. In
the poem "For the Marriage of Faustus and Helen", the
seduction of Helen, who signifies abstract beauty, is accomplished to a jazz orchestra's "snarling hails of melody".
The last poem he wrote celebrated the exalting peal of the
bells announcing an Indian fiesta as "The bell-rope that
gathers God at dawn". An epigraph from Plato's "Symposium", which he renders thus: "Music is then the
knowledge of that which relates to love in harmony and
system." introduces the final section of *The Bridge*. This
suggests Rimbaud's prophecy: "Always full of *Number*
and *Harmony*, poems will be made to last. At bottom this
would be a little like Greek poetry." Both poets revered
the immaterial beauty of ideal patterns, revealed su-
premely in mathematics and in music, which is mathematics embodied.

Crane's imagery, depending as it does on free association, makes his second "Voyage" a richly ambiguous pres-

entation of the sea, one of the most ambiguously rich phenomena of the world we know. The poem is also a love song, but, as in most lyrics about romantic love, the idea of death is not distant. These themes are associated with the sea, the agent of death, the giant womb from which Aphrodite emerged.

More than any of Crane's poems, the series called "Voyages" is suffused with his passion for the sea, which was his chosen symbol for mystic union and which had a curious significance in his personal history. The sea is, of course, the archetypal symbol of birth and death and resurrection. When he was writing "Voyages" he was living in Brooklyn, in the very room once occupied by John Roebling, the engineer who designed the Brooklyn Bridge, overlooking the East River. Crane's companion was a sailor. Ultimately he committed suicide by drowning.

II

It seems natural that Crane's major poem should begin with a vision of Columbus, who takes on the stature of a mythical hero, and that the opening section should speak with the voices of both the navigator and the poet:

> still one shore beyond desire!
> And kingdoms
>   naked in the
>   trembling heart—
>
> Te Deum laudamus
>   O Thou Hand of Fire

It is natural, too, that in looking for a symbol for the conquest of space and of knowledge, Crane should choose that which, in the literal sense of the word, transcends the waters: a bridge. As his poem moved across seascape, landscape, and skyscape, he felt that it was not merely spanning the continent. The physical structure was the visible sign of man's dynamic potentialities, the mechanical extension of his being, and, finally, it became a harp playing the music of ideal horizons. The "Proem", a swift cinematic panorama of the city, with its "gaunt sky-bar-racks" and tunneling subways, as glimpsed from a room overlooking the river and the Brooklyn Bridge, concludes with an apostrophe to the bridge. The dance of atoms in its towers and cables, the play of its tensions, take on a religious significance:

> O Sleepless as the river under thee,
> Vaulting the sea, the prairies' dreaming sod
> Unto us lowliest sometime sweep, descend
> And of the curveship lend a myth to God.

The theme is resumed in the final section, entitled "Atlantis".

The name belongs to an island whose inhabitants, says the Platonic legend, were descended from a god, but, their divine nature being corrupted, their impiety was punished by so fierce a storm that their home was swallowed by the sea. This fabled isle gave its name to the imaginary commonwealth in the Pacific where was established, according to Francis Bacon, "Salomon's House", a college or society devoted to the study "of the works and creatures of God . . . the finding out of the true nature of all things . . . the knowledge of causes, and secret motions of things and the enlarging of the bounds of human empire to the effecting of all things possible."

Although placed at the conclusion of the poem, the "Atlantis" section was the first to be written. In a sense, Crane's "Atlantis", which he identified with the Absolute, suffered a fate like that of Plato's legendary island. As he proceeded with *The Bridge*, the poet had to force his exhausted energies, the treason to his task became self-evident, the glorious conception was lost in a mist of sentimentality, a storm of bombast. Yet at its high points, the poem summons up a vision that the art of painting is too definite, the art of prose too logical, and the art of music too abstract, to present.

On completing the "Atlantis" section Crane felt that

here he had brought together all the separate themes of the sections planned to lead up to it. "The bridge, in becoming a ship, a world, a woman, a tremendous harp (as it does finally) seems really to have a career," he exulted. "I have attempted to induce the same feelings of elation, etc.—like being carried forward and upward simultaneously—both in imagery, rhythm, and repetition, that one experiences in walking across Brooklyn Bridge . . ." "Atlantis" is in effect a more ambitious, more ambiguous, more ecstatic version of Whitman's poem, "Crossing Brooklyn Ferry". It is even more suggestive of Whitman's religous paean on the union of East and West, "Passage to India", inspired by the opening of the Suez Canal and the completion of the Union Pacific Railway. However different his handling of language, Crane's attitude toward the Brooklyn Bridge was that of the elder poet's to those engineering feats. This is clear where the Navigator is identified with Crane's transcendent vision, and Cathay is seen not as the object of physical conquest but as representing what Crane called "an attitude of spirit".

Before the final apotheosis, however, "Atlantis" appears in the third section of the poem as the name of a dream ship. This section, which bears an epigraph from Melville, is called "Cutty Sark", in memory of a famous clipper ship built in 1869 for the China tea trade. The hallucinations of a drunken sailor in a South Street dive are given in erratic rhythms, meant to suggest the lurch of a boat in heavy seas, dramatizing his own unsteadiness. Crane planned the section as a fugue with two voices: that of the world of time, and that of the world of eternity. The second voice was a transmutation of the sound of a nickel-in-the-slot piano playing "Stamboul Nights". An instance of Crane's verbal sleights is the transformation of "O Stamboul Rose—dreams weave the rose!" to "ATLANTIS ROSE drums wreathe the rose." The twist of the phrase proffers the complex of sensations, ideas, and emotions that agitate a modern Platonist drinking with a seaworn derelict in a South Street café, to the sound of a mechanical piano grinding out a popular tune. The word "rose", along with its familiar classical and religious connotations, suggests the old name for the chart of a mariner's compass. The fact that the music is machinemade underscores the tone of regret for an era as lost as Atlantis, in a phantasy that ends with an airy procession of the ghosts of clipper ships.

Crane's verbal telescopy, the close-up of a recent moment opening into scenes rapidly shifting time and place, is particularly successful in parts of the preceding section, "Powhatan's Daughter". Here Pocahontas takes on the aspect of a nature goddess. In identifying her with the American earth, the poet, traveling backward, tries to traverse its history since the white man took possession of it. From the harbor of the empire city we descend into the subway, which is abruptly translated into the Twentieth-century Express, hurtling over the rails, carrying us into the heart of the country where the Mississippi mightily moves. Here we meet the hobo trekkers behind his father's cannery works, and in these childlike vagrants "riding the rods" he finds a parallel to the pioneers who wandered, in the childhood of the American dream, across the Great Valley. However faulty Crane's mythology may be, his compressed language functions admirably for rapid evocations of the native scene.

Not the least memorable of these occur in the section called "The Tunnel". With all its hidden implications, this is grounded in ordinary experience and harks back to commonplace idiom. "The Tunnel" is a journey in the subway, the purgatory to be endured before the discovery of the opening sky of "Atlantis". The motivating idea is the encroachment of machinery upon humanity. Crane found the plainest metaphor for his Dantesque sights:

> The phonographs of hades in the brain
> Are tunnels that re-wind themselves, and love
> A burnt match skating in a urinal—

In this tunnel, quite appropriately, he meets, with "eyes like agate lanterns", Edgar Allan Poe. The scene has the insistent reality of nightmare.

> —And did their riding eyes right through your
>   side,
> And did their eyes like unwashed platters ride?
> And Death, aloft—gigantically down
> Probing through you—toward me, O evermore!

The question that Crane asks that other haunted and haunting poet blends the motion of the train, the pressure of the mob, the hint at the kitchens and cafeterias where they snatch the food that sustains them between dull job and duller play, into one image of needless squalor and meaningless haste. Here, too, is a hint at Christ's unhealing wound. The death theme is emphasized not alone by the references to "The Raven" and to Poe's dread City in the Sea where Death had "reared himself a throne" nor in the allusion to his last night:

> And when they dragged your retching flesh,
> Your trembling hands that night through Baltimore—
> That last night on the ballot rounds, did you
> Shaking, did you deny the ticket, Poe?

The theme is heard in the name of the station at the end of the subway line:

> For Gravesend Manor change at Chambers Street.
> The platform hurries along to a dead stop.

There is like condensation toward the beginning of the section where the poet enters the subway to ride from Times Square to Columbus Circle:

> Be minimum, then, to swim the hiving swarms,
> Out of the Square, the Circle burning bright,—
> Avoid the glass doors gyring at your right,
> Where boxed alone a second, eyes take fright—

Quite unprepared rush naked back to light:
And down beside the turnstile press the coin
Into the slot. The gongs already rattle.

A full understanding of the lines is possible only when
they have behind them the weight of the section, if not of
the poem as a whole. Here is the pressure of the crowd
at Times Square, and the lights and noises of Columbus
Circle, which bring us back to the navigator whose dream
ended so sordidly at the Circle. The difficulty of keeping
a hold on personal identity in the city mob, and the other
terror that lurks in mirrors are also present. Further, the
passage suggests the vain efforts to square the circle.

The impossibility of squaring the circle is one of the
most effective analogies in a poem that is itself a com-
pendious metaphor, *The Divine Comedy*. At the very
close of the Paradiso Dante refers to the geometer's problem in speaking of his own helplessness to describe the
"luce eterna". The radius and the circumference of a circle
being incommensurable, it is impossible to express the
one in terms of the other. Similarly, it is impossible to
express God in human terms.

One might add that Crane's poem is incommensurable
with Dante's. The Florentine was not only the more
greatly gifted, he was also far more learned in the sciences
and the ways of the world of his period. Indeed, *The
Bridge* is sometimes inadvertently funny, as where Crane
addressed Whitman as "Panis Angelicus" or "angelic
bread", under the impression that he was calling the poet
"Holy Pan". But even putting aside genius and learning
and experience, Dante had an immense advantage over
the unschooled American provincial. In spite of the conflict between pope and emperor, between Guelph and
Ghibelline, and within the Guelph party, between the
Blacks and the Whites, the Florentine dealt with a relatively unified world. Crane, hampered by his private confusions and by the dislocation of his times, met his gravest
obstacle in the lack of an accepted cosmology. "How shall

we learn what it is that our hearts believe in?" was the
leading question of "The Hamlet of A. MacLeish". Before
he had finished his poem of affirmation, Crane, who
scarcely thought of himself as a Hamlet, came to realize
that he had no answer.

The Bridge was a tour de force. Nevertheless, the apoc-
alyptic vision on which it closes has a kind of singing
incandescence, and there are times when the poem goes
down into the bowels of our inferno. Throughout are scattered passages in which Crane's condensed language compels acceptance even by those who dissent from his view
of the universe and who recognize the inadequacy of *The
Bridge* as a whole.

Among the weakest parts of that faulty structure are the
few lyrics in it. Though he loved and respected his craft,
Crane was a very uneven writer. Nearly all his poems have
some flaw. Nearly all of them have rare intensities and
luminosities. An instance is the short piece originally
called "Tampa Schooner", composed on a trip to Cuba
and later retitled more appropriately "Repose of Rivers".
Other poets have compared the sound of the wind in the
trees to the sound of the sea, but none as magically as
Crane, who wrests his words so that the steady sound, as
of surf, in the willows of an inland meadow, becomes one
with "wind flaking sapphire" in the summer gulf. Elliptical imagery and verbal music work even more evocatively
in the "Voyages" series. Wind and sea are sovereign in his
poems. "Lo, Lord, Thou ridest!" he cries, in his lines on
"The Hurricane". With a sweep to be matched only by
the author of "The Wreck of *The Deutschland*" they pro-
ceed to their exultant finale:

> Thou ridest to the door, Lord!
> Thou bidest wall nor floor, Lord!

Just when Crane became acquainted with Hopkins'
work is in dispute, but unquestionably he shared that poet's joy in the wildness and wet. It is equally clear that he
felt, "turning, turning on smoked forking spires", an even

stronger revulsion than Hopkins had shown from cities that seemed demoniac to him. Like the Catholic convert, the poet who had to make his own myth plunged into troughs of despair, but Crane, at last, was submerged.

In the sciences, the negative result of an experiment is not without value. So a poetic failure may be an index to what should not be attempted. Crane's work seems not to have influenced that of other poets largely, and no project quite comparable to his has succeeded it. The Bridge crossed to no country fruitful for his fellows. Yet they recognize in him the qualities that poetry demands of its practitioners: an imaginative grasp of language, a longing for order, an integrity that will not be compromised.

Sometimes he is paid the homage of an elegy, sometimes the oblique tribute that he paid to Samuel Greenberg: the incorporation of some phrase, altered to fit its new setting, but recalling its first use in a poem of his. The title poem in James Agee's early book of lyrics, *Permit Me Voyage*, harks back to Crane's "Permit me voyage, Love, into your hands . . ." The second part of Agee's little book is given over to a "Dedication", written in prose, but phrased like a prayer or a litany. It is of interest as the testament of a sensitive American contemporary in his youth, and, in connection with Crane, for a paragraph that sets his name between Ring Lardner's and Lincoln's.

Another poet who offers indirect yet unmistakable reminders of Crane is that intense lyricist, Jean Garrigue. She takes the line from "Voyages" that Agee used and transposes it thus: "Permit me candor of an excited world!" In another of her poems there is a faint but distinct echo of Crane's transposition of Greenberg's line.

More explicitly, John Wheelwright praised Crane in an obituary poem entitled "Fish Pond". Wheelwright's life was abruptly cut off by an accident, but not before he had found time to write some exceedingly knotty poetry. This elegy is no exception. It is a lament for a friend and for a fellow craftsman to whom, in spite of serious differ-

ences, he paid tribute. Wheelwright's intellectualism and
his active concern with the social problems of his time,
one of them the case of Sacco and Vanzetti, helped to
divide him from Crane. Across the gulf that separated
them he held out his hand in hail and farewell.

His "Obituary to Hart Crane" can be read for its simple
surface meanings:

> As you drank deep as Thor, did you think of
>   milk or wine?
> Did you drink blood, while you drank the salt
>   deep?

he asks, and goes on, drily, but feelingly:

> Fishes now look upon you, with eyes which do
>   not gossip.
> Fishes are never shocked.
>
> .   .   .   .   .   .
>
> Now you have willed it, may the Great Wash
>   take you.
>
> .   .   .   .   .   .
>
> What did you see as you fell? What did you hear
>   as you sank?
> Did it make you drunken with hearing?
> I will not ask any more. You saw or heard no evil.

Wheelwright confided the deeper implications of the
piece to a prose postscript. He refers there to the Norse
fable telling how Thor had come, cold and weary, to a
remote cabin, where he found an old crone with a flagon
of ale beside her and a cat on the hearthstone; how the
thirsty god could not drain the flagon nor, for all his giant
strength, move the cat from its place by the fire. Later
Thor learned that when he drank from the flagon, he had
lowered the level of the ocean, and when he lifted three
paws of the cat, he had displaced the tortoise on which
the earth rests. Wheelwright thought of the Flagon as "the
infinite of conceivable sensation", and the Cat as "the uni-

verse of possible act". Crane cared little about the Cat—
for which this socially-minded fellow poet blamed him.
He "vowed himself to the flagon" of infinite sensation,
"drank more than his fill, and was overwhelmed by the ale
fumes."

A later poet, Karl Shapiro, saw Crane's suicide as a leap
"from the deck-rail of his disbelief", the act of a man
who paid for poetry with his blood. Both versions of his
tragedy are true, neither is a complete account. A less
melodramatic and more compassionate poem on Crane's
straining after "the complete vision of love", his confusion
of belief, his heartbreaking failure, was composed by the
British poet, Julian Symons. That rigorous literary mentor, Yvor Winters, has bitterly characterized Crane as "a
poet of great genius, who ruined his life and his talent
by living and writing as the two greatest religious teachers
of our generation [Emerson, Whitman] recommended."
He says much the same thing with the terse authority of
poetry in three stanzas written "In Memory of Hart
Crane" and entitled "Orpheus". The poem is based on
that part of the Greek myth in which the singer is torn to
pieces by enraged Bacchantes, who throw his head and
his lyre into the river, where they float, making continual
music. Winters' tribute concludes: "Crying loud, the immortal tongue, / From the empty body wrung, / Broken
in a bloody dream, / Sang unmeaning down the stream."
Winters was Crane's close contemporary and his friend.
More than a quarter of a century after Crane's death another American poet made his addition to the legend.
Robert Lowell included in his *Life Studies* fourteen casually rhymed pentameters called "Words for Hart Crane".
Lowell, who was a boy of fifteen when Crane drowned
himself, is nevertheless closer to him in spirit than is
Winters. The words he puts into the dead poet's mouth
are as harsh as anything he uttered and more direct. The
last lines run: "My profit was a pocket with a hole. / Who
asks for me, the Shelley of my age, / must lay his heart
out for my bed and board." However one reads the pain-

ful story of Crane's life and death, the poetry, imperfect
and rich, survives.

III

The revolutionary hopes of the poets of the thirties
withered in the fires of the second world war. Their dream
of social regeneration exploded, they turned away from
the rubble around them and the abyss before them, looking inward, seeking to make peace with themselves, or upward, toward a transcendent vision of a Love that would
yet redeem humanity. In the disturbed years that preceded the outbreak of the war in Europe a few young
men, among whom George Fraser, J. F. Hendry, and
Henry Treece were the moving spirits, banded together
as poets of the "Apocalypse". Their dreams had something
of the magnitude and the confused splendor, if not the
esoteric character, of Revelation. Yet if their program,
like their poetry, was disconcertingly vague and evange-
listic, it carried a recognition of what was wrong with their
world. They believed that human development must be
in the direction of an integrity that valued the emotions
no less than the intellect, taking account of the realities
of dream life as well as of the wakeful consciousness. To
poetry they gave a quasi-religious significance. Eager to
rediscover personality, they wanted to free men from the
domination of the machine, and they exalted myth and
imagination. This they took in Coleridge's sense as, in its
primary form, "the living Power and prime Agent of all
human Perception, and as a repetition in the finite mind
of the eternal act of creation in the infinite I AM."
—and in its secondary form that which "dissolves, diffuses,
dissipates, in order to recreate; . . . or where this process
is rendered impossible, . . . it struggles to idealize and
unify." Their religiosity, however publicized, was of a private nature, and eventually they turned toward a "Per-
sonalism" that might be described as a kind of ethical
anarchism, in which a leonine Christianity lay down with

a lamblike Freudianism. The significance of the Apocalypse movement was rather symptomatic than intrinsic,
though a few notable poems were written by some of its
adherents, G. S. Fraser and Vernon Watkins among them.
None of its members, however, has achieved the distinction or the vitality of their literary forebears, D. H. Lawrence, Herbert Read, and the wild Welshman, Dylan
Thomas.

Thomas, too, is a religious poet, not of the dour company that explored the Waste Land, but possessed, as was
Hart Crane, by the revivalist's fervor, and so an exuberant
poet, who heaps image on image as prodigally as he chimes
rhyme with rhyme. Thomas's work presents even more
difficulties than does Crane's because it combines with
equally private references both Freudian and Christian
symbols and allusions to Welsh mythology with which few
outside of Wales are familiar. Further, he was more alive
to the music of his meaning than to the meaning of his
music.

Poetry has a long and honorable history in Wales.
Thomas, though ignorant of Welsh, profited from the literary heritage of his native region even more than from
the rough grandeur of its landscape. He was not a visually-
minded poet, but one with an extraordinarily keen ear.
Among the technical peculiarities of Welsh verse are the
elaborate braiding of rhyme, alliteration, and consonance
known as "cynghanedd". Traces of this are to be found in
the work of Hopkins, to whom the classical Welsh metres
with their dependence on stress and the compound words
of the Cymric bards were also congenial. The richness of
verbal texture that Hopkins rejoiced to discover, were
Thomas's birthright. Gifted, moreover, with a remarkably
resonant voice, he was the better equipped to compose poetry made to be heard.

Some of his most memorable poems divide their beauties between praise of nature and praise of poetry that is
nature's luminous mirror. This, even if, as he assured
Vernon Watkins, he was "not a country man" but a sub-

urban provincial, "making his own weathery world inside;".
Although his imagery derives from astrology as well as
from astronomy, from his interest in magic and in the
cinema, his private weather is governed by nature's. Witness the lyric in which he enumerates what he sees, shut
in his "tower of words", a lyric that gains significance from
its reminder that the root meaning of "poet" is "maker":

> Some let me make you of the vowelled beeches,
> Some of the oaken voices, from the roots
> Of many a thorny shire tell you notes,
> Some let me make you of the water's speeches.

Here, too, is one of his few relatively simple images, the
October wind that "With fists of turnips punishes the
land,". This is an autumnal poem, and ends darkly. Another "Poem in October", far more intricately patterned,
concludes on a note of exaltation frequent with him. It
opens:

> It was my thirtieth year to heaven
> Woke to my hearing from harbour and neighbour wood
> And the mussel pooled and the heron
> Priested shore
> The morning beckon
> With water praying and call of seagull and rook
> And the knock of sailing boats on the net webbed wall
> Myself to set foot
> That second
> In the still sleeping town and set forth.

It is clear that the year woke to his "hearing". The poem
proceeds so resonantly that one scarcely sees, for the sound
of the calling gulls and knocking boats, the simple fisher
scene with its flying birds, rocking masts, and quiet "net
webbed wall". The echo in "harbour" and "neighbour" is
one of many in the first stanza alone. "Heaven" "heron"
"beckon" "second" are woven on one warp of vowels and
"wood" "rook" "foot" are woven on another. But the warp
is a twist of several threads or, not to push the metaphor

too far, there are other repetitive sounds, "woke" alone
having five alliterations, and echoing again in the vowels
of "shore" and "forth", the consonants of "rook" and
"knock". The pattern is far more elaborate than this and
offers delights that no dry sum of vocables can ever suggest. Naturally, the rhymes and half rhymes serve to punc-
tuate the poem meaningfully.

The first line in the second stanza runs: "My birthday
began with the water- / Birds . . ." The word "water"
rhymes with "horse" and "autumn" and finally with "border" in the phrase "Over the border"—the sense of the
windy season stressed by association with the wild seashore
and the poet's setting forth from the just-waking town.
As for the horses, they are white horses, suggesting not so
much farm animals as tumbling breakers. Incidentally, it
seems fitting that the poet's name, "Dylan", should be the
Welsh word for sea, and be linked with the god of the
waves. The strong attraction the sea had for him it has
also for W. S. Graham, whose sea pieces reflect Thomas's
influence. But this Scottish poet, like his compatriot,
Adam Drinan, writes about "The friendly thief sea
wealthy with the drowned" with a bitterness foreign to
the Welshman.

The child of whom Thomas writes in his "Poem in October" is spoken of as long dead, but his joy knows resurrection in the poet, who *was* that child. Like "Fern Hill",
one of his best-known poems, this lyric is suffused with
sensual understanding. "Fern Hill" offers another variation
on the theme of "Intimations of Immortality".

Now as I was young and easy under the apple boughs
About the lilting house and happy as the grass was green,

it begins gaily, with a glance at an early Eden and only a
hint of the advancing shadow of the prison house. Thomas
does not tire of repeating what his predecessors, along with
the author of the Gospel according to Luke, had to say
about "the lamb white days" and their passing. In his study
of the educative values of art, Herbert Read gives a con-

sidered account of the value of that early awareness. Like
other stock themes in poetry, this can be so handled that
it seems utterly fresh. Thus Louis MacNeice, in his lyric,
"Daemonium", expresses his gratitude to his "friendly daemon", more vividly described as his "animal angel", close
to him as his shadow,

> For the mealy buttercup days in the ancient meadow,
> For the days of my teens, the sluice of hearing and
>   seeing,
> The days of topspin drives and physical well-being,

and all its subtler but equally inspiriting gifts. MacNeice's
somewhat wry sophistication and his classical training
combine to make him a poet of a very different temper
from Dylan Thomas. Yet in this lyric as elsewhere he
shows an acute realization of the kind of awareness that
the Welshman celebrates so exuberantly.

The motif recurs in Thomas's quasi-sonnet, "When all
my five and country senses see". This is to be read not
for the novelty of its tenor but for the freshness of its
presentation. It tells us once more, but with what packed
urgency, that as the youth becomes more self-conscious,
his virginal sensuous delight in the world about him de-
cays or is blurred or grows callous, but that the poet's
emotional energy will restore and vivify his responsiveness
and make him as a little child who needs no pass to paradise. "The heart is sensual, . . .". Jean Garrigue uses this
lyric in her angry "Oration against the Orator's Oration".
Her diatribe refers definitely to Thomas's poem at the
close, with its plea for fresh winds that will blow away
the mechanical verbiage of those who cannot bear the "Un-
propped, unbooked, and unreasoned" world, demanding
winds that would restore the world

> All naked, maculate and faulty,
> And five green senses then but all the Word.

One of Thomas's most touching lyrics on this theme is
about a child killed in an air raid. It is obscure enough at

first reading, but illumination comes readily, and indeed, this is one of his few poems that can be roughly translated into prose, however cold and bare. It says that the poet will never mourn the child's death until God, who is named only in a roundabout way as the mankind making, bird, beast, and flower fathering, all humbling darkness, bids *him* die. The last line gives the clue to the poem: "After the first death, there is no other." After this early death, the child will not have to die again, as we who grow up to adulthood repeatedly die: first the child in us, then the young man or woman, one self after another. But this child, dying without much experience of the meanness of life, without having to watch the brightness leak away, in Spender's phrase, is not to be mourned.

The lyric is as remarkable for its imagery as for its harmonies and cadences. Thomas speaks of his own death as the time when he will enter again the round

> Zion of the water bead
> And the synagogue of the ear of corn,

that is, when he again becomes one with the elements, to which he gives a sacramental character. Declaring that he will not lament the child's death, he speaks of lament, too, in his own strange yet persuasive way. To sigh is to "let pray the shadow of a sound"; to weep is to sow the

> salt seed
> In the least valley of sackcloth . . .

The next stanza, which contains a Shakespearean pun on "a grave truth", says that he will not "blaspheme down the stations of the breath", a reference to the stations of the Cross that reinforces the poem's meaning. For life is passion, and passion is suffering; had the child lived, she would have endured evil that her innocence and youth did not know. Only one who remembers childhood as a time of peculiar radiance could write so. Repeatedly Thomas's poems quicken the sense of wonder nowhere caught in prose, save in one of Traherne's Meditations:

Certainly Adam in Paradise had not more sweet and
curious apprehensions of the world, than I when I
was a child . . . I knew nothing of sickness or death
or rents or exaction, either for tribute or bread . . .
The corn was orient and immortal wheat, which
never should be reaped, nor was ever sown. I thought
it had stood from everlasting to everlasting. The dust
and stones of the street were as precious as gold: the
gates were at first the end of the world . . . Boys and
girls tumbling in the street, and playing, were moving
jewels. I knew not that they were born or should die:
But all things abided eternally as they were in their
proper places. Eternity was manifest in the Light of
the Day, and something infinite behind everything
appeared: which talked with my expectation and
moved my desire . . . The streets were mine, the
temple was mine, the people were mine, their clothes
and gold and silver were mine, as much as their
sparkling eyes, fair skins and ruddy faces. The skies
were mine, and so were the sun and moon and stars,
and all the world was mine; and I the only spectator
and enjoyer of it. I knew no churlish proprieties, nor
bounds, nor divisions; but all proprieties and divisions
were mine: all treasures and the possessors of them.
So that with much ado I was corrupted, and made to
learn the dirty devices of this world.

Thomas will not mourn the child killed in the air raid,
because she was prevented from suffering corruption.
That she was nevertheless the victim of an unimaginably
dirty device, the poet does not say, though he wrote a
documentary on the bombing raids so harrowing that it
was not released. The fact that, if the child was not to
lose her innocence, she was likewise never to know the
peculiar joys of maturity, he also ignores. Yet the second
part of another poem on a raid, in the course of which an
infant was murdered, speaks of little else. The poet wonders what possibility denied was the first to die "in the

cinder of the little skull," and laments all that perished
with the dead baby. In a prose tale that is like the tran-
script of a childhood memory, Thomas writes: "There,
playing Indians in the evening, I was aware of me myself
in the exact middle of a living story, and my body was my
adventure and my name." This is the feeling that his
poems of childhood and youth convey with the liveliness
of a throbbing pulse. The loss of that first intensity of
being is more regretted than final dissolution. And this is
not solely because the poet sometimes speaks with credence of resurrection, but also because his lament is like
that of Wordsworth for the irrecoverable "splendour in the
grass" and "glory in the flower", like that of Coleridge for
the spent "beautiful and beauty-making power" of imagination.

IV

Thomas once defined poetry as "the rhythmic, inevita-
bly narrative, movement from an over-clothed blindness to
a naked vision that depends, in its intensity, on the
strength of the labour put into the creation of the poetry."
The word "narrative" is misleading. There is no plot, in
the ordinary sense, in Thomas's poems, save for his "Ballad of the Long-legged Bait", one of his most demanding
performances. Even if one gives the word "narrative" the
largest significance, the myth central to his poetry as a
whole is nowhere so explicit as was Hart Crane's. The beclouded pantheism of his early work gives place to a more
orthodox religiosity, but expressed in the same intensely
personal terms.

The poems entitled "Vision and Prayer", like the early
lyrics, abound in startling imagery: "the wall thin as a
wren's bone" becomes

The Wren
Bone writhes down,

as Christ is born to take on the suffering of the world of men. Here, too, are the poet's reverberant rhymes, his personal vocabulary, and his auditory synesthesia, as "the loud sun"

Christens down
The sky.

and "The sun roars at the prayer's end." But if these poems could have been written only by Thomas, they also recall the devotional lyrics of a less anxious century than ours. As the quoted phrases show, the poet accepts the traditional Christian symbol that identifies the Saviour with the sun. Further, just as George Herbert shaped his devout poems to represent an altar and angelic wings, so Thomas prints his religious lyrics in evocative forms. The first is a blunted diamond shape that may represent a womb or an urn. The central word in the first of this group of poems, which turn on the nativity, is "Child", the last word of the final poem is "Die". The shape of the poems in the second group in the series, which turn on the resurrection, is unmistakably a chalice. The chalice, which is formed of two hour-glasses, so that the idea of time is involved with the idea of eternity, is, of course, a symbol of rebirth. The mere appearance of the poem on the page is open to several interpretations.

Thomas courted ambiguity. His account of the way in which he developed his imagery is instructive. "I let, perhaps, an image be 'made' emotionally in me and then apply to it what intellectual and critical forces I possess,—let it breed another, let that image contradict the first, make, of the third image bred of the other two a fourth contradictory image, and let them all, within my imposed formal limits, conflict . . . Out of the inevitable conflict of images—inevitable, because of the creative, recreative, destructive and contradictory nature of the motivating center, the womb of war—I try to make that momentary peace which is a poem . . ." This is more complicated than the Hegelian dialectic, but it describes with greater veracity what goes on in our minds. It does not explain all of the obscurities in Thomas's poetry, with its fusion of pagan and Freudian and Christian imagery, but insofar as it indicates their genesis, it is helpful. The poet delivered himself over to "the womb of war" in more ways than one. The conflict was not alone between images but between the ideas and attitudes they represent. The Freudian recognized the generous beauty of sexuality. The Christian poet, shadowed by the sense of sin of his chapel-going forebears, was prodded to destroy the body to liberate the spirit. Nearly every poem moves tempestuously among contradictory themes: birth is an act of violence, but the child is born into a world quick with delight; all living is involved with dying, but he would have it that the death of the body means the first free breath of the spirit.

Seldom does he remark thus quietly upon the repetition of the ancient cycle:

> A process in the eye forewarns
> The bones of blindness; and the womb
> Drives in a death as life leaks out.

Rather he envisages the dusty forefathers coming "Out of the urn the size of a man" and crying out at the pangs of Time, bearing another son, and therewith new deaths. Typical is a dialogue between the unborn infant and its mother, where the embryo, pitying the pain it must inflict, cries out:

> "If my bunched, monkey coming is cruel
> Rage me back to the making house. . . ."

But the mother replies that there is no escape, for her or for the unborn, from the joy and the anguish, the life and the death that she carries.

One of his early lyrics speaks wryly of his sympathy with all that grows and flourishes: the blowing flower, the flowing stream, the rising wind, and with all that fades and dies: the crooked rose, the dried-up stream, the slackened wind, the man on the gallows, the lover in the grave (do these refer to Christ?). As in less lucid poems, the hammering effect of alliteration is refined by other consonantal echoes and by the chime of rhyme and assonance throughout. Sometimes Thomas seems to seek violence, whether of music or of metaphor, for its own sake, and to a degree that defies the necessary formal limits. Even those images that have a Dantesque clarity are dense with implications.

In the groin of the natural doorway I crouched like a tailor
Sewing a shroud for a journey
By the light of the meat-eating sun.

Only the initiate know that the manifold meanings in the line about "the meat-eating sun" include allusion to a Welsh fertility ritual. But the reference in the first line to the position of the embryo is obvious, as is the reference to the fact that we are no sooner conceived than we begin to build a body moving towards death. It is less obvious that the tailor represents the world of the flesh as against that of the spirit, the world of time as against that of eternity. The derogatory meanings of this image are clarified by its use elsewhere, as in the allusion to "the clock faced tailors", the line: "Comes, like a scissors stalking, tailor age," or the passage in another poem on his fabulous youth, telling how "up through the lubber crust of Wales" the poet "rocketed to astonish"

> The flashing needle rock of squatters,
> The criers of Shabby and Shorten,
> The famous stitch droppers.

Many of Thomas's lyrics are indecipherable. The fewest have the Yeatsian directness of the poem dealing with his "craft or sullen art". The phrase suggests a sobriety quite foreign to him. He is drunk with the world, with the

grape on the vine as well as in the glass, or he is overwhelmed by the sense of loss, often uttered in a thundering darkness, sometimes expressed in clear sexual imagery:

> Cadaver in the hangar
> Tells the stick, 'fail.'

or with the sad simplicity of the grown man's lament for
"the farm forever fled from the childless land." There are
a few poems that speak with an authority both quiet and
somber. Among them are "The Hunchback in the Park"
and the elegy in memory of Ann Jones.

The first begins with a prose statement that the cadence and the vocables render lyrical:

> The hunchback in the park
> A solitary mister
> Propped between trees and water . . .

The second stanza completes the picture of him

> Eating bread from a newspaper
> Drinking water from the chained cup
> That the children filled with gravel
> In the fountain basin where I sailed my ship . . .

The detail work is masterly, having an apparent simplicity
that is nevertheless open to interpretation. The fountain
basin where a lucky boy sails his ship is the rough answer
to the hunchback's animal need. The chained cup there
that the children filled with gravel is the only cup he has.
This we learn from the concluding lines of the stanza that
tell us how he spent the night in a dog kennel, though
"nobody chained him up." The repetition of "chained",
this time as a verb, is a reminder that the solitary mister
needs no constraint, his hunch is his shackle. The poem
proceeds with a picture of him chased by the boys and
helplessly dodging the park attendant, "With his stick
that picked up leaves", as if the hunchback were fearful

of being mistaken for trash. His loneliness is italicized by the presence of the nurses and the swans no less than by the boys making "tigers jump out of their eyes" and the groves "blue with sailors". We are told that the hunchback made a "woman figure without fault" in his daydream to stand "Straight as a young elm" in his sight when he returned to the kenneled dark, and the last lines remind us that she is his sole protection when the memories of the day follow to assault him there. The piece is the more poignant because there is in it no word or hint of pity, and the hunchback's tormentors are honestly represented as "wild boys innocent as strawberries". Indeed, as G. S. Fraser has observed, they too are "locked out": debarred from the imaginative richness that his deprivation gives the hunchback, a richness of which they are a part.

The poem composed in memory of Ann Jones is written, at least partially, in Thomas's elliptical idiom. Thus, the mourners at the funeral feast are evoked by such phrases as "Windshake of sailshaped ears", "the teeth in black", the

> . . . desolate boy who slits his throat
> In the dark of the coffin and sheds dry leaves, . . .

But suddenly the conjuring verbiage is swept away and we stand with the speaker alone, remembering the dead, "In a room with a stuffed fox and a stale fern,". At once the dense imagery resumes, forcing us into the presence of the poor dead woman,

> Whose hooded, fountain heart once fell in puddles
> Round the parched worlds of Wales and drowned each sun . . .

But then the poet recalls himself:

> (Though this for her is a monstrous image blindly
> Magnified out of praise; her death was a still drop; . . .).

The poem moves back and forth between the monstrous magnifications that are Thomas's signature and a lan-

guage that without sacrificing its density is yet unmistakably plain.

> Her fist of a face clenched on a round pain;
> And sculptured Ann is seventy years of stone.

We are caught up into the speaker's grief for the poverty
and the dignity of this provincial life, so distantly related
to "the ferned and foxy woods", a grief that will not give
over until

> The stuffed lung of the fox twitch and cry Love
> And the strutting fern lay seeds on the black sill.

The miracle is real and it seems as though not the poet
had wrought it, but "dead humped Ann".

Much more straightforward and equally moving is the
poem referred to above on his "craft or sullen art". He
says there that he writes "Not for ambition or bread" nor
for the proud solitary,

> Nor for the towering dead
> With their nightingales and psalms
> But for the lovers, their arms
> Round the griefs of the ages,
> Who pay no praise or wages
> Nor heed my craft or art.

For those who do heed it, his poetry rewards scrutiny. It
also wins immediate response to its rich aural harmonies,
to its profound pathos, and to a radiance like that described by Traherne as having rested on his childhood.
Repeatedly Thomas testifies to a like experience, as where
he tells how the four winds

> Shone in my ears the light of sound,
> Called in my eyes the sound of light.
> And yellow was the multiplying sand,
> Each golden grain spat life into its fellow,
> Green was the singing house.

"You never enjoy the world aright," wrote Traherne, "till you see how a sand exhibiteth the wisdom and power of God." Thomas had a more difficult task: to see the wisdom and power of God exhibited in a world subjected to the fires of a man-made inferno. He wrote at least five poems about air raids. They are no less devout than his poems about childhood. As has been seen, one of them deals, if indirectly, with that theme. Another offers a fine example of Thomas's condensed imagery. This sonnet, "Among Those Killed in the Dawn Raid Was a Man Aged One Hundred", has a Blakean quality, but not even Blake could have made an engraving to illustrate the sestet:

Dig no more for the chains of his grey haired heart.
The heavenly ambulance drawn by a wound
Assembling waits for the spades' ring on the cage.
O keep his bones away from that common cart,
The morning is flying on the wings of his age
And a hundred storks perch on the sun's right hand.

It is unlikely that the poet knew the Swedish legend that this sacred bird got its name because it flew around Christ as He hung on the cross, crying: "Styrka! Styrka!" or "Strengthen! Strengthen!" In any case, the last line is clearly a parable of resurrection. In this poem, as in the others, the political significance of the bombings is scarcely glanced at. Although Thomas took his stand "with any revolutionary body that asserts it to be the right of all men to share, equally and impartially, every production of man from man and from the sources of production at man's disposal", his poetry ignores social issues.

At its rare best it offers the most direct kind of apprehension with an immediacy and intimacy foreign to the adult mind. Certain of his lyrics might be called musical epiphanies. Joyce's word for the illuminated moment seized upon by the artist comes to mind in connection with Thomas because of the way in which he manipulates his vocabulary. This Joycean gift for making his words do

multiple duty, the acknowledged struggle that engendered
his poems, and the conflict within him between the gospel
according to Freud and that according to the saints,
helped frame the poet's dazzling, crowded idiom. Yet the
scenery is the landscape of his childhood, the farms and
the fox-haunted hills, the weather and the sea that the
fisherman knows. Such Christian and Freudian symbols as
fish and cock were as natural to him as the sea and the
barnyard. What is novel is the curious mineral associations he had with flesh, and the many references to tailor-
ing: God is "The cloud perched tailors' master with nerves
for cotton" and himself "The boy of common thread".

v

There is something baroque about the style of such a
poet as Thomas, as about that of Hart Crane, an energy
extravagant to the point of contortion. However individual
their work, the productions of other poets of our day in
search of a God also betray a half-willful dynamism. It is
evident in that of George Barker. His most serious poems
have a boyish boisterousness like Thomas's, and his play
with language is full of tricky puns. The appealing sonnet
to his mother shows her

> Sitting as huge as Asia, seismic with laughter,
> Gin and chicken helpless in her Irish hand,
> Irresistible as Rabelais but most tender for
> The lame dogs and hurt birds that surround her . . .

and ends with the prayer "That she will move from mourning into morning." His "1st American Ode" makes a witty
reference to "Merman Melville", a phrase he likes well
enough to repeat in his "3rd American Ode" where he
hails "The Merman Melville, lashed to the mast of vision". There is both pun and palindrome in the "Sacred
Elegy" that ends "O dog my God!" Barker apostrophizes
Deity in a context suggesting that He can behave like a
dog, but that He is also, as the dog is said to be, man's

best friend, and that He gets much the same treatment. At the same time the poet appears to be bidding his soul follow doglike after his God. The compressed imagery of Barker's "Holy Poems" enhances their quality of tormented ecstasy. The technique is reminiscent of Hopkins', as, more clearly and all naturally, is the syntax in one of his memorial sonnets on two young seamen lost overboard in a mid-Pacific storm.

Barker's poetry combines extravagant language and private symbolism with topical references to current history, as witness his "Requiem for the Austrian Constitution". Such references are the more remarkable when they occur in poems that he calls "elegies", in imitation of that most apolitical of poets, Rainer Maria Rilke. His "Elegy on Spain", dedicated "to the photograph of a child killed in an air-raid on Barcelona", with its characteristically baroque metaphors and echoing vocables, can be understood only in the light of contemporary events. This concern with man as a political and social animal is what chiefly distinguishes his work from that of Dylan Thomas. Not only mortality, but something less intrinsic to the human condition is lamented in his first "Epistle", which was addressed to Thomas. "Meeting a monster of mourning wherever I go," the poet says,

> For whom are you miserable I ask and he murmurs
> I am miserable for innumerable man: for him
> Who wanders through Woolworth's gazing at tin stars;
> I mourn the maternal future tense, Time's mother,
> Who has him in her lap, and I mourn also her,
> Time whose dial face flashes with scars.

The "Epistle" proceeds, in diction half colloquial, half poetic, to give the sad and sordid details of a deprived boyhood, and concludes with the knowledge of how he began by being miserable for himself and now is "miserable for the mass of man." Not misery, but resolution: "the conspiracy of five hundred million / To keep alive and kick" is the theme of a poem on a meeting with the

author of "Resolution and Independence". The first stanza
sets the scene:

I encountered the crowd returning from amusements,
The Bournemouth Pavilion, or the marvellous gardens,
The Palace of Solace, the Empyrean Cinema: and saw
William Wordsworth was one, tawdrily conspicuous,
Obviously emulating the old man of the mountain-moor,
Traipsing along on the outskirts of the noisy crowd.

It should be observed that Wordsworth, defying "The
acute superstition that [he] is after all dead", is not one
of the crowd, but is traipsing on its outskirts. It is the
stuffy old reactionary who is dead. Barker salutes the living Wordsworth: the man who recognized in the ancient
leech gatherer a courage that the poet must emulate, without denying the faith of the joyful young celebrant of the
French Revolution.

Poems of religious affirmation are apt to answer the
Psalmist's command to make a joyful noise. The Trappist,
Thomas Merton, seems to have compensated for his vow
of silence by stationing his poems "on the world's loud
corners" where their rhetoric sounds sadly forced. The
"Divine Poems" of the Philippine poet, José Garcia Villa,
walk delicately, but can dart fierce lightnings from their
eyes. The early poetry of Robert Lowell is eloquent of a
religiosity founded, like Barker's, on tortured sympathy
for his fellows. At first Lowell's startling imagery went
clothed in thunders. He once criticized Dylan Thomas for
not allowing enough "numb or supporting lines" in his
verse. Possibly he recognized this fault because he was inclined to be betrayed into it. Many of his poems rock with
reverberant vocables. Lowell's narrative pieces do not always demand the magnificence of their rhetoric. Yet those
who found his nightmarish vision too singular and the
comfort of his creed unacceptable were nevertheless able
to respond to the power of his presentation. His later
verse is at once more personal and less private. It includes

a poem "To Delmore Schwartz" which is a candid stripping of his friend and himself, drunk on anxiety, ambition, and gin. Some of the more recent lyrics by Schwartz express a euphoric attitude absent from Lowell's case history and recalling rather Edith Sitwell's work in their baroque exaltation.

Poetry expressive of this attitude, like that of Crane and Thomas, can perhaps be written in a secular vein, but so savage an assault upon reality as is made by poets of this stripe argues a religious, or at least a metaphysical, urge. Their attack upon language is like a battering-ram set against the mystery of the universe. It yields not the fraction of an inch to such treatment, and sometimes makes the poetry seem ridiculous. But there are occasions when the opposite is true. Then the poem that cannot shake the door, much less broach it, is like a powerful light illumining some of its details, or an impalpable telescope orienting us with regard to unearthly things. It is nevertheless in his poems praising earthly things and the waters that hold the earth, and the lovers who for a little while rejoice in it, rejoicing in each other, that Dylan Thomas speaks most tellingly.

Three years before he died, he held out the promise of a long poem, only a part of which had been written, and which was to be called "In Country Heaven". It was to be about the self-destruction of one of the worlds of God. With his customary prodigality and only one capitalized noun, Thomas called Him "the godhead, the author, the milky-way farmer, the first cause, the architect, lamplighter, quintessence, the beginning Word, the anthropomorphic bowler-out and black-baller, the stuff of all men, scapegoat, martyr, maker, woe-bearer— . . .". The projected poem was to begin with His weeping on a hill in Heaven because Earth had killed itself: "insanity has blown it rotten;" and on it there was no creature at all. Then, while God weeps, those in Heaven who had been countrymen on Earth, call to one another, remembering the things they had known there. "The poem," said

Thomas, "is made of these tellings. . . . It grows into praise of what is and what could be on this lump in the skies. It is a poem about happiness." So are most of the lyrics on which his reputation is likely to rest. Some sense of what the projected work might have been may be gleaned from three poems that were to have a place in it: "In Country Sleep", "Over St. John's Hill", and "In the White Giant's Thigh", the White Giant being a no mythical kinsman of Goliath but a landmark on a Welsh hill. All three lyrics are plainly "in praise of what is" in the natural world.

In an early poem Thomas wrote, cheering himself up: "The insect fable is a certain promise." Uncertain, we turn back to the boy whispering "the truth of his joy"

> To the trees and the stones and the fish in the tide.
> And the mystery
> Sang alive
> Still in the water and singing birds.

13. Wars and Rumors of Wars

The renaissance that began by bringing poetry back to
common talk and common experience coincided with a
war. World War I was fought on a scale and with a feroc-
ity appalling to a generation that had not been nurtured
on horrors. It brought home to men the need for plain
speech about what they and their fellows must endure. At
the start there was a certain amount of verse written in
ignorance of what the soldiers were to face and with a
confident if vague sense of what they were defending.
Masefield's "August, 1914" opens with a picture of a quiet
cornfield at night, and though it ends with a sad glimpse
of the grasses "Rutted this morning by the passing guns",
it is not before the poet has summoned up a vision of the
New Jerusalem rising on English soil. A patriotism rooted
literally in the land informed poems by men of such different tempers as Thomas Hardy, the aging ironist, that
champion of foreign literary fashions: Ford Madox Ford
(then Hueffer) and the popular young romantic, Rupert
Brooke. The attitude of acceptance, whether dour or serene, was not to prevail. Robert Graves presented a certain cure for lust of blood by painting trench scenes with
the savage veracity of Goya's "Disasters of War". He
prophesied that another war was coming, which "new
foul tricks unguessed before" would "win and justify".
Siegfried Sassoon, obsessed by the agony and the waste
that he had witnessed, poured a hot recital of it into his
verse. Bitterly he indicted those responsible for the horrors
that were the order of the day. But neither he nor more
subdued soldier poets had a control of poetic structure

equal to the emotion it was meant to bear. To some degree this is true even of Isaac Rosenberg and Wilfred Owen.

A very conscious craftsman, whose name was to be repeatedly invoked by those who came after him, Owen spent pains on form in a manner that was apt to draw attention away from the poem to its technical details. Thus, the onomatopoeia in his "Anthem for Doomed Youth" is all too obvious:

> What passing bells for these who died as cattle?
> Only the monstrous anger of the guns,
> Only the stuttering rifles' rapid rattle . . .

The listener forgets the significance of the sound in observing its appropriateness. One of Owen's most memorable poems, "Strange Meeting", which remained unfinished, is similarly flawed by the obtrusiveness of his devices, as well as by irrelevant archaisms. Nevertheless, the validity of this subtle, painful dream of an encounter between two soldiers from opposing lines has become brutally clear. Owen died before he could give right utterance to "the truth untold". But he foresaw what was to come:

> Now men will go content with what we spoiled.
> Or discontent, boil bloody, and be spilled.
> They will be swift with swiftness of the tigress,
> None will break ranks, though nations trek from progress.

One of the weaknesses of this prophetic work is that the couplets, accenting as they do the cleverness of the consonantal rhymes, seem unsuitable to the material. In "The Show" the technical innovations are more effective. This poem gains strength from the fact that it relies not on statement but on metaphor. "From a vague height" where his soul stands with Death, the poet looks down on "a sad land, weak with sweats of dearth". The flatness of the vowels helps to display the barren fields, pocked and scabbed with plagues that are not named. He describes what he sees crawling over that sad land in terms that actualize the hideousness of trench warfare. The imagery is sustained in all its powerful ugliness to the end. This is one of the most terrible poems of the war. Its force is not lessened by the double meaning of the final line, which suggests, perhaps unintentionally, the treason of the intellectuals, and which makes the victim a partner in the guilt.

THE SHOW

My soul looked down from a vague height with Death,
As unremembering how I rose or why,
And saw a sad land, weak with sweats of dearth,
Gray, cratered like the moon with hollow woe,
And pitted with great pocks and scabs of plagues.

Across its beard, that horror of harsh wire,
There moved thin caterpillars, slowly uncoiled.
It seemed they pushed themselves to be as plugs
Of ditches, where they writhed and shrivelled, killed.

By them had slimy paths been trailed and scraped
Round myriad warts that might be little hills.

From gloom's last dregs these long-strung creatures crept,
And vanished out of dawn down hidden holes.

(And smell came up from those foul openings
As out of mouths, or deep wounds deepening.)

On dithering feet upgathered, more and more,
Brown strings, towards strings of gray, with bristling
        spines.
All migrants from green fields, intent on mire.

Those that were gray, of more abundant spawns,
Ramped on the rest and ate them and were eaten.

I saw their bitten backs curve, loop, and straighten,
I watched those agonies curl, lift, and flatten.
Whereat, in terror what that sight might mean,
I reeled and shivered earthward like a feather.

And Death fell with me, like a deepening moan.
And He, picking a manner of worm, which half had hid
Its bruises in the earth, but crawled no further,
Showed me its feet, the feet of many men,
And the fresh-severed head of it, my head.

In the fragmentary notes that prefaced his posthumous
book Owen wrote that he was not concerned with poetry:
"My subject is War, and the pity of War. The Poetry is
in the pity." That phrase has become part of the language.
Thus, the Irish poet, Valentin Iremonger, writing of an
"Evening in Summer" and speaking, not of war, but of
time's treachery, makes it part of his lyrical meditation:

And though, midnight inclining bells over the city
With a shower of sound like tambourines of Spain
Gay in the teeth of the night air, I thought
Of a man who said the truth was in the pity,
Somehow, under the night's punched curtain, I was lost.
I only knew the pity and the pain.

Owen, scribbling against the cruel helplessness of the situation he shared with less articulate men, had felt that all
he could then do was to warn: "That is why true Poets
must be truthful." Perhaps had he lived to revise those
notes, he would have seen the truth more clearly. "Pity
spareth so many an evil thing.", as Artemis complains in
Pound's thirtieth Canto. To make as much of this anemic
emotion as Owen did is to run the danger of producing
poems that have been described as "all blood, dirt, &
sucked sugar stick". The man responsible for that description insisted that passive suffering was not the theme for
poetry. Good poems, including some by Yeats, have been
written on that theme, but pity must come alive in a
kindled indignation. And it is without meaning unless
the poet controls his material with the sensitive power
that the jockey exerts over his horse, the pilot over his
ship. Owen, without achieving Keats's imaginative greatness, was given to his youthful lushness. Some of his com-

panions failed for another reason: they were so outraged
by the wrongs they wanted to castigate that they fumbled
the technical devices which would have helped them to
express what they so passionately felt. They spoke as soldiers and citizens first, as poets afterward.

The Americans, belatedly involved in the war, were,
with some popular exceptions, not so exultant about the
adventure that it promised, nor were they so deeply dis-
illusioned. Sandburg, one of the more vocal, wrote candid
but unilluminated pieces, none of which matched his
elegy on the men busy with their long job of killing,
"Fixed in the drag of the world's heartbreak,". Frost,
building a bonfire of brushwood, paused to observe, emphatically: "*War is for everyone, for children too.*" and
went on with his quiet labors. Only after the signing of
the peace did the younger men cry out against the gutted
values that the war had heaped upon vanquished and
victors alike.

II

During the next decade the poets had an opportunity to
explore the ache a man feels in amputated hopes as well
as in amputated hands and legs. They had not only seen
death wholesale, but they had seen it as a machine affair,
an international industry. They had "walked eye-deep in
hell". Some had limped out of it into the purgatory tellingly described by Ernest Walsh in his tribute to his hospital mate, Kennedy. Those who had not been at the
front were like men who had lived through the plague and
who must suffer the added indignity of survival under the
reign of a plutocracy as dismally vulgar as it was predatory.
Only by becoming grotesque could poetry mirror so grotesque a world.

Cummings paused in the making of delicate love lyrics
to pour out explosively his derision and disgust. Often his
writing on the wall was merely an addition to the literature of the privy. But when he was not amusing himself

by outraging the good burgesses, he communicated his own sense of outrage at the great gaudy parade of death.

Never shy of a romantic lyricism that tends to lapse into sentimentality, he has shown the obverse of it as unmistakably as did Villon, who also lived in a postwar world, his mordant temper finding vent in angrily gay obscenity and incisive satire. Cummings' portraits of "Five Americans"—Liz, Mame, Gert, Marj, and Fran, are as thick with frank detail as the pictures of prostitutes that Villon drew. Nor are Villon's rascally churchmen more sardonically damned than are Cummings' contemporary bigots, prudes, and patrioteers. Sometimes he contents himself with an acid epigram. More often he lets them speak for themselves, accentuating the satire by using conventional forms, as in the sonnet which begins:

> "next to of course god america i
> love you land of the pilgrims and so forth . . ."

and continues as breathlessly:

> "why talk of beauty what could be more beaut-
> iful than these heroic happy dead . . ."

The fractional rhyme: "beaut-" helps to emphasize the fact that the orator is using the American language. This sonnet is an instance of the way in which Cummings will take a pompous platitude and blow it up till the hot air bursts from the shreds of rubber. His behavior is superficially that of a naughty boy. Actually it is that of a moralist, an old-fashioned New England anarchist, protesting against decay.

He turned his candid camera on whatever scene presented itself. Once it was the brutality of the Parisian "*flics*" (cops) toward the local communists. Again, it was the "good kumrads" whom you can always tell "by their altruistic smell" and every one of whom "is a bit / of quite unmitigated hate". He has no social program. He hates the "shrill collective myth" with all his anarchic heart. His future is individual and personal, his freedom is the full realization of the moment that some sages have identified with eternity. But he allied himself naturally with those who were up in arms against an engorging middle class.

Political radicalism in postwar France was an aspect of literary radicalism. The descendants of Rimbaud echoed his boyhood cry: "One is an exile in one's own country!" The Americans who shared that ache, fleeing to Paris, could at least feel at home in the company of their fellow exiles, the French poets. There were other Americans abroad who provided notable targets for the lyrical sharpshooter. Frequently he aimed at the culture hunter from these provincial States.

—O Education:O
thos cook & son

Cummings exclaimed over the virginal Americans descending, complete with Baedeckers, mothers, and kodaks, upon Venice and its environs. Other poets made equally mordant observations on the compatriots they encountered far from home. The satirized ladies and gentlemen had gone abroad to add European culture to their emblems of conspicuous waste. The satirists had also gone abroad, but with other aims. They sought to keep the arts alive under conditions more favorable, in spite of Europe's malaise, than those to be found at home. They felt orphaned of a tradition, whether by loss or lack. Allen Tate made this deprivation the burden of his lay. His own debt to the classics is paid on page after page: in the titles and epigraphs and even passages of his poems, in his frequent Homeric and Virgilian references, in his repeated use of the Platonic parable of the cave. The bitter savor of his lines is that of one who, like his "Aeneas at Washington", is an exile both in his own country and in his own age.

The sense of alienation was to desolate those who had to witness a moral bankruptcy worse than that which followed the first world war. But before this occurred, the victors were presented with the Greek gift of a prosperity out of whose belly, in a night, crept disaster. During the Depression a sonneteer who had exclaimed: "The muse of Darwin! Next, the muse of Freud!" might have observed a younger generation hailing the Muse of Marx. She was invoked sardonically as the Social Muse by Archibald MacLeish, who addressed her successively as Señora, Madame, Fräulein, Lady, and Barinya, thus pointing out her lack of a name and a country. The poem asserts plainly that

> The things of the poet are done to a man alone
> As the things of love are done—or of death. . . .

and that on the bed of love or of death, "Neither his class nor his kind nor his trade may come near him". The "Invocation" is clearly dated by allusions to Marx and Morgan and above all, Hoover. It was during his administration, 1929–33, that MacLeish was writing *Conquistador*, the poem that he declared to be a covert attack upon the men who had conquered and despoiled the world of technology as the Spaniards had conquered and despoiled Mexico. This period of economic disaster took on some of the aspects of war. It meant physical deprivation and death, sometimes from the window of a skyscraper, oftener the starving of body and spirit in a slum or in one of the cold, bare, dirty Hoovervilles scattered across the land. It meant the hopeless tedium that is part of modern warfare. Like war, it was a symptom of moral sickness.

The poets, shaken by the fevers and agues of the times, reacted to this symptom in various ways. Horace Gregory, plunging down tenement-lined streets, along proud avenues, and off into purgatorial suburbs, answered their pressures with a nervous lyricism that drew upon names famous in Greek and Elizabethan tragedy to point up the bleak circumstances of forgotten men, some of them his friends and mentors. Among the latter he counted the poet, James Oppenheim, and the recalcitrant thinker, Randolph Bourne, both of whom had been isolated from their fellows by prophesying—truly, as events were to prove—that World War I was the prelude to more terrible conflicts.

Hammered upon by the obscene forces the action of which these men had foreseen, Gregory pleaded for power *"to stay in no retreat and not to die."* Others, the tone of their irony more aggressive, spoke with growing clarity in the name of a politically biased idealism. Muriel Rukeyser wrote a lyric about a strikers' demonstration and an intimate gathering of sympathizers that demanded: "Make music out of night will change the night." Several of her own ambitious long pieces were an effort, less successful than a few strongly felt lyrics, in just this direction. She was speaking not alone for herself but for her generation when she characterized Jeffers' poetry as "A long and tragic drum-roll beating anger, / Sick of a catapulting nightmare world". As the numbers of the unemployed swelled, a so-called proletarian poetry grew also. The most aloof writers were drawn toward the political and economic vortex. Wallace Stevens, his eyes roving to a picture by Picasso, that " 'hoard / Of destructions',," wondered if this were "an image of our society". Picasso's actual word was not "hoard" but "sum", and he was speaking of the elimination of the unnecessary in a painting. However it is worded, the phrase obviously carries other associations.

The image of our civilization as a "hoard of destructions" is mirrored repeatedly in the blistered glass of Kenneth Fearing's verse. He attacked the violence peculiar to a profit economy in violent parodies of the voices of the high-pressure salesman, the insurance agent, the public relations counselor, the radio announcer advertising whiskys, wars, crises, and cosmetics with the same unctuous glibness. Fearing's medley of slogans and clichés caught the authentic noises of the metropolis (cosmopolis, necropolis?). His details were of the moment, as in the portrait of the man whose soul is at peace, "soothed by Walter Lippmann, and sustained by Haig & Haig", and the "Dirge" for another, also at peace:

With who the hell are you at the corner of his casket, and
      where the hell we're going on the right-hand silver

> knob, and who the hell cares walking second from
> the end with an American Beauty wreath from why
> the hell not,

Very much missed by the circulation staff of the New York
      Evening Post; deeply deeply mourned by the
      B.M.T.,

Wham, Mr. Roosevelt; pow, Sears Roebuck; awk, big dip-
      per; bop, summer rain;
Bong, Mr., bong, Mr., bong, Mr., bong.

Such timely allusions must become as obscure as a good
deal of Villon's verse, while unredeemed by his telling
metaphor and lyric line. Sharing Kenneth Rexroth's sense
of outrage, he also was sometimes too much an iconoclast
to be a poet. Yet Fearing communicated his own desperate
anger by his satiric use of vulgar catchwords, his iteration
of the day-to-day horrors, the endless anonymous casual-
ties in the war against poverty, his shocking substitution of
raw fact for the happy commonplaces of a child's game of
let's pretend. There was a frank admission of panic in his
nervous repetitions and his parodies of newspaper scare-
heads: THE TWENTIETH CENTURY COMES BUT ONCE—YOU
ARE THE VERY MAN WE WANT. Sometimes it is the panic of
those caught in the postwar slump, later on it is that of
prewar disillusion. He spoke for those unable to speak for
themselves as the deliberately alienated writers of the
Beat generation could not do. Occasionally the tone is
quiet, but it is the quiet of suppressed indignation that
burned in the words of Debs: "While there is a soul in
prison, I am not free."

His music is minimal and, where it sounds, comes out
of a juke box. Fearing composed several American rhap-
sodies and though he wrote only one "Twentieth Century
Blues" the title might be given to the coarse plangent discords of his work as a whole. Nothing could be farther from
Wallace Stevens' picture of the poet plucking a blue guitar,
symbol of the imagination, with blue connoting the cool

color of distance. Yet in the confused period between two
world wars, Stevens, chopping his "sullen psaltery",
echoed the sound of ordinary "blues", and there is a reminder of Fearing's queries and of Fearing's cadence, when
he asks:

> Is the spot on the floor, there, wine or blood
> And whichever it may be, is it mine?

Years later, in the midst of overt war, the British poet,
Alex Comfort, was to write, in "Notes for My Son":

> Remember, the smell of burning will not sicken you
> If they persuade you that it will thaw the world

> Beware. The blood of a child does not smell so bitter
> If you have shed it with a high moral purpose.

Here too the cadence is that of Fearing, whose work Comfort probably never read, and whom in no other respect
he resembles. The sardonic intensity is here, too, even if
the music is not "blues". It is as if the same quality of
feeling dictated a like response.

In a book of vignettes of the sharp miseries and edged
pleasures of Negro life, be it on Railroad Avenue or the
Georgia roads, Langston Hughes has a note on the blues.
They have, he says, "a strict poetic pattern: one long line
repeated and a third line to rhyme with the first two.
Sometimes the second line in repetition is slightly changed
and sometimes, but very seldom, it is omitted. The mood
of the *Blues* is almost always despondency, but when they
are sung people laugh." Hughes gave a turn of his own to
this simple form and injected its syncopated effect and the
attendant mood into several pieces. Because she is so scrupulous a craftsman, one or two of Elizabeth Bishop's "Songs
for a Colored Singer" are more telling than some of Hughes'
intimate Negro songs.

With his accustomed restraint Frost once complained
that "poetry's great anti-lure" has been

> to live ungolden with the poor,
> Enduring what the ungolden must endure.

During the Depression many insisted that poetry itself
must live ungolden with the poor. The need for reforming
the world became the "great anti-lure" not because it took
the poets away from the practice of their art but because it
engrossed that art. Only the few realized what Malraux
was to say of a similar movement in France, that the new
academicism of a punch on the jaw was worth no more
than the old academicism of the-young-girl-playing-Bach-
while-looking-at-the-lilies.

                              III

   The convention that poetry must be aggressively revolutionary in tone and its language ordinary to the point of
vulgarity was largely an American one. It was adopted by
young versemakers who were apt to be proletarian in fact
as well as in their sympathies. They cannot have read Mayakovsky's essay, "How to Make Verse", a translation of
which appeared in an obscure periodical during World
War II, but they might well have agreed with him that the
first "datum" for a poem (the scientific term is symptomatic) was the existence of a social problem that could be
solved only by poetry, and the second datum was the will
of the class or group represented by the poet. Mayakovsky
did not go on taking orders from society for his poems. He
shot himself. The ostensible reason was an unhappy love
affair. It may have been with the Communist party. In any
case, his political commitment did not prevent this original
and powerful craftsman from acknowledging in the same
essay that a poet must write verse only when he cannot
speak through any other medium, or from confessing that
"A poet evaluates every meeting, every signboard, every
event, only as material for verbal formations."
   The devotees of the Social Muse in Great Britain were
young men whose social sympathies did not destroy a lively

interest in their craft. When their work first won attention they were loosely united by the conviction that the writer was "not so much the mouthpiece of the community . . . as its conscience, its critical faculty, its generous instinct." Their secular faith, so close to that of the communist poet, did not prevent them from going to school to Hopkins and Eliot. They returned to the simplicities of the nursery rhyme, the easy lilt of the ballad, and found in the vigorous rhythm of Anglo-Saxon verse with its marked alliteration a form suitable to the summons they had to utter. Their eager speech did not wait on grammatical usage, and they reveled as Hopkins had in verbal play and knotty concentration. They accepted the conversational tone and the free associations of Eliot's verse, though their borrowings were different. They exploited the near rhymes with which Wilfred Owen had experimented, and expressed the passionate will to assert human values that he shared with Lawrence. The horrors of the front they had not known. While World War II was still no more than a threat, their poetry had less to say about the anguish that war entails than about the demand for a new social order, to be won, if must be, by fighting.

For some years poetry had been reflecting the mechanical noises, the syncopated tempo of urban life. The younger men were not so conscious of the horns and motors at their backs as of the airplane engine buzzing overhead, the drill grinding at their feet to change a street that might soon be detonated by an enemy bomb or blocked by a revolutionary barricade. Machinery and war were taken for granted in a fashion impossible to their seniors. It was part of the landscape or the "inscape" of the world that they saw rushing toward destruction and rebirth. A distinguishing feature of Auden's early verse was an acceptance of machine warfare that allowed him not merely to introduce it casually and frequently but to convert it into metaphor.

He and his companions took their symbols from our industrialized society and from their study of the natural and

the social sciences, more especially psychopathology. The
scene presented was one of industrial blight: the abandoned works, the ruined farm. Their chief characters were
the labor spy, the thug, the social parasite viewed as a
menace to the healthy organism, the effects of a dominating money power seen as symptoms of disease. Auden repeatedly attacked the Old Gang, the declining middle
class, and therewith attacked everything in himself that
clung to it. The attack—since he was a lively as well as
an angry young man—took the form of buffoonery. The
obscurity of this verse came from sources over and above
the abrupt syntax, the anti-poetic imagery, the puns. It was
due in part to the fact that he turned without warning
from mockery of the social order he despised to mockery
of himself and his friends who, because of their alliance
with that order, were interfering with its defeat.

C. Day Lewis differed from the poets with whom he was
yoked in being more concerned than they were at this time
with metaphysical questions. Witness his references to
Spinoza and to such American writers as Melville, Whitman, and Emily Dickinson, along with his epigraphs from
Hopkins and Blake. Yet he too employed images taken
from modern technology. This was natural in poems designed to give dynamic expression to his faith in social
revolution. It was more remarkable that images derived
from politics and industry should serve intimate lyrics written during the anxious, hopeful months of attendance
upon the arrival of his first-born.

> But think of passion and pain.
> Those absolute dictators will enchain
> The low, exile the princely parts . . .

he writes, and after a stanza on early love which properly
employs metaphors from the natural world, returns, for
allusion to the hours of labor, to the imagery of his own
time and place: "But I shall wait at the railhead alone."

It remained for Stephen Spender to write lyrically of the
beauty of machinery. Like his fellow poets, he went be-

yond this, making metaphors out of the details of the modern scene. He concluded a personal lyric, innocent of political implications, with the reflection that, if certain responses to the beloved were "tricklings through a dam", his love must be great enough to run a factory on, to drive a tram, or give a city power. This is closer to the usage of John Donne, with his maps and compasses, than to that of Shelley, with his violets and mad enchanters. Yet Shelley had recognized that "Hell is a city much like London—", a chief theme with Spender, equally torn with pity for those whose lives were as empty as their pockets. It is the pity with which those lyrics bleed that sets them apart, as the injured are set apart, from the confident or sardonically witty verse of his fellows. He has said that he suffers "from an excess of ideas and a weak sense of form". He might with more truth have said that he suffers from a sense of moral responsibility and metaphysical yearning in excess of his power to handle living language.

Where the young Auden was primarily satirical, Day Lewis hortatory, and MacNeice wryly diffident, Spender expressed the romantic attitude. The locus of his vision of felicity was what seemed to him, as it had to Shelley, a compassable future. His romanticism was fed, and occasionally poisoned, by German sources as well, and his later work was to show other influences, including that of Edith Sitwell, but from the outset his work differed clearly from that of his confrères. He might stand unhappily staring at the unemployed, walk through streets where "Road-drills explore new areas of pain,"—might ask what, living under so heavy a shadow, he could do that mattered. But the grief, the fatigue, the despair, bred by a war remembered and war foreseen, by the boom and the slump, and the insanity of those in power, yielded to another mood. The vagueness of his references, the religious joy that characterizes much of this socially-biased verse, anticipates poetry of another order and points toward the baroque work of a later decade.

If his early lyrics reflected the industrial age, he was less

fearful than his companions of imagery depending on nature. The sun pours through his pages, the actual sun, as
well as the Shelleyan symbol of Promethean triumph. In
one lyric about the hope of revolution Spender alters the
sun symbol by merging it with an image of light: "Clean
and equal like the shine from snow." The simile is repeated in every stanza with new significance. Finally the
poet pleads that the next generation, looking back, may

> Watch the admiring dawn explode like a shell
> Around us, dazing us with its light like snow.

The imagery is not particularly happy here, as one is reminded in reading lines that MacNeice addressed "To a
Communist", telling him that his thoughts made "shape
like snow", a perfect poise, but maintained "For one day
only." Indeed, the shining expectations of these young men
melted rapidly as it became clear that the unemployed
were not to mount defiant barricades, but to prepare for
another world war.

MacNeice was less apt to use snow metaphorically in
poems about social change than to consider it in itself,
with roses blooming against the window of the firelit room
from which he looked out on it, and to realize "The drunk-
enness of things being various." Some of his most exciting
poems have to do with a world that is "suddener . . . more
spiteful and gay than one supposes—". Nevertheless he was
repeatedly drawn back to remind his friends, and himself
with them:

> Minute your gesture but it must be made—
>
> .   .   .   .   .   .
>
> Hatred of hatred, assertion of human values.

This statement comes at the close of his "Eclogue from
Iceland", in which the speakers are an Englishman, an
Irishman, and the ghost of Grettir, hero of an Icelandic
saga. "Is it our only duty?" asks the Englishman, and the
saga hero replies:

>Yes, my friends, it is your only duty.
>And, it may be added, it is your only chance.

The dry prose statement is characteristic of MacNeice, but the abstractions are not. He has said that he enjoys poetry "as one enjoys swimming or swearing," and many of his poems exhibit the swimmer's sensual surrender and control, or a brief intense flare of anger at the malice of things. He is naturally but only temporarily diverted by the day-to-day assaults on freedom from his interest in such matters as time and identity, the incorrigibly plural universe, the artist's attempts at ordering it, and the way in which "the appalling unrest of the soul" exudes from Chardin's dried fish and brown jug and bowl.

His verse, too, is plural, including the forgotten commonplaces of the sensual manifold: "the sluice of hearing and seeing", "the beer-brown water", the fire that flames "with a bubbling sound"; including Belfast and Barcelona, England and Iceland, Connecticut and the Hebrides and Athens; including laughter and terror and brief peace, the pangs of delight and of pain; including the public and the private man. His rhythms are equally various: the lilt of the folk song and the music-hall ditty, a blank verse line so flexible as to be almost free, the strict traditional measures, are all to be met with. His language is usually simple and colloquial, though he is no more averse to the classical allusion and the precise pedantic word when he wants it than he is to the pun. Apparently casual, his work has the restraint, the light touch, of the Latin lyricists he knows so well. The cadences, the vocabulary, the allusions, are different, but one finds the same easy tone and the same wry honesty in the verse of an American classical scholar: Rolfe Humphries, who has translated a few of Edna Millay's sonnets into Latin, the *Aeneid* and the *Metamorphoses* of Ovid into English. For Humphries, as for MacNeice, but more notably for the Irishman, this approach results in exceptionally candid verse about his lack of illusions, his uncertainties, and his unease, which are also ours.

He has reversed the attitude of his companions and
some of his later work has been increasingly hortatory.
Moreover, during the second world war the need for reconciliation with the universe asserted itself, sometimes all
too prosily, in his pages. As an epigraph there, George
Herbert's "Even poisons praise thee" found its place, and
further tribute to the seventeenth-century pietist was paid
in a poem that gave a fresh turn to one of his most touching lyrics: "Sighs and Groans". Herbert's prayer opens:

> O do not use me
> After my sins! Look not on my desert,
> But on Thy glory! then Thou wilt reform,
> And not refuse me; for Thou only art
> The mighty God, but I a silly worm:
> O do not bruise me!

MacNeice, in a poem entitled "Prayer Before Birth",
writes:

> I am not yet born; O hear me.
> Let not the bloodsucking bat or the rat or the stoat
>   or the club-footed ghoul come near me.

Herbert's lyric continues through several stanzas, notable
for the power of the language and the metrical structure,
enforced by rhymes that emphasize such phrases as "O
do not bruise me!" "O do not scourge me!" "O do not
grind me!" and concluding:

> But O reprieve me!
> For Thou hast life and death at Thy command;
> Thou art both Judge and Saviour, feast and rod,
> Cordial and Corrosive; put not Thy hand
> Into the bitter box; but, O my God!
> My God, relieve me!

This is the groan, out of the depths of his guilt, that comes
from a man and a Christian. MacNeice's poem is the cry,
from the dark cavern of the self, uttered by threatened in-

nocence and translated by a humanist who knows more intimately than Herbert against what worldly and fiendish powers, without and within, the soul must contend. The contemporary's poem employs the rolling unmetred cadences of a style that Herbert did not know, rhymes that he would not have recognized, and references that he could not have understood. But the repeated petitions of each stanza: "I am not yet born; O hear me.", "I am not yet born; console me.", "provide me", "forgive me", "rehearse me / In the parts I must play" echo Herbert's prayer. There is a curious reversal of one of his pleas in the final somewhat unwieldy stanza:

I am not yet born; O fill me
With strength against those who would freeze my
    humanity, would dragoon me into a lethal automaton,
      would make me a cog in a machine, a thing with
        one face, a thing, and against all those
          who would dissipate my entirety, would
            blow me like thistledown hither and
              thither or hither and thither
                like water held in the
                  hands would spill me.

Let them not make me a stone and let them not spill me.
Otherwise kill me.

The churchman had sighed to his God: "O do not kill me!" In MacNeice's poem the unborn child, praying to a Power never named, does not mention God except in the plea: "Let not the man who is beast or who thinks he is God come near me." At the close he begs to be saved from becoming an insensate stone or from having his gifts spilled and made nought: otherwise, he says, "Otherwise kill me." The death of the self is so terrible to the humanist that he would prefer not to be born at all.

    This poem was composed during World War II. It appeared with several pieces on "the Trolls", MacNeice's name for the moral and physical monsters that take part in an air raid. He all but identified enemy plane and pilot, fascist ideology and destructive mechanical force. The sound and fury of the raid is roundly conveyed, the moral aspect of it clearly but not searingly indicated.

MacNeice has limited himself largely to occasional poetry, heightened by his intelligent awareness. Such is his *Autumn Sequel,* a long poem about the events, more often personal than public, of the fall of 1953. Technically more interesting than his *Autumn Journal* of fourteen years earlier, the *Sequel* has passages that are far more deeply felt. Such are those about "Gwilym" (the pseudonym for Dylan), from his first puckish appearance to the cantos on the death and burial of this

> spruce and small
> Bow-tied Silenus roistering his way
> Through lands of fruit and fable, well aware
> That even Dionysus has his day,
>
> And cannot take it with him.

Even though this small Silenus was anything but "spruce", the scattered lines about him, taken together, paint a convincing and moving portrait, the more so because MacNeice is a verseman of such a different stripe. He keeps decorum by the casualness of his tone and the live simplicity of his speech. More recently a younger group of poets in England and America, rebelling against Silenus and his kind, have been writing in a deliberately pedestrian style. Neither haunted by a vision nor hankering after a myth, they have set down plainly what they have seen, thought, and, not as plainly, felt. During the thirties many poets had held that desperate diseases require desperate remedies. In the following decades they were more appalled by the disease, more uncertain of the cure.

IV

The poetry of the forties, whether written by noncombatants suffering the horrors of civilian warfare, by soldiers in the thick of the fighting, or by pacifists condemned to their own unspectacular battles, was distinguished from the poetry of the previous great war in its freedom from both romantic enthusiasm and angry disillusion. Physical disaster and moral chaos changed the temper of poetry as they altered the face of the earth and the attitude of all thinking men. There were those who assented to the declaration made in the title poem of John Malcolm Brinnin's first book: "The garden is political," and who interpreted innocence and sin in civic terms. But even the politically-minded were haunted by the general feeling of terrible forlornness. Jean Garrigue paused in her inquiry into the meaning of V-J Day to remark quietly, "Our armless men are all our statues now."

The prevailing tone was quiet. Sometimes it was the hush of confrontation. Sometimes it was the desperate resistance voiced by a few truly Christian poets, of whom Sean Jennett is fairly representative. The third part of his long poem, "The Quick" ("And The Dead" is its fitting pendant), shows Christ's wounds gaping, the "cross rooting in the bloody earth" grow "to the gallows in the conquered city;" and reminds us of the years of war that

> came empty-handed, wolfed, and went their way,
> and paid us only in sharp coins of pain,
> hate and despair, vengeance and revenge.

David Gascoyne demands:

> Whose is this horrifying face,
> This putrid flesh, discoloured, flayed,
> Fed on by flies, scorched by the sun?
> Whose are these hollow red-filmed eyes
> And thorn-spiked head and spear-stuck side?

"Behold the Man," he answers: "He is Man's Son." He
sees Christ "in agony till the world's end," and us as

> onlookers at the crime,
> Callous contemporaries of the slow
> Torture of God.

Robert Lowell, descendant of a long line of New England poets, expressed his convictions as a conscientious objector in dense language employing religious imagery with
more savage daring. In some respects Lowell resembles
John Wheelwright, another revolutionary Bostonian to
whom he is related in more ways than one. Lowell, too,
has identified Protestantism with chauvinistic capitalism,
and repudiated both. He, too, found in Christ the symbol for the holy principle of rebellion against the pharisai-
cal money-changers who dominate the society of which he
is a recalcitrant member. He, too, is close to Blake in his
revolutionary humanism, even when he accepts the in-
stitution of the Church. He, too, has written poetry that
puts heavy demands upon the reader. It differs from
Wheelwright's, however, in important ways. It is not only
more highly charged: it is also immensely more resonant.

Not a few of his poems are shaken by the cold reverberant roll of the north Atlantic. He hears it with the ears
of a familiar of the Nantucket coast. But what, louder than
sea water, batters at his mind is the memory of the old
whalers and of the meaning that Melville read into their
bloody work, and the sound of the guns thundering for the
new Leviathan. The prevalence of puns in his poems is one
index to the richness of the references that crowd them.
But he is also able to produce the exact concrete detail,
as in his "Colloquy in Black Rock", which begins racket-
ingly:

> Here the jack-hammer jabs into the ocean;
> My heart, you race and stagger and demand
> More blood-gangs for your nigger-brass percussions,

and which goes on to evoke the poverty-stricken mud flats
with one plain image:

> Black Mud, a name to conjure with: O mud
> For watermelons gutted to the crust, . . .

Lowell is under no illusion about the power and terror of
the sea, and, with the possible exception of Eliot, who has
enlarged its significance symbolically, no living poet has
realized it more terribly. But he returns repeatedly to the
consoling figure of the Fisher of men walking upon the
waters. As often, however, he shows Christ crucified, the
Saviour condemned, and his early work dwells on the conflict between embodied evil: the greed-inspired or blind,
blundering war makers, and the rejected redeemer, who
symbolizes a love not centered on the self.

In his later work Lowell's outraged attack upon the in-
humanity intrinsic to Puritanism gives place to a more objective examination of the present and the nearer past.
Whether in search of a different style, or because he felt
that density of music and metaphor was unsuitable to his
material, he adopted, in *Life Studies*, a radically simpler
approach. Over half of that slender book is devoted to "An
Autobiographical Fragment" in prose, a title applicable to
most of the poems, some of which read like prose. The
fact that Lowell's family history is involved with the history of New England gives his most personal work an adventitious interest. He moves between covert pride in his
sturdier forebears and sardonic acknowledgment of the
spiritual puniness to which his heritage has dwindled.

That other burly Christian, Dylan Thomas, wrote about
war in the subdued tones of a man harrowed by his experiences as a fire-warden. George Barker, no longer exulting in the rampageous style of his Elegies and Epistles,
asserted:

> This is the only dignity left, the single
> Death without purpose and without understanding
> Like birds boys drop with catapults.

It is an echo of Rilke's perplexity during an earlier war, when he was "always thinking it *must* come to an end, not understanding, not understanding, not understanding! *Not to understand:* yes, that was my entire occupation in these years, I can assure you it was not simple!" Almost alone, Edith Sitwell, however appalled her response to what she too saw as an enduring crucifixion, was able to speak out of a sublime faith in love's regenerative power.

For the most part those poets who had witnessed the evil harvest of the first world war were apt to be outspoken in their attitude toward the second. With the verve of W. S. Gilbert, but without his Victorian urbanity, Cummings thumbed his nose at the

> booted and spurred
> with an apish grin
> (extremely like
> but quite absurd
>
> gloved fist on hip
> & the scowl of a cannibal)
> there's your mineral
> general animal

Jeffers climbed down from the tower where for so long he had been watching the impersonal sea and sky to write a few topical pieces, repeating grimly that "Violence has been the sire of all the world's values." Allen Tate, not given to such heavy pronouncements, composed a witty address in the form of an "Ode to Our Young Pro-Consuls of the Air". This rehearses briefly the past wars in which his compatriots took part, with a glance aside at his private history, and more than one sharp hit at the super-patriots among his own confrères. At the close the poet envisages the bombardier, a "gentle youth", flying above an Everest "Whose mythic crest" resists his "truth": the truth of animal excellence and scientific skill. Let him, then, spying far off

>Upon the Tibetan plain
>A limping caravan,
> Dive, and exterminate
> The Lama, late
>Survival of old pain.
>Go, kill the dying swan.

Appropriately, the ode is dedicated to St.-John Perse, who has so compellingly suggested the mysteries of the Gobi Desert, and the more mysterious deserts of the soul. The "dying swan" recalls Yeats's use of this bird as symbol of the soul, and his concern for a gracious, reckless way of life of which the skillful bombardier is totally ignorant. Even such a poem as Tate's "Ode", however, which attacks the ingenuous blindness of the airman and the blind self-righteousness of those who cheer him on, expresses an attitude more complex than what earlier poets had known. Nor can this be attributed solely to the acumen of the poet speaking.

Years earlier when Yeats had been asked for a war poem he had replied that he thought it better that in times like those,

>A poet's mouth be silent, for in truth
>We have no gift to set a statesman right; . . .

In these later times, when the magnitude of the world's misery could find no image, when there was no power on earth to set the statesmen right, the poets knew that they could say nothing adequate to the catastrophe in which mankind was caught. History was the mirror of each man's meanest and most private shames. The more intimately the writer knew and felt the problems that we must solve or perish, the more his pain and puzzlement wanted utterance, the more stammeringly was he apt to speak. He could say truly only that he was befogged. The agony, the ugliness that surrounded and invaded the poets, were inexpressible. Those who did not hold their tongues often dealt, as Spender frankly confessed to doing, with the "weakness, fantasy and illusion" that are part of the personal life. Many of Delmore Schwartz's poems are such candid self-revelation. He has declared the chief influences on his work to have been Shakespeare and the Depression of 1929. The last must be sought for, but the "prince of Avon", quoted with and more often without inverted commas, haunts his pages. The long poem interlarded with prose commentary, "Coriolanus and his Mother", is not the sole indication that Schwartz tends to identify with that self-regarding hero. Nor is this piece alone in bearing testimony to its author's tutelage by such mentors as Aristotle, Kant, Marx, and Freud, while the shorter lyrics show him employing the strategies of diverse contemporary poets, among them Yeats and Eliot, Auden, Edith Sitwell, and Wallace Stevens. A prolific and versatile writer, Schwartz's more recent poems express a religiously oriented euphoria. His affirmations, like his confessions, are uttered in sophisticated accents and abound in learned allusions. Sometimes his lush language, his repetitive phrasing and undisciplined verbalism destroy the effect he seeks. But he can produce lyrics notable for their grace, their exultation, their honesty. This was evident in an early poem that reminds one of Spender's avowal. Bewildered by the simultaneous contemplation of Plato and of contemporary Europe, he wrote most convincingly about the ego dogging him or about that other "inescapable animal", the body:

> The central ton of every place,
> The hungry beating brutish one
> In love with candy, anger, and sleep, . . .

With imagery not so obsessive, other poets gave vent to a sense of guilt or of alienation, or both. Thus G. S. Fraser laid bare the division between his "simple heart, bred in provincial tenderness," and his "cold mind, that takes the world for theme," and in more penetrating lyrics cried out upon both the world and his own heart. When the personal experience that they took for their subject matter was more or less depersonalized in the great public context of war, soldier poets wrote of it with their senses and their sympathy alive to the interplay of private and public actualities.

The young Greek, Demetrios Capetanakis, who composed a handful of lyrics in English before his too early death, expressed the feeling of his generation in his sonnet, "Abel". Here Abel, representative of the forgiving victim everywhere, is the speaker, and the scene is as contemporary and unreal as the "cinemas half-lit" of the octave. Abel says that he does not blame Cain's nature: "he's my brother;". Nor does he blame "what you call the times:", but rather

> The ageless ambiguity of things
> Which makes our life mean death, our love be hate.
> My blood that streams across the bedroom sings:
> "I am my brother opening the gate."

The poem is fairly typical in its enlargement of the daily commonplace with symbolic reference, its making the legend familiar by dressing it in ordinary details, and, above all, in its acknowledgment of "the ageless ambiguity of things". This is central to the war poems of the forties.

One expects to find it in the poetry of Richard Eberhart, because his concern has steadily been with the incredibility of the actual. His war poems, lyrical in spite of their fierce concision, speak concretely and eloquently of the incongruousness of the concepts of man and of war. He writes with stunning impact of the mindless butchery, the small cruelties, and the greater horror as

> The Earthquake Opens Abrupt the World,
> Cold Dreadful Mass Destruction.

But in the midst of animal anguish and moral disaster he is alive to the dreamlike vision of anti-aircraft seen from a distance: "a controlled kind of falling stars," and he is not afraid to call attention to "the beautiful disrelation of the spiritual."

Poets who were not as intently directed as Eberhart toward metaphysical considerations were constrained by the perversities of war experience to the same tangled consciousness. This is the texture of the war poems of Roy Fuller, to name one among many. Whether he writes of an owl hooting in the winter night, or of giraffes, those creatures whose structure and color and gait are all unbelievable, moving away from him across the dappled plain, or of the grim minutiae of a soldier's life, he writes plainly of the bitter complexity that is the human condition and that war particularly forces upon the humane sensibility.

"The ageless ambiguity of things" is present even in the work of a poet of so different a temper as Karl Shapiro. He has made his own the lessons he has learned from his seniors, among whom Auden appears foremost. His subject matter is whatever, from day to day, falls within his purview: a troop train, an amputation, an unloading of V-mail, or the commonplaces of civilian life. Most of his lyrics have an abounding vigor, as witness "Scyros", the poem that opens his first book. An appropriately savage beat sounds in "Nigger", which pads as softly, leaps as surely, rips as bloodily, as anything in the jungles of Africa or Harlem or Georgia. Shapiro's control is evident if one contrasts the rhythm employed there with that in "Nostalgia" (composed on the Indian Ocean in 1942), where the alternating length of the lines and the clever use of the pause make for a melancholy strain equally free of sentimentality.

> My soul stands at the window of my room,
>   And I ten thousand miles away;
> My days are filled with Ocean's sound of doom,
>   Salt and cloud and the bitter spray.
> Let the wind blow, for many a man shall die.

Along with the vigor goes true tenderness. He writes a poem about "The Fly" which does not shun its most familiar and disgusting aspects. These are emphasized by the choice of metaphors, as in the opening apostrophe: "O hideous little bat, the size of snot,". But the poet is also at pains to present the fly *sub specie aeternatis*, as it were: the fly under the eye of God. He notes that it has "the fine leg of a Duncan-Phyfe", shows how pitiful a creature is this victim of men and children, of housewives and beasts, living precariously, dying nastily. The miracle of the fly's organism, the pathos of its small existence, as well as its ugliness and uselessness or worse from the human viewpoint, make for the poem's complexity.

The lyric on "A Cut Flower" shows a delicate sympathy with another nonhuman form of life. Here the flower itself speaks.

> Who softens the sweet earth about my feet?
> Touches my face so often and brings water?
> Where does she go, taller than any sunflower
> Over the grass like birds? Has she a root?
> These are great animals that kneel to us,
> Sent by the sun perhaps to help us grow.

This is the beginning of the second stanza, which goes on to describe the fading and dying of blossoms as they might understand it. The third stanza has to do with the flower in the vase.

> Yesterday I was well, and then the gleam,
> The thing sharper than frost cut me in half.

That is a flower's view of the shears, as the entire lyric is a flower's view of the world. Here is a distinctly Rilkean approach. To Rilke, no person, indeed, no thing, was an "it", so that he could rightly be called "The poet whom *die Dinge* bless". Shapiro comes closest to him in a series of three sonnets called "The Interlude". The second asks questions that suggest a sonnet in the *Stundenbuch*.

What lives? the proper creatures in their homes?
A weed? the white and giddy butterfly?
Bacteria? necklaces of chromosomes?

What lives? the breathing bell of the clear sky?
The crazed bull of the sea? Andean crags?
Armies that plunge into themselves to die?

Thus Shapiro. Rilke, declaring how strongly he feels that
all life is *lived* ("ALLES LEBEN WIRD GELEBT," he insists)
asks, "But who, then, lives it?" Is it the mute things that
are like a harp's unfingered melody, the winds, the
boughs, the flowers weaving fragrances, the animals, the
birds? "This life—who lives it really? God, do you?" (*"Wer
lebt es denn? Lebst du es, Gott,—das Leben?"*) The question is not framed by the American poet who names such
different forms of life, but it is implicit in his sonnet.

A reverence for life characterizes Shapiro's many war
poems. Of these, among the more memorable is "The
Leg", which, for all its concrete references to iodoform
and rubber hands, the stump and the finest surgical limb,
employs abstractions suggestively, and is at once witty and
religious. His chief fault is carelessness, due to an excessive facility, of which exuberance is another aspect. The
affirmative attitude of one who finds himself happily
bound to the universe expresses itself as often in the
energy of his rhythms as in his avowed sense of kinship
with the least of created things. Yet none of his war poems
has the romantic simplicity of those of an earlier generation. Thus his "Elegy for a Dead Soldier" frankly describes
the death of and brief burial services for one who was
"Neither the victim nor the volunteer," but, as the poem
makes plain, an average, untutored American boy. The
gulf between the circumstances of his life and his death
on a remote Pacific Island, between his understanding
and the possible meaning of his sacrifice, is revealed with
a sad and puzzled tenderness, a hopefulness far from un-
qualified. The "Elegy" is noteworthy for its unrhetorical
setting forth of a small but complex situation, and for the

clarity with which it shows the mixed attitude of the latter-day crusader.

How deeply Shapiro is sensible of this is evidenced in his poem on "The Conscientious Objector". The poem combines, after his own fashion, brusqueness and inwardness. His attitude may have been made possible by the fact that in war he stood between the fighting man and the man of peace, serving as he did with the medical corps. The poem concludes:

> Well might the soldier kissing the hot beach
> Erupting in his face damn all your kind.
> Yet you who saved neither yourselves nor us
> Are equally with those who shed the blood
> The heroes of our cause. Your conscience is
> What we come back to in the armistice.

This is borne out by the unflinching candor of the poets whose war was "inward".

v

Poetry and its changes help to illuminate the complexity of every situation. How much more so that of war, which, even when obviously a lesser evil, is always evil. Among the most famous of Rupert Brooke's sweet and decorous war sonnets is that which begins:

> If I should die, think only this of me:
> That there's some corner of a foreign field
> That is forever England.

Gervase Stewart, who was killed in action in the second world war when he was only twenty, wrote a short lyric on dying for his country which opens:

> I burn for England with a living flame
> In the uncandled darkness of the night.

The piece is remarkable, not for its likeness to Brooke's, but for its difference from it. Stewart recognized, as Brooke

failed to do, England's fault and his own imperfection.
The poem shows that history had taught the younger man
what his predecessor had not learned: the dreadful ambiguity of a war believed to be just.

The ambiguity is absent from the harsh compression of
Randall Jarrell's five lines on "The Death of the Ball Turret Gunner":

From my mother's sleep I fell into the State,
And I hunched in its belly till my wet fur froze.
Six miles from earth, loosed from its dream of life,
I woke to black flak and the nightmare fighters.
When I died they washed me out of the turret with a hose.

His longer poems tend to be discursive and are certainly
less brutal. Indeed, his unflinching grasp of brutal events
is dictated by his compassion. He is like one who, cutting off the dragon's head, grasps his sword below the hilt.
It is natural to mention dragons in connection with Jarrell's poetry because he is at home with *Märchen* and accepts their particulars readily. He does not go in fear of
abstractions, but those he employs oftenest: the State, the
world, justice, are presented so as to take on a magnitude
more awful for being hidden. Along with such obvious
victims as Jews and soldiers, his compassion includes the
enemy, PWs as well as children. His work is sometimes
obsessively repetitive, and no single poem sparkles like his
criticism, but nearly all are redeemed by a tender incisive-
ness. Many of his poems might bear this line from "Mail
Call" as an epigraph: "The soldiers are all haunted by
their lives."

The difference between the poems of World War I and
those of World War II, taking them by and large, might
be said to lie in this fact: the soldier poets of the later
generation were all haunted. Their pages are haunted by
the performance of their literary forebears. You cannot listen to them without recognizing the ghostly presence of
Pound's precise imagery, of Eliot's subterranean music, of
the concentration transmitted through these poets from

the French masters, of Yeats's high talk, of Hopkins' intensity of apprehension and immediacy of language. They were mindful of nearer and less important verse-makers. But the starry-eyed romanticism that had fashioned some dreams of the future was killed before the explosion of the atom bomb. On New Year's Eve, 1940, Auden was writing that

> language may be useless, for
> No words men write can stop the war
> Or measure up to the relief
> Of its intolerable grief.

Years earlier even so aloof a music-maker as Wallace Stevens had heard the noises in the street, and sometimes made statements not unlike those of the proletarian poets who had demanded a decent world here and now. The soldier poets made similar statements, but with greater diffidence. And this precisely because they were haunted—not alone by their own lives but by the lives of their fathers, veterans of the other war, haunted by the bleak lives endured in the interval between the wars, and haunted by those unappeasable specters, the lives of their own unborn children, moving in the shadow of this unforgiveable century.

14. Science and Poetry

When W. H. Auden began writing the collapse of the financial system was affecting men like a series of earthquakes and tidal waves. If here was not literal fire and flood, here was world-wide famine. An alert young poet with a voracious appetite for knowledge and an aggressive sense of fun, he was moved by this spectacle not to thoughts too deep for tears, but to satiric laughter. The Icelandic sagas on which he had been nurtured taught him to find congenial a poetry as cold, craggy, and sulphurous as the country where those epics grew up, and to fill his own verse with roughhousing and riddles. His youthful admirations included three vigorous adversaries of middle-class Christendom. In an early piece, composed in the metre of Tennyson's ambiguous hymn to progress, "Locksley Hall", he refers to all three:

> Lawrence, Blake and Homer Lane, once healers in our
>   English land;
> These are dead as iron forever; these can never
>   hold our hand.

Lane's theories of illness seem to have been a psychosomatic variant of Blakean ideas. They were congenial to a poet who held that his first duty was to be "clinically-minded". Central to Lane's thinking were such "Proverbs of Hell" as "He who desires and acts not, breeds pestilence," and "The tygers of wrath are wiser than the horses of instruction." The psychotherapist had not yet become the deus ex machina of the movie-script writers, but for a time he was a high priest of Auden's religion, and it was in this capacity that Lane appears to have functioned. He had the pitilessness of the saga heroes, prep school boys, and revolutionary plotters who haunt the young poet's pages. Pity he regarded as one of the chief evils of our civilization. When Spender was having a youthful affair with communism he observed that poetry is " 'counter-revolutionary' in the sense that it contains an element of pity." There was nothing counter-revolutionary in Auden's early verse. If it was so much the less poetry, it was so much the more satire, a lively art that tends to poach upon the province of prose. At all events, he made no ado about inviting the muses of Lyell, Marx, and Freud to preside over his performance, and if he induced them to behave like hoydens, this was good evidence that he made them at home.

In the epigraph to his first collection of poems Auden asked that "the vertical man" be honored, though none but "the horizontal one" is valued. The first is obviously the living man, the second is the dead. One might also take it that the vertical man is the man of action, while the horizontal man may be the artist, whose attitude toward the world is that of the receptive, admiring lover. In the epigraph to "The Orators", which dealt boisterously if obscurely with an England where nobody was well, Auden spoke of the charm of private faces in public places. The private and the public man were struggling within him, and his verse was the natural arena for that struggle. In opposition to the revolutionary demand for the "Death of the old gang" was the religious impulse, no less strong because he asked God to behave like a psychotherapist.

> Byron, thou should'st be living at this hour!
> What would you do, I wonder, if you were?

Auden, between two world wars, asked milord in a letter from Iceland. His own poems furnish the answer. The public man defends the private man by the exercise of wit.

Even if one disregards his plays in verse, his poetry is strikingly dramatic. Nor is there only the conflict between one who hopes to be saved by good works and one who hopes to be saved by faith. Paradoxically, the good works are an attack on the status quo, so that they seem wicked to the generality of men. There is also the conflict between the man whose ambition is to "work illegally" (Lenin's phrase) in obedient anonymity, and the poet, whose task is not to wreck a dilapidated social system, but to order his own feelings at the command of his daemon, and whose personality survives as long as his poems are read. There is, further, the conflict between the heart that feels and the mind that thinks.

"Coming out of me living is always thinking," Auden announced at the outset. Hence his interest in the work of Laura Riding, whom he once called "the only living philosophical poet". His early verse carries odd echoes of hers, both in its abrupt cadences and its dry, elliptical style. But his bent is in a different direction. Her poetry explores reality with the zest of an amateur metaphysician. His is a bazaar where the stuffs of our modern ideologies are displayed by a showman given to a sly "caveat emptor". Even in his later poems he dresses the faith of his fathers in a fashion attractive to the skeptical scientist. Unlike other learned contemporaries, Auden does not often append notes to his poems. An exception is the first version of his "New Year Letter" of 1940. It is a remarkable exception, for the notes, some of them in verse, occupy twenty pages more than does the poem itself, which runs to over seventeen hundred lines. It is also furnished with a brief bibliography of its modern sources, which include works on anthropology, history, philosophy, psychoanalysis, and sociology.

His youthful poems are only less representative of his intellectual curiosity. Thus a piece to which he belatedly gave the title: "Venus Will Now Say a Few Words" is a résumé of ideas familiar to students of the natural and social sciences. The speaker is not the goddess of love and beauty celebrated by the lyricists of the ancient world. She bears some resemblance to the paramount deity invoked by Lucretius in his poem on the nature of things, but she looks more like the Bergsonian *élan vital* and not a little like the libido as costumed by Jung. The poem is Venus's address to an unhappy member of a dying class. Toward the close she describes his feeling of dismay as

> That sense of famine, central anguish felt
> For goodness wasted at peripheral fault.

The apparent purport of these lines is that the poor fellow feels remorse because, owing to some superficial error, he did not allow the situation in which he found himself to yield its full measure of good. But the word "fault" has many meanings, among others, a blemish, neglect of duty, the losing of the scent by a hunting dog, a fracture of strata leading to displacement of rock masses. Although the lines obviously have an ethical import, Auden may well have implied the other meanings of the word to give it additional weight. A neglect of duty, which is a moral blemish, may be due to a man's losing the scent where human welfare is concerned, and result in a break between men, while a fracture in the social strata may cause the displacement of masses in a sense not understood by geologists. Like most of Auden's work, the poem indicates that living, for him, is thinking, and since poetry is his métier, his poems embody the ideas that are having the liveliest play in his mind.

An instance is an early piece to which he later gave the name, "Petition". Here he addresses God politely as "Sir," and does not hesitate any more than did Emily Dickinson to refer to the commonplaces of his culture. The fourteen-line poem takes every freedom with the metre, while the rhymes are paired and oblique. The final couplet, however, locks up the whole in sonnetesque fashion:

> Harrow the house of the dead; look shining at
> New styles of architecture, a change of heart.

Originally published during the threatening thirties, the poem states the theme on which Auden was to play

multiple variations. Nearly twenty years later he offered
the theory that a work of art is a mirror which shows the
beholder himself and his world and the relations of his
good and bad feelings. He held that the theory rests on
these beliefs: "a) All created existence is a good. b) Evil
is a negative perversion of created good. c) Man has free
will to choose between good and evil. d) But all men are
sinners with a perverted will."

Read in this light, the poem takes on greater meaning.
"Sir, no man's enemy, forgiving all" it opens cheerfully,
only to add the exception: "But will its negative inversion, . . ." God is no man's enemy. He allows His creature freedom to choose between good and evil. He forgives
every wrong choice, except the negative inversion of the
will. What is that but the death wish? "Be prodigal," the
poet pleads. "Send to us power and light." This is not a
request to reduce to nothing the rates on public utilities,
though it is characteristic that the lines carry such a suggestion. It is a plea recalling a medieval text on the Trinity.
According to one interpretation by the thirteenth-cen-
tury author, the Father is memory, the Son is understanding, the Holy Ghost is the will. It is appropriate to a
twentieth-century poem combining theology and psychopathology that God, represented as memory, should be
asked to give us understanding and will power. According
to authorities in these matters, it is a suppressed memory
that makes for the death wish; and the death wish is the
sin against the Holy Ghost, which is the will. Understanding illuminates memory and frees the will.

As a Christian, Auden is concerned with ethics and so
with action, though the action initially displays itself in
"a change of heart." As a revolutionist he is concerned
with action of the public variety resulting in "New styles
of architecture,". The concluding couplet recognizes the
double need of correcting the cross-eyed gaze of the self-
regarding man and rebuilding a social structure that is ill-
adapted to human needs. Insofar as Auden's later poems
repeat his "Petition" in one form or another, they are an

attempt to reconcile the quarrel between science, which would change the world, and poetry, which mirrors the heart of man.

In his "Christmas Oratorio" he refers like a gland specialist to "the adrenal courage of the tiger" and mentions, in a phrase only a botanist can fully appreciate, "the fern's devotion to spatial necessity". In his "New Year Letter" for 1940 he punningly tells himself not to trust

> the demagogue who raves,
> A quantum speaking to the waves.

Such allusions as these bear out Wordsworth's prophecy about the effect of scientific discoveries on the tenor of poetry. They do not illustrate the fact that Auden is a liaison officer between science and poetry. The method of the first is to measure and to count, to the end of making existence acceptable now and here. The poet, though he counts and measures in his own fashion, does not try to improve life, or, like the religionist, to justify it. He wants to realize it in all its multiplicity and heterogeneity, its meanness and its grandeur. Auden, the naughty schoolboy who has also posed as the haughty schoolmaster, has been steadily concerned with improving the conditions of life, but also, since his talent is for poetry, with realizing it more fully. Indirectly, like all knowledge, this is a way to alter the world.

The word that recurs in his pages again and again is "order". Among his chief mentors is Dante, of whom he speaks admiringly as the poet who grasped the complex "Catholic ecology". What Auden has tried to grasp is the ecology of man in contemporary society: the relation between him and his urban, industrial environment, of which his fellows are an essential part, his adaptation to it, and the possibility of his survival, both physically and morally. The "New Year Letter" might be described as an interior monologue, intended to be overheard, on the subject of an ordered mind in an ordered world. The form itself is orderly. But since the poem is presented as a letter,

the strictness of the pattern is relieved by the free associations and the small explosions of that impenitent confessional. The short, regular lines, clicking with exact
rhymes, are speeded up further by the fact that the poet
is alert to "The situation of our time" which "Surrounds us
like a baffling crime." The reader is kept as constantly on
the *qui vive* as if he were on a kind of intellectual scenic
railway, furnished with some figures from the chamber of
horrors but not lacking in glimpses of a paradisiacal
garden.

The piece was originally prefaced by an epigraph from
Montaigne: "We are, I know not how, double in ourselves,
so that we believe we disbelieve, and cannot rid of ourselves of what we condemn." It is a reflective gentleman's
version of the disciple's cry of abasement: "For the good
which I would I do not, but the evil which I would not,
that I practise." The poet examines this divided creature
in the light of what is known about the psyche. Having
admitted that "Aloneness is man's real condition," he concludes that salvation lies in acknowledging our weaknesses
and in recognizing and loving the uniqueness of each individual. This old neglected truth is made attractive by
the sophisticated accessories to its new costume and by
the delightful if rare music that prepares the way for it.

In the original notes to the poem Auden remarked that
"The Devil, indeed, is the father of Poetry, for poetry
might be defined as the clear expression of mixed feelings." In his own poetry the expression is sometimes too
dazzling for clarity, and one is less aware of feelings than
of ideas, which, if not mixed, are multiple. But the devilish double focus is there, achieved with some assistance
from those masters who "challenge, warn and witness," and
whom Auden has plainly named. First and foremost
among the tribunal before whom he brings his work is
Dante. Other acknowledged masters are Blake, Rimbaud:
"The adolescent with red hands, / Skilful, intolerant,
and quick, / Who strangled an old rhetoric", Dryden,
Tennyson, "Conscious Catullus who made all / His gut-

ter language musical", Baudelaire, Hardy, Rilke, and "horrible old Kipling". Of the ten, only half are English poets. The international character of much modern work, which extends to allusions and symbols as well as to translations, is due largely to Pound. His concern with the poetry of China, as well as with that of the troubadours, and the concern of Eliot and Yeats with the philosophies of India, have had somewhat the same effect on twentieth-century verse that Chaucer's travels in France and Italy had on English verse more than five hundred years ago. Auden was undoubtedly influenced by the poets who affected other members of his generation, and, as always, what his successors owe him is in part what he has chosen to borrow from his own teachers. In his poetic commentary on *The Tempest* he allows Caliban, who represents the unregenerate self, to speak in the accents of yet another mentor, Henry James. Again, standing at the grave of this "Master of nuance and scruple", the poet begs him to suggest and approve.

His elegy in memory of Yeats carries no such personal plea. It is both more objective in approach and more elaborate in form. The first part is a statement, in lively unrhymed free verse, about the day of Yeats's death. The second part is addressed to the dead poet and is a commentary on poetry. It is written in what seems deceptively like syllabic verse; it has one perfect rhyme, one identical rhyme, and several approximate rhymes. The third and final section is the most formal. The increasing coherence and deliberation seem to imply that Auden, disturbed and pained by this death, finally ordered his thoughts about it and about that which survives it: the poetry. Throughout Auden's work are scattered tributes to Yeats. They appear in the skillful use of the refrain, notably one that suggests the old dance tune: "Come ant daunce wyt me in irlaunde." Again there is something of Yeats in the turn of a phrase, or, as in a song set to music by Benjamin Britten, in definite images, definite cadences.

The influence of Eliot is equally apparent, as might be

expected, since Auden, unsatisfied by plans for a new secular architecture, experienced a change of heart that enabled him to follow Eliot into the church of his fathers. Thus, "Autumn 1940", originally published as the epilogue to the religious sonnet series entitled "The Quest", ends on a plea that holds the very substance and spirit of the *Quartets*. Auden asks that

> Time remembered bear witness to time required,
> The positive and negative ways through time
> > Embrace and encourage each other
> > In a brief moment of intersection . . .

This is to pray for what the elder poet sought when he spoke longingly of the memory of those moments in time: "the moment in the rose-garden," and in the rainy arbor, and in the chill dusk of the chapel, which so transcended ordinary experience as to be lifted out of time. It recalls Eliot's view of the saint as devoted to apprehending the Incarnation:

> > The point of intersection of the timeless
> > With time . . .

Auden, however, is less concerned with belief and doubt than with theology. Even his ostensibly religious poems are not notable as expressions of faith. Instead they examine the elements of belief, or interpret Christian ideas in the light of psychotherapy and the writings of that unorthodox if profoundly religious thinker, Sören Kierkegaard. These poems paraphrase the remark of the Danish philosopher that "the God of the Christians is Spirit, and Christianity is Spirit, and discord is posited between flesh and spirit; but 'the flesh' is not sensuousness, it is selfishness . . ." Auden's attack on selfishness is never simple. He knows too well how complex a thing selfhood is. Moreover, he is compelled to arrange his ideas about God in accord with the ideas about creation that his enormous reading and wide-ranging travels have provided. Where Eliot's poetry is apt to embody the words of the saints and

the Church fathers, Auden's is more apt to be colored by
the findings of scientists, and other modern thinkers.

He admires Kierkegaard particularly for having distinguished between "tribulations": the troubles that no effort
of will can alter, and "temptations": the conflicts that in-
volve ethical choice. The aim of science, he observes, is to
turn tribulations into temptations. Poetry, on the contrary,
"makes nothing happen," but makes suffering endurable by
regarding it aesthetically. Auden's work shows him to be
keenly interested in the tasks of science, and steadily concerned with ethics. Yet his pleasure in playing with ideas
and the demands of his art tend to make him treat ethical
problems as merely material for verse.

Our disordered worlds, inner and outer, clamor for ethical work. "Set Love in order, Thou that lovest Me," commands Christ in a canticle by St. Francis. It was a familiar
plea in the middle ages. Auden composed an elaborate
sestina, entitled "Kairos and Logos", in which the repeated
end words of the first stanza are: time, world, order, condemned, self-love, and death, which is a modern version of
this prayer. In another poem he asserted that "order never
can be willed," being "the state of the fulfilled." It would
appear to be man's perpetual duty, if hopeless task, to
seek to achieve it.

II

As might be expected, Auden, for all his preoccupation
with morality, keeps recurring to the arts, and particularly
that of music. When he speaks of it, one seems to be listening to a man who accepts not Christian orthodoxy but
the more venerable religions expounded so persuasively for
the Western world by Schopenhauer. That bitter philosopher found in music the means of reconciliation with the
miseries and ennui of existence. For him music, like the
phenomenal world, was an expression of the Will at the
heart of things, but free of the world's tensions and dis-
satisfactions. Here, he said in effect, is reality, to be con-

templated innocently. Music alone allows us to feel ourselves at one with the governing principle of the universe,
but sympathetically and understandingly, not as involved
with the activities, anxieties, and passions of the world
in which the Will takes substantial form. This union, this
remoteness, are together the source of our solace and our
joy. So Auden, in the midst of irruptions of violence cul-
minating in all the horrors of the second world war, could
take refuge in a passacaglia of Buxtehude which made the
minds of its hearers

> a *civitas* of sound
> Where nothing but assent was found,
> For art had set in order sense
> And feeling and intelligence,
> And from its ideal order grew
> Our local understanding too.

He has written a number of songs and what he calls
"other musical pieces". One of the loveliest is an untitled
lyric, melodious, melancholy, and not without its moral.

> As I walked out one evening,
>   Walking down Bristol Street,
> The crowds upon the pavement
>   Were fields of harvest wheat.
>
> And down by the brimming river
>   I heard a lover sing
> Under an arch of the railway:
>   Love has no ending.
>
> "I'll love you, dear, I'll love you
>   Till China and Africa meet,
> And the river jumps over the mountain
>   And the salmon sing in the street.
>
> I'll love you till the ocean
>   Is folded and hung up to dry,
> And the seven stars go squawking
>   Like geese about the sky.

The years shall run like rabbits,
    For in my arms I hold
The Flower of the Ages,
    And the first love of the world."

But all the clocks in the city
    Began to whirr and chime:
"O let not Time deceive you,
    You cannot conquer Time.

In the burrows of the Nightmare
    Where Justice naked is,
Time watches from the shadow
    And coughs when you would kiss.

In headaches and in worry
    Vaguely life leaks away,
And Time will have his fancy
    Tomorrow or today.

Into many a green valley
    Drifts the appalling snow;
Time breaks the threaded dances
    And the diver's brilliant bow.

O plunge your hands in water,
    Plunge them in up to the wrist;
Stare, stare in the basin
    And wonder what you've missed.

The glacier knocks in the cupboard,
    The desert sighs in the bed,
And the crack in the tea-cup opens
    A lane to the land of the dead,

Where the beggars raffle the banknotes
    And the Giant is enchanting to Jack,
And the Lily-white Boy is a Roarer,
    And Jill goes down on her back.

O look, look in the mirror,
  O look in your distress;
Life remains a blessing
  Although you cannot bless.

O stand, stand at the window
  As the tears scald and start;
You shall love your crooked neighbor
  With your crooked heart."

It was late, late in the evening,
  The lovers they were gone;
The clocks had ceased their chiming,
  And the deep river ran on.

Here are echoes of folksong and of Housman harmonized
with Auden's personal idiom, and freighted with symbolic
meaning. The "deep river" suggests the conscienceless
stream of life. The "desert" is associated with a loveless industrial civilization, and the line about the desert sighing
in the bed might be a telescoped version of the passage on
the mechanical act of love in *The Waste Land*. Central to
the poem is the injunction:

O look, look in the mirror,
  O look in your distress;
Life remains a blessing
  Although you cannot bless.

Auden's range is great, from relatively simple ballads
and "Blues" to elaborate fugues and chorales. His "Refugee
Blues" is characteristic in the sad immediacy of its details,
the grimness of its humor. His signature is equally plain
in the "Song for St. Cecilia's Day", with its intricate rhyme
pattern and skillfully manipulated rhythms, its juncture of
the vulgar particular and the grand abstraction, its speculative interest, its puns and gaiety. The first part relates to
the patron saint of music, whom legend credits with having
been loved by an angel and further with having invented

the organ. In his Ode Auden, like Dryden before him, alludes to both stories. At the start he tells us how

> In a garden shady this holy lady
> With reverent cadence and subtle psalm,
> Like a black swan as death came on
> Poured forth her song in perfect calm:
> And by ocean's margin this innocent virgin
> Constructed an organ to enlarge her prayer,
> And notes tremendous from her great engine
> Thundered out on the Roman air.

One is tempted to read "organ" figuratively here, and think not of an early Christian martyr creating a new instrument but of life itself evolving in humankind the capacity for music, the art which above all others seems to intimate a superhuman excellence and so to make prayer acceptable. The resonance of that thunder on the Roman air is dissipated in the next stanza by a flight of phrases in the treble and by the introduction of blonde Aphrodite rising up excited,

> Moved to delight by the melody,
> White as an orchid she rode quite naked
> In an oyster shell on top of the sea; . . .

The first part concludes with an invocation to the blessed Cecilia, asking her to descend and inspire all composers, including presumably the poet himself.

This is followed by a curt section open to more than one interpretation. Take the third quatrain:

> I am defeat
> When it knows it
> Can now do nothing
> By suffering.

This might be a definition of the art of music. It can also be read as the voice of Beethoven's final quartets, specifically the famous one in which is heard the question and answer: *"Muss es sein?" "Es muss sein."*—a phrase which

may be taken as referring to the necessity for paying an
overdue laundry bill or paying the death one owes to nature. The final, formally organized section brings in the
theme of setting love in order. It is quite Audenesque in
its familiar use of abstractions, as in the reference to Sorrow's "adolescent gaucheness" and in its treatment of the
Christian myth. Again, there seems an allusion to Beethoven's *"Heiliger Dankgesang"* in the last stanza:

> O flute that throbs with the thanksgiving breath
> Of convalescents on the shores of death.

The lines show how cleverly Auden can make the most of
an outworn rhyme, like a jeweler enhancing an old stone
by the beauty of the new setting. Here, too, in the final
italicized line, apostrophizing the soul of man, the poet
returns to the Kierkegaardian motif that haunts him, crying: *"O wear your tribulation like a rose."*

The variety of his musical pieces is only one index to his
virtuosity. He has revived interest in the freedoms of the
nursery rhyme and of folk song and also in the discipline
of such formal patterns as villanelle and terza rima, the
ballade, with its twenty-eight lines on only three rhymes,
and the sestina, with six stanzas and a tercet ringing the
changes on six end words. Moreover, his scheme for the
end words is far from arbitrary. Thus, in an early sestina,
as the order of the words alters, their symbolic meaning alters, or, as the poet explains: "their part in the action
changes; clock turns from safeguard to fetter, the pro-
hibited wood becomes a source of fresh life, love, from
passive grown active, points to a new country." Thus the
poem is an "attack on habit and docility." This seems to
be the moral of his work as a whole.

His employment of French forms has not meant a cor-
responding interest in French verse. More narrowly than
most contemporary poets he has devoted himself to the
native tradition. He has followed the lead of Hopkins in
the direction of the muscular rhythms and ruggedly consonantal style of Anglo-Saxon verse, he likes to use the slant

rhyme introduced by Wilfred Owen, and his pages ring
with echoes of English balladry. Karl Shapiro notes in his
Essay on Rime Auden's deft usage of "proselike forms" to
brace the older measures, and is eloquent on the subject of
his vocabulary. It was Auden, says the poet-critic, who first
introduced the radio, the car, the sofa, and the new highway into the poem as things, rather than as symbols. He
might more truly have said that Auden presented them as
both things and symbols. When Shapiro declares that

> The scenery changed
> To absolute present and the curtain rose
> On the actual place, not Crane's demonic city
> Nor Eliot's weird unreal metropolis,
> But that pedestrian London with which prose
> Alone had previously dealt,

he is again telling only half the story. For Auden, less
concerned with pedestrian London than with decaying industrial centers and ruined country houses, raised the curtain on an actual place that symbolized a time on the revolutionist's calendar.

Karl Shapiro has an energy and a facility reminiscent of
Auden's and, like him, a pleasure in technical experiment
and a strong feeling for rhythm. He is singular in his preference for the dancing anapest and the hammering dactyl.
His satirical verse shows him similarly responsive to the
Zeitgeist. If he lacks Auden's intellectual athleticism, he
has improved on the master's ability to bring the car and
the highway into poetry. His lyrics offer a startlingly fresh
view of many details of the American pattern: the drug-
store, the movie, the university, the suburban Sunday, and
the meaning in that pattern of Jefferson and Franklin, of
"Nigger" and "Jew". His approach to his material has a
stereopticon clarity and yet remains sympathetic.

In an early piece called "Poet" he brilliantly sets forth
the complex peculiarities of this oddity, whose motto he
gives as "Sentio, ergo sum:" I feel, therefore I am. Where
Auden's verse offers several references to Rilke, his junior

adopts, quite simply and naturally, the Rilkean attitude of unembarrassed, universal sympathy, as in his poems on "The Fly" and "The Cut Flower". His tenderness helps to distinguish his work from that of the poet to whom it owes much, Wystan Hugh Auden.

III

Prominent in the poetry of our time is its endless concern with poetry. Shapiro, whose *Essay on Rime* wittily touches off a number of contemporaries, makes much of the question:

> At what point in the history of art
> Has such a cleavage between audience
> And poet existed?

Eliot, composing his grave *Quartets*, passes from a religious lyric on the Passion of Christ to talk of the effort of the twenty years behind him:

Twenty years largely wasted, the years of *l'entre deux guerres*—
Trying to learn to use words, and every attempt
Is a wholly new start, and a different kind of failure . . .

Almost the final statement in the fourth *Quartet* is a repetition of what more than one of his fellows have found to be required of them:

> An easy commerce of the old and the new,
> The common word exact without vulgarity,
> The formal word precise but not pedantic,

every phrase and every sentence being, he says, at once an end and a beginning.

William Carlos Williams devotes his most ambitious work, *Paterson*, as he explicitly says, to "a search for the redeeming language by which a man's premature death . . . might have been prevented." In Book I he cries out: "the language . . . the language!" and, expressed or latent, the words echo, with what eagerness, what exasperation, what anger, what love, through the rest of the poem, notably in Book III, which centers on the desiccation of language in the Library, that museum of what was once living speech. He repeats here in his own terms something of Eliot's thought:

> The past above, the future below
> and the present pouring down: the roar,
> the roar of the present, a speech—
> is, of necessity, my sole concern.
>
> .   .   .   .   .   .
>
>   I must
> find my meaning and lay it, white,
> beside the sliding water: myself—
> comb out the language—or succumb . . .

In conclusion he insists, honestly,

>   this rhetoric
>   is real!

Similarly, Wallace Stevens, not alone in his essays on aesthetics and the radiant aphorisms he called "Adagia", but in poem after poem, discusses questions relating to the practice of his art.

> The poem, through candor, brings back a power again
> That gives a candid kind to everything.
>
> .   .   .   .   .   .
>
> The poem goes from the poet's gibberish to
> The gibberish of the vulgate and back again.
>
> .   .   .   .   .   .
>
> That's it: the more than rational distortion,
> The fiction that results from feeling. Yes, that.

With gay imagery taken from the sky and the seasons, from the garden and the exotic feast in the garden, with sophisticated music, "idiot minstrelsy", and metaphysical talk, Stevens elaborates upon the several aspects and uses of "the supreme fiction", the art which helps the practitioner, and, to a lesser extent, those who can follow him, to explore reality. More gravely, Hugh MacDiarmid, in his meditative elegy, "Lament for the Great Music", declares:

> The mind creates only to destroy:
> Amid the desolation language rises, and towers
> Above the ruins: . . . .

The leader of the Scottish renaissance, MacDiarmid draws upon various dialects, as well as on English and the literary Scots of Chaucer's time. His poetry should therefore make verbal difficulties for the reader, aside from the intellectual problems presented by the work of this ranging, aggressive mind. Yet while acknowledging that the most difficult synthetic Scots is as obscure as any modern poetry, MacDiarmid insists that, being grounded in the speech and expressive of the emotions of the folk, it remains open to them. Eagerer than most to speak to and rouse his fellows, he is no more sharply conscious of the transcendent value and the practical uses of language than of its helplessness:

> The trouble is that words
> Are a' but useless noo
> To span the gulf atween
> The human and 'highbrow' view
> —Victims at ilka point
> O' optical illusions,
> Brute Nature's limitations,
> And inherited confusions.

Out of a more intimate distress of heart, D. S. Savage confesses:

> I walk among men
> With my labour and pain,
> Blood on the pen,
> Ink in the vein.

In a poetic dialogue that takes its themes from the Pound controversy, Shapiro has the Chorus of Poets claim that they can turn water to wine. But they end by lamenting "a failure of the word" as Williams and MacDiarmid lament the decay of language, Stevens and Eliot the difficulty of the traffic between fictive music and common speech.

Perhaps because he so readily effects an unlikely union between the two, Auden shows little dismay over the poet's problem. Nevertheless, he frequently writes about poetry, which, though it "makes nothing happen," nevertheless, in the midst of our faults and failures, can "Still persuade us to rejoice." Is not this an event? The joy it affords is in part due to its granting release, like a game, from the practical routine demands of everyday living. To the poet, of course, it resembles a game even more closely, since the work of composition offers him certain chancy choices within the limits of a strict set of rules. The acceptance of that necessity gives the craftsman his freedom. "The most difficult game conceivable to man" is Auden's definition of art. Poetry might be said to be the most serious game in which man engages. If it does not seek by conscious or unconscious magic to persuade or convince, it may be, for the poet, a form of play. For the reader, accepting it as one experience among others, to be enjoyed without necessary assent to its intellectual premises or its ethical implications, it is also play. Yet the most frivolous and trivial game affects both the participants and the spectators. Poetry, even more than the other arts, realizes the contradictions that lie at the heart of human experience. That is what makes it such a serious game.

The contradictions are plain enough. The disparity between our technology and our morality is nothing new. Millenniums before it became so present to us, man felt himself to be intimately involved with a universe from which, as a self-conscious being, he was also isolated. This truism, seized upon in concrete instances by the imagination, is the tenor of many fine poems. As the most primi-

tive religions and the most sophisticated philosophies testify, man would like to bring his short, harassed, disorderly
life into relation with the permanence and the harmony
that, until recently, he found in the movements of the
planets, the organization of the atom, and other exemplars
of the laws of nature. In exploring the human condition,
the poet must draw upon the facts that the sciences coldly
furnish. But his poem, though fed by fact, is rooted in
emotion and shaped by an ordering imagination.

Prominent in the work of Auden and his successors is
the return to the fairy tale. If the fairies, elves, and witches
are reduced and vulgarized gods and goddesses, the fairy
tales themselves are reduced and vulgarized myths. These
in any form the poets lay claim to, because, expressing
fears and desires inherited from our primitive past, they
continue to have emotional validity for us. Hart Crane's
myth did not have deep enough foundations and so failed
to support his work. Yeats's religion, though more solidly
grounded, remained a home-made construct of which others cannot avail themselves. Eliot's *Quartets*, while reaffirming religious values, are threaded with doubt. Auden
mocked the cry:

> Intervene. O descend as a dove or
> A furious papa or a mild engineer: but descend.

Yet he has spoken of God in equally dubious terms.
Heresy, dissent, and doubt notwithstanding, contemporary
poetry is filled with appeals to the mild engineer, the
furious papa, or the dove.

There is a kinship between poetry and religion that has
led some critics to transfer the quarrel between religion
and science to a quarrel between science and poetry. The
gulf between these two is obviously growing. The findings
of the biochemist and the mathematical physicist are too
abstract to be translatable into words. The scientist doubt-
less finds aesthetic pleasure in the elegance of his pro-
cedures and is excited by their results. Poems, elegant or
barbaric, which excite emotion, are, however, composed

not of formulas but of words, and only by poets. Empson, with his knowledge of the exact sciences, has made his own verse the vehicle of their understandings, but he has had to explain them to the reader, as he himself deplores, in supplementary notes. Today poets seem less likely to be supplied with new subject matter by the progress of science than to be deprived of themes that have been throning it for millennia in hundreds of languages. Only a few years ago the Scottish poet, Sidney Goodsir Smith, spoke, in a lyric, of having met the smile of "A lassie frae the mune—direct!" in a bar in Rose Street. He pleaded: "Goddess, help us baith / On this fell pilgrimage." But the Moon-Goddess is no longer likely to be helpful to poets. Already the countless songs and sonnets in which the moon figures begin to have an outmoded look. That planet, to hold its place in poetry, must become available to the writer in a fresh fashion: to be celebrated as another Cathay, a new world to be explored, or else to be mourned as a lost, corrupted source of myth, as the pagan gods are said to have been mourned on the advent of Christianity. The scientific revolution is changing our lives with a rapidity that affects us radically. It is not astonishing that the poet has more than ordinary difficulty in finding words for his sense of the world when the world alters so fast and confronts him with so much that is too large, too abstract, too remote from human experience for imagination to cope with it.

Even before that revolution it was clear that the scientist and the poet have diverse ends. Poetry cannot cure cancer, nor put an end to fire, famine, and flood. But it can provide a fusion of relaxation and excitement without the penalties attaching to either. To a greater degree than the other arts, it can reveal the conditions of living. This should help us to amend them. Its bonds with religion are subtler and more various than its bonds with science and so with control of the physical world. The appeal of poetry, except in the instance of drama, which seems to begin and end in the church, is primarily to the individual. It is not as likely as music, the dance, or even architecture, to unite him with his equally self-regarding fellows. Indeed, it may sometimes define his sense of isolation. Curiously and significantly, however, it will not, thereby, increase it. Quite the contrary. James Stephens, telling the "sad all" of weakness, wrong, and loss to his good friends, Raftery, O'Brien, Rahilly, poets who had had their troubles too, cared his grief into song, and "cared his grief away." Jeffers speaks of "The honey peace in old poems," and they are not apt to be jolly ones.

> Sing of human unsuccess
> In a rapture of distress,

Auden commands in his elegy for Yeats. The poet tries, on the one hand, to realize an unusually comprehensive experience more intensely. On the other hand, he tries to realize an unusually intense, if sometimes trivial, experience more comprehensively. This is to add to our knowledge, which is the procedure of science; this is also to deepen our understanding, which has been the effort of religion. Is it impossible that in the poem these two old enemies may be, even briefly, reconciled?

In the foreword to a collection of his poems, MacNeice speaks of a long, rambling, topical piece written in the autumn of 1938 as having failed in depth. The failure had been foreseen. "We shall not be capable of depth—of tragedy or *great* poetry—until we have made sense of our world," he says truly. Recognizing that they could not make sense of their world, certain British poets who came forward in the fifties have been content not to attempt "*great* poetry". In reaction against the allusive symbolism of Eliot and the romantic enthusiasm of Dylan Thomas, they make wry statements in a subdued tone about the facts of their lives. The seniors whose names have been invoked in discussions of these poets include William Empson and the American moralist, Yvor Winters. Indeed, "To Yvor Winters, 1955" is the title of a poem by one of the more notable of the younger men, Thom Gunn.

He admires Winters for his discipline and his energy, and because, knowing "the force of death", he nevertheless remains "tough in will". The word "will" occurs on page after page of Gunn's first book. A line in the opening poem might be taken as a punning reference to the poets of what has been called "the New Movement", though the poem itself is about motorcyclists: "One joins in the movement in a valueless world." The title poem of his second book, "My Sad Captains", shows how different his stance is from that of the young Stephen Spender, declaring: "I think continually of those who were truly great." Spender's poem concludes: "Born of the sun they travelled a short while towards the sun, / And left the vivid air signed with their honour." Gunn's poem, more than a quarter of a century and several wars later, begins: "One by one they appear in / the darkness: a few friends, and / a few with historical / names." In the end he sees them ". . . turn with disinterested / hard energy, like the stars." Horror and despair are more overt in his later poems, which deal with some of the features of this monstrous age and also with the eternal monstrous mystery. His manipulation of rhyme and metre, his wit, his severe economy, are servants of his acuteness. He might be speaking of himself, of his whole generation, when he writes, of Odysseus in Hades, that, without comfort, watching the dead, he "was alive / Because he had no comfort." He describes himself and his fellows when he says of one of the "Black Jackets": "The present was the things he stayed among." He differs from the leather-coated cyclists evoked in this poem in being intensely conscious of what went to the making of the present and what it forebodes. In lines called "Flying Above California" Gunn's description of the "cold hard light without break" might be applied to his own poetry, which also

>   reveals merely what is—no more
>   and no less.

It is a tribute to his gifts that no American has more successfully presented the particular magic of Muir Woods than Gunn in his "Lights Among Redwoods". One of the most admired poems of the decade is Philip Larkin's "Church Going"—a title that conceals a pun. It is the account of a casual visit to an empty old church, the speaker being a professed agnostic, who envisages its becoming "completely out of use", declares that "superstition, like belief, must die," and wonders "what remains when disbelief has gone?" In the end he acknowledges the building as "A serious house on serious earth" and comes to feel that there will always be someone hungering for greater seriousness who will turn to this place, "Which, he once heard, was proper to grow wise in, / If only that so many dead lie round." The seven stanzas that compose this piece, each of nine loosely iambic lines skilfully rhymed, are not "*great* poetry", but they are an honest, fully realized, thoughtful narrative. The harsh candor of some work by this generation of poets recalls a like vein in that of Robert Graves, whose devotion to the Great White Goddess they are far from sharing. Their temper seems closer to that of a less bristly, equally honest poet: Louis MacNeice. He concludes the foreword to one of his books mentioned above with the statement that he writes poetry because he enjoys it, and also because it is his "road to freedom and knowledge". They might well say the same.

Writing his "New Year Letter" on the grim eve of 1940, Auden concluded Part I with the plea that

> such heart and intelligence
> As huddle now in conference
> Whenever an impasse occurs
> Use the good offices of verse;

which seems a direct denial of his assertion that poetry makes nothing happen. Certainly its influence is apt to be indirect, unforeseen, complex. Certainly, too, there is one thing that it can do. It can help us in a task on the necessity of which philosophers, saints, and physicians agree, that of self-discovery. A compulsion to discover or recover the self has always animated poetry and is singularly overt in recent work. It expresses itself in William Carlos Williams' need to continue and extend *Paterson,* and is prominent in the performance of such diverse practitioners among his juniors as Robert Lowell and Theodore Roethke.

A divided man, like another, the poet tries to reconcile what he feels with what he knows. He will never, in Coleridge's phrase, bring the whole soul of man into activity, because this is to describe the performance as it never occurs: "in *ideal* perfection". He will not be capable, as Yeats dreamed, of holding in one thought reality and justice. Yet with a new and deeper meaning the poet today repeats the words of a forgotten harper of ancient Egypt: "I have seen violence, I have seen violence— / Give thy heart after letters." In the poem, sound and image, emotion and idea, work together to enrich the simple experience, to order as they may the confused elements in the more complicated. This is to speak against violence in the only way possible. If on occasion the poem speaks for it, it is in the interests of a more inclusive harmony.

We have seen violence undreamed of by the old Egyptian. And it appears to have no limits. Unpeopled outer space and the secret places of the human personality are alike being assaulted, with unforeseeable results. The contemporary, confronting these hazards, recognizes, too, the divergence between himself, with his consciousness of death, his curiosity about destiny, his delight, his awe, his grief, and that impersonal world of which he is a part. He does not compel himself to tolerate a situation that appears nauseating or absurd. He gives his heart after letters. And not by way of escape. Rather, he tries to order words, which stand for things and for thoughts, which speak and sing, so as to reconcile those two alien existences, that of man and that of the mindless universe.

Here, then, is an art that variously accomplishes a meeting of contraries. At its outer margins lie two enormous realms to which it can never attain. The one is pure music. "All others translate," says Auden, in a lyric addressed to "The Composer", whose gift he rightly declares supreme. Music needs no logic, no form, no substance in the world but its own. As poetry can express what is beyond the power of any other words, so music can express what even poetry is too clumsy to say. On the opposite shore lies the other realm, more insubstantial, more immense, that of silence. There men go in their extreme moments. When they leave that region, they are fortunate if they can turn to poetry. For of those things that most concern us it speaks intimately—of the activity of soul and body, of justice and reality, of death, and of love.

Note to Index of Poets

Below are the names and dates of those poets who have died since the first printing of the Index.

Conrad Aiken (1889-1973)
Kenneth Slade Alling (1887-19??)
W. H. Auden (1907-73)
R. P. Blackmur (1904-65)
Louise Bogan (1897-1970)
Emanuel Carnevali (1897-1942)
Padraic Colum (1881-1972)
Hubert Creekmore (1907-66)
T. S. Eliot (1888-1965)
Robert Frost (1875-1963)
Jean Garrigue (1913-73)
Langston Hughes (1902-69)
Rolfe Humphries (1894-1969)
Randall Jarrell (1914-65)
Patrick Kavanagh (1905-67)
Alfred Kreymborg (1883-1966)
C. Day Lewis (1904-72)
Louis MacNeice (1907-63)
Marianne Moore (1887-1972)
Ogden Nash (1902-71)
Pablo Neruda (1904-73)
Ezra Pound (1885-1972)
John Crowe Ransom (1888-1974)
Theodore Roethke (1908-63)
Carl Sandburg (1878-1967)
Delmore Schwartz (1913-66)
Edith Sitwell (1887-1964)
Sir Osbert Sitwell (1892-1969)
Mark Van Doren (1894-1973)
William Carlos Williams (1883-1963)
Yvor Winters (1900-68)

Index of Poets

Adams, Léonie (b. 1899): 261–65, 266

Agee, James (1909–55): 366

Aiken, Conrad (b. 1889): 195–97

Aldington, Richard (1892–1962): 87–88

Alling, Kenneth Slade (b. 1887): xv, 71

Anderson, Patrick (b. 1915): 127–28

Apollinaire, Guillaume (1880–1918): 99, 122, 157, 269

Arnold, Matthew (1882–88): 13, 17

Auden, W. H. (b. 1907): xi, 15, 32, 57, 90, 118, 163, 202, 240, 293, 311, 321, 339, 402, 414, 416, 421, 423–39, 442–43, 445, 447, 449

Barker, George (b. 1913): 384–86, 411

Barnes, William (1800–86): 68

Baudelaire, Charles (1821–67): 171, 186, 244, 430

Belitt, Ben (b. 1911): 163

Benét, Stephen (1898–1943): 47

Betjeman, John (b. 1916): 234

Bishop, Elizabeth (b. 1911): 100–2, 399

Bishop, John Peale (1892–1944): 206, 208–12, 216

Blackmur, R. P. (b. 1904): 213

Blake, William (1757–1827): 55, 90, 96, 248, 252, 253, 287, 293, 383, 402

Blunt, Wilfrid Scawen (1840–1922): 155

Bogan, Louise (b. 1897): 265–67

Booth, Philip (b. 1925): 102

Born, Bertran de (c. 1140–c. 1215): 137, 211

Bridges, Robert (1844–1930): 321, 327, 328, 337, 341

Brinnin, John M. (b. 1916): 409

Brontë, Emily (1818–48): 245

Brooke, Rupert (1887–1915): 68, 69, 389, 419

Browning, Robert (1812–61): 59, 129–30, 133, 163

Bunting, Basil (fl. 1933): 162

Burns, Robert (1759–96): 67, 234

Calderon de la Barca, Pedro (1600–81): 301

Campbell, Joseph ·(1879–1944): 318

Campbell, Roy (1902–57): 39

Cannell, Skipwith (fl. 1914): 88

Capetanakis, Demetrios (1912–44): 415

Carnevali, Emanuel (b. 1897): 91–93

Catullus (B.C. 87–54): 88

Cavalcanti, Guido (c. 1259–1300): 151

Char, René (b. 1907): 119

Chaucer, Geoffrey (1340?–1400): xi, 31, 41, 88, 430, 441

Clare, John (1793–1864): 68

Coleridge, S. T. (1772–1834): 165, 227, 376, 448

Colum, Padraic (b. 1881): 41, 318

Comfort, Alex (b. 1920): 34, 399

Corbière, Tristan (1845–75): 140, 171, 195

Cornford, Frances (1886–1943): 234

Cournos, John (b. 1881): 88

Crabbe, George (1754–1832): 61

Crane, Hart (1899–1932): 48, 118, 210, 213, 232, 349–69, 370, 376, 384, 387, 443

Crapsey, Adelaide (1878–1914): 91–92

Crashaw, Richard (1612–49): 192

Creekmore, Hubert (b. 1907): 163

Cummings, E. E. (1894–1962): 92, 121–27, 393–95, 412

Daiken, Leslie (b. 1912): 346

Dante Alighieri (1265–1321): 51, 146, 151, 153, 172, 174–75, 179, 181, 185, 203, 213, 217, 218, 232, 291, 349, 352, 364, 428, 429

Davies, W. H. (1870–1940): 69, 255

de la Mare, Walter (1873–1956): xi, 69, 255–57

Devlin, Denis (1908–59): 91, 239, 318, 345

Dickinson, Emily (1830–86): 100, 118, 235, 245, 253, 260, 330, 344, 350, 402, 426

Divus, Andreas (fl. 1538): 144, 229

Donne, John (1573–1631): 168–70, 234, 253, 293, 338, 403

Doolittle, Hilda. See H. D.

Drinan, Adam, pseud. Joseph Todd Gordon Macleod (b. 1903): 372

Dryden, John (1631–1700): 235, 429, 436

Eberhart, Richard (b. 1904): 235, 346, 415–16

Eliot, T. S. (b. 1888): 16, 39, 52, 90, 118, 120–21, 156–57, 163, 165–95, 197, 198, 200–3, 206–7, 213–14, 220, 229–30, 235, 269, 290, 349, 351, 401, 411, 414, 420, 430, 431, 439–40, 442, 443, 445

Empson, William (b. 1906): 232–33, 444, 445

Engle, Paul (b. 1910): 47

Evans, Abbie Huston (b. 1881): 260

Fearing, Kenneth (1902–61): 52, 56, 123, 220, 397–99

Ferlingetti, Lawrence (b. 1920): 46

Fitzgerald, Robert (b. 1910): 127, 160

Flecker, James Elroy (1884–1915): 255

Fletcher, John Gould (1886–1951): 88, 205

Flint, F. S. (1885–1960): 88
Ford, Ford Madox, née Hueffer (1873–1939): 88, 389
Fraser, G. S. (b. 1915): 68, 369, 381, 414
Frost, Robert (b. 1875): xi, 59, 63, 65–84, 128, 235, 393, 399
Fuller, Roy (b. 1912): 68, 416

Garrett, George (b. 1929): 73
Garrigue, Jean (b. 1913): 103–4, 366, 409
Gascoyne, David (b. 1916): 409
Gautier, Théophile (1811–72): 87–88, 137, 140, 163, 172–73
Gilbert, W. S. (1836–1911): 412
Ginsberg, Allen (b. 1926): 53, 117
Goethe, Johann Wolfgang von (1749–1832): 140
Gogarty, Oliver St. John (1878–1957): 318
Goldsmith, Oliver (1728–74): 175
Graham, W. S. (b. 1917): 372
Graves, Robert (b. 1895): xi, 227–28, 389
Greenberg, Samuel (1893–1917): 356, 366
Gregory, Horace (b. 1898): 52, 396
Gunn, Thom (b. 1929): 445–47
Gustafson, Ralph (b. 1909): 346

Hall, Donald (b. 1928): 163
Hardy, Thomas (1840–1928): 1–12, 19–23, 40–41, 64, 69, 72, 96, 128, 138, 221, 292, 389, 430

H. D., pen name of Hilda Doolittle (1886–1961): 87, 91, 105–8
Heine, Heinrich (1797–1856): 17, 88
Hendry, J. F. (b. 1912): 369
Henley, W. E. (1849–1903): 90
Henryson, Robert (1430?–1506?): 49
Herbert, George (1593–1633): 336, 377, 406–7
Higgins, F. R. (1896–1941): 318
Hillyer, Robert (1895–1961): 328
Homer (fl. B.C. 9th c.): 146, 163, 174
Hopkins, G. M. (1844–89): 16, 75, 265, 321–43, 344, 345–47, 348, 365–66, 370, 401, 402, 421
Housman, A. E. (1859–1936): 12–19, 435
Howes, Barbara (b. 1914): 73
Hughes, Langston (b. 1902): 56, 399
Hugo, Victor (1802–85): 310
Hulme, T. E. (1883–1917): 85–86

Iremonger, Valentin (b. 1918): 319

Jarrell, Randall (b. 1914): 420
Jeffers, Robinson (1887–1962): 19–25, 72, 292, 344, 397, 412, 445
Jennett, Sean (b. 1912): 409
Jennings, Elizabeth (b. 1926): 104
Jones, David (b. 1895): 239
Jonson, Ben (1573?–1637): 63, 171
Joyce, James (1882–1941): 88, 114, 187, 244, 312–17, 346,

Joyce, James (cont'd)
383
Kavanagh, Patrick (b. 1905):
318
Keats, John (1795–1821): 72,
165, 290, 392
Kipling, Rudyard (1865–1936):
31–40, 41, 44, 57–58, 61,
138, 187, 278, 430
Kreymborg, Alfred (b. 1883):
235
Kunitz, Stanley (b. 1905):
238–39

Laforgue, Jules (1860–87):
140, 170, 195
Landor, Walter Savage (1775–
1864): 37
Larkin, Philip (b. 1922): 447
Lawrence, D. H. (1885–1930):
5, 24–25, 69, 88, 93–98, 323,
370, 401
Leonard, William Ellery (1876–
1944): 196
Levertov, Denise (b. 1923):
120
Lewis, C. Day (b. 1904): 15,
32–33, 232, 339–40, 402–3
Lindsay, Vachel (1879–1931):
44–49, 57, 108
Li Po (700–62): 89, 91, 137,
141–42, 163
Lowell, Amy (1874–1925): 88,
140
Lowell, Robert (b. 1917): 84,
386–87, 410–11, 448
Lucretius (B.C. 96–55): 70,
426

MacDiarmid, Hugh, pseud. C.
M. Grieve (b. 1892): 27–
28, 342–44, 441, 442
McGreevy, Thomas (b. 1893):
91, 318
MacLeish, Archibald (b. 1892):
85, 157–60, 180, 365, 396

MacNeice, Louis (b. 1907):
290, 318, 339, 373, 403,
404–8, 447
Mallarmé, Stéphane (1842–98):
24, 87, 171, 186, 214
Manifold, John (b. 1915): 39,
257
Marvell, Andrew (1621–78):
40, 221
Masefield, John (b. 1875): 31,
41–44, 57, 61, 66, 69, 389
Masters, Edgar Lee (1869–
1951): 48–52, 57, 109, 137
Mayakovsky, Vladimir (1893–
1930): 257, 400
Melville, Herman (1819–91):
402, 410
Meredith, George (1828–
1909): 196
Merton, Thomas (b. 1915):
386
Merwin, W. S. (b. 1927): 284
Meun, Jean de (1240?–1305?):
92
Mew, Charlotte (1869–1928):
6
Millay, Edna St. Vincent
(1892–1951): 14–15, 405
Milton, John (1608–74): 187,
323, 349
Moore, Marianne (b. 1887):
99–101, 103, 229–31, 278
Moore, Merrill (1903–57): 234
Morris, William (1834–96):
304
Muir, Edwin (1887–1959):
258–60

Nash, Ogden (b. 1902): 234
Neruda, Pablo (b. 1904): 101
Nicholson, Norman (b. 1914):
16, 43

O'Bruadair, David (1650–94):
41, 318

Olson, Elder (b. 1909): 263, 346

Oppenheim, James (1882–1932): 396

Ovid (B.C. 43–A.D. 17): 146

Owen, Wilfred (1893–1918): 16, 143, 390–92, 401, 438

Patmore, Coventry (1823–96): 323

Perse, St.-John, *pseud.* Alexis St. Léger Léger (b. 1889): 157, 187, 188, 413

Po Chü-i (772–846): 292

Poe, Edgar Allan (1809–49): 44, 186, 241, 351–53, 363

Pope, Alexander (1688–1744): 244

Pound, Ezra (b. 1885): 50, 85, 87, 88, 91, 108, 117, 129–57, 158, 159, 161, 162–63, 165, 166, 195, 201, 229, 235, 293, 340, 420, 442, 430

Praed, Winthrop Mackworth (1802–39): 59–60

Prévert, Jacques (b. 1900): 46

Propertius (B.C. 50?–15?): 137

Raftery, Antoine (1784?–1835): 318, 445

Rahilly, Egan (d. 1725?): 445

Raine, Kathleen (b. 1908): 259

Ransom, John Crowe (b. 1888): 205, 206, 221–27, 228, 299

Read, Herbert (b. 1893): 85, 370, 372

Reese, Lizette Woodworth (1856–1935): 14

Rexroth, Kenneth (b. 1905): 25–27, 92, 99, 398

Richards, I. A. (b. 1893): 232

Ridge, Lola (1883–1941): 91

Riding, Laura (b. 1901): 123, 227, 425

Rilke, Rainer Maria (1875–1926): 120, 243, 385, 412, 417–18, 438

Rimbaud, Jean Arthur (1854–91): 94, 211, 248, 353–54, 355, 358, 429

Robinson, E. A. (1869–1935): 59, 64, 65, 292

Rodgers, W. R. (b. 1911): 318, 344–45

Roethke, Theodore (b. 1908): 197–200, 448

Rosenberg, Isaac (1890–1918): 390

Rukeyser, Muriel (b. 1913): 397

St. Francis (1182–1226): 432

St. John of the Cross (1542–91): 185

Sandburg, Carl (b. 1878): 48, 53–57, 109, 393

Sappho (*fl.* B.C. 600?): 88, 106, 117, 175

Sassoon, Siegfried (b. 1886): 289

Savage, D. S. (b. 1917): 68, 441

Scarfe, Francis (b. 1911): 68

Schwartz, Delmore (b. 1913): 387, 414

Scott, Tom (b. 1918): 162

Shakespeare (1564–1616): xi, 17, 51

Shapiro, Karl (b. 1913): 15, 33, 77, 368, 416–19, 438, 442

Shelley, Percy Bysshe (1792–1822): 51, 165, 288, 293, 403

Simonides (B.C. 556?–468?): 48

Simpson, Louis (b. 1923): 17

Sitwell, Edith (b. 1887): 243–51, 252, 387, 403, 412, 414

Sitwell, Sir Osbert (b. 1892): 247

Sitwell, Sacheverell (b. 1897): 247

Skelton, John (1460–1529): 323

Smith, Sidney Goodsir (b. 1915): 444

Smith, William Jay (b. 1918): 73

Snodgrass, W. D. (b. 1926): 73

Sordello (c. 1180–c. 1255): 147

Spender, Stephen (b. 1909): 1, 32, 402–3, 413, 446

Spenser, Edmund (1552?–1599?): 288

Stein, Gertrude (1872–1946): 123–24, 214, 244

Stephens, James (1882–1950): 69, 257–58, 318, 445

Stevens, Wallace (1879–1955): xi, xii, xiii, 27, 84, 104, 109, 269–85, 397, 398–99, 414, 421, 440

Stevenson, R. L. (1850–94): 210

Stewart, Gervase (1920–41): 419

Stuart, Jesse (b. 1907): 234

Surrey, Henry Howard, Earl of (1517?–47): 165

Swenson, May (b. 1919): 103

Swift, Jonathan (1667–1745): 41, 318, 323

Symons, Julian (b. 1912): 368

Synge, John (1871–1909): 41, 44, 289, 318

Tate, Allen (b. 1899): 205, 207, 212–19, 220, 228, 293, 395, 413

Teasdale, Sara (1884–1933): 14

Tennyson, Alfred, Lord (1809–92): 60, 423, 429

Thomas, Dylan (1914–53): 248, 370–84, 385, 387–88, 411, 445

Thomas, Edward (1878–1917): 70

Tomlinson, Charles (b. 1927): 271

Traherne, Thomas (1652–74): 248, 336, 374–75, 382, 383

Treece, Henry (b. 1912): 369

Turner, W. J. (1889–1946): 255

Upward, Allen (1863–1926): 88

Valéry, Paul (1871–1945): 187

Van Doren, Mark (b. 1894): 71, 73, 235

Verlaine, Paul (1844–96): 61, 172, 312

Villa, José Garcia (b. 1914): 284, 386

Villon, François (1431–53?): 88, 148, 162, 224, 394

Virgil (B.C. 70–19): 70, 172

Walsh, Ernest (1895–1926): 92, 99, 393

Warren, Robert Penn (b. 1905): xii, 73, 98, 205, 219–22

Watkins, Vernon (b. 1906): 370

Wheelock, John Hall (b. 1886): 258

Wheelwright, John (1897–1940): 84, 201, 231, 366–67

Whitman, Walt (1819–92): 19, 53, 95, 135–36, 163, 287, 322, 327, 350, 352, 361, 364, 402

Wilbur, Richard (b. 1921): 284, 347–48

Williams, William Carlos (b. 1883): xiii, 84, 88, 90, 92, 98–99, 105, 108–21, 149, 156, 235, 275, 439, 442, 448

Winters, Yvor (b. 1900): 231, 368, 445–46

Wordsworth, William (1770–1850): 42, 67, 114, 165, 191,

Wordsworth (*cont'd*)
  376, 386, 428
Wright, James (b. 1927): 76
Wyatt, Sir Thomas (1503?-42):
  165
Wylie, Elinor (1886-1929):
  251-54, 263, 267

Yeats, W. B. (1865-1939): xii,
  xiii, 14, 28, 31, 41, 55, 78,
  119, 133-34, 149, 195, 235,
  251, 256, 262, 263, 287-312,
  315, 319, 349, 392, 413, 414,
  421, 430, 443, 445, 448

Zaturenska, Marya (b. 1902):
  267-68
Zukofsky, Louis (b. 1904): 99,
  162

Below are a few names and page references inadvertently omitted from the Index of Poets.

George Gordon, Lord Byron (1788-1824): 203, 424
Tram Combs (b. 1924): 128
Edward Field (b. 1924): 128
Rolfe Humphries (1894-1969): 405
Gary Snyder (b. 19??): 128
References to Robert Lowell should include p. 368.

The Foreword to the present edition offers a further reference to John Hall Wheelock and introduces the names of John Berryman, Anthony Hecht and Howard Nemerov.